MICROSOFT

Office 2000

Essential Concepts and Techniques

WORD 2000   EXCEL 2000   ACCESS 2000   POWERPOINT 2000

MICROSOFT

Office 2000

Essential Concepts and Techniques

WORD 2000   EXCEL 2000   ACCESS 2000   POWERPOINT 2000

Gary B. Shelly
Thomas J. Cashman
Misty E. Vermaat

Contributing Authors
Steven G. Forsythe
Mary Z. Last
Philip J. Pratt
James S. Quasney
Susan L. Sebok
Denise M. Woods

COURSE TECHNOLOGY
ONE MAIN STREET
CAMBRIDGE MA 02142

an International Thomson Publishing company   **I(T)P**

SHELLY
CASHMAN
SERIES®

CAMBRIDGE • ALBANY • BONN • CINCINNATI • LONDON • MADRID • MELBOURNE

MEXICO CITY • NEW YORK • PARIS • SAN FRANCISCO • TOKYO • TORONTO • WASHINGTON

COURSE
TECHNOLOGY

Course Technology
One Main Street
Cambridge, Massachusetts 02142, USA

ITP GmbH
Konigswinterer Strasse 418
53227 Bonn, Germany

ITP Europe
Berkshire House
168-173 High Holborn
London, WC1V 7AA, United Kingdom

International Thomson Editores
Saneca, 53
Colonia Polanco
11560 Mexico D.F. Mexico

ITP Asia
60 Albert Street, #15-01
Albert Complex
Singapore 189969

ITP Australia
102 Dodds Street
South Melbourne
Victoria 3205 Australia

ITP Nelson Canada
1120 Birchmount Road
Scarborough, Ontario
Canada M1K 5G4

ITP Japan
Hirakawa-cho Kyowa Building, 3F
2-2-1 Hirakawa-cho, Chiyoda-ku
Tokyo 102, Japan

PHOTO CREDITS: **Microsoft Windows 98** *Project 1, pages INT 1.2-3* Cardinal, computer, rose, tree, Courtesy of International Microcomputer Software, Inc.; Illustrations, Ellana Russo; **Microsoft Word 2000** *Project 1, pages WD 1.4-5* Illustrations, Chris Schneider; **Microsoft Excel 2000** *Project 1, pages E 1.4-5* Background swirls, building doorway, business man photo, circuit board, hand, library, man at ATM, man talking on telephone, people with groceries, stack of books, student on steps, student with books, woman at computer, woman holding garment, Courtesy of PhotoDisc, Inc.; parking meter, Courtesy of KPT Metatools; Illustrations, Ellana Russo; **Microsoft Access 2000** *Project 1, pages A 1.4-5* Children in school, log wheels, man painting, ship, teacher at chalkboard, woman and child, woman at computer, Courtesy of PhotoDisc, Inc.; Trojan horse, Courtesy of Corel Professional Photos CD-ROM Image Usage; Illustrations, Ellana Russo; **Microsoft PowerPoint 2000** *Project 1, pages PP 1.4-5* COMDEX/Canada, COMDEX/Las Vegas, conference presentation, Courtesy of 2D Events; IBM computer, Courtesy of International Business Machines; First Apple computer, Courtesy of Apple Computer, Inc.; portable computer, Courtesy of Compaq Computer Corporation; Illustrations, Chris Schneider.

ISBN 0-7895-4652-3

2 3 4 5 6 7 8 9 10   BC   04 03 02 01 00

MICROSOFT

Office 2000

Essential Concepts and Techniques

WORD 2000   EXCEL 2000   ACCESS 2000   POWERPOINT 2000

C O N T E N T S

Microsoft Access 2000

Microsoft PowerPoint 2000

Preface

The Shelly Cashman Series® offers the finest textbooks in computer education. We are proud of the fact that our Microsoft Office 4.3, Microsoft Office 95, and Microsoft Office 97 textbooks have been the most widely used books in education. Each edition of our Office textbooks has included innovations, many based on comments made by the instructors and students who use our books. The Microsoft Office 2000 books continue with the innovation, quality, and reliability that you have come to expect from the Shelly Cashman Series.

Office 2000 is the most significant upgrade ever to the Office suite. Microsoft has enhanced Office 2000 in the following areas: (1) interface changes; (2) application-specific features; (3) multi-language pack; (4) round tripping HTML files back to an Office 2000 application; (5) collaboration; and (6) new applications. Each one of these enhancements is discussed in detail.

In our Office 2000 books, you will find an educationally sound and easy-to-follow pedagogy that combines a step-by-step approach with corresponding screens. All projects and exercises in this book are designed to take full advantage of the Office 2000 enhancements. The popular Other Ways and More About features offer in-depth knowledge of Office 2000. The project openers provide a fascinating perspective on the subject covered in the project. The project material is developed carefully to ensure that students will see the importance of learning Office 2000 applications for future course work.

The Shelly Cashman Approach

Features of the Shelly Cashman Series Office 2000 books include:

- **Project Orientation:** Each project in the book uses the unique Shelly Cashman Series screen-by-screen, step-by-step approach.

- **Screen-by-Screen, Step-by-Step Instructions:** Each of the tasks required to complete a project is identified throughout the development of the project. The steps are accompanied by full-color screens.

- **Thoroughly Tested Projects:** Every screen in the book is correct because it is produced by the author only after performing a step, resulting in unprecedented quality.

- **Other Ways Boxes and Quick Reference Summary:** Office 2000 provides a variety of ways to carry out a given task. The Other Ways boxes displayed at the end of most of the step-by-step sequences specify the other ways to do the task completed in the steps. Thus, the steps and the Other Ways box make a comprehensive reference unit. In addition, a Quick Reference Summary, available on the Web, summarizes the way application-specific tasks can be completed.

- **More About Feature:** These marginal annotations provide background information that complements the topics covered, adding depth and perspective to the learning process.

- **Integration of the World Wide Web:** We have integrated the World Wide Web into the students' Office 2000 learning experience in different ways. For example, we have added (1) More Abouts that send students to Web sites for up-to-date information and alternative approaches to tasks; (2) a MOUS information Web page and a MOUS map Web page so students can better prepare for the Microsoft Office Use Specialist (MOUS) Certification examinations; (3) an

---

Other Ways

1. Click Format Picture button on Picture toolbar, click Size tab, enter desired height and width, click OK button

2. On Format menu click Picture, click Size tab, enter desired height and width, click OK button

---

More About 2000

Navigation

For more information on selecting cells that contain certain entries, such as constants or formulas, visit the Excel 2000 More About Web page (www.scsite.com/ex2000/more.htm) and click Using Go To Special.

Office 2000 Quick Reference Summary Web page that summarizes the ways to complete tasks (mouse, menu, shortcut menu, and keyboard); and (4) project reinforcement Web pages in the form of true/false, multiple choice, and short answer questions, and other types of student activities.

Organization of This Textbook

Microsoft Office 2000: Essential Concepts and Techniques is divided into five projects and four appendices as follows:

An Introduction to Windows 98 and Microsoft Office 2000 Students learn about user interfaces, Windows 98, Windows Explorer, and each Office 2000 application. Topics include using the mouse; minimizing, maximizing, and restoring windows; sizing and scrolling windows; launching and quitting an application; displaying the contents of a folder; creating a folder; selecting and copying a group of files; renaming and deleting a file and a folder; using Windows 98 Help; and shutting down Windows 98. Topics pertaining to Office 2000 include a brief explanation of Word 2000, Excel 2000, Access, 2000, PowerPoint 2000, Publisher 2000, FrontPage 2000, PhotoDraw 2000, and Outlook 2000, and examples of how these applications take advantage of the Internet and World Wide Web.

Microsoft Word 2000 - Creating and Editing a Word Document Students are introduced to Word terminology and the Word window by preparing an announcement. Topics include starting and quitting Word; entering text; checking spelling while typing; saving a document; selecting characters, words, lines, and paragraphs; changing the font and font size of text; centering, right-aligning, and formatting text in bold and italic; undoing commands and actions; inserting clip art into a document; resizing a graphic; printing a document; opening a document; correcting errors; and using the Word Help system.

Microsoft Excel 2000 - Creating a Worksheet and Embedded Chart Students are introduced to Excel terminology, the Excel window, and the basic characteristics of a worksheet and workbook. Topics include starting and quitting Excel; entering text and numbers; selecting a range; using the AutoSum button; copying using the fill handle; changing font size; formatting in bold; centering across columns; using the AutoFormat command; charting using the ChartWizard; saving and opening a workbook; editing a worksheet; using the AutoCalculate area; and using the Excel Help system.

Microsoft Access 2000 — Creating a Database Using Design and Datasheet Views Students are introduced to the concept of a database and shown how to use Access to create a database. Topics include creating a database; creating a table; defining the fields in a table; opening a table; adding records to a table; closing a table; and previewing and printing the contents of a table. Additional topics include using a form to view data; using the Report Wizard to create a report; and using the Access Help system. Students also learn how to design a database to eliminate redundancy.

Microsoft PowerPoint 2000 - Using a Design Template and AutoLayouts to Create a Presentation Students are introduced to PowerPoint terminology, the PowerPoint window, and the basics of creating a multi-level bulleted list presentation. Topics include selecting a design template; increasing font size; changing font style; ending a slide show with a black slide; saving a presentation; viewing the slides in a presentation; checking a presentation for spelling and style errors; changing line spacing on the Slide Master; printing copies of the slides; and using the PowerPoint Help system.

Appendices The book concludes with four appendices. Appendix A presents a detailed step-by-step introduction to the Microsoft Office Help system. Students learn how to use the Office Assistant, as well as the Contents, Answer Wizard, and Index sheets in the Help window. Appendix B describes how to publish Office Web pages to a Web server. Appendix C shows students how to reset the menus and toolbars in any Office application. Appendix D introduces students to the Microsoft Office User Specialist (MOUS) Certification program.

End-of-Project Student Activities

A notable strength of the Shelly Cashman Series Office 2000 books is the extensive student activities at the end of each project. Well-structured student activities can make the difference between students merely participating in a class and students retaining the information they learn. The activities in the Shelly Cashman Series Office 2000 books include the following.

- **What You Should Know** A listing of the tasks completed within a project together with the pages where the step-by-step, screen-by-screen explanations appear. This section provides a perfect study review for students.

- **Project Reinforcement on the Web** Every project has a Web page accessible from www.scsite.com/off2000/reinforce.htm. The Web page includes true/false, multiple choice, and short answer questions, and additional project-related reinforcement activities that will help students gain confidence in their Office 2000 abilities.

- **Apply Your Knowledge** This exercise requires students to open and manipulate a file on the Data Disk for the Office 2000 books. To obtain a copy of the Data Disk, follow the instructions on the inside back cover of this textbook.

- **In the Lab** Three in-depth assignments per project require students to apply the knowledge gained in the project to solve problems on a computer.

- **Cases and Places** Up to seven unique case studies that require students to apply their knowledge to real-world situations.

Shelly Cashman Series Teaching Tools

A comprehensive set of Teaching Tools accompanies this textbook in the form of a CD-ROM. The CD-ROM includes an Instructor's Manual and teaching and testing aids. The CD-ROM (ISBN 0-7895-4636-1) is available through your Course Technology representative or by calling one of the following telephone numbers: Colleges and Universities, 1-800-648-7450; High Schools, 1-800-824-5179; and Career Colleges, 1-800-477-3692. The contents of the CD-ROM are listed below.

- **Instructor's Manual** The Instructor's Manual is made up of Microsoft Word files. The files include lecture notes, solutions to laboratory assignments, and a large test bank. The files allow you to modify the lecture notes or generate quizzes and exams from the test bank using your own word processing software. Where appropriate, solutions to laboratory assignments are embedded as icons in the files. When an icon appears, double-click it and the application will start and the solution will display on the screen. The Instructor's Manual includes the following for each project: project objectives; project overview; detailed lesson plans with page number references; teacher notes and activities; answers to the end-of-project exercises; test bank of 110 questions for every project (25 multiple-choice, 50 true/false, and 35 fill-in-the-blank) with page number references; and transparency references. The transparencies are available through the Figures in the Book. The test bank questions are numbered the same as in Course Test Manager. Thus, you can print a copy of the project test bank and use the printout to select your questions in Course Test Manager.

- **Figures in the Book** Illustrations of the figures and tables in the textbook are available in Figures in the Book. Use this ancillary to create a slide show from the illustrations for lecture or to print transparencies for use in lecture with an overhead projector.

- **Course Test Manager** Course Test Manager is a powerful testing and assessment package that enables instructors to create and print tests from the large test bank. Instructors with access to a networked computer lab (LAN) can administer, grade, and track tests online. Students also can take online practice tests, which generate customized study guides that indicate where in the textbook students can find more information for each question.

- **Lecture Success System** Lecture Success System files are for use with the application software, a personal computer, and projection device to explain and illustrate the step-by-step, screen-by-screen development of a project in the textbook without entering large amounts of data.

- **Instructor's Lab Solutions** Solutions and required files for all the In the Lab assignments at the end of each project are available.

- **Lab Tests/Test Outs** Tests that parallel the In the Lab assignments are supplied for the purpose of testing students in the laboratory on the material covered in the project or testing students out of the course.

- **Student Files** All the files that are required by students to complete the Apply Your Knowledge exercises are included.

- **Interactive Labs** Eighteen hands-on interactive labs that take students from ten to fifteen minutes each to step through help solidify and reinforce mouse and keyboard usage and computer concepts. Student assessment is available in each interactive lab by means of a Print button. The assessment requires students to answer questions.

Microsoft Office 2000 Supplements

Three supplements can be used in combination with the Shelly Cashman Series Microsoft Office 2000 books. These supplements reinforce the concepts and techniques presented in the books.

Microsoft Office 2000 Workbook

This highly popular supplement (ISBN 0-7895-4690-6) includes a variety of activities that help students recall, review, and master Office 2000 concepts and techniques. The workbook complements the end-of-project material with a guided project outline, a self-test consisting of true/false, multiple choice, short answer, fill-in, and matching questions, an entertaining puzzle, and other challenging exercises.

Course Assessment Live

Course Assessment Live (ISBN 0-619-00147-X) is a performance-based testing program that measures students' proficiency in Microsoft Office 2000. Previously known as SAM, Course Assessment Live is available for Office 2000 in both live and simulated environments. You can use Course Assessment Live to place students into or out of courses, monitor their performance throughout a course, and help prepare them for the MOUS certification exams.

Course CBT

Enhance your students' Office 2000 classroom learning experience with self-paced computer-based training on CD-ROM (ISBN 0-619-00151-8). Course CBT engages students with interactive multimedia and hands-on simulations that reinforce and complement the concepts and skills covered in the textbook. All the content is aligned with the Microsoft Office User Specialist (MOUS) program, making it a great preparation tool for the certification exams. Course CBT also includes extensive pre- and post-assessments that test students' mastery of skills. These pre- and post-assessments automatically generate a custom learning path through the course that highlights only the topics with which students need help.

Shelly Cashman Series MOUS Web Page

The Shelly Cashman Series MOUS Web page has more than fifteen Web pages you can visit to obtain additional information on the MOUS Certification Program. The Web page (www.scsite.com/off2000/cert.htm) includes links to general information on certification, choosing an application for certification, preparing for the certification exam, and taking and passing the certification exam.

Acknowledgments

The Shelly Cashman Series would not be the leading computer education series without the contributions of outstanding publishing professionals. First, and foremost, among them is Becky Herrington, director of production and designer. She is the heart and soul of the Shelly Cashman Series, and it is only through her leadership, dedication, and tireless efforts that superior products are made possible. Becky created and produced the award-winning Windows series of books.

Under Becky's direction, the following individuals made significant contributions to these books: Doug Cowley, production manager; Ginny Harvey, series specialist and developmental editor; Ken Russo, senior Web designer; Mike Bodnar, associate production manager; Stephanie Nance, graphic artist, Mark Norton, Web designer; Jeanne Black and Betty Hopkins, Quark experts; Nancy Lamm and Lyn Markowicz, copy editors; Marilyn Martin, Mary Steinman, and Kim Kosmatka, proofreaders; Cristina Haley, indexer; Sarah Evertson of Image Quest, photo researcher; and Susan Sebok and Ginny Harvey, contributing writers.

Special thanks go to Richard Keaveny, managing editor; Jim Quasney, series consultant; Lora Wade, product manager; Meagan Walsh, associate product manager; Francis Schurgot, Web product manager; Tonia Grafakos, associate Web product manager; Scott Wiseman, online developer; Rajika Gupta, marketing manager; and Erin Bennet, editorial assistant. Special mention must go to Suzanne Biron, Becky Herrington, and Michael Gregson for the outstanding book design; Becky Herrington for the cover design; and Stephanie Nance for the cover illustrations.

Gary B. Shelly
Thomas J. Cashman
Misty E. Vermaat

Shelly Cashman Series – Traditionally Bound Textbooks

The Shelly Cashman Series presents the following computer subjects in a variety of traditionally bound textbooks. For more information, see your Course Technology representative or call 1-800-648-7450. For Shelly Cashman Series information, visit Shelly Cashman Online at **www.scseries.com**

COMPUTERS	
Computers	Discovering Computers 2000: Concepts for a Connected World, Web and CNN Enhanced
	Discovering Computers 2000: Concepts for a Connected World, Web and CNN Enhanced Brief Edition
	Teachers Discovering Computers: A Link to the Future, Web and CNN Enhanced
	Discovering Computers 98: A Link to the Future, World Wide Web Enhanced
	Discovering Computers 98: A Link to the Future, World Wide Web Enhanced Brief Edition
	Exploring Computers: A Record of Discovery 2e with CD-ROM
	Study Guide for Discovering Computers 2000: Concepts for a Connected World, Web and CNN Enhanced
	Essential Introduction to Computers 3e (32-page)

WINDOWS APPLICATIONS	
Microsoft Office	Microsoft Office 2000: Essential Concepts and Techniques (5 projects)
	Microsoft Office 2000: Brief Concepts and Techniques (9 projects)
	Microsoft Office 2000: Introductory Concepts and Techniques (15 projects)
	Microsoft Office 2000: Advanced Concepts and Techniques (11 projects)
	Microsoft Office 2000: Post Advanced Concepts and Techniques (11 projects)
	Microsoft Office 97: Introductory Concepts and Techniques, Brief Edition (6 projects)
	Microsoft Office 97: Introductory Concepts and Techniques, Essentials Edition (10 projects)
	Microsoft Office 97: Introductory Concepts and Techniques, Enhanced Edition (15 projects)
	Microsoft Office 97: Advanced Concepts and Techniques
Microsoft Works	Microsoft Works 4.5[1] • Microsoft Works 3.0[1]
Windows	Microsoft Windows 98: Essential Concepts and Techniques (2 projects)
	Microsoft Windows 98: Introductory Concepts and Techniques (3 projects)
	Microsoft Windows 98: Introductory Concepts and Techniques Web Style Edition (3 projects)
	Microsoft Windows 98: Complete Concepts and Techniques (6 projects)
	Microsoft Windows 98: Comprehensive Concepts and Techniques (9 projects)
	Introduction to Microsoft Windows NT Workstation 4
	Microsoft Windows 95: Introductory Concepts and Techniques (2 projects)
	Introduction to Microsoft Windows 95 (3 projects)
	Microsoft Windows 95: Complete Concepts and Techniques
Word Processing	Microsoft Word 2000[2] • Microsoft Word 97[1] • Microsoft Word 7[1]
	Corel WordPerfect 8 • Corel WordPerfect 7 • WordPerfect 6.1[1]
Spreadsheets	Microsoft Excel 2000[2] • Microsoft Excel 97[1] • Microsoft Excel 7[1] • Microsoft Excel 5[1] • Lotus 1-2-3 97[1]
Database	Microsoft Access 2000[2] • Microsoft Access 97[1] • Microsoft Access 7[1]
Presentation Graphics	Microsoft PowerPoint 2000[2] • Microsoft PowerPoint 97[1] • Microsoft PowerPoint 7[1]
Desktop Publishing	Microsoft Publisher 2000[1]

PROGRAMMING	
Programming	Microsoft Visual Basic 6: Complete Concepts and Techniques[1]
	Microsoft Visual Basic 5: Complete Concepts and Techniques[1]
	QBasic • QBasic: An Introduction to Programming • Microsoft BASIC
	Structured COBOL Programming

INTERNET	
Browser	Microsoft Internet Explorer 5: An Introduction • Microsoft Internet Explorer 4: An Introduction
	Netscape Navigator 4: An Introduction
Web Page Creation	HTML: Complete Concepts and Techniques[1] • Microsoft FrontPage 98: Complete Concepts and Techniques[1] • Netscape Composer • JavaScript: Complete Concepts and Techniques[1]

SYSTEMS ANALYSIS	
Systems Analysis	Systems Analysis and Design, Third Edition

DATA COMMUNICATIONS	
Data Communications	Business Data Communications: Introductory Concepts and Techniques, Second Edition

[1]Also available as an Introductory Edition, which is a shortened version of the complete book
[2]Also available as an Introductory Edition, which is a shortened version of the complete book and also as a Comprehensive Edition, which is an extended version of the complete book

Shelly Cashman Series – Custom Edition™ Program

If you do not find a Shelly Cashman Series traditionally bound textbook to fit your needs, the Shelly Cashman Series unique **Custom Edition** program allows you to choose from a number of options and create a textbook perfectly suited to your course. Features of the **Custom Edition** program are:

- Textbooks that match the content of your course

- Windows- and DOS-based materials for the latest versions of personal computer applications software

- Shelly Cashman Series quality, with the same full-color materials and Shelly Cashman Series pedagogy found in the traditionally bound books

- Affordable pricing so your students receive the **Custom Edition** at a cost similar to that of traditionally bound books

The table on the right summarizes the available materials.

For more information, see your Course Technology representative or call one of the following telephone numbers: Colleges and Universities, 1-800-648-7450; High Schools, 1-800-824-5179; and Career Colleges, 1-800-477-3692.

For Shelly Cashman Series information, visit Shelly Cashman Online at **www.scseries.com**

COMPUTERS	
Computers	Discovering Computers 2000: Concepts for a Connected World, Web and CNN Enhanced
	Discovering Computers 2000: Concepts for a Connected World, Web and CNN Enhanced Brief Edition
	Discovering Computers 98: A Link to the Future, World Wide Web Enhanced
	Discovering Computers 98: A Link to the Future, World Wide Web Enhanced Brief Edition
	A Record of Discovery for Exploring Computers 2e (available with CD-ROM)
	Study Guide for Discovering Computers 2000: Concepts for a Connected World, Web and CNN Enhanced
	Essential Introduction to Computers 3e (32-page)

OPERATING SYSTEMS	
Windows	Microsoft Windows 98: Essential Concepts and Techniques (2 projects)
	Microsoft Windows 98: Introductory Concepts and Techniques (3 projects)
	Microsoft Windows 98: Introductory Concepts and Techniques Web Style Edition (3-project)
	Microsoft Windows 98: Complete Concepts and Techniques (6 projects)
	Microsoft Windows 98: Comprehensive Concepts and Techniques (9 projects)
	Microsoft Windows 95: Introductory Concepts and Techniques (2 projects)
	Introduction to Microsoft Windows NT Workstation 4
	Introduction to Microsoft Windows 95 (3 projects)
	Microsoft Windows 95: Complete Concepts and Techniques
DOS	Introduction to DOS 6 (using DOS prompt)

WINDOWS APPLICATIONS	
Microsoft Office	Microsoft Office 2000: Brief Concepts and Techniques (5 projects)
	Microsoft Office 97: Introductory Concepts and Techniques, Brief Edition (396-pages)
	Microsoft Office 97: Introductory Concepts and Techniques, Essentials Edition (672-pages)
	Object Linking and Embedding (OLE) (32-page)
	Microsoft Outlook 97 • Microsoft Schedule+ 7
	Using Microsoft Office 97 (16-page)
	Using Microsoft Office 95 (16-page)
	Introduction to Integrating Office 97 Applications (48-page)
	Introduction to Integrating Office 95 Applications (80-page)
Word Processing	Microsoft Word 2000* • Microsoft Word 97* • Microsoft Word 7* Corel WordPerfect 8 • Corel WordPerfect 7 •
Spreadsheets	Microsoft Excel 2000* • Microsoft Excel 97* • Microsoft Excel 7* Lotus 1-2-3 97* • Quattro Pro 6
Database	Microsoft Access 2000* • Microsoft Access 97* • Microsoft Access 7*
Presentation	Microsoft PowerPoint 2000* • Microsoft PowerPoint 97*
Graphics	Microsoft PowerPoint 7*

INTERNET	
Internet	The Internet: Introductory Concepts and Techniques (UNIX)
Browser	Netscape Navigator 4 • Netscape Navigator 3
	Microsoft Internet Explorer 5 • Microsoft Internet Explorer 4
	Microsoft Internet Explorer 3
Web Page Creation	Netscape Composer

*Also available as a mini-module

Microsoft Windows 98 and Office 2000

P R O J E C T

1

An Introduction to Windows 98 and Office 2000

O B J E C T I V E S

You will have mastered the material in this project when you can:

- Describe the Microsoft Windows 98 user interface
- Identify the objects on the Microsoft Windows 98 desktop
- Perform the basic mouse operations: point, click, right-click, double-click, drag, and right-drag
- Open, minimize, maximize, restore, scroll, and close a window
- Move and resize a window on the desktop
- Understand keyboard shortcut notation
- Identify the three desktop views: Classic style, Web style, and Custom style
- Launch and quit an application program
- Identify the elements of the Exploring – My Computer window
- Create. expand, and collapse a folder
- Select and copy one file or a group of files
- Rename and delete a folder or file
- Use Windows 98 Help
- Quit Windows Explorer and shut down Windows 98
- Identify each application in Microsoft Office 2000
- Define World Wide Web, intranet, and Internet
- Explain how each Microsoft Office 2000 application uses the Internet
- Understand the Microsoft Office 2000 Help system

Doing Windows
Graphical Computing
Clicks with Users

Doing Windows" has an entirely new meaning since Bill Gates announced plans to add graphical capabilities to the IBM personal computer in 1983. The Microsoft CEO decided to take this step to help current personal computer users work more effectively and entice others to buy systems.

Up until this time, users were typing cumbersome disk operating system (DOS) commands to run their computers. When IBM decided to design a personal computer in 1980, corporate executives approached Gates to develop its new operating system. Gates declined the offer and suggested that IBM contact Gary Kildall at Digital Research, a leading microcomputer software developer. Kildall had developed a widely used operating system called CP/M.

Kildall, however, decided not to attend the meeting at IBM headquarters. The frustrated IBM executives contacted Gates once again, and this time he reconsidered, even though he knew very little about operating systems. By chance, a neighboring company in Washington named Seattle Computer Products was developing an operating system it called QDOS (QDOS was an acronym for Quick and Dirty Operating System). Bill Gates made a proposal to the company, and in December 1980, Microsoft obtained nonexclusive rights to QDOS. Later, Microsoft acquired all rights for a total purchase price of $1 million, and renamed the system MS-DOS (an

MS-DOS

acronym for Microsoft Disk Operating System).

Microsoft modified the program, and then shipped it in the first IBM personal computer, the IBM PC, unveiled in August 1981. The sale of millions of IBM PCs and consequently millions of copies of the operating system, propelled Microsoft to the world's largest software company.

Gates's graphical intentions were fueled by work being done at Xerox's Palo Alto Research Center in California. He saw researchers there using an invention they called a mouse to move a pointer instead of using arrow keys on the keyboard to move a cursor.

Then, working with Apple, Microsoft developed software for the Macintosh computer. Combining its original innovations with those of Xerox, Microsoft created the graphical user interface and experimented with the use of various icons and fonts to make the screen user-friendly. In addition, Microsoft introduced Word and Excel for the Macintosh platform. When the Mac was released in 1984, it became a success among users, particularly students.

Microsoft's next step was to develop these applications for the IBM PC and IBM-compatible computers. The company's innovations resulted in the release of Windows 3.1 and Windows 95 prior to Windows 98. Currently more than 100 million computers worldwide use the Windows operating system.

Programmers at Microsoft use a process the corporation calls continuous reinvention to constantly add new features to enhance Windows performance. Microsoft also allows anyone to write programs for the Windows platform without requiring prior permission. Indeed, today many of the thousands of Windows-based programs compete with Microsoft's own programs.

Gates predicts his company will continue to release new Windows versions every two or three years. He is convinced that individuals will want to take advantage of user interface enhancements and innovations that make computing easier, more reliable, faster, and integrated with the Internet.

Using Windows 98 in this project, you will launch an application, create folders and documents, and access Windows Help. The latest enhancements to the applications in the Office 2000 suite are introduced including new programs, integration with the World Wide Web, and the extensive Office Help system.

Windows 98/Office 2000

Microsoft Windows 98 and Office 2000

An Introduction to Windows 98 and Office 2000

PROJECT 1

CASE PERSPECTIVE

After weeks of planning, your organization finally switched from Microsoft Windows 95 to Microsoft Windows 98 and installed Microsoft Office 2000 on all computers. As the computer trainer for the upcoming in-house seminar, you realize you should know more about Windows 98 and Office 2000. Since installing Windows 98 and Office 2000, many employees have come to you with questions. You have taken the time to answer their questions by sitting down with them at their computers and searching for the answers using the Microsoft Help system.

From their questions, you determine the seminar should cover the basics of Windows 98, including basic mouse operations, working within a window, launching an application, performing file maintenance using Windows Explorer, and searching for answers to employees' questions using Windows 98 Help. In addition, the seminar should familiarize the participants with each of the Office 2000 applications. Your goal in this project is to become familiar with Windows 98 and the Office 2000 applications in order to teach the seminar.

Introduction

Microsoft Windows 98 is a widely used version of the Microsoft Windows operating system. Microsoft Windows 98 is an easy-to-use program that allows you to communicate with and control your computer readily and customize it to fit your individual needs.

In this project, you will learn about Microsoft Windows 98 and how to use the Windows 98 graphical user interface to simplify the process of working with documents and applications, transfer data between documents, organize the manner in which you interact with your computer, and use your computer to access information on the Internet and/or intranet.

In the first part of this project, you will work with the desktop and the windows available on the desktop, learn the basic mouse operations, launch an application program, and create and modify documents using Microsoft Word 2000. Using Windows Explorer, you will learn to view the contents of files and folders, create and delete folders, select and copy files and folders, rename and delete files, and use Microsoft Windows 98 Help.

Microsoft Office 2000, the latest edition of the world's best-selling office suite, is a collection of the more popular Microsoft application software products that work similarly and together as if they were a single program. Microsoft Office 2000 integrates these applications and combines them with the power of the Internet so you can move quickly among applications, transfer text and graphics easily among them, and interact seamlessly with the World Wide Web. An explanation of each of the application software programs in Microsoft Office 2000 is given at the end of this project.

What Is Microsoft Windows 98?

An **operating system** is the set of computer instructions, called a computer program, that controls the allocation of computer hardware, such as memory, disk devices, printers, and CD-ROM and DVD drives, and provides you with the capability of communicating with your computer. The most popular and widely used operating system for personal computers is **Microsoft Windows 98** (called **Windows 98** for the rest of this book).

Windows 98 is an operating system that performs every function necessary to enable you to communicate with and use your computer. Windows 98 is called a **32-bit operating system** because it uses 32 bits for addressing and other purposes, which means the operating system can address more than four gigabytes of RAM (random-access memory) and perform tasks faster than older operating systems. Windows 98 includes **Microsoft Internet Explorer (IE)**, a browser software program developed by Microsoft Corporation, that integrates the Windows 98 desktop and the Internet. Internet Explorer allows you to work with programs and files in a similar fashion, whether they are located on your computer, a local network, or the Internet.

Windows 98 is designed to be compatible with all existing **application programs**, which are programs that perform an application-related function such as word processing. To use the application programs that can be executed under Windows 98, you must know about the Windows 98 user interface.

More *About*

Windows

For information about the Windows operating system, visit the Office 2000 More About Web page (www.scsite.com/off2000/more.htm) and then click Windows.

What Is a User Interface?

A **user interface** is the combination of hardware and software that you use to communicate with and control your computer. Through the user interface, you are able to make selections on your computer, request information from your computer, and respond to messages displayed by your computer. Thus, a user interface provides the means for dialogue between you and your computer.

Hardware and software together form the user interface. Among the hardware devices associated with a user interface are the monitor, keyboard, and mouse (Figure 1-1). The **monitor** displays messages and provides information. You respond by entering data in the form of a command or other response using the **keyboard** or **mouse**. Among the responses available to you are responses that specify what application program to run, what document to open, when to print, and where to store data for future use.

USER INTERFACE

monitor

COMPUTER HARDWARE

keyboard

mouse

MAIN MEMORY

Display messages ⎫ USER
Accept responses ⎬ INTERFACE
Determine actions ⎭ PROGRAMS

FIGURE 1-1

COMPUTER SOFTWARE

INT 1.5

The Windows 98 Interface

The Windows 98 graphical user interface, although similar to the Windows 95 graphical user interface, has been improved greatly. Thousands of hours were spent accomplishing this. Of tremendous importance to the development of this version were the usability labs where all levels of users interacted with the various versions of the interface. One of the most significant improvements that emerged from the labs was the Quick Launch toolbar.

The computer software associated with the user interface consists of the programs that engage you in dialogue (Figure 1-1 on the previous page). The computer software determines the messages you receive, the manner in which you should respond, and the actions that occur based on your responses.

The goal of an effective user interface is to be **user friendly**, meaning that the software can be used easily by individuals with limited training. Research studies have indicated that the use of graphics can play an important role in aiding users to interact effectively with a computer. A **graphical user interface**, or **GUI** (pronounced gooey), is a user interface that displays graphics in addition to text when it communicates with the user.

The Windows 98 graphical user interface was designed carefully to be easier to set up, simpler to learn, faster and more powerful, and better integrated with the Internet than previous versions of Microsoft Windows.

Launching Microsoft Windows 98

When you turn on your computer, an introductory screen consisting of the Windows logo and Windows 98 name displays on a blue sky and clouds background in the middle of the screen. The screen clears and several items display on a background called the **desktop.** The default color of the desktop background is green, but your computer may display a different color. Your screen will display as shown in Figure 1-2. It may also display without the Welcome screen shown in Figure 1-2.

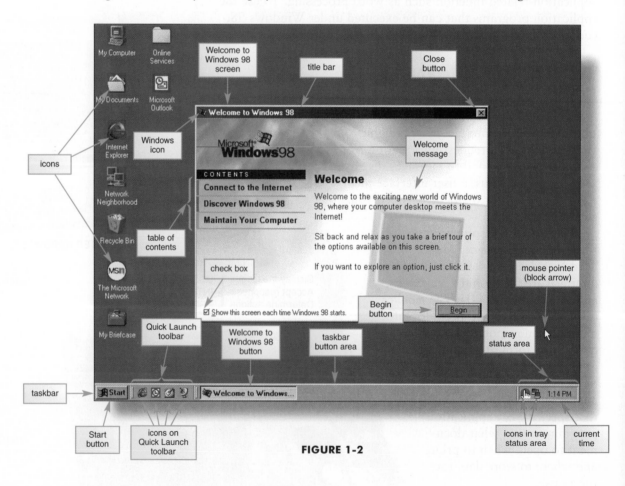

FIGURE 1-2

The items on the desktop shown in Figure 1-2 include nine icons and their titles on the left side of the desktop and the taskbar at the bottom of the desktop. Using the nine **icons**, you can view the contents of your computer (**My Computer**), store documents in one location (**My Documents**), connect to and browse the Internet (**Internet Explorer**), work with other computers connected to your computer (**Network Neighborhood**), discard unneeded objects (**Recycle Bin**), connect to The Microsoft Network online service (**The Microsoft Network**), transfer documents or folders to and from a portable computer (**My Briefcase**), investigate other online services (**Online Services**), and receive and send e-mail (**Microsoft Outlook**). Your computer's desktop may contain more, fewer, or some different icons because the desktop of the computer can be customized.

The **taskbar** at the bottom of the screen shown in Figure 1-2 contains the Start button, Quick Launch toolbar, taskbar button area, and the tray status area. The **Start button** allows you to launch a program quickly, find or open a document, change your computer's settings, shut down the computer, and perform many more tasks. The **Quick Launch toolbar** contains four icons that allow you to launch Internet Explorer (**Launch Internet Explorer Browser**), launch Microsoft Outlook (**Launch Microsoft Outlook**), view an uncluttered desktop at any time (**Show Desktop**), and view a list of channels (**View Channels**).

The **taskbar button area** contains buttons to indicate which windows are open on the desktop. In Figure 1-2, the Welcome to Windows 98 screen displays on the desktop and the Welcome to Windows 98 button displays in the taskbar button area. The **tray status area** contains **The Microsoft Network icon** to connect to The Microsoft Network online service, the **Internet connection icon** to indicate a modem is being used to connect to the Internet, and the current time (1:14 PM). The tray status area on your desktop may contain more, fewer, or some different icons because the contents of the tray status area change.

The Welcome to Windows 98 screen that may display on your desktop when you launch Windows 98 is shown in Figure 1-2. The **title bar** at the top of the screen, which is dark blue in color, contains the Windows icon, identifies the name of the screen (Welcome to Windows 98), and contains the Close button to close the Welcome to Windows 98 screen.

On the Welcome to Windows 98 screen, a table of contents contains three options (Connect to the Internet, Discover Windows 98, and Maintain Your Computer). The options in the table of contents allow you to perform different tasks such as connecting to the Internet, learning Windows 98 using the Discover Windows 98 tutorial, and improving the performance of your computer. A welcome message (Welcome) to the right of the table of contents welcomes you to the world of Windows 98. Pointing to an option in the table of contents replaces the Welcome message with an explanation of the option. The **Begin button** in the lower-right corner begins the process of connecting to the Internet, and a check mark in the **check box** in the left corner of the screen indicates the Welcome to Windows 98 screen will display each time you start Windows 98.

In the lower-right corner of the desktop is the mouse pointer. On the desktop, the **mouse pointer** is the shape of a block arrow. The mouse pointer allows you to point to objects on the desktop and may change shape as it points to different objects.

Nearly every item on the Windows 98 desktop is considered an object. Even the desktop itself is an object. Every **object** has properties. The **properties** of an object are unique to that specific object and may affect what can be done to the object or what the object does. For example, the properties of an object may be the color of the object, such as the color of the desktop.

More *About*

The Windows 98 Desktop

Because Windows 98 is customized easily, the desktop on your computer may not resemble the desktop in Figure 1-2. For example, the icon titles on the desktop may be underlined or objects not shown in Figure 1-2 may display on your desktop. If this is the case, contact your instructor for instructions for selecting the default desktop view settings to change the desktop view.

More *About*

Windows Tips and Tricks

For undocumented Windows tips and tricks, visit the Office 2000 More About Web page (www.scsite.com/off2000/more.htm) and then click Tips and Tricks.

More *About*

Windows Performance

To improve Windows performance and view information about Windows Second Edition, visit the Office 2000 More About Web page (www.scsite.com/off2000/more.htm) and then click Windows Performance.

Closing the Welcome Screen

As noted, the Welcome screen may display when you launch Windows 98. If the Welcome screen does display on the desktop, you should close it prior to beginning any other operations using Windows 98. To close the Welcome screen, complete the following step.

TO CLOSE THE WELCOME SCREEN

 Press and hold the ALT key on the keyboard and then press the F4 key on the keyboard. Release the ALT key.

The Welcome to Windows 98 screen closes.

The Desktop as a Work Area

The Windows 98 desktop and the objects on the desktop were designed to emulate a work area in an office or at home. You may think of the Windows desktop as an electronic version of the top of your desk. You can move objects around on the desktop, look at them and then put them aside, and so on. In Project 1, you will learn how to interact with the Windows 98 desktop.

Communicating with Microsoft Windows 98

The Windows 98 interface provides the means for dialogue between you and your computer. Part of this dialogue involves your requesting information from your computer and responding to messages displayed by your computer. You can request information and respond to messages using either a mouse or a keyboard.

cable

primary
mouse button

wheel
button

IntelliMouse

Microsoft

secondary
mouse button

FIGURE 1-3

Mouse Operations

A **mouse** is a pointing device that is attached to the computer by a cable. Although not required when using Windows 98, Windows supports the use of the **Microsoft IntelliMouse** (Figure 1-3). The IntelliMouse contains three buttons; the primary mouse button, the secondary mouse button, and the wheel button between the primary and secondary mouse buttons. Typically, the **primary mouse button** is the left mouse button and the **secondary mouse button** is the right mouse button although Windows 98 allows you to switch them. In this book, the left mouse button is the primary mouse button and the right mouse button is the secondary mouse button. The functions the **wheel button** and wheel perform depends on the software application being used. If the mouse connected to your computer is not an IntelliMouse, it will not have a wheel button between the primary and secondary mouse buttons.

Using the mouse, you can perform the following operations: (1) point; (2) click; (3) right-click; (4) double-click; (5) drag; and (6) right-drag. These operations are demonstrated on the following pages.

Point and Click

Point means you move the mouse across a flat surface until the mouse pointer rests on the item of choice on the desktop. As you move the mouse across a flat surface, the movement of a ball on the underside of the mouse (Figure 1-4) is sensed electronically, and the mouse pointer moves across the desktop in the same direction.

Click means you press and release the primary mouse button, which in this book is the left mouse button. In most cases, you must point to an item before you click. To become acquainted with the use of the mouse, perform the following steps to point to and click various objects on the desktop.

single ball on underside of mouse

FIGURE 1-4

 To Point and Click

1 **Point to the Start button on the taskbar by moving the mouse across a flat surface until the mouse pointer rests on the Start button.**

The mouse pointer on the Start button displays a **ScreenTip** *(Click here to begin.) (Figure 1-5). The ScreenTip, which provides instructions, displays on the desktop for approximately five seconds. Other Screen-Tips display on the screen until you move the mouse pointer off the object.*

Start button

ScreenTip

Click here to begin.

mouse pointer

FIGURE 1-5

2 **Click the Start button on the taskbar by pressing and releasing the left mouse button.**

The *Start menu* displays and the Start button is recessed on the taskbar (Figure 1-6). A *menu* is a list of related commands. A *command* directs Windows 98 to perform a specific action such as shutting down the operating system. Each command on the Start menu consists of an icon and a command name. A *right arrow* follows some commands to indicate pointing to the command will open a submenu. Three commands (Run, Log Off Steven Forsythe, and Shut Down) are followed by an *ellipsis* (...) to indicate more information is required to execute these commands.

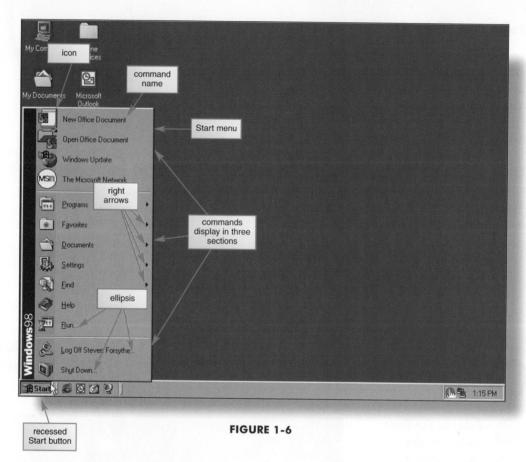

FIGURE 1-6

3 **Point to Programs on the Start menu.**

When you point to Programs, Windows 98 highlights the Programs command on the Start menu and the *Programs submenu* displays (Figure 1-7). A *submenu, or cascading menu,* is a menu that displays when you point to a command that is followed by a right arrow. Whenever you point to a command on a menu, the command is highlighted.

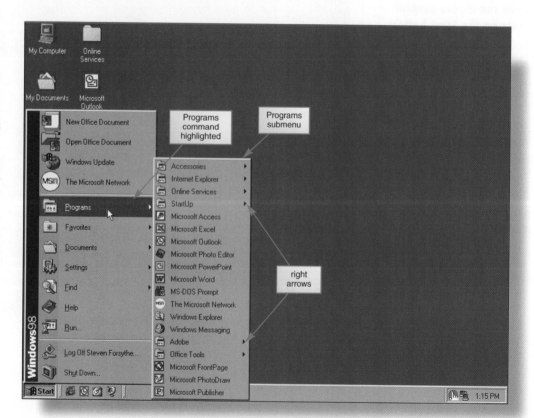

FIGURE 1-7

4 **Point to an open area of the desktop and then click the open area of the desktop.**

The Start menu and Programs submenu close (Figure 1-8). The mouse pointer points to the desktop. To close a menu anytime, click any open area of the desktop except on the menu itself. The Start button is no longer recessed.

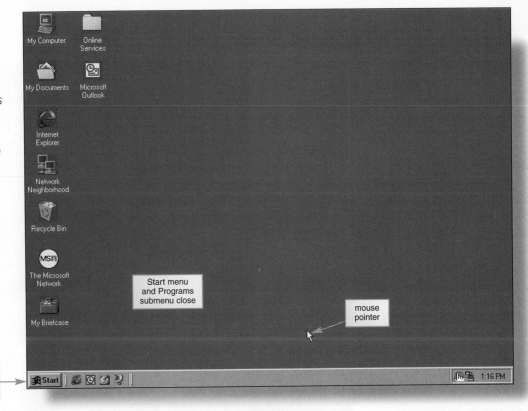

Start menu and Programs submenu close

mouse pointer

Start button no longer recessed

Start   1:16 PM

FIGURE 1-8

The Start menu shown in Figure 1-6 is divided into three sections. The top section contains commands to create or open a Microsoft Office document (New Office Document and Open Office Document), launch the Windows Update application (Windows Update), and connect to The Microsoft Network (The Microsoft Network); the middle section contains commands to launch an application, work with documents or Web sites, customize options, and search for files or Help (Programs, Favorites, Documents, Settings, Find, Help, and Run); and the bottom section contains basic operating tasks (Log Off Steven Forsythe and Shut Down).

When you click an object such as the Start button in Figure 1-6, you must point to the object before you click. In the steps that follow, the instruction that directs you to point to a particular item and then click is, Click the particular item. For example, Click the Start button means point to the Start button and then click.

Right-Click

Right-click means you press and release the secondary mouse button, which in this book is the right mouse button. As directed when using the primary mouse button for clicking an object, normally you will point to an object before you right-click it. Perform the steps on the next page to right-click the desktop.

More About

Buttons

Buttons on the desktop and in programs are an integral part of Windows 98. When you point to them, their function displays in a ScreenTip. When you click them, they appear to recess on the screen to mimic what would happen if you pushed an actual button. All buttons in Windows 98 behave in the same manner.

More About

The Right Mouse Button

The earliest versions of Microsoft Windows made little use of the right mouse button. In Windows 98, you will find using the right mouse button essential.

Steps **To Right-Click**

1 **Point to an open area of the desktop and then press and release the right mouse button.**

A shortcut menu displays (Figure 1-9). The shortcut menu consists of eight commands. Right-clicking an object, such as the desktop, opens a **shortcut menu** that contains a set of commands specifically for use with that object. When a command on a menu appears dimmed, such as the Paste command and the Paste Shortcut command, that command is unavailable.

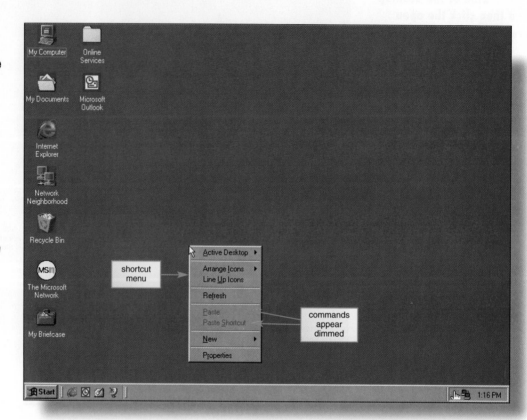

FIGURE 1-9

2 **Point to New on the shortcut menu.**

When you move the mouse pointer to the New command, Windows 98 highlights the New command and opens the New submenu (Figure 1-10). The New submenu contains a variety of commands. The number of commands and the actual commands that display on your computer may be different.

3 **Point to an open area of the desktop and click the open area to close the shortcut menu and the New submenu.**

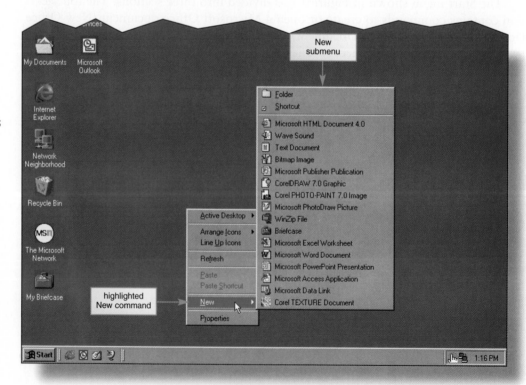

FIGURE 1-10

Whenever you right-click an object, a shortcut menu (also referred to as an object menu) will display. As you will see, the use of shortcut menus speeds up your work and adds flexibility to your interface with the computer.

Double-Click

To **double-click**, you quickly press and release the left mouse button twice without moving the mouse. In most cases, you must point to an item before you double-click. Perform the following step to open the My Computer window on the desktop by double-clicking the My Computer icon.

More About

Right-Clicking

Right-clicking an object other than the desktop will display a different shortcut menu with commands useful to that object. Right-clicking an object is thought to be the fastest method of performing an operation on an object.

Steps **To Open a Window by Double-Clicking**

1 **Point to the My Computer icon on the desktop and then double-click by quickly pressing and releasing the left mouse button twice without moving the mouse.**

The My Computer window opens (Figure 1-11). The recessed My Computer button is added to the taskbar button area.

FIGURE 1-11

The My Computer window, the only open window, is the active window. The **active window** is the window currently being used. Whenever you click an object that can be opened, such as the My Computer icon, Windows 98 will open the object; and the open object will be identified by a recessed button in the taskbar button area. The recessed button identifies the active window.

The contents of the My Computer window on your computer may be different from the contents of the My Computer window in Figure 1-11.

More About

Double-Clicking

When double-clicking, many people have a tendency to move the mouse before they click a second time. You should find, however, that with a little practice, double-clicking becomes quite natural.

My Computer

The trade press and media have poked fun at the icon name, My Computer. One wag said no one should use Windows 98 for more than five minutes without changing the name (which is easily done). Microsoft responds that in their usability labs, beginning computer users found the name, My Computer, easier to understand.

The My Computer Window

Because Windows 98 is customized easily, the My Computer window on your computer may not resemble the window in Figure 1-11 on the previous page. If this is the case, check the commands on the View menu by clicking View on the menu bar. If a check mark precedes the as Web Page command, click the as Web Page command. If a large dot does not precede the Large Icons command, click the Large Icons command.

Minimizing Windows

Windows management on the Windows 98 desktop is important in order to keep the desktop uncluttered. You will find yourself frequently minimizing windows and then later reopening them with a click of a button in the taskbar button area.

My Computer Window

The thin line, or **window border**, surrounding the My Computer window shown in Figure 1-11 on the previous page determines its shape and size. The **title bar** at the top of the window contains a small icon that is the same as the icon on the desktop and the **window title** (My Computer) that identifies the window. The color of the title bar (dark blue) and the recessed My Computer button in the taskbar button area indicate the My Computer window is the active window. The color of the active window on your computer may be different from the dark blue color shown in Figure 1-11.

Clicking the icon at the left on the title bar will open the **System menu**, which contains commands to carry out the actions associated with the My Computer window. At the right on the title bar are three buttons, the Minimize button, the Maximize button, and the Close button, that can be used to specify the size of the window and close the window.

The **menu bar**, which is the horizontal bar below the title bar of a window (see Figure 1-11 on the previous page), contains a list of menu names for the My Computer window: File, Edit, View, Go, Favorites, and Help. One letter in each menu name is underlined. You can open a menu by clicking the menu name on the menu bar or by typing the corresponding underlined letter on the keyboard in combination with the ALT key. At the right end of the menu bar is a button containing the Windows logo. Clicking this button starts the Microsoft Internet Explorer Web browser and displays one of the Web pages in the Microsoft Web site in the browser window.

Below the menu bar is the **Standard Buttons toolbar** containing buttons that allow you to navigate through open windows on the desktop (Back, Forward, and Up) and copy and move text within a window or between windows (Cut, Copy, and Paste). Additional buttons display when the size of the window is increased or the double right arrow button is clicked. Each button contains a **text label** and an icon describing its function.

The area below the Standard Buttons toolbar contains 10 icons. A title below each icon identifies the icon. The five icons in the top row, called **drive icons**, represent a 3½ Floppy (A:) drive, a Hard disk (C:) drive, a different area on the same hard disk (D:), a Removable Disk (E:) drive, and a CD-ROM drive (F:).

The first four icons in the second row are folders on your computer. A **folder** is an object created to contain related documents, applications, and other folders. A folder in Windows 98 contains items in much the same way a folder on your desk contains items. The Web folders icon, which is associated with Microsoft Office, allows you to publish documents for viewing in a Web browser.

A message at the left on the **status bar** located at the bottom of the window indicates the right panel contains ten objects (see Figure 1-11 on the previous page). The My Computer icon and My Computer icon title display to the right of the message on the status bar.

Minimize Button

Two buttons on the title bar of a window, the Minimize button and the Maximize button, allow you to control the way a window displays or does not display on the desktop. When you click the **Minimize button** (see Figure 1-11 on the previous page), the My Computer window no longer displays on the desktop and the recessed My Computer button in the taskbar button area changes to a non-recessed button. A minimized window still is open but it does not display on the screen. To minimize and then redisplay the My Computer window, complete these steps.

Steps **To Minimize and Redisplay a Window**

1 Point to the Minimize button on the title bar of the My Computer window.

The mouse pointer points to the Minimize button on the My Computer window title bar (Figure 1-12). A ScreenTip displays below the Minimize button and the My Computer button in the taskbar button area is recessed.

FIGURE 1-12

2 Click the Minimize button.

When you minimize the My Compuer window, Windows 98 removes the My Computer window from the desktop and the My Computer button changes to a non-recessed button (Figure 1-13).

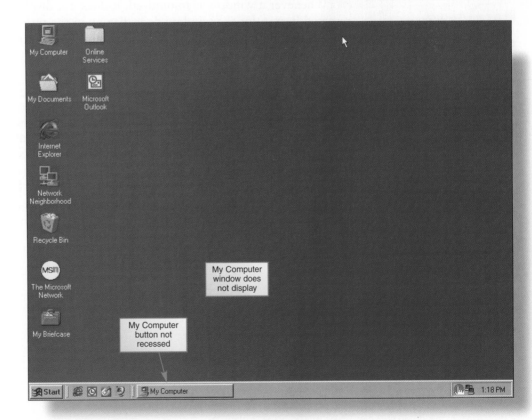

FIGURE 1-13

3 Click the My Computer button in the taskbar button area.

The My Computer window displays on the desktop in the same place and size as it was before being minimized (Figure 1-14). In addition, the My Computer window is the active window because it contains the dark blue title bar, and the My Computer button in the taskbar button area is recessed.

My Computer window opens

My Computer button recessed

mouse pointer

FIGURE 1-14

Whenever a window is minimized, it does not display on the desktop but a non-recessed button for the window does display in the taskbar button area. Whenever you want a minimized window to display and be the active window, click its button in the taskbar button area.

Maximize and Restore Buttons

Sometimes when information is displayed in a window, the information is not completely visible. One method to display the entire contents of a window is to enlarge the window using the **Maximize button**. The Maximize button maximizes a window so the window fills the entire screen, making it easier to see the contents of the window. When a window is maximized, the **Restore button** replaces the Maximize button on the title bar. Clicking the Restore button will return the window to its size before maximizing. To maximize and restore the My Computer window, complete the following steps.

Steps To Maximize and Restore a Window

1 **Point to the Maximize button on** the title bar of the My Computer window (Figure 1-15).

FIGURE 1-15

2 **Click the Maximize button.**

The My Computer window expands so it and the taskbar fill the entire screen (Figure 1-16). The Restore button replaces the Maximize button and the My Computer button in the taskbar button area remains recessed. The My Computer window still is the active window and additional buttons display on the Standard Buttons toolbar that allow you to undo a previous action (Undo), delete text (Delete), display the properties of an object (Properties), and change the desktop view (Views).

FIGURE 1-16

3 Point to the Restore button on the title bar of the My Computer window (Figure 1-17).

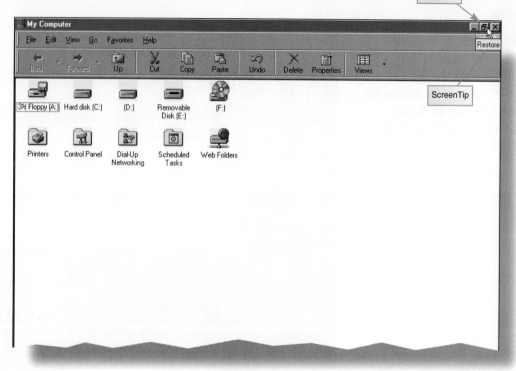

FIGURE 1-17

4 Click the Restore button.

The My Computer window returns to the size and position it occupied before being maximized (Figure 1-18). The My Computer button does not change. The Maximize button replaces the Restore button.

FIGURE 1-18

PROJECT 1

When a window is maximized, such as shown in Figure 1-16 on page INT 1.17, you also can minimize the window by clicking the Minimize button. If, after minimizing the window, you click its button in the taskbar button area, the window will return to its maximized size.

Close Button

The **Close button** on the title bar of a window closes the window and removes the window button from the taskbar. To close and then reopen the My Computer window, complete the following steps.

More About

The Close Button

The Close button was new in Windows 95. Before Windows 95, the user had to double-click a button or click a command on a menu to close the window. The choice of how to perform an operation such as closing a window is a matter of personal preference. In most cases, you will want to choose the easiest method.

Steps To Close a Window and Reopen a Window

 1 Point to the Close button on the title bar of the My Computer window (Figure 1-19).

FIGURE 1-19

2 Click the Close button.

The My Computer window closes and the My Computer button no longer displays in the taskbar button area (Figure 1-20).

FIGURE 1-20

3 **Double-click the My Computer icon on the desktop.**

The My Computer window opens and displays on the screen (Figure 1-21). The My Computer button displays in the taskbar button area.

FIGURE 1-21

More About

Dragging

Dragging is the second-most difficult skill to learn with a mouse. You may want to practice dragging a few times so you are comfortable with it.

Drag

Drag means you point to an item, hold down the left mouse button, move the item to the desired location, and then release the left mouse button. You can move any open window to another location on the desktop by pointing to the title bar of the window and dragging the window. To drag the My Computer window to another location on the desktop, perform the following steps.

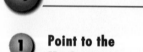

To Move an Object by Dragging

1 **Point to the My Computer window title bar (Figure 1-22).**

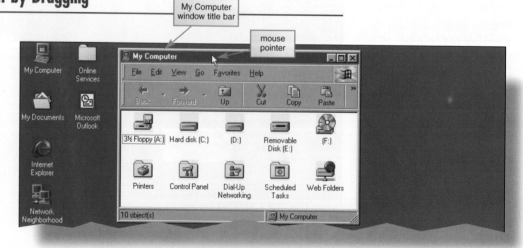

FIGURE 1-22

2 Hold down the left mouse button, move the mouse so the window moves to the center of the desktop, and release the left mouse button.

As you drag the mouse, the My Computer window moves across the desktop. When you release the left mouse button, the window displays in its new location (Figure 1-23).

FIGURE 1-23

Sizing a Window by Dragging

You can use dragging for more than just moving an object. For example, you can drag the border of a window to change the size of the window. To change the size of the My Computer window, perform the following step.

 To Size a Window by Dragging

1 Position the mouse pointer over the lower-right corner of the My Computer window until the mouse pointer changes to a two-headed arrow. Drag the lower-right corner upward and to the right until the window on your desktop resembles the window shown in Figure 1-24.

As you drag the lower-right corner, the window changes size and a vertical scroll bar displays (Figure 1-24). Five of the ten icons in the window are visible in the resized window in Figure 1-24.

FIGURE 1-24

A scroll bar is a bar that displays at the right edge and/or bottom edge of a window when the window contents are not completely visible. A vertical scroll bar contains an **up scroll arrow**, a **down scroll arrow**, and a **scroll box** that enable you to view areas of the window not currently visible. A vertical scroll bar displays in the My Computer window shown in Figure 1-24 on the previous page.

The size of the scroll box in any window is dependent on the amount of the window that is not visible. The smaller the scroll box, the more of the window that is not visible. In Figure 1-24, the scroll box occupies approximately half of the scroll bar. This indicates that approximately half of the contents of the window are not visible. If the scroll box were a tiny rectangle, a large portion of the window would not be visible.

In addition to dragging a corner of a window, you also can drag any of the borders of a window. If you drag a vertical border, such as the right border, you can move the border left or right. If you drag a horizontal border, such as the bottom border, you can move the border of the window up or down.

As mentioned earlier, maximizing a window is one method to enlarge a window and display more information in the window. Dragging a window to enlarge the window is a second method to display information in a window that is not visible.

Scrolling in a Window

Previously, two methods were shown to display information that was not completely visible in the My Computer window. These methods were maximizing the My Computer window and changing the size of the My Computer window. A third method uses the scroll bar in the window.

Scrolling can be accomplished in three ways: (1) click the scroll arrows; (2) click the scroll bar; and (3) drag the scroll box. On the following pages, you will use the scroll bar to scroll the contents of the My Computer window. Perform the following steps to scroll the My Computer window using the scroll arrows.

Steps: To Scroll a Window Using Scroll Arrows

1 Point to the down scroll arrow on the vertical scroll bar (Figure 1-25).

FIGURE 1-25

2 **Click the down scroll arrow one time.**

The window scrolls down (the icons move up in the window) and displays the tops of the icons previously not visible (Figure 1-26). Because the window size does not change when you scroll, the contents of the window will change, as seen in the difference between Figure 1-25 and Figure 1-26.

FIGURE 1-26

3 **Click the down scroll arrow two more times.**

The scroll box moves to the bottom of the scroll bar and the remaining icons in the window display (Figure 1-27).

FIGURE 1-27

You can scroll continuously through a window using scroll arrows by pointing to the up or down scroll arrow and holding down the left mouse button. The window continues to scroll until you release the left mouse button or you reach the top or bottom of the window. You also can scroll by clicking the scroll bar itself. When you click the scroll bar, the window moves up or down a greater distance than when you click the scroll arrows.

The third way in which you can scroll through a window to view its contents is by dragging the scroll box. When you drag the scroll box, the window moves up or down as you drag.

Being able to view the contents of a window by scrolling is an important Windows 98 skill because in many cases the entire contents of a window are not visible.

Resizing a Window

After moving and resizing a window, you may wish to return the window to approximately its original size. To return the My Computer window to about its original size, complete the following steps.

TO RESIZE A WINDOW

 Position the mouse pointer over the lower-right corner of the My Computer window border until the mouse pointer changes to a two-headed arrow.

 Drag the lower-right corner of the My Computer window until the window is the same size as shown in Figure 1-23 on page INT 1.21, and then release the mouse button.

The My Computer window is approximately the same size as before you made it smaller.

Closing a Window

After you have completed your work in a window, normally you will close the window. To close the My Computer window, complete the following steps.

TO CLOSE A WINDOW

 Point to the Close button on the right of the title bar in the My Computer window.

 Click the Close button.

The My Computer window closes and the desktop contains no open windows.

Right-Drag

Right-drag means you point to an item, hold down the right mouse button, move the item to the desired location, and then release the right mouse button. When you right-drag an object, a shortcut menu displays. The shortcut menu contains commands specifically for use with the object being dragged. To right-drag the My Briefcase icon to the right of its current position on the desktop, perform the following steps. If the My Briefcase icon does not display on your desktop, choose another icon and follow the procedure in the following steps.

To Right-Drag

1 **Point to the My Briefcase icon on the desktop, hold down the right mouse button, drag the icon to the right toward the middle of the desktop, and then release the right mouse button.**

The dimmed My Briefcase icon and a shortcut menu display in the middle of the desktop (Figure 1-28). The My Briefcase icon remains at its original location. The shortcut menu contains four commands: Move Here, Copy Here, Create Shortcut(s) Here, and Cancel. The Move Here command in bold (dark) type identifies what would happen if you were to drag the My Briefcase icon with the left mouse button.

FIGURE 1-28

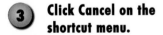

2 **Point to Cancel on the shortcut menu.**

The Cancel command is highlighted (Figure 1-29).

3 **Click Cancel on the shortcut menu.**

The shortcut menu and the dragged My Briefcase icon disappear from the screen.

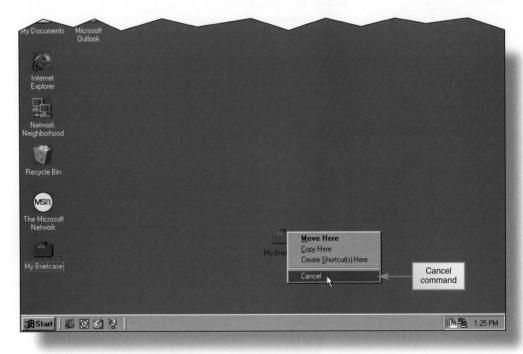

FIGURE 1-29

Whenever you begin an operation but do not want to complete the operation, you can click Cancel on a shortcut menu or click the Cancel button in a dialog box. The **Cancel** command will reset anything you have done in the operation.

If you click **Move Here** on the shortcut menu shown in Figure 1-28 on the previous page, Windows 98 will move the icon from its current location to the new location. If you click **Copy Here**, the icon will be copied to the new location and two icons will display on the desktop. Windows 98 automatically will give the second icon a different title. If you click **Create Shortcut(s) Here**, a special object called a shortcut will be created.

Although you can move icons by dragging with the primary (left) mouse button and by right-dragging with the secondary (right) mouse button, it is strongly suggested you right-drag because a menu displays and you can specify the exact operation you want to occur. When you drag using the left mouse button, a default operation takes place and the operation may not do what you want.

Summary of Mouse and Windows Operations

You have seen how to use the mouse to point, click, right-click, double-click, drag, and right-drag in order to accomplish certain tasks on the desktop. The use of a mouse is an important skill when using Windows 98. In addition, you have learned how to move around and display windows on the Windows 98 desktop.

The Keyboard and Keyboard Shortcuts

The **keyboard** is an input device on which you manually key, or type, data. Figure 1-30a shows the enhanced IBM 101-key keyboard, and Figure 1-30b shows a Microsoft Natural keyboard designed specifically for use with Windows. Many tasks you accomplish with a mouse also can be accomplished using a keyboard.

To perform tasks using the keyboard, you must understand the notation used to identify which keys to press. This notation is used throughout Windows 98 to identify **keyboard shortcuts**.

FIGURE 1-30a

FIGURE 1-30b

Keyboard shortcuts consist of: (1) pressing a single key (example: press the ENTER key); or (2) pressing and holding down one key and then pressing a second key, as shown by two key names separated by a plus sign (CTRL+ESC). For example, to obtain Help about Windows 98, you can press the F1 key; to open the Start menu, hold down the CTRL key and then press the ESC key (press CTRL+ESC).

Often, computer users will use keyboard shortcuts for operations they perform frequently. For example, many users find pressing the F1 key to launch Windows 98 Help easier than using the Start menu as shown later in this project. As a user, you probably will find the combination of keyboard and mouse operations that particularly suit you, but it is strongly recommended that generally you use the mouse.

The Windows 98 Desktop Views

Windows 98 provides several ways to view your desktop and the windows that open on the desktop. The three desktop views are the Web style, Classic style, and Custom style. The desktop view you choose will affect the appearance of your desktop, how you open and work with windows on the desktop, and how you work with the files and folders on your computer.

The **Classic style** causes the desktop and the objects on the desktop to display and function as they did in Windows 95, the previous version of Windows. The icon titles are not underlined and you double-click an icon to open the window associated with the icon. In **Web style**, the icon titles on the desktop are underlined and you click, instead of double-click, an icon to open its window. Additional desktop items that are designed to allow you to access information on the Internet easily also may display on the desktop.

The **Custom style** is a combination of Classic style and Web style settings. The icon titles on the desktop may display with or without an underline, and you either click or double-click an icon to open its window. Unless you change the settings after installing Windows 98, the desktop will display in the Custom style as shown in the figures illustrated previously in this project.

For more information about desktop views and how to change the desktop view, read the instructions in the Using Windows Help section later in this project and then use Windows Help to search for information about desktop views.

Launching an Application Program

One of the basic tasks you can perform using Windows 98 is to launch an application program. A **program** is a set of computer instructions that carries out a task on your computer. An **application program** is a program that allows you to accomplish a specific task for which that program is designed. For example, a **word processing program** is an application program that allows you to create written documents; a **presentation graphics program** is an application program that allows you to create graphic presentations for display on a computer; and a **Web browser program** is an application program that allows you to search for and display Web pages.

The most popular activity using a computer is launching an application program to accomplish tasks. Windows allows you to launch an application in a variety of ways. When several methods are available, you have the opportunity to select the method that best fits your needs.

Launching an Application Using the Start Button

One method to launch an application program is to use the Start menu. Perform the steps on the next page to launch Internet Explorer using the Start menu and Internet Explorer command.

More About

Desktop Views

The Classic style was included in the Windows 98 operating system to allow Windows 95 users to upgrade easily to the newer Windows 98 operating system. Responses from people in the Beta Test program, which is a program designed to test software prior to the public sale of the software, indicated that most Windows 95 users had little difficulty switching to Windows 98, and experienced users liked the Web style.

More About

Application Programs

Some application programs, such as Internet Explorer, are part of Windows 98. Most application programs, however, such as Microsoft Office, Lotus SmartSuite, and others must be purchased separately from Windows 98.

To Launch a Program Using the Start Menu

1 **Click the Start button on the taskbar. Point to Programs on the Start menu. Point to Internet Explorer on the Programs submenu. Point to Internet Explorer on the Internet Explorer submenu.**

The Start menu, Programs submenu, and Internet Explorer submenu display (Figure 1-31). The Internet Explorer submenu contains the **Internet Explorer command** *to launch the Internet Explorer program. You may find a different set of commands on the submenus on your computer.*

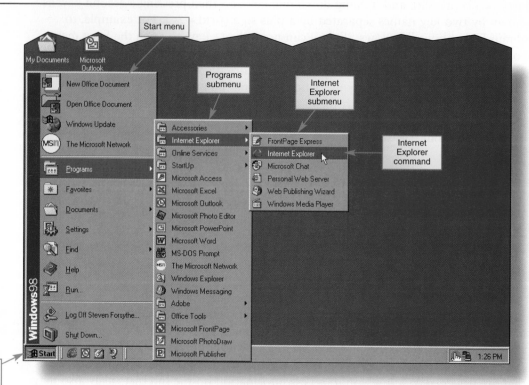

FIGURE 1-31

2 **Click Internet Explorer.**

Windows 98 launches the Internet Explorer program by opening the MSN.COM window on the desktop, displaying the MSN Web page in the window, and adding a recessed button to the taskbar button area (Figure 1-32). The URL for the Web page displays on the Address bar. Because Web pages are modified frequently, the Web page that displays on your desktop may be different from the Web page in Figure 1-32.

Other Ways

1. Click Launch Internet Explorer icon on Quick Launch toolbar

2. Double-click Internet Explorer icon on desktop

FIGURE 1-32

After you have launched Internet Explorer, you can use the program to search for and display different Web pages.

Windows 98 provides a number of ways to accomplish a particular task. In the previous section, one method to launch the Internet Explorer program was illustrated, and then alternate methods were listed in the Other Ways box. The remainder of this book will use the same format: a single set of steps will illustrate how to accomplish a task; and if you can perform the same task using other methods, the Other Ways box will specify the other methods. In each case, the method shown in the steps is the preferred method, but it is important for you to be aware of all the techniques you can use.

Quitting a Program

When you have completed your work using a program, you should quit the program. Perform the following steps to quit the Internet Explorer program.

 ### To Quit a Program

Close button

1 **Point to the Close button in the Internet Explorer window (Figure 1-33).**

2 **Click the Close button.**

Windows 98 quits Internet Explorer, closes the Internet Explorer window, and removes the Internet Explorer button from the taskbar.

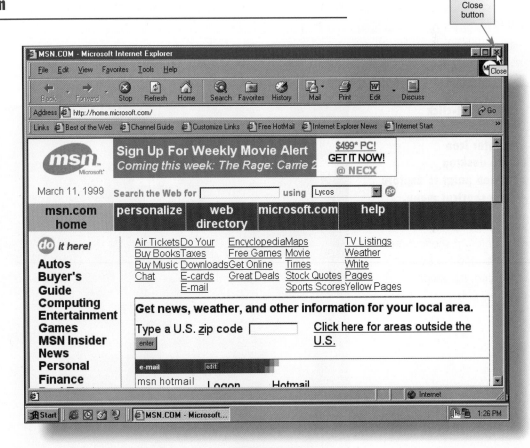

FIGURE 1-33

In the preceding sections, you launched Internet Explorer and then quit the Internet Explorer program. In the next section, you will launch the Windows Explorer application program. Windows Explorer is another application program included with Windows 98. This program allows you to view the contents of the computer, the hierarchy of folders on the computer, and the files and folders in each folder.

Other **Ways**

1. Double-click Internet Explorer logo on title bar
2. On File menu click Close
3. Press ALT+F4

Windows Explorer

Windows Explorer is an application program included with Windows 98 that allows you to view the contents of the computer, the hierarchy of folders on the computer, and the files and folders in each folder.

Windows Explorer also allows you to organize the files and folders on the computer by copying and moving the files and folders. In this project, you will use Windows Explorer to (1) work with the files and folders on your computer; (2) select and copy a group of files between the hard drive and a floppy disk; (3) create, rename, and delete a folder on a floppy disk; and (4) rename and delete a file on a floppy disk. These are common operations that you should understand how to perform.

Starting Windows Explorer and Maximizing Its Window

To explore the files and folders on the computer, start Windows Explorer and maximize its window by performing the following steps.

 To Start Windows Explorer and Maximize Its Window

1 **Right-click the My Computer icon on the desktop and then point to Explore on the shortcut menu.**

The My Computer icon is highlighted, a shortcut menu displays, and the Explore command is highlighted (Figure 1-34).

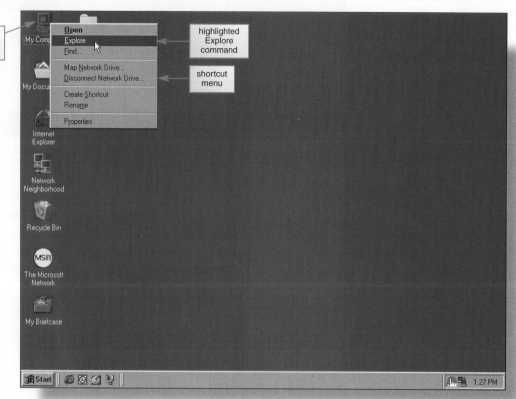

FIGURE 1-34

2 **Click Explore and then click the Maximize button on the Exploring - My Computer title bar.**

The Exploring - My Computer window opens and is maximized. The recessed Exploring - My Computer button is added to the taskbar button area (Figure 1-35).

Exploring - My Computer window opened and maximized

Exploring - My Computer button

FIGURE 1-35

The Exploring – My Computer Window

When you start Windows Explorer by right-clicking the My Computer icon and then clicking the Explore command on the shortcut menu, Windows 98 opens the Exploring - My Computer window (Figure 1-36 on the next page). The menu bar contains the File, Edit, View, Go, Favorites, Tools, and Help menu names. These menus contain commands to organize and work with the drives on the computer and the files and folders on those drives. Below the menu bar is the Standard Buttons toolbar.

Other Ways

1. Right-click Start button, click Explore on shortcut menu

2. Click Start button, point to Programs, click Windows Explorer

3. Right-click any icon on desktop (except The Microsoft Network icon and Microsoft Outlook icon), click Explore on shortcut menu

4. Right-click any icon on desktop except The Microsoft Network icon and Microsoft Outlook icon, press E

FIGURE 1-36

The main window is divided into two panes separated by a bar. The left pane of the window, identified by the Folders title, contains a **hierarchy** of folders on the computer. The right pane of the window displays the contents of the My Computer folder. In Figure 1-36, the Contents pane contains the icons and folder names of ten folders (3½ Floppy (A:), Hard disk (C:), (D:), Removable Disk (E:), (F:), Printers, Control Panel, Dial-Up Networking, Scheduled Tasks, and Web Folders) in the My Computer folder. These folders may be different on your computer. You can change the size of the Folders and Contents panes by dragging the bar that separates the two panes.

Each folder in the Folders pane is represented by an icon and folder name. The first folder, consisting of an icon and the Desktop folder name, represents the desktop of the computer. The seven folders indented and aligned below the Desktop folder name (My Computer, My Documents, Internet Explorer, Network Neighborhood, Recycle Bin, My Briefcase, and Online Services) are connected to the vertical line below the Desktop icon. These folders correspond to seven of the nine icons displayed on the left edge of the desktop (see Figure 1-2 on page INT 1.6). These folders may be different on your computer.

Windows 98 displays a minus sign (–) in a box to the left of an icon in the Folders pane to indicate the corresponding folder contains one or more folders that are visible in the Folders pane. These folders, called **subfolders**, are indented and aligned below the folder name.

In Figure 1-36, a minus sign precedes the My Computer icon, and 10 subfolders are indented and display below the My Computer folder name. The 10 subfolders (3½ Floppy (A:), Hard disk (C:), (D:), Removable Disk (E:), (F:), Printers, Control Panel, Dial-Up Networking, Scheduled Tasks, and Web Folders) correspond to the 10 folders in the Contents pane. Clicking the minus sign, referred to as **collapsing the folder**, removes the indented subfolders from the hierarchy of folders in the Folders pane and changes the minus sign to a plus sign.

Windows 98 displays a plus sign (+) in a box to the left of an icon to indicate the corresponding folder consists of one or more subfolders that are not visible in the Folders pane. In Figure 1-36, a plus sign precedes the first five icons indented and aligned below the My Computer name (3½ Floppy (A:), Hard disk (C:), (D:), Removable Disk (E:), and (F:) icons). Clicking the plus sign, referred to as **expanding the folder**, displays a list of indented subfolders and changes the plus sign to a minus sign.

If neither a plus sign nor a minus sign displays to the left of an icon, the folder does not contain subfolders. In Figure 1-36, the Printers, Control Panel, Dial-Up Networking, Scheduled Tasks, Recycle Bin, and My Briefcase icons are not preceded by a plus or minus sign and do not contain subfolders.

The status bar at the bottom of the Exploring - My Computer window indicates the number of folders, or objects, displayed in the Contents pane of the window (10 object(s)). Depending on the objects displayed in the Contents pane, the amount of disk space the objects occupy and the amount of unused disk space also may display on the status bar. If the status bar does not display in the Exploring - My Computer window on your computer, click View on the menu bar and then click Status Bar.

In addition to using Windows Explorer to explore your computer by right-clicking the My Computer icon, you also can use Windows Explorer to explore different aspects of your computer by right-clicking the Start button on the taskbar and the My Documents, Internet Explorer, Network Neighborhood, Recycle Bin, My Briefcase, and Online Services icons on the desktop.

Displaying the Contents of a Folder

In Figure 1-36, the Contents pane contains the subfolders in the My Computer folder. In addition to displaying the contents of the My Computer folder, the contents of any folder in the Folders pane can be displayed in the Contents pane. Perform the steps on the next page to display the contents of the Hard disk (C:) folder.

To Display the Contents of a Folder

1 Point to the Hard disk (C:) folder name in the Folders pane of the Exploring - My Computer window (Figure 1-37).

FIGURE 1-37

2 Click the Hard disk (C:) folder name.

The highlighted Hard disk (C:) folder name displays in the Folders pane, the contents of the Hard disk (C:) folder display in the Contents pane, the window title and button in the taskbar button area change to reflect the folder name, and the messages on the status bar change (Figure 1-38).

FIGURE 1-38

Other Ways

1. Double-click Hard disk (C:) icon in Contents pane

2. Press TAB to select any icon in Folders pane, press DOWN ARROW or UP ARROW to select Hard disk (C:) icon in Contents pane

The status bar messages shown in Figure 1-38 indicate 45 objects, the objects occupy 5.64MB of disk space, and the amount of unused (free) disk space is 230MB. The contents of the Hard disk (C:) folder may be different on your computer.

In addition to displaying the contents of the Hard disk (C:) folder, you can display the contents of the other folders by clicking the corresponding icon or folder name in the Folders pane. The contents of the folder you click then will display in the Contents pane of the window.

Expanding a Folder

Currently, the Hard disk (C:) folder is highlighted in the Folders pane of the Exploring - Hard disk (C:) window, and the contents of the Hard disk (C:) folder display in the Contents pane. Windows 98 displays a plus sign (+) to the left of the Hard disk (C:) icon to indicate the folder contains subfolders that are not visible in the hierarchy of folders in the Folders pane. To expand the Hard disk (C:) folder and display its subfolders, perform the following steps.

 To Expand a Folder

1 **Point to the plus sign to the left of the Hard disk (C:) icon in the Folders pane (Figure 1-39).**

FIGURE 1-39

2 **Click the plus sign to display the subfolders in the Hard disk (C:) folder.**

A minus sign replaces the plus sign preceding the Hard disk (C:) icon, a vertical scroll bar displays, and the Hard disk (C:) folder expands (Figure 1-40). The window title and the files and folders in the Contents pane remain unchanged.

FIGURE 1-40

Other Ways

1. Double-click the folder icon
2. Select folder icon, press PLUS SIGN on numeric keypad (or RIGHT ARROW)

The subfolders in the expanded Hard disk (C:) folder shown in Figure 1-40 on the previous page are indented and aligned below the Hard disk (C:) folder name. A closed folder icon and folder name identify each subfolder in the Hard disk (C:) folder.

Collapsing a Folder

Currently, the subfolders in the Hard disk (C:) folder display indented and aligned below the Hard disk (C:) folder name (see Figure 1-40 on the previous page). Windows 98 displays a minus sign (–) to the left of the Hard disk (C:) icon to indicate the folder is expanded. To collapse the Hard disk (C:) folder and then remove its subfolders from the hierarchy of folders in the Folders pane, perform the following steps.

 To Collapse a Folder

1 **Point to the minus sign preceding the Hard disk (C:) icon in the Folders pane (Figure 1-41).**

FIGURE 1-41

2 **Click the minus sign to display the Hard disk (C:) folder without its subfolders.**

A plus sign replaces the minus sign preceding the Hard disk (C:) icon and the subfolders in the Hard disk (C:) folder are removed from the hierarchy of folders (Figure 1-42).

FIGURE 1-42

Other **Ways**

1. Double-click folder icon
2. Select folder icon, press MINUS SIGN on numeric keypad (or LEFT ARROW)

Copying Files to a Folder on a Floppy Disk

One common operation that every student should understand how to perform is copying a file or group of files from one disk to another disk or from one folder to another folder. On the following pages, you will create a new folder, named My Files, on the floppy disk in drive A, select a group of files in the Windows folder on drive C, and copy the files from the Windows folder on drive C to the My Files folder on drive A.

When copying files, the drive and folder containing the files to be copied are called the **source drive** and **source folder**, respectively. The drive and folder to which the files are copied are called the **destination drive** and **destination folder**, respectively. Thus, the Windows folder is the source folder, drive C is the source drive, the My Files folder is the destination folder, and drive A is the destination drive.

Creating a New Folder

In preparation for selecting and copying files from a folder on the hard drive to a folder on the floppy disk in drive A, a new folder with the name of My Files will be created on the floppy disk. Perform the following steps to create the new folder.

 To Create a New Folder

1 **Insert a formatted floppy disk into drive A on your computer.**

2 **Click the 3½ Floppy (A:) folder name in the Folders pane and then point to an open area of the Contents pane.**

The 3½ Floppy (A:) folder name is highlighted, the contents of the 3½ Floppy (A:) folder display in the Contents pane, and the messages on the status bar change (Figure 1-43). The 3½ Floppy (A:) folder name displays in the window title and on the button in the taskbar button area. Currently, no files or folders display in the Contents pane. The files and folders may be different on your computer.

FIGURE 1-43

3 **Right-click the open area of the Contents pane and then point to New on the shortcut menu.**

A shortcut menu and the New submenu display and the New command is highlighted on the shortcut menu (Figure 1-44). Although no subfolders display in the Contents pane and no plus sign should precede the 3½ Floppy (A:) icon in the Folders pane, a plus sign precedes the icon.

FIGURE 1-44

4 **Point to Folder on the New submenu.**

The Folder command is highlighted on the New submenu (Figure 1-45). Clicking the Folder command will create a folder in the Contents pane using the default folder name, New Folder.

FIGURE 1-45

5 **Click Folder on the New submenu.**

The New Folder icon displays in the Contents pane (Figure 1-46). The text box below the icon contains the highlighted default folder name, New Folder, and an insertion point. A plus sign continues to display to the left of the 3½ Floppy (A:) icon to indicate the 3½ Floppy (A:) folder contains the New Folder subfolder. The message on the status bar indicates one object is selected in the Contents pane.

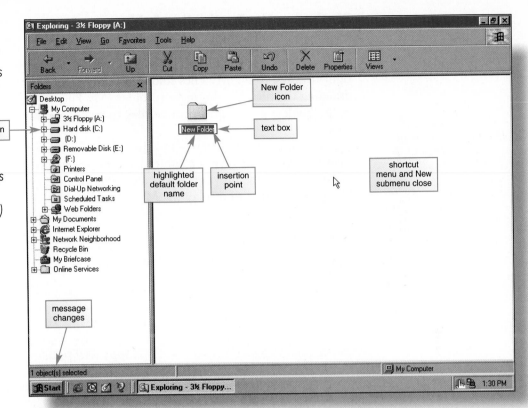

FIGURE 1-46

6 **Type** My Files **in the text box and then press the ENTER key.**

The new folder name, My Files, is entered and the text box is removed (Figure 1-47).

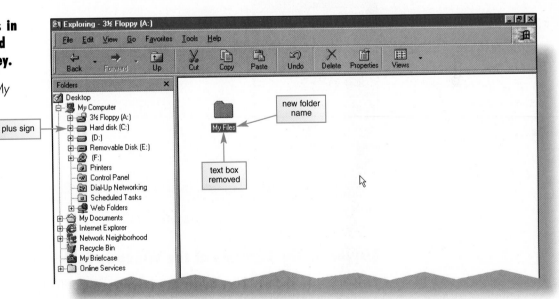

FIGURE 1-47

After creating the My Files folder on the floppy disk in drive A, you can save files in the folder or copy files from other folders to the folder. On the following pages, you will copy a group of files consisting of the Black Thatch, Bubbles, and Circles files from the Windows folder on drive C to the My Files folder on drive A.

Other Ways

1. Select drive in Folders pane, on File menu point to New, click Folder on New submenu

Displaying the Destination Folder

To copy the three files from the Windows folder on drive C to the My Files folder on drive A, the files to be copied will be selected in the Contents pane and right-dragged to the My Files folder in the Folders pane. Prior to selecting and right-dragging the files, the destination folder (My Files folder on drive A) must be visible in the Folders pane, and the three files to be copied must be visible in the Contents pane.

Currently, the plus sign (+) to the left of the 3½ Floppy (A:) icon indicates the folder contains one or more subfolders that are not visible in the Folders pane (see Figure 1-47 on the previous page). Perform the following steps to expand the 3½ Floppy (A:) folder to display the My Files subfolder.

TO EXPAND A FOLDER

1 Point to the plus sign to the left of the 3½ Floppy (A:) icon in the Folders pane.

2 Click the plus sign to display the subfolders in the 3½ Floppy (A:) folder.

A minus sign replaces the plus sign preceding the 3½ Floppy (A:) folder, the folder name is highlighted, and the My Files subfolder displays in the 3½ Floppy (A:) folder, indented and aligned below the 3½ Floppy (A:) folder name (Figure 1-48).

FIGURE 1-48

Displaying the Contents of the Windows Folder

Currently, the My Files folder displays in the Contents pane of the Exploring - 3½ Floppy (A:) window. To copy files from the source folder (Windows folder on drive C) to the My Files folder, the Windows folder must be visible in the Folders pane. To make the Windows folder visible, you must expand the Hard disk (C:) folder and then click the Windows folder name to display the contents of the Windows folder in the Contents pane. Perform the following steps to display the contents of the Windows folder.

Steps To Display the Contents of a Folder

1 **Click the plus sign to the left of the Hard disk (C:) icon in the Folders pane and then point to the Windows folder name.**

A minus sign replaces the plus sign to the left of the Hard disk (C:) icon and the subfolders in the Hard disk (C:) folder display (Figure 1-49). In addition to folders and other files, the Windows folder contains a series of predefined graphics, called **clip art files,** *that can be used with application programs.*

FIGURE 1-49

2 **Click the Windows folder name.**

The Windows folder name is highlighted in the Folders pane, the closed folder icon to the left of the Windows folder name changes to an open folder icon, and the contents of the Windows folder display in the Contents pane (Figure 1-50).

FIGURE 1-50

3 **Scroll the Contents pane to make the files in the Windows folder visible.**

The files in the Windows folder display in the Contents pane (Figure 1-51). Each file is identified by a large icon and a file name. The files in the Windows folder may be different and file extensions may display as part of the file names on your computer.

FIGURE 1-51

Changing the View

In Figure 1-51, the files in the Contents pane of the Exploring - Windows window display in Large Icons view. In **Large Icons view**, each file is represented by a large icon and a file name. Other views include Small Icons, List, and Details. List view often is useful when copying or moving files from one location to another location. In **List view**, each file is represented by a smaller icon and name, and the files are arranged in columns. Perform the following steps to change from Large Icons view to List view.

 To Change to List View

1 **Right-click an open area in the Contents pane, point to View on the shortcut menu, and then point to List on the View submenu.**

A shortcut menu displays, the View command is highlighted on the shortcut menu, the View submenu displays, and the List command is highlighted on the View submenu (Figure 1-52). A large dot to the left of the Large Icons command indicates files and folders in the Contents pane display in Large Icons view.

FIGURE 1-52

files and
folders display
in List view

② Click List.

The files and folders in the Contents pane display in List view (Figure 1-53).

FIGURE 1-53

Selecting a Group of Files

You easily can copy a single file or group of files from one folder to another folder using Windows Explorer. To copy a single file, select the file in the Contents pane and right-drag the highlighted file to the folder in the Folders pane where the file is to be copied. Group files are copied in a similar fashion by clicking the icon or file name of the first file in a group of files to select it. You select the remaining files in the group by pointing to each file icon or file name, holding down the CTRL key, and clicking the file icon or file name. Perform the following steps to select the group of files consisting of the Black Thatch, Bubbles, and Circles files.

Other Ways

1. Click Views button on Standard Buttons toolbar repeatedly until files and folder display in List view
2. Click Views button arrow on Standard Buttons toolbar, click List
3. On View menu click List
4. Press ALT+V, press L

 ## To Select a Group of Files

① Select the Black Thatch file by clicking the Black Thatch file name, and then point to the Bubbles file name.

The Black Thatch file is highlighted in the Contents pane and two messages display on the status bar (Figure 1-54). The messages indicate that one file is selected (1 object(s) selected) and the size of the file is 182 bytes.

FIGURE 1-54

2 Hold down the CTRL key, click the Bubbles file name, release the CTRL key, and then point to the Circles file name.

The Black Thatch and Bubbles files are highlighted and the two messages on the status bar change to reflect the additional file selected (Figure 1-55). The messages indicate two files are selected (2 object(s) selected) and the size of the two files (2.24KB).

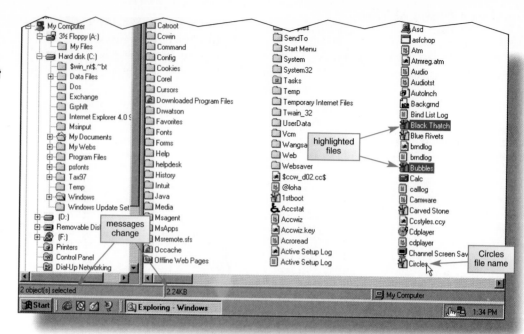

FIGURE 1-55

3 Hold down the CTRL key, click the Circles file name, and then release the CTRL key.

The group of files consisting of the Black Thatch, Bubbles, and Circles files is highlighted and the messages on the status bar change to reflect the selection of a third file (Figure 1-56). The messages indicate three files are selected (3 object(s) selected) and the size of the three files (2.43KB).

FIGURE 1-56

Other Ways

1. To select contiguous files, select first file name, hold down SHIFT key, click last file name
2. To select all files, on Edit menu click Select All

Copying a Group of Files

After selecting a group of files, copy the files to the My Files folder on drive A by pointing to any highlighted file name in the Contents pane and right-dragging the file name to the My Files folder in the Folders pane. Perform the following steps to copy a group of files.

 Steps | **To Copy a Group of Files**

1 If necessary, scroll the Folders pane to make the My Files folder visible. Point to the highlighted Black Thatch file name in the Contents pane.

The pointer points to the highlighted Black Thatch file name in the Contents pane and the My Files folder is visible in the Folders pane (Figure 1-57).

FIGURE 1-57

2 Right-drag the Black Thatch file over the My Files folder name in the Folders pane.

As you drag the file, an outline of three icons and three horizontal lines displays and the My Files folder name is highlighted (Figure 1-58). The mouse pointer contains a plus sign to indicate the group of files is being copied, not moved.

FIGURE 1-58

3 Release the right mouse button and then point to Copy Here on the shortcut menu.

A shortcut menu displays and the Copy Here command is highlighted (Figure 1-59).

FIGURE 1-59

4 Click Copy Here.

*The Copying dialog box displays and remains on the screen while each file is copied to the My Files folder (Figure 1-60). A **dialog box** displays whenever Windows 98 needs to supply information to you or requires you to enter information or select among several options. The Copying dialog box shown in Figure 1-60 indicates the Bubbles.bmp file is being copied.*

FIGURE 1-60

Other Ways

1. Drag file to copy from Contents pane to folder icon in Folders pane
2. Select file to copy in Contents pane, click Copy button on Standard Buttons toolbar, select folder icon to receive copy, click Paste button on Standard Buttons toolbar
3. Select file to copy in Contents pane, on Edit menu click Copy, select folder icon to receive copy, on Edit menu click Paste
4. Select file to copy, press CTRL+C, select folder icon to receive copy, press CTRL+V

Displaying the Contents of the My Files Folder

After copying a group of files, you should verify the files were copied into the correct folder. To view the files that were copied to the My Files folder, perform the following steps.

TO DISPLAY THE CONTENTS OF A FOLDER

1 Point to the My Files folder name in the Folders pane.

2 Click the My Files folder name.

The highlighted My Files folder name displays in the Folders pane, the open folder icon replaces the closed folder icon to the left of the My Files folder name, the contents of the My Files folder display in the Contents pane, and the message on the status bar changes (Figure 1-61). The status bar message indicates 1.38MB of free disk space on the disk in drive A.

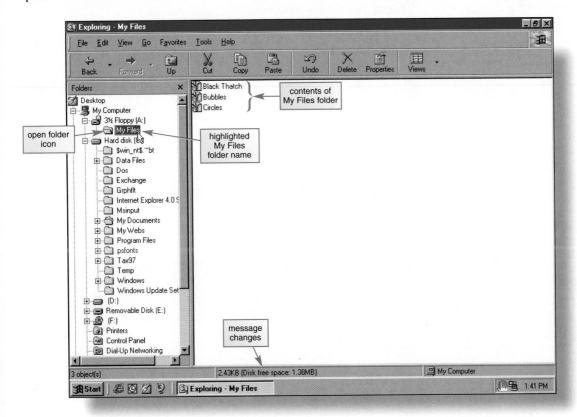

FIGURE 1-61

Renaming a File or Folder

For various reasons, you may wish to change the name of a file or folder on disk. Perform the following steps to change the name of the Circles file on drive A to Blue Circles.

 To Rename a File

 Point to the Circles file name in the Contents pane (Figure 1-62).

The mouse pointer points to the Circles file name.

FIGURE 1-62

2 **Click the Circles file name twice (do not double-click the file name).**

A text box containing the highlighted Circles file name and insertion point displays (Figure 1-63).

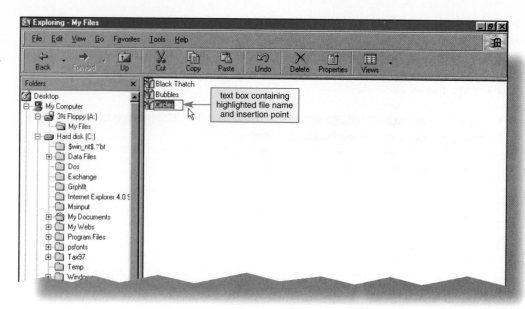

FIGURE 1-63

3 **Type** Blue Circles **and then press the ENTER key.**

The file name changes to Blue Circles and the text box surrounding the file name is removed (Figure 1-64).

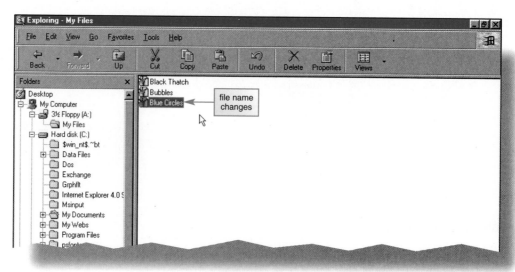

FIGURE 1-64

Other Ways

1. Right-click file name in Contents pane, click Rename on shortcut menu, type new name, press ENTER

2. Select file name in Contents pane, on File menu click Rename, type new name, press ENTER

3. Select file name in Contents pane, press F2, type new name, press ENTER

4. Select file name, press ALT+F, press M, type new name, press ENTER

Follow the same procedure to change a folder name. The following steps change the name of the My Files folder to Clip Art Files.

TO RENAME A FOLDER

1 Point to the My Files folder name in the Folders pane.

2 Click the My Files folder name twice (do not double-click the folder name).

3 Type Clip Art Files and then press the ENTER key.

The folder name changes to Clip Art Files and the text box surrounding the folder name is removed (Figure 1-65). The new folder name replaces the old folder name in the window title and on the button in the taskbar button area.

FIGURE 1-65

Deleting a File or Folder

When you no longer need a file or folder, you can delete it. When you delete a file or folder on the hard drive using the Recycle Bin, Windows 98 temporarily stores the deleted file or folder in the Recycle Bin until you permanently discard the contents of the Recycle Bin by emptying the Recycle Bin. Until the Recycle Bin is emptied, you can retrieve the files and folders you have deleted previously by mistake or other reasons. Unlike deleting files or folders on the hard drive, when you delete a file or folder located on a floppy disk, the file or folder is deleted immediately and not stored in the Recycle Bin.

Deleting a File by Right-Clicking Its File Name

Right-clicking a file name produces a shortcut menu that contains the Delete command. To illustrate how to delete a file by right-clicking, perform the steps on the next two pages to delete the Bubbles file.

To Delete a File by Right-Clicking

1 **Right-click the Bubbles file name in the Contents pane and then point to the Delete command on the shortcut menu.**

The Bubbles file name is highlighted and a shortcut menu displays (Figure 1-66).

FIGURE 1-66

2 **Click Delete. When the Confirm File Delete dialog box displays, point to the Yes button.**

The Confirm File Delete dialog box displays (Figure 1-67). The dialog box contains the message, Are you sure you want to delete 'Bubbles'?, and the Yes and No command buttons.

FIGURE 1-67

3 **Click the Yes button.**

A Deleting dialog box displays while the file is being deleted, and then the Bubbles file is removed from the Contents pane (Figure 1-68).

FIGURE 1-68

Other Ways

1. Click file name, click Delete button on Standard Buttons toolbar, click Yes button
2. Right-drag file name over Recycle Bin icon, click Move Here, click Yes button
3. Drag file name over Recycle Bin icon, click Yes button

You can use the file selection techniques illustrated earlier in this project to delete a group of files. When deleting a group of files, click the Yes button in the Confirm Multiple File Delete dialog box to confirm the deletion of the group of files.

Deleting a Folder

Follow the same procedure to delete a folder. When you delete a folder, Windows 98 deletes any files or subfolders in the folder. Perform the following steps to delete the Clip Art Files folder on drive A.

TO DELETE A FOLDER

1 Right-click the Clip Art Files folder name in the Folders pane.

2 Click Delete on the shortcut menu.

3 Click the Yes button in the Confirm Folder Delete dialog box.

4 Remove the floppy disk from drive A.

A Deleting dialog box displays while the folder is being deleted, the Clip Art Files folder is removed from the Folders pane, and a plus sign replaces the minus sign preceding the 3½ Floppy (A:) icon (Figure 1-69).

FIGURE 1-69

Quitting Windows Explorer

After completing your work with Windows Explorer, you should quit Windows Explorer. Perform the following steps to quit Windows Explorer.

TO QUIT A PROGRAM

1 Point to the Close button on the Exploring window title bar.

2 Click the Close button.

Windows 98 closes the Windows Explorer window and quits Windows Explorer.

More About

Windows 98 Help

If you purchased an operating system or application program five years ago, you received thick, heavy technical manuals that explained the software. With Windows 98, you receive a skinny manual less than 100 pages in length. The online Help feature of Windows 98 replaces reams and reams of printed pages in hard-to-understand technical manuals.

Using Windows Help

One of the more powerful application programs for use in Windows 98 is Windows Help. Windows Help is available when using Windows 98, or when using any application program running under Windows 98, to assist you in using Windows 98 and the various application programs. It contains answers to many questions you can ask with respect to Windows 98.

Contents Sheet

Windows Help provides a variety of ways in which to obtain information. One method to find a Help topic involves using the **Contents sheet** to browse through Help topics by category. To illustrate this method, you will use Windows Help to determine how to find a topic in Help. To launch Help, complete the following steps.

Steps) To Launch Windows Help

1 Click the Start button on the taskbar. Point to Help on the Start menu (Figure 1-70).

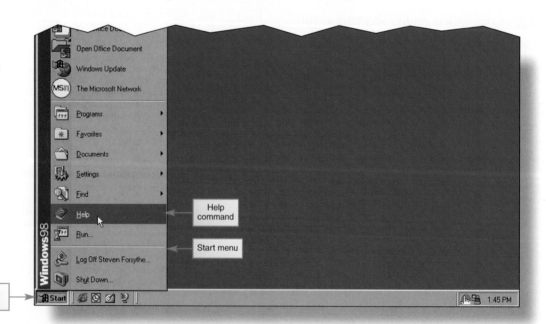

FIGURE 1-70

2 **Click Help.
Click the
Maximize button on the
Windows Help title bar. If
the Contents sheet does not
display, click the Contents
tab.**

*The Windows Help window
opens and maximizes (Figure
1-71). The window contains
the Help toolbar and two
frames. The left frame contains three **tabs** (Contents,
Index, and Search). The
Contents sheet is visible in
the left frame. The right
frame contains information
about the Welcome to Help
topic.*

FIGURE 1-71

Other Ways

1. Press F1
2. Press WINDOWS+H (WINDOWS
key on Microsoft Natural
keyboard)

The Contents sheet contains a **Help topic** preceded by a question mark icon and
followed by 10 books. Each book consists of a closed book icon followed by a book
name. The Help topic, Welcome to Help, is highlighted. In the left frame, a closed
book icon indicates that Help topics or more books are contained in the book. The
question mark icon indicates a Help topic without any further subdivisions. Clicking
either the Index tab or the Search tab in the left frame opens the Index or Search
sheet, respectively.

In addition to launching Help by using the Start button, you also can launch
Help by pressing the F1 key.

After launching Help, the next step is to find the topic in which you are interested. To find the topic that describes how to find a topic in Help, complete the
steps on the next two pages.

To Use Help to Find a Topic in Help

1 Point to the Introducing Windows 98 closed book icon.

The mouse pointer changes to a hand when positioned on the icon and the Introducing Windows 98 book name displays in blue font and underlined (Figure 1-72).

FIGURE 1-72

2 Click the Introducing Windows 98 closed book icon and then point to the How to Use Help closed book icon.

Windows 98 opens the Introducing Windows 98 book, changes the closed book icon to an open book icon, highlights the Introducing Windows 98 book name, underlines the How to Use Help book name, and displays the name and underline in blue font (Figure 1-73).

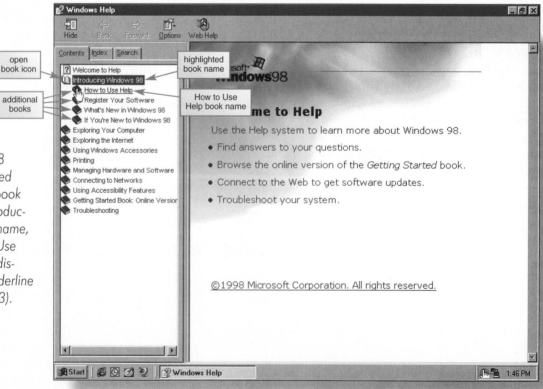

FIGURE 1-73

3 **Click the How to Use Help closed book icon and then point to Find a topic in the opened How to Use Help book.**

Windows 98 opens the How to Use Help book and displays several Help topics in the book, changes the closed book icon to an open book icon, highlights the How to Use Help book name, underlines the Find a topic Help topic name, and displays the topic name and underline in blue font (Figure 1-74).

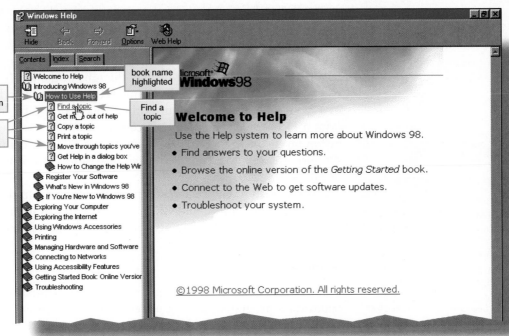

FIGURE 1-74

4 **Click Find a topic. Read the information about finding a Help topic in the right frame of the Windows Help window.**

Windows 98 highlights the Find a topic Help topic and displays information about finding a Help topic in the right frame of the Windows Help window (Figure 1-75).

FIGURE 1-75

Other **Ways**

1. Press DOWN ARROW key until book or topic is highlighted, press ENTER, continue until Help topic displays, read Help topic

In Figure 1-75 on the previous page, if you click the **Hide button** on the Help toolbar, Windows 98 hides the tabs in the left frame and displays only the right frame in the Windows Help window. Clicking the **Back button** or **Forward button** displays a previously displayed Help topic in the right frame. Clicking the **Options button** allows you to hide or display the tabs in the left frame, display previously displayed Help topics in the right frame, return to the Help home page, stop the display of a Help topic, refresh the currently displayed Help topic, access Web Help, and print a Help topic. The **Web Help command** on the Options menu and the **Web Help button** on the Help toolbar allow you to use the Internet to obtain technical support, answers to frequently asked questions, and tips about working with Windows 98.

Notice also in Figure 1-75 that the Windows Help title bar contains a Minimize button, Restore button, and Close button. You can minimize or restore the Windows Help window as needed and also close the Windows Help window.

Index Sheet

A second method of finding answers to your questions about Windows 98 or application programs running under Windows 98 is the Index sheet. The **Index sheet** lists a large number of index entries, each of which references one or more Help screens. To learn more about the Classic style and Web style, complete the following steps.

More About

The Index Sheet

The Index sheet probably is the best source of information in Windows Help because you can enter the subject you are interested in. Sometimes, however, you will have to be creative to discover the index entry that answers your question because the most obvious entry will not always lead to your answer.

Steps **To Use the Help Index Sheet**

1 **Click the Index tab. Type** classic style **(the flashing insertion point is positioned in the text box) in the text box. Point to the Display button at the bottom of the left frame.**

The Index sheet displays in the left frame and includes a list of entries that can be referenced (Figure 1-76). When you type an entry, the list automatically scrolls and the entry you type, such as classic style, is highlighted. To see additional entries, use the scroll bar at the right of the list. To highlight an entry in the list, click the entry.

FIGURE 1-76

2 Click the Display button in the Windows Help window. Point to the Display button in the Topics Found dialog box.

The Topics Found dialog box displays on top of the Windows Help window and two Help topics display in the dialog box (Figure 1-77). The first topic, Choosing Web or Classic style for folders, is highlighted. This topic contains information about the Web and Classic styles.

FIGURE 1-77

3 Click the Display button.

Information about the Web and Classic style and several hyperlinks display in the right frame of the Windows Help window (Figure 1-78).

FIGURE 1-78

After viewing the index entries, normally you will close Windows Help. To close Windows Help, complete the following step.

TO CLOSE WINDOWS HELP

1 Click the Close button on the title bar of the Windows Help window.

Windows 98 closes the Windows Help window.

Shutting Down Windows 98

After completing your work with Windows 98, you may want to shut down Windows 98 using the **Shut Down command** on the Start menu. If you are sure you want to shut down Windows 98, perform the following steps. If you are not sure about shutting down Windows 98, read the following steps without actually performing them.

 To Shut Down Windows 98

1 **Click the Start button on the taskbar and then point to Shut Down on the Start menu (Figure 1-79).**

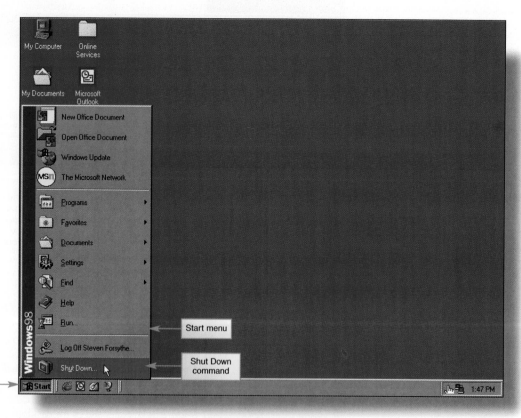

FIGURE 1-79

2 **Click Shut Down. Point to the OK button in the Shut Down Windows dialog box.**

The desktop darkens and the Shut Down Windows dialog box displays (Figure 1-80). The dialog box contains three option buttons. The selected option button, Shut down, indicates that clicking the OK button will shut down Windows 98.

3 **Click the OK button.**

Windows 98 is shut down.

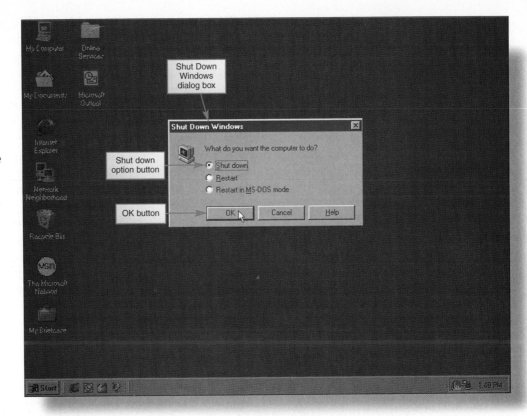

FIGURE 1-80

Two screens display while Windows 98 is shutting down. The first screen containing the Windows logo, Windows 98 name, and the text, Windows is shutting down, displays momentarily while Windows 98 is being shut down. Then, a second screen containing the text, It's now safe to turn off your computer, displays. At this point you can turn off your computer. Some computers are programmed to turn off automatically at this point. When shutting down Windows 98, you should never turn off your computer before these two screens display.

If you accidentally click Shut Down on the Start menu and you do not want to shut down Windows 98, click the Cancel button in the Shut Down Windows dialog box to return to normal Windows 98 operation.

What Is Microsoft Office 2000?

Microsoft Office 2000, the latest edition of the world's best-selling office suite, is a collection of the more popular Microsoft application software products. Microsoft Office 2000 is available in Standard, Small Business, Professional, Premium, and Developer editions. The **Microsoft Office 2000 Premium Edition** includes Microsoft Word 2000, Microsoft Excel 2000, Microsoft Access 2000, Microsoft PowerPoint 2000, Microsoft Publisher 2000, Microsoft FrontPage 2000, Microsoft PhotoDraw 2000, Microsoft Outlook 2000, and Internet Explorer. Microsoft Office 2000 allows you to work more efficiently, communicate better, and improve the appearance of the documents you create.

Other **Ways**

1. Press CTRL+ESC, press U, Press UP ARROW or DOWN ARROW key to select Shut down option button, press ENTER
2. Press ALT+F4, press UP ARROW or DOWN ARROW key to select Shut down option button, press ENTER

More About

Office 2000

For more information about any Microsoft Office 2000 application, click Help on the menu bar of any Office 2000 application window, and click Office on the Web. Explore a Web page by clicking a hyperlink. After clicking a hyperlink, click the Back button to display the last Web page.

One of the CD-ROMs that accompanies Microsoft Office 2000 contains a clip art gallery that you can use in any of the applications to enhance the appearance of a document. The gallery contains over 16,000 clip art images, sounds, photographs, animations, themes, and backgrounds. In addition, thousands of additional images are available from the Microsoft Clipart Gallery Live found on the Microsoft Web site. Hundreds of new images are added each month to this collection.

Menus and toolbars adjust to the way in which you work. As Microsoft Office detects which commands you use more frequently, these commands display at the top of the menu, and the infrequently used commands are placed in reserve. A button at the bottom of the menu allows you to expand the menu in order to view all its commands. More frequently used buttons on a toolbar display on the toolbar, while less frequently used buttons are not displayed.

Microsoft Office applications are self-repairing. If you accidentally delete a file that is needed to run an Office application, the Self-Repairing Application feature automatically finds the deleted file and reinstalls the file. This feature reduces the number of calls to technical support and increases user productivity.

In addition, Microsoft Office 2000 integrates its applications with the power of the Internet so you can share information, collaborate on projects, and conduct online meetings.

The Internet, World Wide Web, and Intranets

Microsoft Office 2000 allows you to take advantage of the Internet, the World Wide Web, and intranets. The **Internet** is a worldwide network of thousands of computer networks and millions of commercial, educational, government, and personal computers. The **World Wide Web** is an easy-to-use graphical interface for exploring the Internet. The World Wide Web consists of many individual Web sites. A **Web site** can consist of a single **Web page** or multiple Web pages linked together. The first Web page in the Web site is called the **home page** and a unique address, called a **Uniform Resource Locator (URL)**, identifies each Web page. Web sites are located on computers called **Web servers**.

A software tool, called a **browser**, allows you to locate and view a Web page. One method of viewing a Web page is to use the browser to enter the URL for the Web page. A widely used browser, called **Microsoft Internet Explorer**, is included with Microsoft Office 2000. Another method of viewing Web pages allows you to click a hyperlink. A **hyperlink** is colored or underlined text or a graphic that, when clicked, connects to another Web page.

An **intranet** is a special type of Web that is available only to the users of a particular type of computer network, such as a network used within a company or organization for internal communication. Like the Internet, hyperlinks are used within an intranet to access documents, pages, and other destinations on the intranet.

Microsoft Office 2000 and the Internet

Microsoft Office 2000 was designed in response to customer requests to streamline the process of information sharing and collaboration within their organizations. Organizations that, in the past, made important information available only to a select few, now want their information accessible to a wider range of individuals who are using tools such as Microsoft Office and Microsoft Internet Explorer. Microsoft Office 2000 allows users to utilize the Internet or an intranet as a central location to view documents, manage files, and work together.

Each of the Microsoft Office 2000 applications makes publishing documents on a Web server as simple as saving a file on a hard disk. Once the file is placed on the Web server, users can view and edit the documents, and conduct Web discussions and live online meetings.

More About

Microsoft Office 2000

To subscribe to a free Office 2000 weekly newsletter delivered via e-mail, visit the Office 2000 More About Web page (www.scsite.com/off2000/more.htm) and then click Office 2000 Newsletter.

An explanation of each Microsoft Office 2000 application software program in the Premium Edition along with how it is used to access an intranet or the Internet is given on the following pages.

Microsoft Word 2000

Microsoft Word 2000 is a full-featured word processing program that allows you to create many types of personal and business communications, including announcements, letters, memos, business documents, and academic reports, as well as other forms of written documents. Figure 1-81 illustrates the top portion of the announcement that students create in one of the exercises in Project 1 of the Microsoft Word section of this book. The steps to create an announcement are shown in Project 1 of Microsoft Word 2000.

More About

Microsoft Word 2000

For more information about Microsoft Word 2000, click Help on the menu bar of the Microsoft Word window, and click Office on the Web. Explore a Web page by clicking a hyperlink. After clicking a hyperlink, click the Back button to display the last Web page.

FIGURE 1-81

The Microsoft Word AutoCorrect, Spelling, and Grammar features allow you to proofread documents for errors in spelling and grammar by identifying the errors and offering corrections as you type. As you create a specific document, such as a business letter or resume, Word provides wizards, which ask questions and then use your answers to format the document before you type the text of the document.

The Collect and Paste feature allows you to cut or copy as many as 12 objects (text, pictures, e-mail messages, and so on) and collect them on the Office Clipboard. Then you can paste them into the same document or different documents. Collect and Paste can be used within a single Office 2000 application or among multiple Office 2000 applications.

Microsoft Word automates many often-used tasks and provides you with powerful desktop publishing tools to use as you create professional-looking brochures, advertisements, and newsletters. The drawing tools allow you to design impressive 3-D effects by including shadows, textures, and curves. Floating tables permit you to position a table in an exact location on a page and then wrap text around the table.

Microsoft Word 2000 and the Internet

Microsoft Word makes it possible to access Web pages and search for information, design and publish Web pages on an intranet or the Internet, insert a hyperlink to a Web page in a word processing document, and retrieve pictures from other Web pages. Figure 1-82 illustrates the top portion of a cover letter that contains a hyperlink (e-mail address) that allows you to send an e-mail message to the sender.

Clicking the hyperlink starts the Microsoft Outlook mail program and allows you to send an e-mail message to the author of the cover letter. In Figure 1-83, the Resume and Cover Letter - Message [Rich Text] window that allows you to compose a new e-mail message contains the recipient's e-mail address (brandon@lenox.com), subject of the e-mail message (Resume and Cover Letter), and a brief message.

FIGURE 1-82

FIGURE 1-83

Microsoft Excel 2000

Microsoft Excel 2000 is a spreadsheet program that allows you to organize data, complete calculations, make decisions, graph data, develop professional looking reports, publish organized data on the Web, and access real-time data from Web sites. Figure 1-84 illustrates the Microsoft Excel window that contains the worksheet and 3-D column chart created in Project 1 of the Microsoft Excel section of this book.

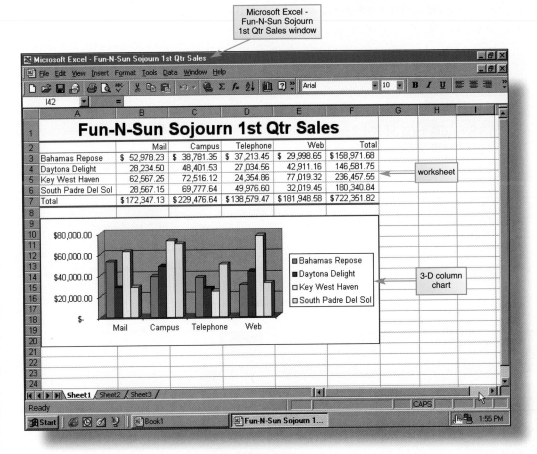

FIGURE 1-84

Microsoft Excel 2000 and the Internet

Using Microsoft Excel, you can create hyperlinks within a worksheet to access other Office 2000 documents on the network, an organization's intranet, or the Internet. You also can save worksheets as static and dynamic Web pages that can be viewed using your browser. Static Web pages cannot be changed by the person viewing them. Dynamic Web pages give the person viewing them many Excel capabilities in their browser. In addition, you can create and run queries to retrieve information from a Web page directly into a worksheet.

Figure 1-85 illustrates a worksheet created by running a Web query to retrieve stock market information for two stocks (CMGI, Inc. and America Online, Inc.). The two hyperlinks were created using the Insert HyperLink button on the Standard toolbar, and the information in the worksheet was obtained from the Microsoft Investor Web site. The Refresh All button on the External Data toolbar allows you to update the last price of the stocks (Last).

Clicking the Refresh All button locates the Microsoft Investor Web site, retrieves current information for the stocks in the worksheet, and displays the updated information in the worksheet (Figure 1-86). Notice that the stock prices and information in this worksheet differ from what was displayed in the worksheet in Figure 1-85.

FIGURE 1-85

FIGURE 1-86

Microsoft Access 2000

Microsoft Access 2000 is a comprehensive **database management system (DBMS)**. A **database** is a collection of data organized in a manner that allows access, retrieval, and use of that data. Microsoft Access allows you to create a database; add, change, and delete data in the database; sort data in the database; retrieve data from the database; and create forms and reports using the data in the database.

The database created in Project 1 of the Microsoft Access section of this book displays in the Microsoft Access - [Marina : Table] window illustrated in Figure 1-87. The steps to create this database are shown in Project 1 of Access.

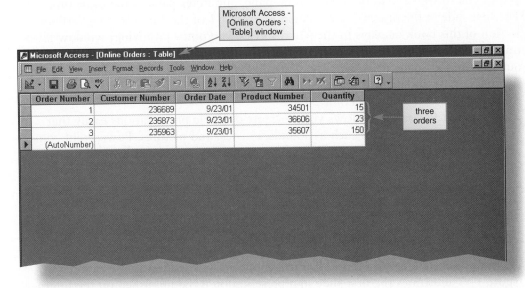

FIGURE 1-87

Microsoft Access 2000 and the Internet

Databases provide a central location to store related pieces of information. Microsoft Access simplifies the creation of databases with a wizard that can build one of more than a dozen types of databases quickly. You also can transform lists or worksheets into databases using Access wizards. Data access pages allow you to share a database with other computer users on a network, intranet, or over the Internet, as well as allowing the users to view and edit the database. The database shown in Figure 1-88 contains information (order number, customer number, order date, product number, and quantity) about three orders entered over the Internet using the Microsoft Internet Explorer browser.

FIGURE 1-88

Figure 1-89 illustrates a simple online order form created to enter order information into the database shown in Figure 1-88 on the previous page. The order form, containing information about order number 4, displays in the Online Orders - Microsoft Internet Explorer window.

FIGURE 1-89

Microsoft PowerPoint 2000

For more information about Microsoft PowerPoint 2000, click Help on the menu bar of the Microsoft PowerPoint window, and click Office on the Web. Explore a Web page by clicking a hyperlink. After clicking a hyperlink, click the Back button to display the last Web page.

Microsoft PowerPoint 2000

Microsoft PowerPoint 2000 is a complete **presentation graphics program** that allows you to produce professional-looking presentations. PowerPoint gives you the flexibility to make informal presentations using overhead transparencies, make electronic presentations using a projection device attached to a personal computer, make formal presentations using 35mm slides, or run virtual presentations on the Internet.

In PowerPoint 2000, you create a presentation in Normal view. Normal view allows you to view the outline pane, slide pane, and notes pane at the same time. The first slide in the presentation created in Project 1 of the Microsoft PowerPoint section of this book displays in the Microsoft PowerPoint - [Studying] window illustrated in Figure 1-90. The window contains the outline pane with the presentation outline, the slide pane displaying the first slide in the presentation, and the note pane showing a note about the presentation. The steps to create this presentation are shown in Project 1 of PowerPoint 2000.

Microsoft PowerPoint allows you to create dynamic presentations easily that include multimedia features such as sounds, movies, and pictures. PowerPoint comes with templates that assist you in designing a presentation that can be used to create a slide show. PowerPoint also contains formatting for tables, so that you do not have to create the tables using Excel or Word. The Table Draw tool used in Word to draw tables also is available in PowerPoint.

Microsoft PowerPoint 2000 and the Internet

PowerPoint allows you to publish presentations on the Internet or an intranet. Figure 1-91 illustrates the first slide in a presentation to be published on the Internet. The slide displays in Slide view and contains a title (Microsoft Office 2000), subtitle (Guide to Office Applications), and creation date (Created: October 2001). The additional slides in this presentation do not display in Figure 1-91.

FIGURE 1-90

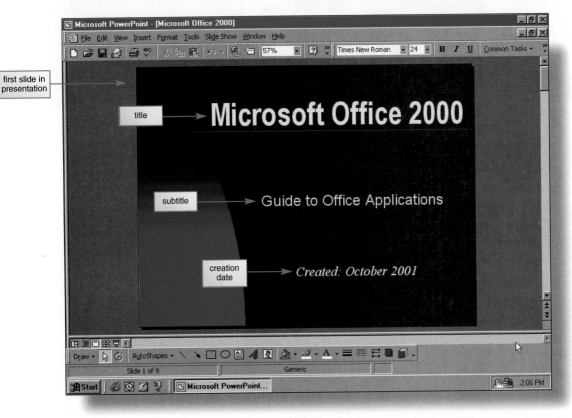

FIGURE 1-91

Figure 1-92 shows the first Web page in a series of Web pages created from the presentation illustrated in Figure 1-91 on the previous page. The Web page displays in the Microsoft Office 2000 - Microsoft Internet Explorer window. Navigation buttons below the Web page allow you to view additional Web pages in the presentation.

FIGURE 1-92

The Web Toolbar

The easiest method of navigating an intranet or the Internet is to use the Web toolbar. The Web toolbar allows you to search for and open Microsoft Office 2000 documents that have been placed on an intranet or the Internet. The Web toolbar in the Paulette Brandon Cover Letter - Microsoft Word window shown in Figure 1-93 is available in all Microsoft Office 2000 applications except Microsoft Publisher, Microsoft PhotoDraw, and Microsoft FrontPage. Currently, a Word document (cover letter) displays in the window, and the path and file name of the document display in the text box on the Web toolbar.

The buttons and text box on the Web toolbar allow you to jump to Web pages you have viewed previously, cancel a jump to a Web page, update the contents of the current Web page, or replace all other toolbars with the Web toolbar. In addition, you can view the first Web page displayed, search the Web for new Web sites, and add any Web pages you select to the Favorites folder, so you can return to them quickly in the future.

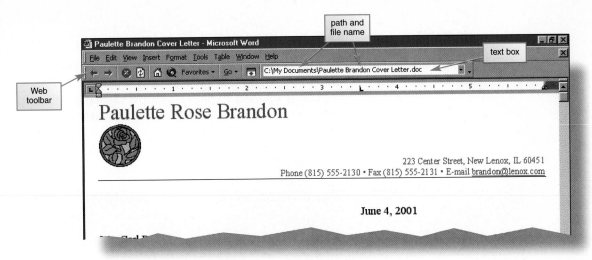

FIGURE 1-93

Microsoft Publisher 2000

Microsoft Publisher 2000 is a **desktop publishing (DTP) program** that allows you to design and produce professional-quality documents (newsletters, flyers, brochures, business cards, Web sites, and so on) that combine text, graphics, and photographs. Desktop publishing software provides a variety of tools, including design templates, graphic manipulation tools, color schemes or libraries, and various page wizards and templates. For large jobs, businesses use desktop publishing software to design publications that are **camera ready**, which means the files are suitable for production by outside commercial printers.

Publisher allows you to design a unique image, or logo, using one of more than 1,600 professional-looking design sets. This, in turn, permits you to use the same design for all your printed documents (letter, business cards, brochures, and advertisements) and Web pages. Microsoft Publisher includes 60 coordinated color schemes, more than 10,000 high-quality clip art images, 1,500 photographs, 1,000 Web-art graphics, 175 fonts, 340 animated graphics, and hundreds of unique Design Gallery elements (quotations, sidebars, and so on). In addition, you can download an additional 100 images from Microsoft Clipart Gallery Live on the Microsoft Web site each month.

In the Business Card - Hank Landers - Microsoft Publisher window shown in Figure 1-94, a business card that was created using the Business Card wizard and the Arcs design set displays.

FIGURE 1-94

Microsoft Publisher and the Internet

Microsoft Publisher allows you to create a multi-page Web site with custom color schemes, photo images, animated images, and sounds easily. Figure 1-95 illustrates the Superior Graphics - Microsoft Internet Explorer window displaying the top portion of the home page in a Web site created using the Web page wizard and Arcs design set.

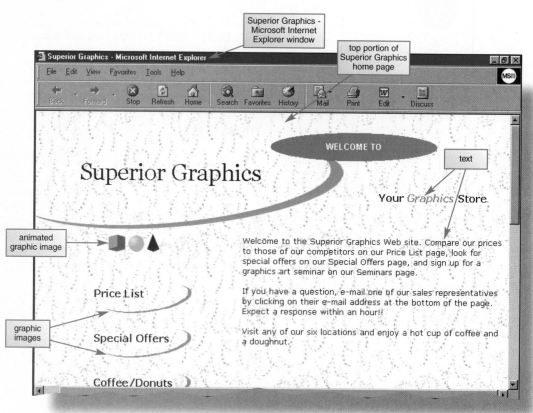

FIGURE 1-95

The home page in the Superior Graphics Web site contains text, graphic images, animated graphic images, and displays using the same design set (Arcs) as the business card illustrated in Figure 1-94 on the previous page.

More About 2000

Microsoft FrontPage 2000

For more information about Microsoft FrontPage 2000, click Help on the menu bar of the Microsoft FrontPage window, and click Office on the Web. Explore a Web page by clicking a hyperlink. After clicking a hyperlink, click the Back button to display the last Web page.

Microsoft FrontPage 2000

Microsoft FrontPage 2000 is a Web page authoring and site management program that allows you to create and manage professional-looking Web sites on the Internet or an intranet. You can create and edit Web pages without knowing HyperText Markup Language (HTML), view the pages and files in the Web site and control their organization, manage existing Web sites, import and export files, and diagnose and fix problems. A variety of templates, including the new Workgroup Web template that allows you to set up and maintain the basic structure of a workgroup Web, are available to facilitate managing a Web site.

Figure 1-96 illustrates the top portion of a Web page created using Microsoft FrontPage 2000 that contains information about the Discovering Computers 2000 textbook published by Course Technology. It displays in the Discovering Computers 2000 - Microsoft Internet Explorer window.

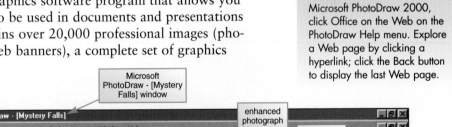

FIGURE 1-96

More About

Microsoft PhotoDraw 2000

For more information about Microsoft PhotoDraw 2000, click Office on the Web on the PhotoDraw Help menu. Explore a Web page by clicking a hyperlink; click the Back button to display the last Web page.

Microsoft PhotoDraw 2000

Microsoft PhotoDraw 2000 is a business graphics software program that allows you to create eye-catching business graphics to be used in documents and presentations on the Web. Microsoft PhotoDraw contains over 20,000 professional images (photos, logos, three-dimensional text, and Web banners), a complete set of graphics tools, 200 built-in special effects, and 300 professionally designed templates. Figure 1-97 illustrates the Microsoft PhotoDraw - [Mystery Falls] window displaying an enhanced, or retouched, photograph that has been outlined using the Soft Edges tool.

FIGURE 1-97

Microsoft Outlook 2000

For more information about Microsoft Outlook 2000, click Help on the menu bar of the Microsoft Outlook window, and click Office on the Web. Explore a Web page by clicking a hyperlink. After clicking a hyperlink, click the Back button to display the last Web page.

Microsoft Outlook 2000

Microsoft Outlook 2000 is an integrated **desktop information management (DIM)** program that helps you organize information on the desktop and share information with others. Microsoft Outlook allows you to manage personal and business information such as e-mail, appointments, contacts, tasks, and documents, and keep a journal of your activities. Outlook organizes and stores this information in folders on your desktop.

When you start Microsoft Outlook, the Inbox - Microsoft Outlook window displays and the contents of the Inbox folder (your e-mail messages) display in the window (Figure 1-98).

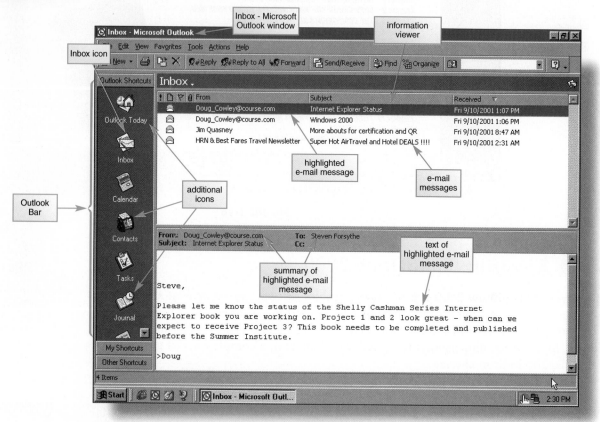

FIGURE 1-98

The Inbox icon, representing the Inbox folder, displays on the Outlook Bar on the left side of the window and the information viewer displays on the right side of the window. The contents of the Inbox folder (one highlighted e-mail message and three e-mail messages) display at the top of the information viewer. Summary information (From:, To:, Subject:, and Cc:) and the text of the highlighted e-mail message displays at the bottom of the information viewer. Also visible on the Outlook Bar are the Outlook Today, Calendar, Contacts, Tasks, and Journal icons. Clicking an icon in the Outlook Bar displays the contents of the associated folder in the information viewer.

When you click the Outlook Today button on the Outlook Bar, the Personal Folders - Microsoft Outlook window displays (Figure 1-99). The window contains the current date (Monday, September 10, 2001); a list of scheduled events, appointments, and meetings for the week; a list of tasks to perform; and a summary of the e-mail messages.

FIGURE 1-99

Microsoft Outlook also allows you to click the Calendar icon to schedule activities (events, appointments, and meetings), click the Contacts icon to maintain a list of contacts and e-mail addresses, and click the Tasks button to view a detailed list of tasks. In addition, you can click the Journal button to view a log of your Outlook activities and store and click the Notes button to make and review electronic reminders, or notes.

More About

Assistant

To change the Office Assistant, right-click the Office Assistant window, click Options on the shortcut menu, if necessary click Gallery tab, click Next button to select Office Assistant, and click the OK button.

The Microsoft Office 2000 Help System

At any time while you are using one of the Microsoft Office 2000 applications, you can interact with the Help system for that application and display information on any topic associated with the application. Several categories of help are available to you. One of the easiest methods to obtain help is to use the Office Assistant. The **Office Assistant** answers your questions and suggests more efficient ways to complete a task. The Office Assistant and balloon display whenever you start any Microsoft Office 2000 application. The Office Assistant and balloon that display in the Notes - Microsoft Outlook window are illustrated in Figure 1-100.

FIGURE 1-100

The Office Assistant (an animated two-dimensional paper clip) is completely customizable so you can select one of nine Office Assistants and the options that best suit the way you work. Detailed instructions for using the Office Assistant and the other categories of Help are explained in Appendix A of this book.

C A S E   P E R S P E C T I V E   S U M M A R Y

While continuing to answer questions about Windows 98 and Office 2000 in the workplace, you spent nearly every free moment in the next two weeks learning about the newly installed operating system and application software. Then, the daily training sessions kept you busy for the following three months. You taught 37 workshops and trained all of the 473 employees in the company. Your supervisor, who attended the Windows 98 and Excel 2000 seminars, complimented your success by giving you a sizeable pay raise and time off to attend the Shelly Cashman Institute at Purdue University.

Project Summary

Project 1 illustrated the Microsoft Windows 98 graphical user interface and the Microsoft Office 2000 applications. You started Windows 98, learned the components of the desktop and the six mouse operations. You opened, closed, moved, resized, minimized, maximized, and scrolled a window. You used Windows Explorer to select and copy a group of files, display the contents of a folder, create a folder, expand and collapse a folder, and rename and delete a file and a folder. You obtained help about using Microsoft Windows 98 and shut down Windows 98.

Brief explanations of the Microsoft Word, Microsoft Excel, Microsoft Access, Microsoft PowerPoint, Microsoft Publisher, Microsoft FrontPage, Microsoft PhotoDraw, and Microsoft Outlook applications and examples of how these applications interact with the Internet, World Wide Web, and intranets were given. With this introduction, you are ready to begin a more in-depth study of each of the Microsoft Office 2000 applications explained in this book.

What You Should Know

Having completed this project, you now should be able to perform the following tasks:

▶ Change to List View *(INT 1.42)*
▶ Close a Window *(INT 1.24)*
▶ Close a Window and Reopen a Window *(INT 1.19)*
▶ Close the Welcome Screen *(INT 1.8)*
▶ Close Windows Help *(INT 1.58)*
▶ Collapse a Folder *(INT 1.36)*
▶ Copy a Group of Files *(INT 1.45)*
▶ Create a New Folder *(INT 1.37)*
▶ Delete a File by Right-Clicking *(INT 1.50)*
▶ Delete a Folder *(INT 1.51)*
▶ Display the Contents of a Folder *(INT 1.34, INT 1.41, INT 1.46)*
▶ Expand a Folder *(INT 1.35, INT 1.40)*
▶ Launch a Program Using the Start Menu *(INT 1.28)*
▶ Launch Windows Help *(INT 1.52)*
▶ Maximize and Restore a Window *(INT 1.17)*
▶ Minimize and Redisplay a Window *(INT 1.15)*

▶ Move an Object by Dragging *(INT 1.20)*
▶ Open a Window by Double-Clicking *(INT 1.13)*
▶ Point and Click *(INT 1.9)*
▶ Quit a Program *(INT 1.29, INT 1.52)*
▶ Rename a File *(INT 1.47)*
▶ Rename a Folder *(INT 1.48)*
▶ Resize a Window *(INT 1.24)*
▶ Right-Click *(INT 1.12)*
▶ Right-Drag *(INT 1.25)*
▶ Scroll a Window Using Scroll Arrows *(INT 1.22)*
▶ Select a Group of Files *(INT 1.43)*
▶ Shut Down Windows 98 *(INT 1.58)*
▶ Size a Window by Dragging *(INT 1.21)*
▶ Start Windows Explorer and Maximize Its Window *(INT 1.30)*
▶ Use Help to Find a Topic in Help *(INT 1.54)*
▶ Use the Help Index Sheet *(INT 1.56)*

In the Lab

1 Improving Your Mouse Skills

Instructions: Use a computer to perform the following tasks.

1. If necessary, start Microsoft Windows 98.
2. Click the Start button on the taskbar, point to Programs on the Start menu, point to Accessories on the Programs submenu, point to Games on the Accessories submenu, and then click Solitaire on the Games submenu. If you cannot find the Games command on the Accessories submenu, ask your instructor if the games have been removed from your computer.
3. Click the Maximize button in the Solitaire window.
4. Click Help on the Solitaire menu bar and then click Help Topics.
5. If the Contents sheet does not display, click the Contents tab.
6. Review the Playing Solitaire and Choosing a scoring system topics on the Contents sheet.
7. After reviewing the Help topics, close the Solitaire Help window.
8. Play the game of Solitaire.
9. Click the Close button on the Solitaire title bar to close the game.

2 Using the Discover Windows 98 Tutorial

Instructions: To use the Discover Windows 98 tutorial, you will need a copy of the Windows 98 CD-ROM. If this CD-ROM is not available, skip this lab assignment. Otherwise, use a computer and the CD-ROM to perform the following tasks.

1. If necessary, start Microsoft Windows 98.
2. Insert the Windows 98 CD-ROM in your CD-ROM drive. If the Windows 98 CD-ROM window displays, click the Close button on the title bar to close the window.
3. Click the Start button on the taskbar, point to Programs on the Start menu, point to Accessories on the Programs submenu, point to System Tools on the Accessories submenu, and then click Welcome to Windows on the System Tools submenu.
4. Click Discover Windows 98 in the Welcome to Windows 98 window to display the Discover Windows 98 Contents.
5. Click the Computer Essentials title (hyperlink) in the Discover Windows 98 Contents screen (Figure 1-101). The Computer Essentials tutorial starts and fills the desktop. The left panel contains a list of lessons. A left-pointing arrow to the right of a lesson indicates the current lesson. Pressing the RIGHT ARROW key on the keyboard displays the next screen in the lesson. Pressing the UP ARROW key quits the Computer Essentials tutorial. Clicking the Contents button displays the Table of Contents in the Discover Windows 98 Contents screen.
6. Press the RIGHT ARROW key to begin the Introduction.
7. When appropriate, press the number 1 key to begin the Meeting Your Computer section. Complete this lesson. The lesson takes approximately 10 minutes.

In the Lab

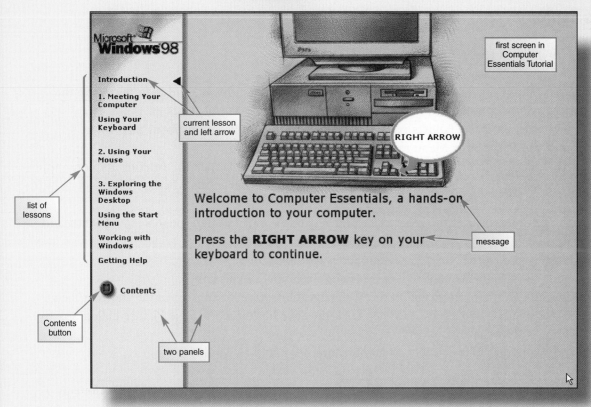

FIGURE 1-101

8. Click the Contents button to display the Discover Windows 98 Contents screen.

9. If you have experience using Windows 3.0 or Windows 3.1 and are learning to use Windows 98, click the Windows 98 Overview title. Otherwise, go to Step 10. This lesson takes approximately 10 minutes.

10. If you have experience using Windows 95 and are learning to use Windows 98, click the What's New title. Otherwise, go to Step 11. Press any key on the keyboard to begin the lesson. Features are organized into five groups. Click each feature (hyperlink) in each group to view a demonstration. When you have finished, click the Exit button. This lesson takes approximately 20 minutes.

11. If time permits, click the More Windows 98 Resources title. Click the Microsoft Windows 98 Starts Here title (1) and then click the Microsoft Press title (2) to view additional information about Windows 98. Click each of the three hyperlinks below the Resources title to explore three Windows-related Web sites. When you have finished, click the Close button in the Microsoft Internet Explorer window and click the Contents button.

12. Click the Close button in the Discover Windows 98 Contents screen.

13. Click the Yes button in the Discover Windows 98 dialog box.

14. Click the Close button in the Welcome to Windows 98 window.

15. Remove the Windows 98 CD-ROM from your CD-ROM drive.

In the Lab

3 Windows Explorer

Instructions: Use a computer to perform the following tasks.

1. Start Microsoft Windows 98 and connect to the Internet.
2. Right-click the Start button on the taskbar, click Explore on the shortcut menu, and then maximize the Exploring - Start Menu window.
3. If necessary, scroll to the left in the Folders pane so the Start Menu and Programs icons are visible.
4. Click the Programs icon in the Start Menu folder.
5. Double-click the Internet Explorer shortcut icon in the Contents pane to launch the Internet Explorer application. What is the URL of the Web page that displays in the Address bar in the Microsoft Internet Explorer window? _____
6. Click the URL in the Address bar in the Internet Explorer window to select it. Type www.scsite.com and then press the ENTER key.
7. Scroll the Web page to display the Shelly Cashman Series textbook titles.
8. Click the Microsoft Windows 98 Complete Concepts and Techniques hyperlink.
9. Right-click the Space Needle clip art image on the Web page, click Save Picture As on the shortcut menu, type Space Needle in the File name box, and then click the Save button in the Save Picture dialog box to save the image in the My Documents folder.
10. Click the Close button in the Windows 98 - Microsoft Internet Explorer window.
11. Scroll to the top of the Folders pane to make the drive C icon visible.
12. Click the minus sign in the box to the left of the drive C icon. The 3½ Floppy (A:) and My Documents icons should be visible.
13. Click the My Documents icon.
14. Right-click the Space Needle icon and then click Properties on the shortcut menu.
    a. What type of file is the Space Needle file? _____
    b. When was the file last modified? _____
    c. What is the size of the file in bytes? _____
15. Click the Cancel button in the Properties dialog box.
16. Insert a formatted floppy disk in drive A of your computer.
17. Right-drag the Space Needle icon over the 3½ Floppy (A:) icon in the Folders pane. Click Move Here on the shortcut menu. Click the 3½ Floppy (A:) icon in the Folders pane. Is the Space Needle file stored on drive A? _____
18. Click the Close button in the Exploring - 3½ Floppy (A:) window.

4 Using Windows Help

Instructions: Use Windows Help and a computer to perform the following tasks.

Part 1: *Using the Question Mark Button*

1. If necessary, start Microsoft Windows 98.
2. Click the Start button on the taskbar.
3. Point to Settings on the Start menu.

In the Lab

4. Click Folder Options on the Settings submenu.
5. Click the General tab in the Folder Options dialog box.
6. Click the Question Mark button on the title bar. The mouse pointer changes to a block arrow with a question mark (Figure 1-102).
7. Click the preview monitor in the General sheet. A pop-up window displays explaining the contents of the preview monitor. Read the information in the pop-up window.

FIGURE 1-102

8. Click an open area of the General sheet to remove the pop-up window.
9. Click the Question Mark button on the title bar and then click the Web style option button. A pop-up window displays explaining what happens when you select this option. Read the information in the pop-up window. Click an open area on the General sheet to remove the pop-up window.
10. Click the Question Mark button on the title bar and then click the Classic style option button. A pop-up window displays explaining what happens when you select this option. Read the information in the pop-up window. Click an open area on the General sheet to remove the pop-up window.
11. Click the Question Mark button on the title bar and then click the Custom style option button. A pop-up window displays explaining what happens when you select this option. Read the information in the pop-up window. Click an open area on the General sheet to remove the pop-up window.
12. Click the Question Mark button on the title bar and then click the Settings button. A pop-up window displays explaining the function of the button. Read the information in the pop-up window. Click an open area on the General sheet to remove the pop-up window.
13. Summarize the function of the Question Mark button. _____
14. Click the Close button in the Folder Options dialog box.

Part 2: *Finding What's New in Windows 98*

1. Click the Start button and then click Help on the Start menu.
2. Click the Maximize button on the Windows Help title bar.
3. If the Contents sheet does not display, click the Contents tab. Click the Introducing Windows 98 closed book icon.
4. Click the What's New in Windows 98 closed book icon.

(continued)

In the Lab

Using Windows Help *(continued)*

5. Click the True Web integration Help topic. Seven hyperlinks display in the right frame (Figure 1-103).

6. Click the Active Desktop hyperlink in the right frame and read the information about the Active Desktop.

7. Click the Channels hyperlink and read the information about channels.

8. Click the Options button on the Help toolbar to display the Options menu and then click Print.

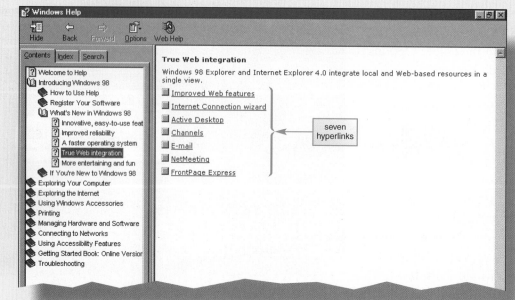

FIGURE 1-103

9. Click the OK button in the Print Topics dialog box to print the True Web integration screen.

Part 3: *Reading About the Online Getting Started Manual*

1. Click the Getting Started Book: Online Version closed book icon in the left frame.

2. Click the Microsoft Windows 98 Getting Started Book Help topic. Read the information Windows 98 displays about the Getting Started Book in the right frame. The Getting Started Book is the online version of the printed manual for Windows 98.

3. Click the Click here hyperlink in the right frame to open the Getting Started window.

4. If the Contents sheet does not display, click the Contents tab. Click the Introducing Getting Started closed book icon. Click and read each of the four Help topics that display.

5. Click the Welcome closed book icon. Three Help topics and two closed book icons display in the open book. Click and read the Overview, Windows 98 at a Glance, and If You're New to Windows topics.

6. Click the Where to Find Information closed book icon.

7. Click the Resources Included with Windows 98 closed book icon. Click and read the Overview topic.

8. Click the Online Tutorial: Discover Windows 98 topic. Read the information about the topic.

9. Click the Troubleshooters topic. Read the information about the topic.

10. Click the Back button on the Help toolbar to display the previous screen (Online Tutorial: Discover Windows 98) in the right frame.

11. Click the Options button on the Help toolbar, click Print, and then click the OK button to print the Help topic.

12. Click the Close button in the Getting Started window.

13. Click the Close button in the Windows Help window.

Word 2000

Microsoft **Word 2000**

Microsoft Word 2000

Creating and Editing a Word Document

You will have mastered the material in this project when you can:

OBJECTIVES

- Start Word
- Describe the Word window
- Zoom page width
- Change the default font size of all text
- Enter text into a document
- Check spelling as you type
- Scroll through a document
- Save a document
- Select text
- Change the font of selected text
- Change the font size of selected text
- Bold selected text
- Right-align a paragraph
- Center a paragraph
- Undo commands or actions
- Italicize selected text
- Underline selected text
- Insert clip art into a document
- Resize a graphic
- Print a document
- Open a document
- Correct errors in a document
- Use Microsoft Word Help
- Quit Word

Wobbling Words

Help for the Spelling Challenged

*" My spelling is Wobbly.
It's good spelling, but it Wobbles,
and the letters get in the wrong places. "*

Winnie-the-Pooh

ough

ought
ouch
dough
bough
cough

Ignore All

Add

AutoCorrect

Language

o wonder Pooh has a difficult time trying to spell words correctly. If he pronounces the words bough, cough, rough, though, and through, he realizes that despite the fact they all end with the letters, ough, they all are pronounced quite differently.

If you share Pooh's spelling dilemma, you are not alone. Most people have difficulty remembering how to spell some words. One study reports 20 percent of writers do not spell well because they cannot visualize words. Even remembering the simple rules such as, i before e except after c, does not offer much assistance because of the slew of exceptions such as the words, weird science.

A spelling error in a flyer distributed on campus, a resume sent to a potential employer, or an e-mail message forwarded to an associate

exceptions - exceptions - exc

does not offer much help because

even remembering simple rules such as, i before e except after c,

gazebo

could lessen your credibility, cause a reader to doubt the accuracy of your statements, and leave a negative impression. In this project, Microsoft Word will check your typing for possible spelling errors as you create an announcement for the Student Government Association's upcoming winter break ski trip at Summit Peak Resort.

If you type a word that does not appear in Word's dictionary, Word will flag the possible error with a wavy red underline. If the spelling is correct, you can instruct Word to ignore the flagged word. If it is misspelled, the spelling feature will offer a list of suggested corrections. Despite this assistance from the spelling checker, one study indicates college students repeatedly ignore or override the flagged words.

Word's spelling checker is a useful alternative to a dictionary, but you must not rely on it 100 percent. It will not flag commonly misused homophones, which are words that are pronounced alike but are spelled differently. For example, it is easy to confuse the homophones in the sentence, The Web site contains an incorrect cite to the reference materials discussing regaining sight after experiencing blindness.

Then what is a spelling-challenged writer to do? English teachers emphasize that you can learn to spell better, but not by strictly memorizing long lists or having someone mark all the errors in a paper. Instead, you need to try the following strategies to improve awareness of spelling difficulties.

First, identify error patterns. For example, do you misspell the same words repeatedly? If so, write them in a list and have a friend dictate them to you. Then write the words again. If you involve your senses, hear the words spelled correctly, and then visualize the words, you increase your awareness of the problem.

Next, always consult a dictionary when you are uncertain of a word's spelling. Note the word's etymology — its origin and history. For example, the word, science, originated from the Latin word, scientia, a form of the verb to know.

As you proofread, read from right to left. Use a pencil to point at each word as you say it aloud.

Using Microsoft Word's spelling checker and a good dictionary should enhance your spelling skills, and stop your words from *Wobbling*.

Microsoft Word 2000

Creating and Editing
a Word Document

P R O J E C T

1

C A S E   P E R S P E C T I V E

Jackie Peterson is this year's Activities Chairperson for the Student Government Association (SGA) at Hilltop Community College. Each year, the Activities Chairperson coordinates vacation plans for the winter break and then prepares fliers announcing the exciting plans. SGA members post these announcements in locations throughout the school, print them in the school newspaper, and mail them to each student.

Because of Jackie's avid love of skiing and snowboarding, she attempts to locate a ski resort in the Midwest designed to accommodate all tastes and budgets. She succeeds! Summit Peak Resort has over 5,200 acres of groomed slopes and pristine lakes for skiing, sledding, snowboarding, ice skating, and ice fishing.

As a Marketing major, you have learned the guidelines for designing announcements. Jackie asks for your assistance with this assignment. You recommend using large, bold characters for the headline and title. To attract attention to the announcement, you suggest including a graphic of a skier sailing down the slopes. Together, you begin designing the announcement.

What Is Microsoft Word 2000?

Microsoft Word is a full-featured word processing program that allows you to create professional looking documents such as announcements, letters, resumes, and reports, and revise them easily. You can use Word's desktop publishing features to create high-quality brochures, advertisements, and newsletters. Word also provides many tools that enable you to create Web pages with ease. From within Word, you even can place these Web pages directly on a Web server.

Word has many features designed to simplify the production of documents. With Word, you easily can include borders, shading, tables, graphics, pictures, and Web addresses in your documents. You can instruct Word to create a template, which is a form you can use and customize to meet your needs. While you are typing, Word can perform tasks automatically. For example, Word can detect and correct spelling and grammar errors in a variety of languages. Word also can format text such as headings, lists, fractions, borders, and Web addresses as you type them. Word's thesaurus allows you to add variety and precision to your writing. Within Word, you can e-mail a copy of your Word document to an e-mail address.

Project One — Summit Peak Announcement

To illustrate the features of Word, this book presents a series of projects that use Word to create documents similar to those you will encounter in academic and business environments. Project 1 uses Word to produce the announcement shown in Figure 1-1.

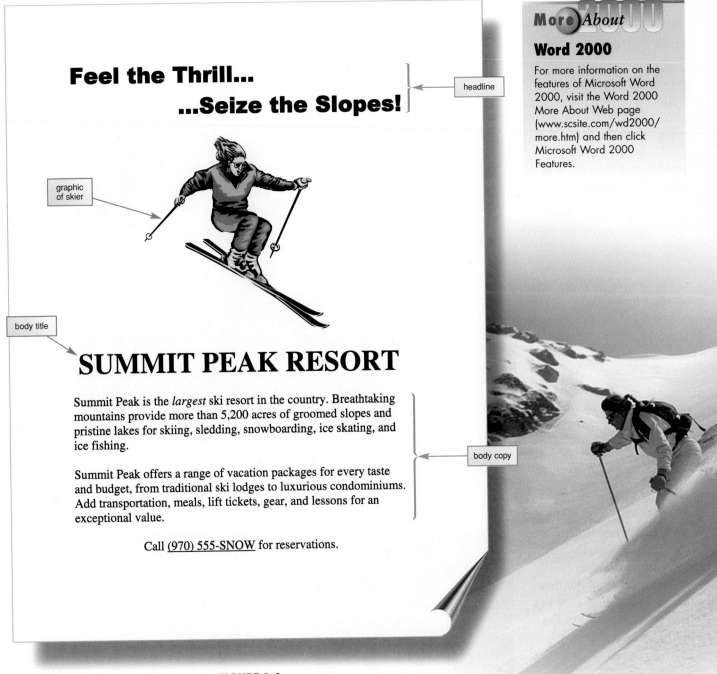

More *About*

Word 2000

For more information on the features of Microsoft Word 2000, visit the Word 2000 More About Web page (www.scsite.com/wd2000/more.htm) and then click Microsoft Word 2000 Features.

Feel the Thrill...
...Seize the Slopes!

headline

graphic of skier

body title

SUMMIT PEAK RESORT

Summit Peak is the *largest* ski resort in the country. Breathtaking mountains provide more than 5,200 acres of groomed slopes and pristine lakes for skiing, sledding, snowboarding, ice skating, and ice fishing.

body copy

Summit Peak offers a range of vacation packages for every taste and budget, from traditional ski lodges to luxurious condominiums. Add transportation, meals, lift tickets, gear, and lessons for an exceptional value.

Call (970) 555-SNOW for reservations.

FIGURE 1-1

The announcement informs students about exciting vacation packages offered by Summit Peak Resort during winter break. The announcement begins with a headline that is followed by a graphic of a skier. Below the graphic of the skier is the body title, SUMMIT PEAK RESORT, followed by the body copy that consists of a brief paragraph about the resort and another paragraph about the vacation packages. Finally, the last line of the announcement lists the resort's telephone number. The appearance of the text and graphic in the announcement is designed to catch the attention of the reader.

Starting Word

Follow these steps to start Word, or ask your instructor how to start Word for your system.

 To Start Word

1 **Click the Start button on the taskbar and then point to New Office Document.**

*The programs on the Start menu display above the Start button (Figure 1-2). The New Office Document command is highlighted on the Start menu. A **highlighted command** displays as light text on a dark background.*

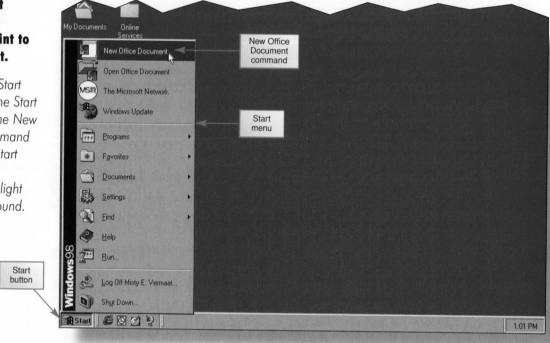

FIGURE 1-2

2 **Click New Office Document. If necessary, click the General tab when the New Office Document dialog box first displays. Point to the Blank Document icon.**

Office displays several icons in the General sheet in the New Office Document dialog box (Figure 1-3). The icons are large because the Large Icons button is selected. Each icon represents a different type of document you can create in Microsoft Office.

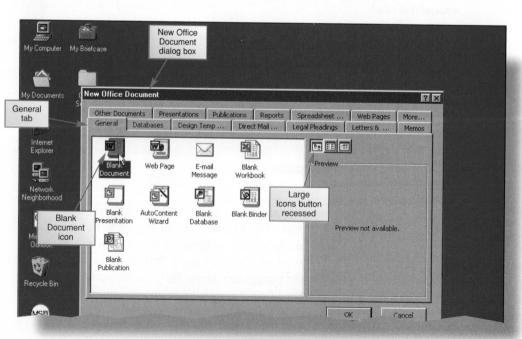

FIGURE 1-3

3 Double-click the Blank Document icon.

Office starts Word. While Word is starting, the mouse pointer changes to the shape of an hourglass. After a few moments, an empty document titled Document1 displays in the Word window (Figure 1-4).

4 If the Word window is not maximized, double-click its title bar to maximize it. If the Office Assistant displays, right-click it and then click Hide on the shortcut menu. If your screen differs from Figure 1-4, click View on the menu bar and then click Normal.

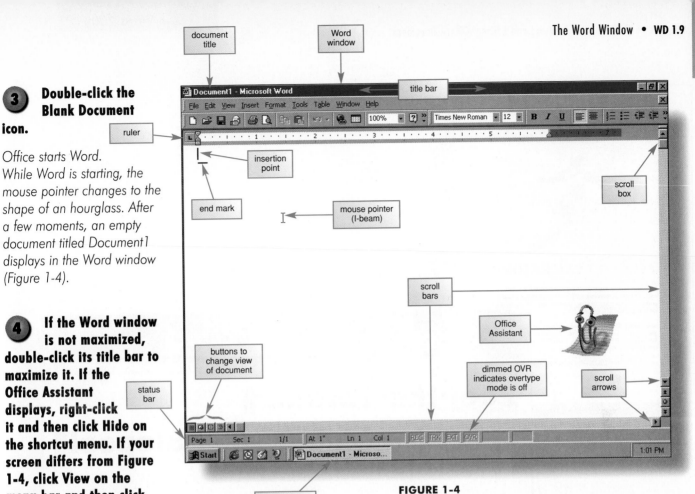

FIGURE 1-4

The Windows taskbar at the bottom of the screen displays the Word program button, indicating the Word program is open.

The Word Window

The **Word window** (Figure 1-4) consists of a variety of components to make your work more efficient and documents more professional. The following sections discuss these components.

Document Window

The document window displays text, tables, graphics, and other items as you type or insert them into a document. Only a portion of your document, however, displays on the screen at one time. You view the portion of the document displayed on the screen through the **document window** (Figure 1-5 on the next page).

Other **Ways**

1. Right-click Start button, click Open, double-click New Office Document, click General tab, double-click Blank Document icon

2. Click New Office Document button on Microsoft Office Shortcut Bar, click General tab, double-click Blank Document icon

3. On Start menu point to Programs, click Microsoft Word

FIGURE 1-5

The document window contains several elements commonly found in other applications, as well as some elements unique to Word. The main elements of the Word document window are the insertion point, end mark, mouse pointer, rulers, scroll bars, and status bar (see Figure 1-4 on the previous page).

INSERTION POINT The **insertion point** is a blinking vertical bar that indicates where text will be inserted as you type. As you type, the insertion point moves to the right and, when you reach the end of a line, it moves downward to the next line. You also can insert graphics, tables, and other items at the location of the insertion point.

END MARK The **end mark** is a short horizontal line that indicates the end of your document. Each time you begin a new line, the end mark moves downward.

MOUSE POINTER The **mouse pointer** becomes different shapes depending on the task you are performing in Word and the pointer's location on the screen. The mouse pointer in Figure 1-4 has the shape of an I-beam. Other mouse pointer shapes are described as they appear on the screen during this and subsequent projects.

RULERS At the top edge of the document window is the **horizontal ruler**. You use the horizontal ruler, sometimes simply called the **ruler**, to set tab stops, indent paragraphs, adjust column widths, and change page margins.

An additional ruler, called the **vertical ruler**, sometimes displays at the left edge of the window when you perform certain tasks. The purpose of the vertical ruler is discussed as it displays on the screen in a later project. If your screen displays a vertical ruler, click View on the menu bar and then click Normal.

SCROLL BARS You use the **scroll bars** to display different portions of your document in the document window. At the right edge of the document window is a vertical scroll bar, and at the bottom of the document window is a horizontal scroll bar. On both the vertical and horizontal scroll bars, the position of the **scroll box** reflects the location of the portion of the document displaying in the document window.

On the left edge of the horizontal scroll bar are four buttons you use to change the view of your document, and on the bottom of the vertical scroll bar are three buttons you can use to scroll through a document. These buttons are discussed as they are used in later projects.

STATUS BAR The status bar displays at the bottom of the document window, above the Windows taskbar. The **status bar** presents information about the location of the insertion point, the progress of current tasks, as well as the status of certain commands, keys, and buttons.

From left to right, the following information displays on the status bar in Figure 1-5: the page number, the section number, the page containing the insertion point followed by the total number of pages in the document, the position of the insertion point in inches from the top of the page, the line number and column number of the insertion point, followed by several status indicators. If you perform a task that requires several seconds (such as saving a document), the status bar displays a message informing you of the progress of the task.

You use the **status indicators** to turn certain keys or modes on or off. Four of these status indicators (REC, TRK, EXT, and OVR) display darkened when on and dimmed when off. For example, the dimmed OVR indicates overtype mode is off. To turn these four status indicators on or off, double-click the status indicator. These status indicators are discussed as they are used in the projects.

The next status indicators display icons as you perform certain tasks. When you begin typing in the document window, a Spelling and Grammar Status icon displays. When Word is saving your document, a Background Save Status icon displays. When you print a document, a Background Print Status icon displays.

When you point to various areas on the status bar, Word displays a ScreenTip to help you identify it. A **ScreenTip** is a short descriptive name of a button, icon, or command associated with the item to which you are pointing.

Menu Bar and Toolbars

The menu bar displays at the top of the screen just below the title bar (Figure 1-6a on the next page). The Standard toolbar and Formatting toolbar are preset to share a single row that displays immediately below the menu bar.

More About

The Horizontal Ruler

If the horizontal ruler does not display on your screen, click View on the menu bar and then click Ruler. To hide the ruler, also click View on the menu bar and then click Ruler.

More About

Scroll Bars

You can use the vertical scroll bar to scroll through multi-page documents. As you drag the scroll box up or down the scroll bar, Word displays a page indicator to the left of the scroll box. If you release the mouse button, Word displays the page referenced by the page indicator in the document window.

More About

Language Mode

If system support for multiple languages was installed on your computer, the status bar also displays the Language mode indicator, which shows the name of the language you are using to create the document.

FIGURE 1-6a

More About 2000

Shortcut Menus

Right-clicking an object displays a shortcut menu (also called a context-sensitive or object menu). Depending on the object, the commands in the shortcut menu vary.

MENU BAR The **menu bar** displays the Word menu names. Each menu contains a list of commands you can use to perform tasks such as retrieving, storing, printing, and formatting data in your document. When you click a menu name on the menu bar, a **short menu** displays that lists your most recently used commands (Figure 1-6b). To display a menu, such as the View menu, click the menu name on the menu bar. If you point to a command on a menu with an arrow to its right, a submenu displays from which you choose a command.

FIGURE 1-6b

If you wait a few seconds or click the arrows at the bottom of the short menu, it expands into a full menu. A **full menu** lists all the commands associated with a menu (Figure 1-6c). You also can display a full menu immediately by double-clicking the menu name on the menu bar. In this book, when you display a menu, always display the full menu using one of these techniques:

1. Click the menu name on the menu bar and then wait a few seconds.
2. Click the menu name and then click the arrows at the bottom of the short menu.
3. Click the menu name and then point to the arrows at the bottom of the short menu.
4. Double-click the menu name.

When a full menu displays, some of the commands are recessed into lighter gray background and some also are unavailable. A recessed command is called a **hidden command** because it does not display on a short menu. As you use Word, it automatically personalizes the short menus for you based on how often you use commands. That is, as you use hidden commands, Word *unhides* them and places them on the short menu. An **unavailable command** displays dimmed, which indicates it is not available for the current selection.

FIGURE 1-6c

TOOLBARS Word has many pre-defined, or built-in, toolbars. A **toolbar** contains buttons, boxes, and menus that allow you to perform tasks more quickly than using the menu bar and related menus. For example, to print a document, you click the Print button on the toolbar. Each button on a toolbar displays an image to help you remember its function. Also, when you point to a button or box on a toolbar, a ScreenTip (the item's name) displays below the mouse pointer (see Figure 1-10 on page WD 1.15).

Two built-in toolbars are the Standard toolbar and the Formatting toolbar. Figure 1-7a illustrates the Standard toolbar and identifies its buttons and boxes. Figure 1-7b illustrates the Formatting toolbar. Each button and box is explained in detail as it is used in the projects throughout the book.

The Standard toolbar and Formatting toolbar are preset to display docked on the same row immediately below the menu bar. A **docked toolbar** is one that is attached to the edge of the Word window. Because both of these toolbars cannot fit entirely on a single row, a portion or all of the Standard toolbar displays on the left of the row and a portion or all of the Formatting toolbar displays on the right (Figure 1-8a). The buttons that display on the toolbar are the more frequently used buttons.

FIGURE 1-7a Standard Toolbar

FIGURE 1-7b Formatting Toolbar

FIGURE 1-8a

To display the entire Standard toolbar, double-click its **move handle**, which is the vertical bar at the left edge of a toolbar. When you display the complete Standard toolbar, only a portion of the Formatting toolbar displays (Figure 1-8b). To display the entire Formatting toolbar, double-click its move handle. When you display the complete Formatting toolbar, only a portion of the Standard toolbar displays (Figure 1-8c on the next page).

FIGURE 1-8b

FIGURE 1-8c

An alternative to double-clicking the move handle to display an entire toolbar is to click the More Buttons button at the right edge of the toolbar. When you click a toolbar's **More Buttons** button, Word displays a **More Buttons list** that contains the toolbar's hidden buttons (Figure 1-8d).

FIGURE 1-8d

As with menus, Word personalizes toolbars. That is, once you click a hidden button in the More Buttons list, Word removes the button from the More Buttons list and places it on the toolbar. For example, if you click the Drawing button in Figure 1-8d, Word displays this button on the Standard toolbar and removes a less frequently used button to make room for the Drawing button. By adapting to the way you work, this intelligent personalization feature of Word is designed to increase your productivity.

Additional toolbars may display on the Word screen, depending on the task you are performing. These additional toolbars display either stacked below the row containing the Standard and Formatting toolbars or floating in the Word window. A **floating toolbar** is not attached to an edge of the Word window. You can rearrange the order of docked toolbars and can move floating toolbars anywhere in the Word window. Later in this book, steps are presented that show you how to float a docked toolbar or dock a floating toolbar.

Resetting Menus and Toolbars

Each project in this book begins with the menu bars and toolbars appearing as they did at the initial installation of the software. To reset your menus and toolbars so they appear exactly as shown in this book, follow the steps in Appendix C.

Displaying the Entire Standard Toolbar

Perform the following step to display the entire Standard toolbar.

To Display the Entire Standard Toolbar

1 **Double-click the move handle on the Standard toolbar.**

Word displays the entire Standard toolbar (Figure 1-9).

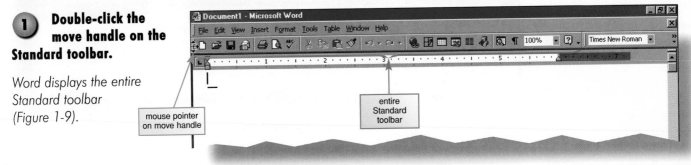

FIGURE 1-9

Zooming Page Width

Depending on your Windows and Word settings, the horizontal ruler at the top of the document window may show more inches or fewer inches than the ruler shown in Figure 1-9. The more inches of ruler that display, the smaller the text will be on the screen. The fewer inches of ruler that display, the larger the text will be on the screen. To minimize eyestrain, the projects in this book display the text as large as possible without extending the right margin beyond the right edge of the document window.

Two factors that affect how much of the ruler displays in the document window are the Windows screen resolution and the Word zoom percentage. The screens in this book use a resolution of 800 x 600. With this resolution, you can increase the preset zoom percentage beyond 100% so that the right margin extends to the edge of the document window. To increase or decrease the size of the displayed characters to a point where both the left and right margins are at the edges of the document window, use the **zoom page width** command as shown in the following steps.

 To Zoom Page Width

1 **Point to the Zoom box arrow on the Standard toolbar.**

The mouse pointer shape is a left-pointing block arrow when positioned on a toolbar button or box (Figure 1-10). When you point to a toolbar button or box, Word displays a ScreenTip.

FIGURE 1-10

2 **Click the Zoom box arrow.**

Word displays a list of available zoom percentages and the Page Width option in the Zoom list (Figure 1-11).

FIGURE 1-11

3 **Point to Page Width in the Zoom list.**

Word highlights Page Width in the Zoom list (Figure 1-12).

FIGURE 1-12

4 **Click Page Width.**

Word extends the right margin to the right edge of the document window (Figure 1-13).

FIGURE 1-13

Other Ways

1. On View menu click Zoom, select Page Width, click OK button

More About

Zooming

If you want to zoom to a percentage not displayed in the Zoom list, you can click the Zoom box on the Standard toolbar, type the desired percentage, and then press the ENTER key; or click view on the menu bar, click Zoom, and then enter the desired zoom percentage.

If your Zoom list (Figure 1-12) displayed additional options, click View on the menu bar and then click Normal.

The Zoom box in Figure 1-13 displays 127%, which Word computes based on a variety of settings. Your percentage may be different depending on your system configuration.

Changing the Default Font Size

Characters that display on the screen are a specific shape, size, and style. The **font**, or typeface, defines the appearance and shape of the letters, numbers, and special characters. The preset, or **default**, font is Times New Roman (Figure 1-14). **Font size** specifies the size of the characters. Font size is determined by a measurement system called points. A single **point** is about 1/72 of one inch in height. Thus, a character with a font size of ten is about 10/72 of one inch in height.

If Word 2000 is installed on a new computer, then the default font size most likely is 12. If, however, you upgrade from a previous version of Word when installing Word 2000, your default font most likely is 10.

If more of the characters in your document require a larger font size than the default, you easily can change the default font size before you type. In Project 1, many of the characters in the announcement are a font size of 16. Follow these steps to increase the font size before you begin entering text.

 To Increase the Default Font Size Before Typing

1 **Double-click the move handle on the Formatting toolbar to display the entire toolbar. Click the Font Size box arrow on the Formatting toolbar and then point to 16.**

A list of available font sizes displays in the Font Size list (Figure 1-14). The available font sizes depend on the current font, which is Times New Roman.

FIGURE 1-14

2 **Click 16.**

The font size for characters in this document changes to 16 (Figure 1-15). The size of the insertion point increases to reflect the new font size.

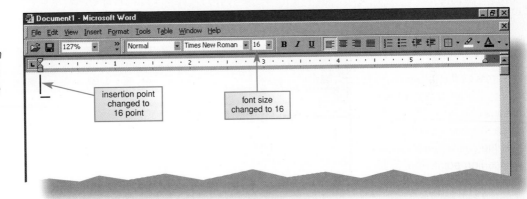

FIGURE 1-15

The new font size takes effect immediately in your document. Word uses this font size for characters you type into this announcement.

Entering Text

To create a document that contains text, you enter the text by typing on the keyboard. The example on the next page explains the steps to enter both lines of the headline of the announcement. These lines will be positioned at the left margin. Later in this project, you will format the headline so that both lines are bold and enlarged and the second line is positioned at the right margin.

 Ways

1. Right-click above end mark, click Font on shortcut menu, click Font tab, select desired font size in Size list, click OK button
2. On Format menu click Font, click Font tab, select desired font size in Size list, click OK button
3. Press CTRL+SHIFT+P, type desired font size, press ENTER
4. Press CTRL+SHIFT+>

To Enter Text

1 **Type** Feel the Thrill **and then press the PERIOD key (.) three times. If you make an error while typing, press the BACKSPACE key until you have deleted the text in error and then retype the text correctly.**

As you type, the insertion point moves to the right (Figure 1-16).

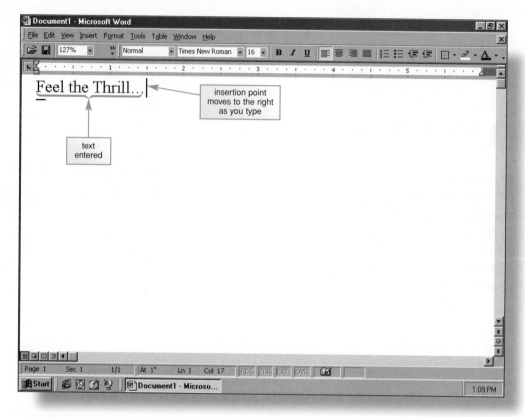

FIGURE 1-16

2 **Press the ENTER key.**

Word moves the insertion point to the beginning of the next line (Figure 1-17). Notice the status bar indicates the current position of the insertion point. That is, the insertion point currently is on line 2 column 1.

FIGURE 1-17

3 **Press the PERIOD key three times and then type** Seize the Slopes! **Press the ENTER key.**

The headline is complete (Figure 1-18). The insertion point is on line 3.

Feel the Thrill…
…Seize the Slopes!

headline entered

insertion point

FIGURE 1-18

When you begin entering text into a document, the **Spelling and Grammar Status icon** displays at the right of the status bar (Figure 1-17). As you type, the Spelling and Grammar Status icon shows an animated pencil writing on paper, which indicates Word is checking for possible errors. When you stop typing, the pencil changes to either a red check mark or a red X. In Figure 1-17, the Spelling and Grammar Status icon displays a red check mark.

In general, if all of the words you have typed are in Word's dictionary and your grammar is correct, a red check mark displays on the Spelling and Grammar Status icon. If you type a word not in the dictionary (because it is a proper name or misspelled), a red wavy underline displays below the word. If you type text that may be grammatically incorrect, a green wavy underline displays below the text. When Word flags a possible spelling or grammar error, it also changes the red check mark on the Spelling and Grammar Status icon to a red X. As you enter text into the announcement, your Spelling and Grammar Status icon may show a red X instead of a red check mark. Later in this project, you will check the spelling of these words. At that time, the red X will return to a red check mark.

Entering Blank Lines into a Document

To enter a blank line into a document, press the ENTER key without typing any text on the line. The following example explains how to enter three blank lines below the headline.

 To Enter Blank Lines into a Document

1 **Press the ENTER key three times.**

Word inserts three blank lines into your document below the headline (Figure 1-19).

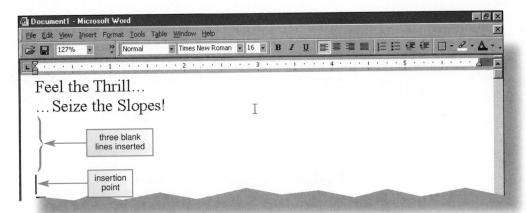

Feel the Thrill…
…Seize the Slopes!

three blank lines inserted

insertion point

FIGURE 1-19

Displaying Formatting Marks

To indicate where in the document you press the ENTER key or SPACEBAR, you may find it helpful to display formatting marks. A **formatting mark**, sometimes called a **nonprinting character**, is a character that displays on the screen but is not visible on a printed document. For example, the paragraph mark (¶) is a formatting mark that indicates where you pressed the ENTER key. A raised dot (•) shows where you pressed the SPACEBAR. Other formatting marks are discussed as they display on the screen.

Depending on settings made during previous Word sessions, your screen may already display formatting marks (see Figure 1-21). If the formatting marks are not already displaying on your screen, perform the following steps to display them.

To Display Formatting Marks

1 **Double-click the move handle on the Standard toolbar to display the entire toolbar. Point to the Show/Hide ¶ button on the Standard toolbar (Figure 1-20).**

FIGURE 1-20

2 **If it is not already recessed, click the Show/Hide ¶ button.**

Word **recesses**, or pushes in, the Show/Hide ¶ button on the Standard toolbar and displays formatting marks on the screen (Figure 1-21).

FIGURE 1-21

Other Ways

1. On Tools menu click Options, click View tab, click All, click OK button
2. Press CTRL+SHIFT+*

Notice several changes to your Word document window (Figure 1-21). A paragraph mark displays at the end of each line to indicate you pressed the ENTER key. Each time you press the ENTER key, Word creates a new paragraph. Because you changed the font size, the paragraph marks are 16 point. Notice Word places a paragraph mark above the end mark – you cannot delete this paragraph mark. Between each word, a raised dot appears, indicating you pressed the SPACEBAR. A small square at the beginning of the first line in the announcement indicates it is formatted using the Heading 1 style. Styles are discussed in a later project. Finally, the Show/Hide ¶ button is recessed to indicate it is selected.

If you feel the formatting marks clutter your screen, you can hide them by clicking the Show/Hide ¶ button again. It is recommended that you display formatting marks; therefore, the document windows presented in this book show the formatting marks.

Entering More Text

The body title (SUMMIT PEAK RESORT) in the announcement is capitalized. The next step is to enter this body title in all capital letters into the document window as explained below.

TO ENTER MORE TEXT

(1) Press the CAPS LOCK key on the keyboard to turn on capital letters. Verify the CAPS LOCK indicator is lit on your keyboard.

(2) Type SUMMIT PEAK RESORT and then press the CAPS LOCK key to turn off capital letters.

(3) Press the ENTER key twice.

The body title displays on line 6 as shown in Figure 1-22 below.

Using Wordwrap

Wordwrap allows you to type words in a paragraph continually without pressing the ENTER key at the end of each line. When the insertion point reaches the right margin, Word positions it automatically at the beginning of the next line. As you type, if a word extends beyond the right margin, Word also positions that word automatically on the next line with the insertion point.

Thus, as you enter text using Word, do not press the ENTER key when the insertion point reaches the right margin. Because Word creates a new paragraph each time you press the ENTER key, press the ENTER key only in these circumstances:

1. To insert blank lines into a document
2. To begin a new paragraph
3. To terminate a short line of text and advance to the next line
4. In response to certain Word commands

Perform the following step to become familiar with wordwrap.

Steps To Wordwrap Text as You Type

(1) **Type** Summit Peak is the largest ski resort in the country. Breathtaking mountains provide **as the beginning of the body copy.**

Word wraps the word, mountains, to the beginning of line 9 because it is too long to fit on line 8 (Figure 1-22). Your document may wordwrap differently depending on the type of printer you are using.

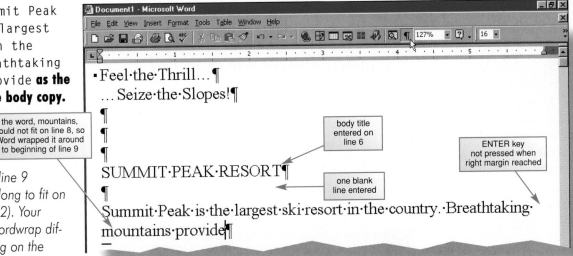

FIGURE 1-22

Checking Spelling Automatically as You Type

As you type text into the document window, Word checks your typing for possible spelling and grammar errors. If a word you type is not in the dictionary, a red wavy underline displays below it. Likewise, if text you type contains possible grammar errors, a green wavy underline displays below the text. In both cases, the Spelling and Grammar Status icon on the status bar displays a red X, instead of a check mark. Although you can check the entire document for spelling and grammar errors at once, you also can check these errors immediately.

To verify that the check spelling as you type feature is enabled, right-click the Spelling and Grammar Status icon on the status bar and then click Options on the shortcut menu. When the Spelling & Grammar dialog box displays, be sure Check spelling as you type has a check mark and Hide spelling errors in this document does not have a check mark.

When a word is flagged with a red wavy underline, it is not in Word's dictionary. A flagged word, however, is not necessarily misspelled. For example, many names, abbreviations, and specialized terms are not in Word's main dictionary. In these cases, you tell Word to ignore the flagged word. As you type, Word also detects duplicate words. For example, if your document contains the phrase, to the the store, Word places a red wavy underline below the second occurrence of the word, the. To display a list of suggested corrections for a flagged word, you right-click it.

In the following example, the word, sledding, has been misspelled intentionally as sleding to illustrate Word's check spelling as you type feature. If you are doing this project on a personal computer, your announcement may contain different misspelled words, depending on the accuracy of your typing.

Entering Sentences

Word processing documents use variable character fonts; for example, the letter w takes up more space than the letter i. With these fonts, it often is difficult to determine how many times the SPACEBAR has been pressed between sentences. Thus, the rule is to press the SPACEBAR only once after periods, colons, and other punctuation marks.

Steps **To Check Spelling as You Type**

---

1 **Press the SPACEBAR once. Type** more than 5,200 acres of groomed slopes and pristine lakes for skiing, sleding, **and then press the SPACEBAR.**

Word flags the misspelled word, sleding, by placing a red wavy underline below it (Figure 1-23). Notice the Spelling and Grammar Status icon on the status bar now displays a red X, indicating Word has detected a possible spelling or grammar error.

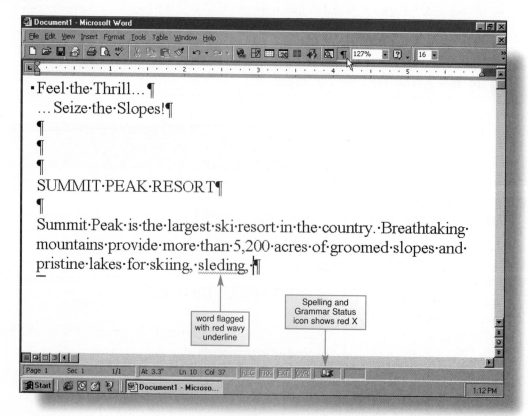

FIGURE 1-23

2 Position the mouse pointer in the flagged word (sleding, in this case).

The mouse pointer's shape is an I-beam when positioned in a word (Figure 1-24).

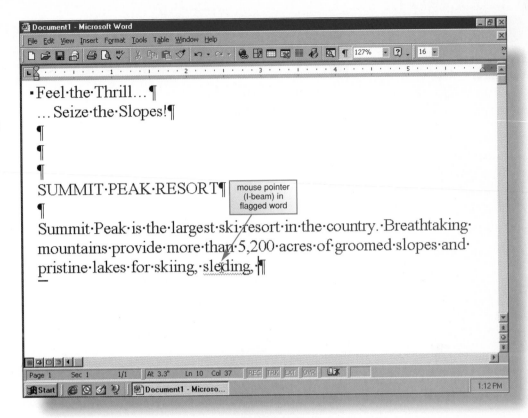

FIGURE 1-24

3 Right-click the flagged word, sleding. When the shortcut menu displays, point to sledding.

Word displays a shortcut menu that lists suggested spelling corrections for the flagged word (Figure 1-25).

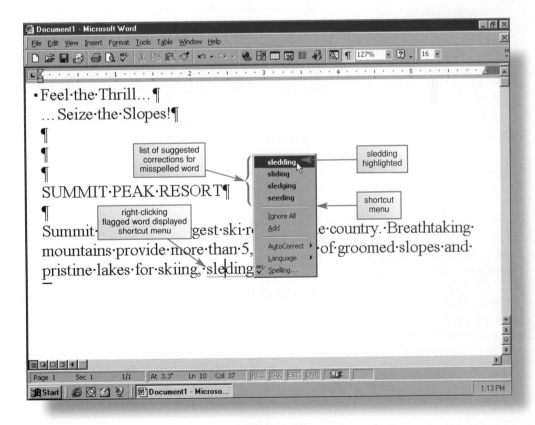

FIGURE 1-25

4 **Click sledding. Press the END key and then type the remainder of the sentence:** snowboarding, ice skating, and ice fishing.

Word replaces the misspelled word with the selected word on the shortcut menu (Figure 1-26). Word replaces the red X with a check mark on the Spelling and Grammar Status icon.

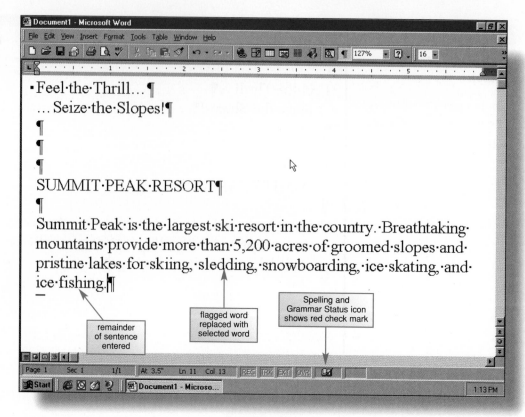

FIGURE 1-26

If the word actually is spelled correctly and, for example, is a proper name, you can right-click it and then click Ignore All on the shortcut menu (Figure 1-25 on the previous page). If, when you right-click the misspelled word, your desired correction is not in the list on the shortcut menu, you can click outside the shortcut menu to make the menu disappear and then retype the correct word, or you can click Spelling on the shortcut menu to display the Spelling dialog box. The Spelling dialog box is discussed in Project 2.

If you feel the wavy underlines clutter your document window, you can hide them temporarily until you are ready to check for spelling errors. To hide spelling errors, right-click the Spelling and Grammar Status icon on the status bar and then click Hide Spelling Errors on the shortcut menu. To hide grammar errors, right-click the Spelling and Grammar Status icon on the status bar and then click Hide Grammatical Errors on the shortcut menu.

Entering Text that Scrolls the Document Window

As you type more lines of text than Word can display in the document window, Word **scrolls** the top portion of the document upward off the screen. Although you cannot see the text once it scrolls off the screen, it remains in the document. You have learned that the document window allows you to view only a portion of your document at one time (Figure 1-5 on page WD 1.10).

Perform the following step to enter text that scrolls the document window.

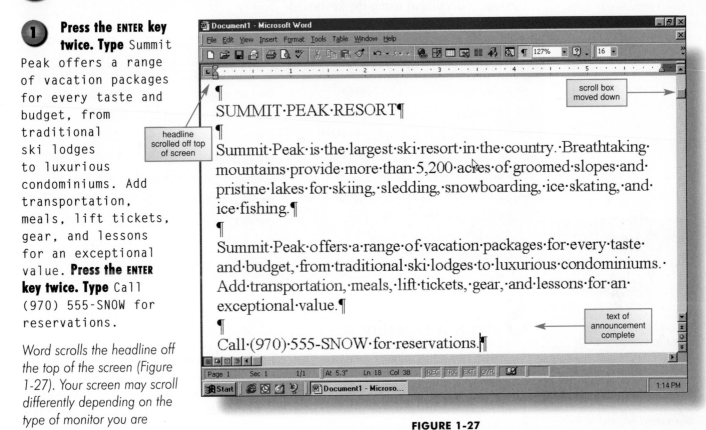

Steps To Enter Text that Scrolls the Document Window

1 **Press the ENTER key twice. Type** Summit Peak offers a range of vacation packages for every taste and budget, from traditional ski lodges to luxurious condominiums. Add transportation, meals, lift tickets, gear, and lessons for an exceptional value. **Press the ENTER key twice. Type** Call (970) 555-SNOW for reservations.

Word scrolls the headline off the top of the screen (Figure 1-27). Your screen may scroll differently depending on the type of monitor you are using.

FIGURE 1-27

When Word scrolls text off the top of the screen, the scroll box on the scroll bar at the right edge of the document window moves downward (Figure 1-27). The **scroll box** indicates the current relative location of the insertion point in the document. You may use either the mouse or the keyboard to move the insertion point to a different location in a document.

With the mouse, you use the scroll arrows or the scroll box to display a different portion of the document in the document window, and then click the mouse to move the insertion point to that location. Table 1-1 explains various techniques for vertically scrolling with the mouse.

Table 1-1 Techniques for Scrolling with the Mouse

SCROLL DIRECTION	MOUSE ACTION
Up	Drag the scroll box upward.
Down	Drag the scroll box downward.
Up one screen	Click anywhere above the scroll box on the vertical scroll bar.
Down one screen	Click anywhere below the scroll box on the vertical scroll bar.
Up one line	Click the scroll arrow at the top of the vertical scroll bar.
Down one line	Click the scroll arrow at the bottom of the vertical scroll bar.

When you use the keyboard to scroll, the insertion point moves automatically when you press the appropriate keys. Table 1-2 outlines various techniques to scroll through a document using the keyboard.

Table 1-2 Techniques for Scrolling with the Keyboard

SCROLL DIRECTION	KEY(S) TO PRESS	SCROLL DIRECTION	KEY(S) TO PRESS
Left one character	LEFT ARROW	Down one paragraph	CTRL+DOWN ARROW
Right one character	RIGHT ARROW	Up one screen	PAGE UP
Left one word	CTRL+LEFT ARROW	Down one screen	PAGE DOWN
Right one word	CTRL+RIGHT ARROW	To top of document window	ALT+CTRL+PAGE UP
Up one line	UP ARROW	To bottom of document window	ALT+CTRL+PAGE DOWN
Down one line	DOWN ARROW	Previous page	CTRL+PAGE UP
To end of a line	END	Next page	CTRL+PAGE DOWN
To beginning of a line	HOME	To the beginning of a document	CTRL+HOME
Up one paragraph	CTRL+UP ARROW	To the end of a document	CTRL+END

More About

Saving

When you save a document, you use meaningful file names. A file name can be up to 255 characters, including spaces. The only invalid characters are backslash (\), slash (/), colon (:), asterisk (*), question mark (?), quotation mark ("), less than symbol (<), greater than symbol (>), and vertical bar (|).

Saving a Document

As you create a document in Word, the computer stores it in memory. If you turn off the computer or if you lose electrical power, the document in memory is lost. Hence, it is mandatory to save on disk any document that you will use later. The following steps illustrate how to save a document on a floppy disk inserted in drive A using the Save button on the Standard toolbar.

Steps To Save a New Document

1 Insert a formatted floppy disk into drive A. Click the Save button on the Standard toolbar.

Word displays the Save As dialog box (Figure 1-28). The first line from the document displays highlighted in File name text box as the default file name. With this file name selected, you can change it by immediately typing the new name.

FIGURE 1-28

2 **Type** Summit Peak Announcement **in the File name text box. Do not press the ENTER key after typing the file name.**

The file name, Summit Peak Announcement, displays in the File name text box (Figure 1-29). Notice that the current save location is the My Documents folder. A **folder** is a specific location on a disk. To change to a different save location, you use the Save in box.

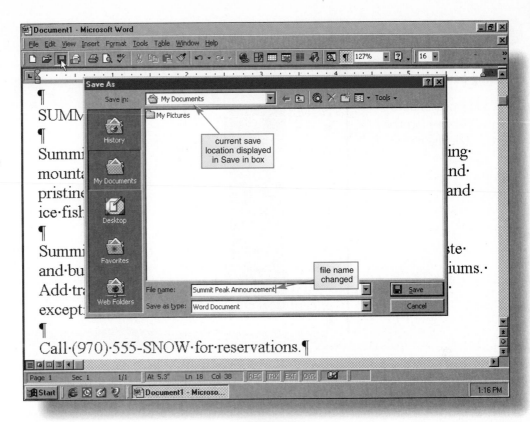

FIGURE 1-29

3 **Click the Save in box arrow and then point to 3½ Floppy (A:).**

A list of the available save locations displays (Figure 1-30). Your list may differ depending on your system configuration.

FIGURE 1-30

4 **Click 3½ Floppy (A:) and then point to the Save button in the Save As dialog box.**

The 3½ Floppy (A:) drive becomes the save location (Figure 1-31). The names of existing files stored on the floppy disk in drive A display. In Figure 1-31, no Word files currently are stored on the floppy disk in drive A.

FIGURE 1-31

5 **Click the Save button in the Save As dialog box.**

Word saves the document on the floppy disk in drive A with the file name Summit Peak Announcement (Figure 1-32). Although the announcement is saved on a floppy disk, it also remains in main memory and displays on the screen.

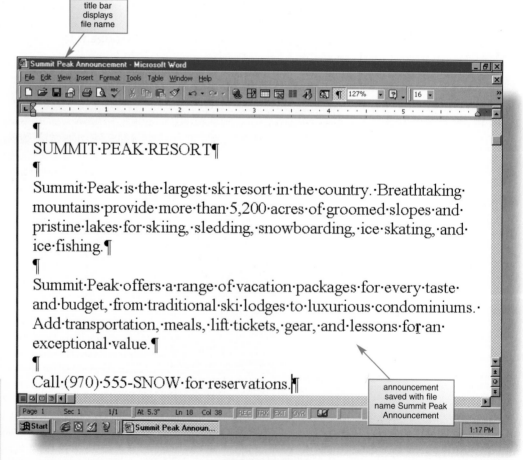

FIGURE 1-32

Formatting Paragraphs and Characters in a Document

The text for Project 1 now is complete. The next step is to format the characters and paragraphs in the announcement. Paragraphs encompass the text up to and including a paragraph mark (¶). **Paragraph formatting** is the process of changing the appearance of a paragraph. For example, you can center or indent a paragraph.

Characters include letters, numbers, punctuation marks, and symbols. **Character formatting** is the process of changing the way characters appear on the screen and in print. You use character formatting to emphasize certain words and improve readability of a document.

With Word, you can format before you type or apply new formats after you type. Earlier, you changed the font size before you typed any text, and then you entered the text. In this section, you format existing text.

Figure 1-33a shows the announcement before formatting the paragraphs and characters. Figure 1-33b shows the announcement after formatting. As you can see from the two figures, a document that is formatted not only is easier to read, but it looks more professional.

More *About*

Formatting

Character formatting includes changing the font, font style, font size; adding an underline, color, strikethrough, shadow, outline; embossing; engraving; making a superscript or subscript; and changing the case of the letters. Paragraph formatting includes alignment; indentation; and spacing above, below, and in between lines.

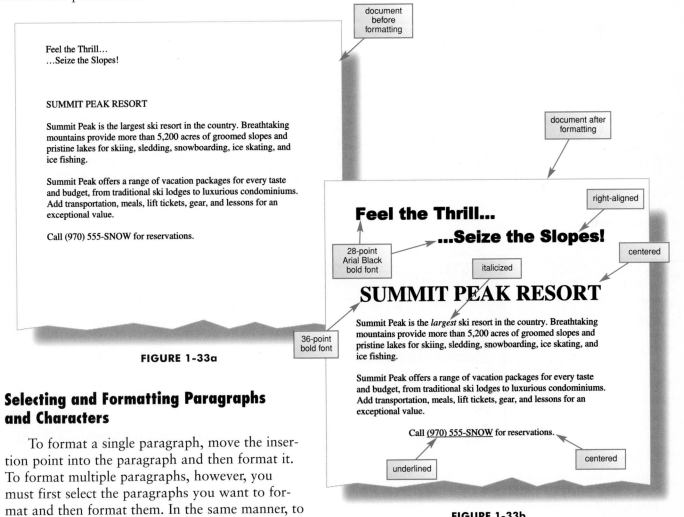

FIGURE 1-33a

FIGURE 1-33b

Selecting and Formatting Paragraphs and Characters

To format a single paragraph, move the insertion point into the paragraph and then format it. To format multiple paragraphs, however, you must first select the paragraphs you want to format and then format them. In the same manner, to format characters, a word, or words, you first must select the characters, word, or words to be formatted and then format your selection.

Selected text is highlighted. That is, if your screen normally displays dark letters on a light background, then selected text displays light letters on a dark background.

Selecting Multiple Paragraphs

The first formatting step in this project is to change the font of the characters in the headline. The headline consists of two separate lines, each ending with a paragraph mark. You have learned that each time you press the ENTER key, Word creates a new paragraph. Thus, the headline actually is two separate paragraphs.

To change the font of the characters in the headline, you must first **select**, or highlight, both paragraphs in the headline as shown in the following steps.

To Select Multiple Paragraphs

1 Press CTRL+HOME; that is, press and hold the CTRL key, then press the HOME key, and then release both keys. Move the mouse pointer to the left of the first paragraph to be selected until the mouse pointer changes to a right-pointing block arrow.

The mouse pointer changes to a right-pointing block arrow when positioned to the left of a paragraph (Figure 1-34). CTRL + HOME positions the insertion point at the top of the document.

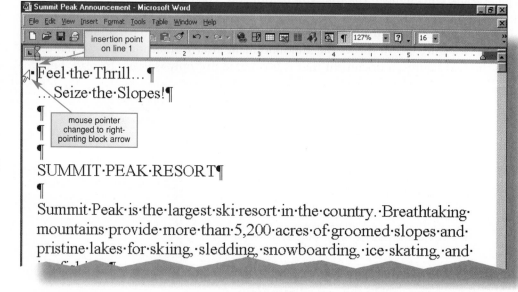

FIGURE 1-34

2 Drag downward until both paragraphs are highlighted.

Word selects both of the paragraphs (Figure 1-35). Recall that dragging is the process of holding down the mouse button while moving the mouse and finally releasing the mouse button.

FIGURE 1-35

1. With insertion point at beginning of first paragraph, press CTRL+SHIFT+DOWN ARROW repeatedly

Changing the Font of Selected Text

You have learned that the default font is Times New Roman. Word, however, provides many other fonts to add variety to your documents. Thus, change the font of the headline in the announcement to Arial Black as shown in these steps.

Steps **To Change the Font of Selected Text**

1 **Double-click the move handle on the Formatting toolbar to display the entire toolbar. While the text is selected, click the Font box arrow on the Formatting toolbar, scroll through the list until Arial Black displays, and then point to Arial Black.**

Word displays a list of available fonts (Figure 1-36). Your list of available fonts may differ, depending on the type of printer you are using.

FIGURE 1-36

2 **Click Arial Black.**

Word changes the font of the selected text to Arial Black (Figure 1-37).

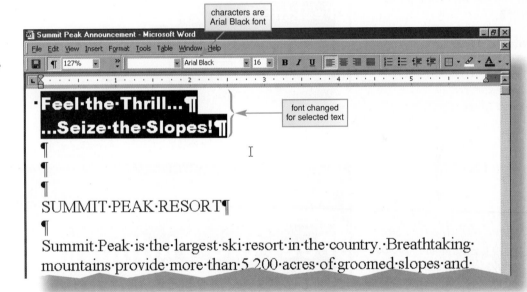

FIGURE 1-37

Changing the Font Size of Selected Text

The next step is to increase the font size of the characters in the selected headline. Recall that the font size specifies the size of the characters. Earlier in this project, you changed the font size for characters in the entire announcement to 16. To give the headline more impact, it has a font size larger than the body copy. Follow the steps on the next page to increase the font size of the headline from 16 to 28 points.

Other **Ways**

1. Right-click selected text, click Font on shortcut menu, click Font tab, select desired font in Font list, click OK button

2. On Format menu click Font, click Font tab, select desired font in Font list, click OK button

3. Press CTRL+SHIFT+F, press DOWN ARROW key until desired font displays, press ENTER

Steps ## To Change the Font Size of Selected Text

1 While the text is selected, click the Font Size box arrow on the Formatting toolbar and then point to the down scroll arrow on the Font Size scroll bar.

Word displays a list of the available font sizes (Figure 1-38). Available font sizes vary depending on the font and printer driver.

FIGURE 1-38

2 Click the down scroll arrow on the scroll bar until 28 displays in the list and then point to 28.

Word highlights 28 in the list (Figure 1-39).

FIGURE 1-39

3 Click 28.

Word increases the font size of the headline from 16 to 28 (Figure 1-40). The Font Size box on the Formatting toolbar displays 28, indicating the selected text has a font size of 28.

FIGURE 1-40

 Other Ways

1. Right-click selected text, click Font on shortcut menu, click Font tab, select desired point size in Size list, click OK button
2. On Format menu click Font, click Font tab, select desired point size in Size list, click OK button
3. Press CTRL+SHIFT+P, type desired point size, press ENTER

Bold Selected Text

Bold characters display somewhat thicker than those that are not bold. To further emphasize the headline of the announcement, perform the following step to bold its characters.

To Bold Selected Text

1 **While the text is selected, click the Bold button on the Formatting toolbar.**

Word formats the headline in bold (Figure 1-41). The Bold button is recessed.

FIGURE 1-41

When the selected text is bold, the Bold button on the Formatting toolbar is recessed. If, for some reason, you wanted to remove the bold format of the selected text, you would click the Bold button a second time.

Right-Align a Paragraph

The default alignment for paragraphs is **left-aligned**; that is, flush at the left edge of the document with uneven right edges. In Figure 1-42, the Align Left button is recessed to indicate the current paragraph is left-aligned.

The second line of the headline, however, is to be **right-aligned**; that is, flush at the right edge of the document with uneven left edges. Recall that the second line of the headline is a paragraph and that paragraph formatting does not require you to select the paragraph prior to formatting. Just position the insertion point in the paragraph to be formatted and then format it accordingly.

Perform the following steps to right-align the second line of the headline.

 To Right-Align a Paragraph

1 **Click somewhere in the paragraph to be right-aligned. Point to the Align Right button on the Formatting toolbar.**

Word positions the insertion point at the location you clicked (Figure 1-42).

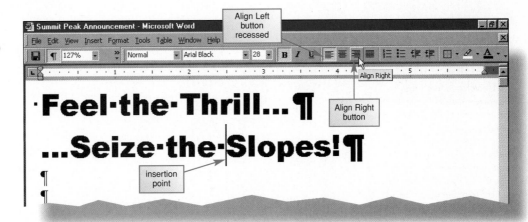

FIGURE 1-42

Other Ways

1. Right-click selected text, click Font on shortcut menu, click Font tab, click Bold in Font style list, click OK button
2. On Format menu click Font, click Font tab, click Bold in Font style list, click OK button
3. Press CTRL+B

2 **Click the Align Right button.**

The second line of the headline is right-aligned (Figure 1-43). Notice that you did not have to select the paragraph before right-aligning it; paragraph formatting only requires the insertion point be positioned somewhere in the paragraph.

FIGURE 1-43

When a paragraph is right-aligned, the Align Right button on the Formatting toolbar is recessed. If, for some reason, you wanted to return the selected paragraphs to left-aligned, you would click the Align Left button on the Formatting toolbar.

Center a Paragraph

The body title currently is left-aligned. Perform the following step to **center** it, that is, position the body title horizontally between the left and right margins on the page.

More About
Centering

The Center button on the Formatting toolbar centers text horizontally. You also can center text vertically between the top and bottom margins. To do this, click File on the menu bar, click Page Setup, click the Layout tab, click the Vertical alignment box arrow, click Center in the list, and then click the OK button.

Steps **To Center a Paragraph**

1 **Click somewhere in the paragraph to be centered. Click the Center button on the Formatting toolbar.**

Word centers the body title between the left and right margins (Figure 1-44). The Center button on the Formatting toolbar is recessed, which indicates the paragraph containing the insertion point is centered.

FIGURE 1-44

When a paragraph is centered, the Center button on the Formatting toolbar is recessed. If, for some reason, you wanted to return the selected paragraphs to left-aligned, you would click the Align Left button on the Formatting toolbar.

Undoing Commands or Actions

Word provides an **Undo button** on the Standard toolbar that you can use to cancel your recent command(s) or action(s). For example, if you format text incorrectly, you can *undo* the format and try it again. If, after you undo an action, you decide you did not want to perform the undo, you can use the **Redo button** to undo the undo. Some actions, such as saving or printing a document, cannot be undone or redone.

Perform the steps on the next page to *uncenter* the body title and then re-center it.

Other **Ways**

1. Right-click paragraph, click Paragraph on shortcut menu, click Indents and Spacing tab, click Alignment box arrow, click Centered, click OK button

2. On Format menu click Paragraph, click Indents and Spacing tab, click Alignment box arrow, click Centered, click OK button

3. Press CTRL+E

To Undo an Action

1 **Double-click the move handle on the Standard toolbar to display the entire toolbar. Click the Undo button on the Standard toolbar.**

Word left-aligns the body title (Figure 1-45). Word returns the body title to its formatting prior to you issuing the command to center it.

2 **Click the Redo button on the Standard toolbar.**

Word re-applies the center format to the body title (see Figure 1-46).

FIGURE 1-45

Other Ways

1. On Edit menu click Undo
2. Press CTRL+Z

You also can cancel a series of prior actions by clicking the Undo button arrow (Figure 1-45) to display the undo actions list and then dragging through the actions you wish to be undone.

Whereas undo cancels an action you did not want to perform, Word also provides a **Repeat command**, which duplicates an action you wish to perform again. For example, if you format a paragraph and wish to format another paragraph the exact same way, you could click in the second paragraph to format and then click Repeat on the Edit menu.

Selecting a Line and Formatting It

The next series of steps selects the body title, SUMMIT PEAK RESORT, and formats the characters in it. First, you select the body title. To select the body title, perform the following step.

To Select a Line

1 **Move the mouse pointer to the left of the line to be selected (SUMMIT PEAK RESORT) until it changes to a right-pointing block arrow and then click.**

The entire line to the right of the mouse pointer is highlighted (Figure 1-46).

FIGURE 1-46

The next step is to increase the font size of the selected characters to 36 point and bold the selected characters, as explained in the following steps.

TO FORMAT A LINE OF TEXT

1 Double-click the move handle on the Formatting toolbar to display the entire toolbar. While the text is selected, click the Font Size box arrow on the Formatting toolbar and then scroll to 36 in the list. Click 36.

2 Click the Bold button on the Formatting toolbar.

The characters in the body title are enlarged and bold (Figure 1-47 on the next page).

Selecting a Word

To format characters in a word, you must select the entire word first. Follow the steps on the next page to select the word, largest, so you can italicize it.

Other **Ways**

1. Drag through the line
2. With insertion point at beginning of desired line, press SHIFT+DOWN ARROW

More *About*

The Formatting Toolbar

Many of the buttons on the Formatting toolbar are toggles; that is, click them once to format the selected text; and click them again to remove the format from the selected text. For example, clicking the Bold button bolds selected text; clicking the Bold button again removes the bold.

Steps **To Select a Word**

1 **Position the mouse pointer somewhere in the word to be formatted (largest, in this case).**

The mouse pointer's shape is an I-beam when you position it in unselected text in the document window (Figure 1-47).

FIGURE 1-47

2 **Double-click the word to be selected.**

The word, largest, is high-lighted (Figure 1-48). Notice that when the mouse pointer is positioned in a selected word, its shape is a left-pointing block arrow.

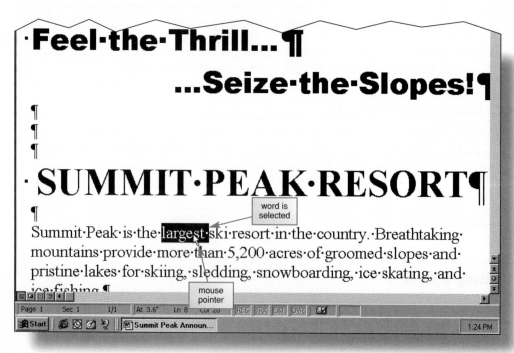

Other **Ways**

1. Drag through the word
2. With insertion point at beginning of desired word, press CTRL+SHIFT+RIGHT ARROW

FIGURE 1-48

Italicize Selected Text

To italicize the word, largest, perform the following step.

 To Italicize Selected Text

1 **With the text still selected, click the Italic button on the Formatting toolbar.**

Word italicizes the text (Figure 1-49). The Italic button on the Formatting toolbar is recessed.

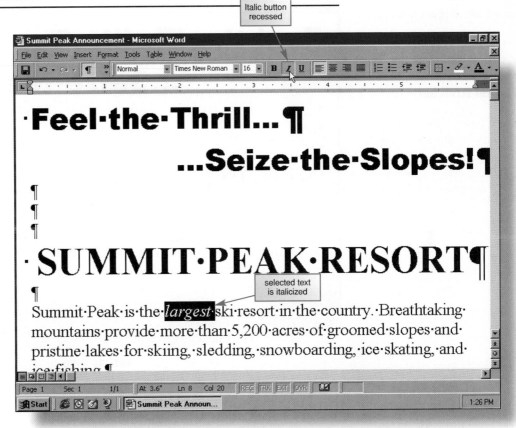

FIGURE 1-49

When the selected text is italicized, the Italic button on the Formatting toolbar is recessed. If, for some reason, you wanted to remove the italics from the selected text, you would click the Italic button a second time, or you immediately could click the Undo button on the Standard toolbar.

Scrolling

Continue formatting the document by scrolling down one screen so the bottom portion of the announcement displays in the document window. Perform the steps on the next page to display the lower portion of the document.

Other Ways

1. Right-click selected text, click Font on shortcut menu, click Font tab, click Italic in Font style list, click OK button
2. On Format menu click Font, click Font tab, click Italic in Font style list, click OK button
3. Press CTRL+I

To Scroll Through the Document

1 **Position the mouse pointer below the scroll box on the vertical scroll bar (Figure 1-50).**

2 **Click below the scroll box on the vertical scroll bar.**

Word scrolls down one screenful in the document (see Figure 1-51). Depending on your monitor type, your screen may scroll differently.

FIGURE 1-50

Other Ways

1. Drag scroll box on vertical scroll bar
2. Click scroll arrows on vertical scroll bar
3. Press PAGE DOWN or PAGE UP
4. See Tables 1-1 and 1-2 on pages WD 1.25 and WD 1.26

The next step is to center the last line of the announcement as described in the following steps.

TO CENTER A PARAGRAPH

1 Click somewhere in the paragraph to be centered.

2 Click the Center button on the Formatting toolbar.

Word centers the last line of the announcement (see Figure 1-51).

Selecting a Group of Words

The next step is to underline the telephone number in the last line of the announcement. Because the telephone number contains spaces and other punctuation, Word considers it a group of words. Thus, the telephone number is a group of words. Select the telephone number by performing the following steps.

To Select a Group of Words

1 **Position the mouse pointer immediately to the left of the first character of the text to be selected.**

The mouse pointer, an I-beam, is to the left of the parenthesis in the telephone number (Figure 1-51).

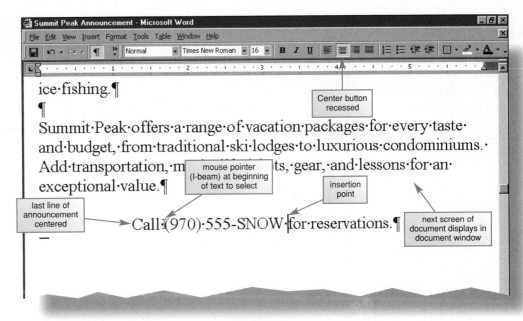

FIGURE 1-51

2 **Drag the mouse pointer through the last character of the text to be selected.**

Word highlights the telephone number (Figure 1-52).

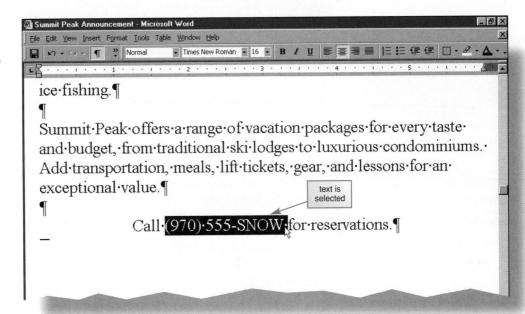

FIGURE 1-52

Underlining Selected Text

Underlined text prints with an underscore (_) below each character. Like bold, it used to emphasize or draw attention to specific text. Follow the step on the next page to underline the selected telephone number.

Other Ways

1. With insertion point at beginning of first word in the group, press CTRL+SHIFT+RIGHT ARROW until words are selected

Steps **To Underline Selected Text**

1 **With the text still selected, click the Underline button on the Formatting toolbar. Click inside the selected text to remove the highlight.**

Word underlines the text and positions the insertion point inside the underlined text (Figure 1-53). When the insertion point is inside the underlined text, the Underline button is recessed.

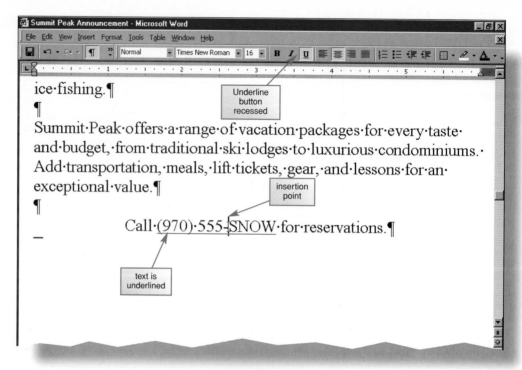

FIGURE 1-53

Other **Ways**

1. Right-click selected text, click Font on shortcut menu, click Font tab, click Underline style box arrow, click desired underline style, click OK button
2. On Format menu click Font, click Font tab, click Underline style box arrow, click desired underline style, click OK button
3. Press CTRL+U

To remove a highlight, click the mouse. If you click inside the highlight, the Formatting toolbar displays the formatting characteristics of the characters and paragraphs containing the insertion point.

When the selected text is underlined, the Underline button on the Formatting toolbar is recessed. If, for some reason, you wanted to remove the underline from the selected text, you would click the Underline button a second time, or you immediately could click the Undo button on the Standard toolbar.

In addition to the basic underline shown in Figure 1-53, Word has many decorative underlines that are available in the Font dialog box. For example, you can use double underlines, dotted underlines, and wavy underlines. You also can change the color of an underline and instruct Word to underline only the words and not the spaces between the words.

The formatting for the announcement is now complete. The next step is to insert a graphical image into the document and then resize the image.

More *About*

The Font Dialog Box

If a character formatting operation is not available on the Formatting toolbar, use the Font dialog box to perform the operation. To display the Font dialog box, click Format on the menu bar and then click Font.

Inserting Clip Art into a Word Document

Files containing graphical images, also called **graphics**, are available from a variety of sources. Word 2000 includes a series of predefined graphics called **clip art** that you can insert into a Word document. Clip art is located in the **Clip Gallery**, which contains a collection of **clips**, including clip art, as well as photographs, sounds, and video clips. The Clip Gallery contains its own Help system to assist you in locating clips suited to your application.

More *About*

Clip Galleries

For more information on the clip galleries available for purchase, visit the Word 2000 More About Web page (www.scsite.com/wd2000/more.htm) and then click Clip Galleries.

Inserting Clip Art

The next step in the project is to insert a graphic of a skier into the announcement. Perform the following steps to insert a graphic into the document.

 Steps **To Insert Clip Art into a Document**

1 **To position the insertion point where you want the clip art to be located, press CTRL+HOME and then press the DOWN ARROW key three times. Click Insert on the menu bar.**

The insertion point is positioned on the second paragraph mark below the headline, and the Insert menu displays (Figure 1-54). Remember that a short menu initially displays, which expands into a full menu after a few seconds.

FIGURE 1-54

2 **Point to Picture and then point to Clip Art.**

The Picture submenu displays (Figure 1-55). You have learned that when you point to a command that has a small arrow to its right, Word displays a submenu associated with that command.

FIGURE 1-55

3 **Click Clip Art. When the Insert ClipArt window opens, click the Search for clips text box.**

Word opens the Insert ClipArt window (Figure 1-56). The text in the Search for clips text box is highlighted. When you enter a description of the desired graphic in this text box, Word searches the Clip Gallery for clips that match the description.

FIGURE 1-56

4 **Type** ski **and then press the ENTER key.**

A list of clips that match the description, ski, displays (Figure 1-57).

FIGURE 1-57

5 **Click the desired image and then point to the Insert clip button on the Pop-up menu.**

Word displays a Pop-up menu (Figure 1-58). The Pop-up menu contains four buttons: (1) Insert clip, (2) Preview clip, (3) Add clip to Favorites or other category, and (4) Find similar clips.

FIGURE 1-58

6 **Click the Insert clip button. Click the Close button at the right edge of the Insert ClipArt window's title bar. Press the UP ARROW key twice to display part of the headline.**

Word inserts the clip into the document at the location of the insertion point (Figure 1-59). The graphic of the skier displays below the headline in the announcement.

FIGURE 1-59

Obtaining Graphics

If you have a scanner or digital camera attached to your computer, Word can insert a graphic directly from these devices.

The clip art in the document is part of a paragraph. Because that paragraph is left-aligned, the clip art also is left-aligned. You can, however, use any of the paragraph alignment buttons on the Formatting toolbar to reposition the clip art.

Selecting and Centering a Graphic

To center a graphic, you first must select it. Perform the following steps to select and then center the graphic.

 To Select a Graphic

1 **Click anywhere in the graphic. If your screen does not display the Picture toolbar, click View on the menu bar, point to Toolbars, and then click Picture.**

*Word selects the graphic (Figure 1-60). A selected graphic displays surrounded by a **selection rectangle** that has small squares, called **sizing handles**, at each corner and middle location. You use the sizing handles to change the size of the graphic. When a graphic is selected, the Picture toolbar automatically displays on the screen.*

FIGURE 1-60

Graphics

Emphasize a graphic by placing it at the optical center of the page. To determine optical center, divide the page in half horizontally and vertically. The optical center is located one third of the way up the vertical line from the point of intersection of the two lines.

If the Picture toolbar covers the Standard and Formatting toolbars you can drag the title bar of the Picture toolbar to move the toolbar to a different location.

TO CENTER A SELECTED GRAPHIC

1 With the graphic still selected, click the Center button on the Formatting toolbar.

Word centers the selected graphic between the left and right margins of the document (see Figure 1-61). The Center button is recessed.

When you center the graphic, Word may scroll down so the graphic is positioned at the top of the document window. The graphic is a little too large for this announcement. The next step is to resize the graphic.

Resizing a Graphic

Once you have inserted a graphic into a document, you easily can change its size. **Resizing** includes both enlarging and reducing the size of a graphic. To resize a graphic, you first must select it. The following steps show how to resize the graphic you just inserted and selected.

More About

Resizing Graphics

When you drag the sizing handles to resize a graphic, you might distort its proportions. To maintain the proportions of the graphic, press the SHIFT key while you drag a corner sizing handle.

 To Resize a Graphic

1 **With the graphic still selected, point to the upper-left corner sizing handle.**

The mouse pointer changes to a two-headed arrow when it is on a sizing handle (Figure 1-61). To resize a graphic, you drag the sizing handles until the graphic is the desired size.

FIGURE 1-61

2 **Drag the sizing handle diagonally toward the center of the graphic until the dotted selection rectangle is positioned approximately as shown in Figure 1-62.**

FIGURE 1-62

3 **Release the mouse button. Press**

CTRL + HOME.

Word resizes the graphic (Figure 1-63). When you click outside of a graphic or press a key to scroll through a document, Word deselects the graphic. The Picture toolbar disappears from the screen when you deselect the graphic.

FIGURE 1-63

Instead of resizing a selected graphic with the mouse, you also can use the Format Picture dialog box to resize a graphic by clicking the Format Picture button (Figure 1-62 on the previous page) on the Picture toolbar and then clicking the Size tab. Using the Size sheet, you enter exact height and width measurements. If you have a precise measurement for a graphic, use the Format Picture dialog box; otherwise, drag the sizing handles to resize a graphic.

Restoring a Resized Graphic to Its Original Size

Sometimes you might resize a graphic and realize it is the wrong size. In these cases, you may want to return the graphic to its original size and start again. You could drag the sizing handle until the graphic resembles its original size. To restore a resized graphic to its exact original size, click the graphic to select it and then click the Format Picture button on the Picture toolbar to display the Format Picture dialog box. Click the Size tab and then click the Reset button. Finally, click the OK button.

Saving an Existing Document with the Same File Name

The announcement for Project 1 now is complete. To transfer the modified document with formatting changes and graphic to your floppy disk in drive A, you must save the document again. When you saved the document the first time, you assigned a file name to it (Summit Peak Announcement). If you use the following procedure, Word automatically assigns the same file name to the document each time you subsequently save it.

Steps To Save an Existing Document with the Same File Name

1 Double-click the move handle on the Standard toolbar to display the entire toolbar. Click the Save button on the Standard toolbar.

Word saves the document on a floppy disk inserted in drive A using the currently assigned file name, Summit Peak Announcement (Figure 1-64).

FIGURE 1-64

While Word is saving the document, the Background Save Status icon displays at the right edge of the status bar. When the save is complete, the document remains in memory and on the screen.

If, for some reason, you want to save an existing document with a different file name, click Save As on the File menu to display the Save As dialog box. Then, fill in the Save As dialog box as discussed in Steps 2 through 5 on pages WD 1.27 and WD 1.28.

Printing a Document

The next step is to print the document you created. A printed version of the document is called a **hard copy** or **printout**. Perform the steps on the next page to print the announcement created in Project 1.

Other Ways

1. On File menu click Save
2. Press CTRL+S

More About

Save As

In the Save As dialog box, you can create a new Windows folder by clicking the Create New Folder button. You also can delete or rename files by selecting the file and then clicking the Tools button arrow in the Save As dialog box. To display the Save As dialog box, click File on the menu bar and then click Save As.

Steps **To Print a Document**

1 **Ready the printer according to the printer instructions. Click the Print button on the Standard toolbar.**

The mouse pointer briefly changes to an hourglass shape as Word prepares to print the document. While the document is printing, a printer icon displays in the tray status area on the taskbar (Figure 1-65).

2 **When the printer stops, retrieve the printout (see Figure 1-1 on page WD1.7).**

FIGURE 1-65

 Other Ways

1. On File menu click Print, click OK button
2. Press CTRL+P, press ENTER

More About

Print Preview

To view a document before you print it, click the Print Preview button on the Standard toolbar. To return to the document window, click the Close Preview button on the Print Preview toolbar.

When you use the Print button to print a document, Word prints the entire document automatically. You then may distribute the hard copy or keep it as a permanent record of the document.

If you wanted to print multiple copies of the document, click File on the menu bar and then click Print to display the Print dialog box. This dialog box has several printing options, including specifying the number of copies to print.

If you wanted to cancel your job that is printing or one you have waiting to be printed, double-click the printer icon on the taskbar (Figure 1-65). In the printer window, click the job to be canceled and then click Cancel Printing on the Document menu.

Quitting Word

After you create, save, and print the announcement, Project 1 is complete. To quit Word and return control to Windows, perform the following steps.

To Quit Word

Close button

① Point to the Close button in the upper-right corner of the title bar (Figure 1-66).

② Click the Close button.

The Word window closes.

FIGURE 1-66

If you made changes to the document since the last save, Word displays dialog box asking if you want to save the changes. Clicking the Yes button saves the changes; clicking the No button ignores the changes; and clicking the Cancel button returns to the document. If you did not make any changes since you saved the document, this dialog box does not display.

You created and formatted the announcement, inserted clip art into it, printed it, and saved it. You might decide, however, to change the announcement at a later date. To do this, you must start Word and then retrieve your document from the floppy disk in drive A.

Opening a Document

Earlier, you saved the Word document created in Project 1 on a floppy disk using the file name Summit Peak Announcement. Once you have created and saved a document, you often will have reason to retrieve it from the disk. For example, you might want to revise the document or print it. The steps on the next page illustrate how to open the file Summit Peak Announcement.

More *About*

Opening Files

In Word, you can open a recently used file by clicking File on the menu bar and then clicking the file name on the File menu. To instruct Word to show the recently used documents on the File menu, click Tools on the menu bar, click Options, click the General tab, click Recently used file list, and then click the OK button.

To Open a Document

1 **Click the Start button on the taskbar and then point to Open Office Document (Figure 1-67).**

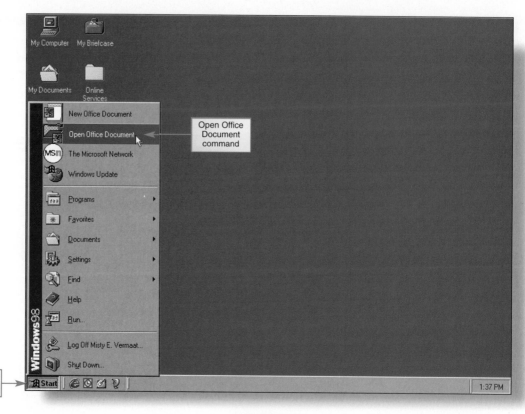

FIGURE 1-67

2 **Click Open Office Document. If necessary, click the Look in box arrow and then click 3½ Floppy (A:). If it is not selected already, click the file name Summit Peak Announcement. Point to the Open button.**

Office displays the Open Office Document dialog box (Figure 1-68). Office displays the files on the floppy disk in drive A.

FIGURE 1-68

③ Click the Open button.

Office starts Word, and then Word opens the document, Summit Peak Announcement, from the floppy disk in drive A and displays the document on the screen (Figure 1-69).

document name on title bar

Summit Peak Announcement displays

FIGURE 1-69

Correcting Errors

After creating a document, you often will find you must make changes to it. Changes can be required because the document contains an error or because of new circumstances.

Types of Changes Made to Documents

The types of changes made to documents normally fall into one of the three following categories: additions, deletions, or modifications.

ADDITIONS Additional words, sentences, or paragraphs may be required in a document. Additions occur when you omit text from a document and want to insert it later. For example, you may want to insert the word, winter, in front of vacation packages to differentiate winter packages from summer packages.

DELETIONS Sometimes, text in a document is incorrect or is no longer needed. For example, the resort might remove transportation from their package deals. In this case, you would delete the word, transportation, from the list.

MODIFICATIONS If an error is made in a document or changes take place that affect the document, you might have to revise the word(s) in the text. For example, the resort might purchase more land and have 6,500 acres of slopes and lakes; thus, you would change the number from 5,200 to 6,500.

Word provides several methods for correcting errors in a document. For each of the error correction techniques, you first must move the insertion point to the error.

Other Ways

1. In Microsoft Word, click Open button on Standard toolbar, select file name, click Open button in dialog box

2. In Microsoft Word, on File menu click Open, select file name, click Open button in dialog box

3. In Microsoft Word, press CTRL+O, select file name, press ENTER

Inserting Text into an Existing Document

If you leave a word or phrase out of a sentence, you can include it in the sentence by positioning the insertion point where you intend to insert the text. Word is preset to insert the text to the left of the insertion point. The text to the right of the insertion point moves to the right and downward to accommodate the new text.

TO INSERT TEXT INTO AN EXISTING DOCUMENT

1 Click to left of location to insert new text.

2 Type new text.

In Word, the default typing mode is insert mode. In **insert mode**, as you type a character, Word inserts the character and moves all the characters to the right of the typed character one position to the right. You can change to overtype mode by double-clicking the **OVR status indicator** on the status bar (see Figure 1-4 on page WD 1.9). In **overtype mode**, Word replaces characters to the right of the insertion point. Double-clicking the OVR status indicator a second time returns you to insert mode.

Deleting Text from an Existing Document

It is not unusual to type incorrect characters or words in a document. You have learned that you can click the Undo button on the Standard toolbar to undo a command or action – this includes typing. Word also provides other methods of correcting typing errors. For example, you may want to delete certain letters or words.

TO DELETE AN INCORRECT CHARACTER IN A DOCUMENT

1 Click next to the incorrect character.

2 Press the BACKSPACE key to erase to the left of the insertion point; or press the DELETE key to erase to the right of the insertion point.

TO DELETE AN INCORRECT WORD OR PHRASE IN A DOCUMENT

1 Select the word or phrase you want to erase.

2 Right-click the selected word or phrase, and then click Cut on the shortcut menu; or click the Cut button on the Standard toolbar (Figure 1-7a on page WD 1.13); or press the DELETE key.

Closing the Entire Document

Sometimes, everything goes wrong. If this happens, you may want to close the document entirely and start over. You also may want to close a document when you are finished with it so you can begin your next document.

TO CLOSE THE ENTIRE DOCUMENT AND START OVER

1 Click File on the menu bar and then click Close.

2 If Word displays a dialog box, click the No button to ignore the changes since the last time you saved the document.

3 Click the New Blank Document button (see Figure 1-7a on page WD 1.13) on the Standard toolbar.

You also can close the document by clicking the Close button at the right edge of the menu bar.

ord Help System

At any time while you are using Word, you can get answers to questions by using the **Word Help system**. Used properly, this form of online assistance can increase your productivity and reduce your frustrations by minimizing the time you spend learning how to use Word.

The following section shows how to obtain answers to your questions using the Office Assistant. For additional information on using help, see Appendix A.

Using the Office Assistant

The **Office Assistant** answers your questions and suggests more efficient ways to complete a task. With the Office Assistant active, for example, you can type a question, word, or phrase in a text box and the Office Assistant provides immediate help on the subject. Also, as you create a document, the Office Assistant accumulates tips that suggest more efficient ways to do the tasks you completed while creating a document, such as formatting, printing, and saving. This tip feature is part of the **IntelliSense technology** that is built into Word, which understands what you are trying to do and suggests better ways to do it. When the light bulb displays above the Office Assistant, click it to see a tip.

The following steps show how to use the Office Assistant to obtain information on changing the size of a toolbar.

Help

If you purchased an application program five years ago, you probably received one or more thick technical manuals explaining the software. With Microsoft Word 2000, you receive a small manual. The online Help feature of Microsoft Word 2000 replaces the reams and reams of printed pages in complicated technical manuals.

Steps To Obtain Help Using the Office Assistant

1 **If the Office Assistant is not on the screen, click Help on the menu bar and then click Show the Office Assistant. With the Office Assistant on the screen, click it. Type** change toolbar size **in the What would you like to do? text box. Point to the Search button (Figure 1-70).**

FIGURE 1-70

2 **Click the Search button. Point to Resize a toolbar in the list of topics.**

The Office Assistant displays a list of topics relating to the typed question, change toolbar size (Figure 1-71). The mouse pointer changes to a pointing hand.

FIGURE 1-71

3 **Click Resize a toolbar. When Word opens the Word Help window, click its Maximize button. If necessary, drag the Office Assistant out of the way of the Help text.**

The Office Assistant opens a Word Help window that provides Help information on resizing toolbars (Figure 1-72).

4 **Click the Close button on the Word Help window title bar.**

The Word Help window closes and the Word document window again is active.

FIGURE 1-72

Other **Ways**

1. If the Office Assistant is on, click Microsoft Word Help button or click Microsoft Word Help on the Help menu

You can use the Office Assistant to search for Help on any topic concerning Word.

Table 1-3 summarizes the nine categories of help available to you. Because of the way the Word Help system works, please review the right-most column of Table 1-3 if you have difficulties activating the desired category of help.

Table 1-3	Word Help System		
TYPE	DESCRIPTION	HOW TO ACTIVATE	TURNING THE OFFICE ASSISTANT ON AND OFF
Answer Wizard	Similar to the Office Assistant in that it answers questions that you type in your own words.	Click the Microsoft Word Help button on the Standard toolbar. If necessary, maximize the Help window by double-clicking its title bar. Click the Answer Wizard tab.	If the Office Assistant displays, right-click it, click Options, click Use the Office Assistant to remove the check mark, click the OK button.
Contents sheet	Groups Help topics by general categories. Use when you know only the general category of the topic in question. Similar to a table of contents in a book.	Click the Microsoft Word Help button on the Standard toolbar. If necessary, maximize the Help window by double-clicking its title bar. Click the Contents tab.	If the Office Assistant displays, right-click it, click Options, click Use the Office Assistant to remove the check mark, click the OK button.
Detect and Repair	Automatically finds and fixes errors in the application.	Click Detect and Repair on the Help menu.	
Hardware and Software Information	Shows Product ID and allows access to system information and technical support information.	Click About Microsoft Word on the Help menu and then click the appropriate button.	
Index sheet	Similar to an index in a book; use when you know exactly what you want.	Click the Microsoft Word Help button on the Standard toolbar. If necessary, maximize the Help window by double-clicking its title bar. Click the Index tab.	If the Office Assistant displays, right-click it, click Options, click Use the Office Assistant to remove the check mark, click the OK button.
Office Assistant	Answers questions that you type in your own words, offers tips, and provides Help for a variety of Word features.	Click the Microsoft Word Help button on the Standard toolbar or double-click the Office Assistant icon. Some dialog boxes also include the Microsoft Word Help button.	If the Office Assistant does not display, click Show the Office Assistant on the Help menu.
Office on the Web	Used to access technical resources and download free product enhancements on the Web.	Click Office on the Web on the Help menu.	
Question Mark button and What's This? command	Used to identify unfamiliar items on the screen.	In a dialog box, click the Question Mark button and then click an item in the dialog box. Click What's This? on the Help menu, and then click an item on the screen.	
WordPerfect Help	Used to assist WordPerfect users who are learning Microsoft Word.	Click WordPerfect Help on the Help menu.	

The final step in this project is to quit Word.

TO QUIT WORD

1 Click the Close button in the Word window.

The Word window closes.

More About

Quick Reference

For a table that lists how to complete the tasks covered in this book using the mouse, menu, shortcut menu, and keyboard, visit the Shelly Cashman Series Office Web page (www.scsite.com/off2000/qr.htm) and then click Microsoft Word 2000.

CASE PERSPECTIVE SUMMARY

Jackie is thrilled with the completed announcement. The characters in the headline and body title are large enough so students can read them from a distance and the graphic is quite eye-catching. She takes the announcement to the school's Promotions Department and receives approval to post it in several locations around campus, have it printed in the school newspaper, and mailed to each student's home. Members of the SGA assist Jackie with these activities.

Project Summary

Project 1 introduced you to starting Word and creating a document. Before entering any text in the document, you learned how to change the font size. You also learned how to save and print a document. You used Word's check spelling as you type feature. Once you saved the document, you learned how to format its paragraphs and characters. Then, you inserted and resized clip art. You learned how to move the insertion point so you could insert, delete, and modify text. Finally, you learned one way to use Word Help.

What You Should Know

Having completed this project, you now should be able to perform the following tasks:

▶ Bold Selected Text *(WD 1.33)*
▶ Center a Paragraph *(WD 1.35 and WD 1.40)*
▶ Center a Selected Graphic *(WD 1.46)*
▶ Change the Font of Selected Text *(WD 1.31)*
▶ Change the Font Size of Selected Text *(WD 1.32)*
▶ Check Spelling as You Type *(WD 1.22)*
▶ Close the Entire Document and Start Over *(WD 1.54)*
▶ Delete an Incorrect Character in a Document *(WD 1.54)*
▶ Delete an Incorrect Word or Phrase in a Document *(WD 1.54)*
▶ Display Formatting Marks *(WD 1.20)*
▶ Displays the Entire Standard Toolbar *(WD 1.15)*
▶ Enter Blank Lines into a Document *(WD 1.19)*

▶ Enter More Text *(WD 1.21)*
▶ Enter Text *(WD 1.18)*
▶ Enter Text that Scrolls the Document Window *(WD 1.25)*
▶ Format a Line of Text *(WD 1.37)*
▶ Increase the Default Font Size Before Typing *(WD 1.17)*
▶ Insert Clip Art into a Document *(WD 1.43)*
▶ Insert Text into an Existing Document *(WD 1.54)*
▶ Italicize Selected Text *(WD 1.39)*
▶ Obtain Help Using the Office Assistant *(WD 1.55)*
▶ Open a Document *(WD 1.52)*
▶ Print a Document *(WD 1.50)*
▶ Quit Word *(WD 1.51)*
▶ Resize a Graphic *(WD 1.47)*
▶ Right-Align a Paragraph *(WD 1.33)*
▶ Save a New Document *(WD 1.26)*
▶ Save an Existing Document with the Same File Name *(WD 1.49)*
▶ Scroll Through the Document *(WD 1.40)*
▶ Select a Graphic *(WD 1.46)*
▶ Select a Group of Words *(WD 1.41)*
▶ Select a Line *(WD 1.37)*
▶ Select a Word *(WD 1.38)*
▶ Select Multiple Paragraphs *(WD 1.30)*
▶ Start Word *(WD 1.8)*
▶ Underline Selected Text *(WD 1.42)*
▶ Undo an Action *(WD 1.36)*
▶ Wordwrap Text as You Type *(WD 1.21)*
▶ Zoom Page Width *(WD 1.15)*

More *About*

Microsoft Certification

The Microsoft Office User Specialist (MOUS) Certification program provides an opportunity for you to obtain a valuable industry credential — proof that you have the Word 2000 skills required by employers. For more information, see Appendix D or visit the Shelly Cashman Series MOUS Web page at www.scsite.com/off2000/cert.htm.

Apply Your Knowledge

Project Reinforcement at www.scsite.com/off2000/reinforce.htm

1 Checking Spelling of a Document

Instructions: Start Word. Open the document, Meeting Announcement, on the Data Disk. If you did not download the Data Disk, see the inside back cover for instructions for downloading the Data Disk or see your instructor.

As shown in Figure 1-73, the document is a meeting announcement that contains many spelling and grammar errors. You are to right-click each of the errors and then click the appropriate correction on the shortcut menu.

You have learned that Word flags spelling errors with a red wavy underline. A green wavy underline indicates that Word has detected a possible grammar error. *Hint:* If your screen does not display the grammar errors, use the Word Help System to determine how to enable the check grammar feature. Perform the following tasks:

1. Position the insertion point at the beginning of the document. Right-click the flagged word, Notise. Change the incorrect word, Notise, to Notice by clicking Notice on the shortcut menu.
2. Right-click the flagged word, Januery. Change the incorrect word, Januery, to January by clicking January on the shortcut menu.
3. Right-click the flagged word, be. Click Delete Repeated Word on the shortcut menu to remove the duplicate occurrence of the word, be.

> spelling and grammar errors are flagged on printout to help you identify them

Meeting Notise
All Employees

NEW HEALTH INSURANCE PLAN

Effective Januery 1, Kramer Enterprises will be be switching to a new insurance providor for major medical coverage. At that time, all employees must begin submitting claims and directing all claim-related questions to ofr new provider, Health America.

Representative's from Health America will be visiting our office on Friday, December 1, to discuss our nesw insurance plan. Please plan to attend either the morning session at 9:00 a.m. or the afternoon session at 2:00 p.m. Both session will be in the lunchroom.

insurance cards will be distributed at these meetings!

FIGURE 1-73

4. Right-click the flagged word, providor. Change the incorrect word, providor, to provider by clicking provider on the shortcut menu.
5. Right-click the flagged word, ofr. Because the shortcut menu does not display the correct word, click outside the shortcut menu to remove it from the screen. Correct the misspelled word, ofr, to the correct word, our, by removing the letter f and replacing it with the letter u.
6. Right-click the flagged word, Representative's. Change the word, Representative's, to its correct plural by clicking the word, Representatives, on the shortcut menu.
7. Right-click the incorrect word, nesw. Change the incorrect word, nesw, to new by clicking new on the shortcut menu.
8. Right-click the flagged word, session. Change the incorrect word, session, to its plural by clicking sessions on the shortcut menu.
9. Right-click the flagged word, insurance. Capitalize the word, insurance, by clicking Insurance on the shortcut menu.
10. Click File menu on the menu bar and then click Save As. Save the document using Corrected Meeting Announcement as the file name.
11. Print the revised document.

In the Lab

1 Creating an Announcement with Clip Art

Problem: The Director of the Harbor Theatre Company at your school has requested that each student in your Marketing 102 class prepare an announcement for auditions of its upcoming play. The student that creates the winning announcement will receive five complimentary tickets to the play. You prepare the announcement shown in Figure 1-74. *Hint:* Remember, if you make a mistake while formatting the announcement, you can click the Undo button on the Standard toolbar to undo your mistake.

Instructions:

1. Change the font size from 10 to 18 by clicking the Font Size box arrow on the formatting toolbar and then clicking 18.

2. If necessary, click the Show/Hide ¶ button on Standard toolbar to display formatting marks.

3. Create the announcement shown in Figure 1-74. Enter the document first without clip art and unformatted; that is without any bold, underlined, italicized, right-aligned, or centered text. If Word flags any misspelled words as you type, check the spelling of these words and correct them.

4. Save the document on a floppy disk with Grease Announcement as the file name.

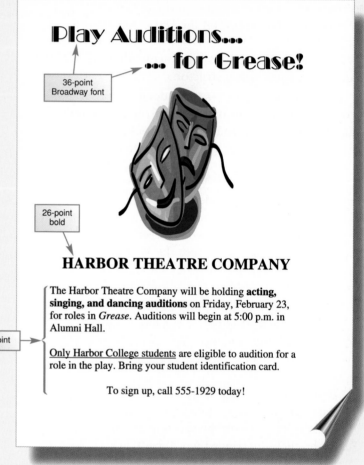

FIGURE 1-74

5. Select the two lines of the headline. Change their font to Broadway, or a similar font. Change their font size from 18 to 36.

6. Click somewhere in the second line of the headline. Right-align it.

7. Click somewhere in the body title line. Center it.

8. Select the body title line. Increase its font size from 18 to 26. Bold it.

9. In the first paragraph of the body copy, select the following phrase: acting, singing, and dancing auditions. Bold the phrase.

10. In the same paragraph, select the word, Grease. Italicize it.

11. In the second paragraph of the body copy, select the following phrase: Only Harbor College students. Underline the phrase.

12. Click somewhere in the last line of the announcement. Center it.

13. Insert the graphic of the drama masks between the headline and the body title line. Search for the text, drama, in the Clip Gallery to locate the graphic.

14. Click the graphic to select it. Center the selected graphic.

15. Save the announcement again with the same file name.

16. Print the announcement.

2 Creating an Announcement with Resized Clip Art

Problem: You are an assistant for the Marketing Manager at Taylor Business School. She has asked you to prepare an announcement for Fall Registration. The announcement must include clip art. You prepare the announcement shown in Figure 1-75. *Hint:* Remember, if you make a mistake while formatting the announcement, you can click the Undo button on the Standard toolbar to undo your mistake.

Instructions:

1. Change the font size from 10 to 18 by clicking the Font Size box arrow on the Formatting toolbar and then clicking 18.
2. If it is not already selected, click the Show/Hide ¶ button on the Standard toolbar to display formatting marks.
3. Create the announcement shown in Figure 1-75. Enter the document first without the clip art and unformatted; that is without any bold, underlined, italicized, right-aligned, or centered text. If Word flags any misspelled words as you type, check the spelling of these words and correct them.
4. Save the document on a floppy disk with Registration Announcement as the file name.
5. Select the two lines of the headline. Change their font to Arial, or a similar font. Change their font size from 20 to 36. Bold both lines.
6. Click somewhere in the second line of the headline. Right-align it.
7. Click somewhere in the body title line. Center it.
8. Select the body title line. Increase its font size from 18 to 28. Bold it.
9. Select the words, and much more, in the first paragraph of the body copy. Italicize the words.
10. Select the word, variety, in the second paragraph of the body copy. Underline it.
11. Click somewhere in the last line of the announcement. Center it.
12. Insert the graphic of the classroom between the headline and the body title line. Search for the text, classroom, in the Clip Gallery to locate the graphic.
13. Enlarge the graphic of the classroom. If you make the graphic too large, the announcement may flow onto two pages. If this occurs, reduce the size of the graphic so the announcement fits on a single page. *Hint*: Use Help to learn about **print preview**, which is a way to see the page before you print it. To exit print preview and return to the document window, click the Close button on the Print Preview toolbar.
14. Click the graphic to select it. Center the selected graphic.
15. Save the announcement again with the same file name.
16. Print the announcement.

FIGURE 1-75

In the Lab

3 Creating an Announcement with Resized Clip Art and a Bulleted List

Problem: You are the secretary of The Computer Club at your school. One of your responsibilities is to announce the monthly meetings. For the February meeting, you prepare the announcement shown in Figure 1-76. *Hint:* Remember, if you make a mistake while formatting the announcement, you can click the Undo button on the Standard toolbar to undo your mistake.

Instructions:

1. Change the font size from 10 to 18.
2. If they are not already showing, display formatting marks.
3. Create the announcement shown in Figure 1-76. Enter the document first without the clip art and unformatted; that is without any bulleted, bold, underlined, italicized, right-aligned, or centered text. Check spelling as you type.
4. Save the document on a floppy disk with February Announcement as the file name.
5. Format the two lines of the headline to 28-point Arial Rounded MT Bold or a similar font.
6. Right-align the second line of the headline.
7. Center the body title line. Format the body title line to 22-point Courier New bold or a similar font.

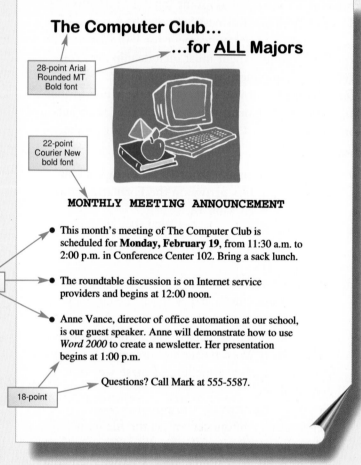

FIGURE 1-76

8. Add bullets to the three paragraphs of body copy. A **bullet** is a symbol positioned at the beginning of a paragraph. In Word, the default bullet symbol is a small darkened circle. A list of paragraphs with bullets is called a **bulleted list**. *Hint*: Use Help to learn how to add bullets to a list of paragraphs.
9. Bold the date, Monday, February 19, in the first paragraph of the body copy.
10. Italicize the phrase, Word 2000, in the third paragraph of the body copy.
11. Center the last line of the announcement.
12. Insert the graphic of the computer between the headline and the body title line. Search for the text, academic computer, in the Clip Gallery to locate the graphic.
13. Enlarge the graphic of the computer. If you make the graphic too large, the announcement may flow onto two pages. If this occurs, reduce the size of the graphic so the announcement fits on a single page. *Hint:* Use Help to learn about **print preview**, which is a way to see the page before you print it. To exit print preview and return to the document window, click the Close button on the Print Preview toolbar.
14. Center the graphic.
15. Save the announcement again with the same file name.
16. Print the announcement.

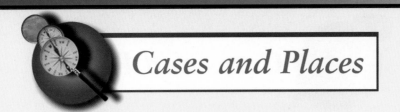

Cases and Places

The difficulty of these case studies varies:
▶ are the least difficult; ▶▶ are more difficult; and ▶▶▶ are the most difficult.

1 ▶ You have been assigned the task of preparing an announcement for Starport Airlines. The announcement is to contain a graphic of an airplane from the Clip Gallery. Use the following text: first line of headline – Fly With Us...; second line of headline – ... We Have Your Ticket; body title – Starport Airlines; first paragraph of body copy – For the month of October, we are offering flights to 25 cities nationwide for the unbelievable rate of $100 per person round trip.; second paragraph of body copy – Take advantage of these low, low rates and make your travel arrangements now for a vacation, a business trip, or a family reunion.; last line – For reservations, call 555-9898. Use the concepts and techniques presented in this project to create and format this announcement. Ask your instructor if you should bullet the list of paragraphs of the body copy.

2 ▶ You have been assigned the task of preparing an announcement for the Lake Shore Carnival. The announcement contains a graphic of a carnival from the Clip Gallery. Use the following text: first line of headline – It's Time...; second line of headline – ...for Our Carnival; body title – Lake Shore Carnival; first paragraph of body copy – Join us for fun, food, entertainment, crafts, contests, and rides at the Lake Shore Carnival on the weekend of July 21 and 22.; second paragraph of body copy – Admission is $10 per adult and $5 for children under 10 years old. Gates open at 8:00 a.m. each day and close at midnight.; last line – For information, call 555-9383. Use the concepts and techniques presented in this project to create and format this announcement. Ask your instructor if you should bullet the list of paragraphs of the body copy.

3 ▶▶ Your Uncle John, a graduate of Eagle High School, will be celebrating his twenty-fifth high school reunion this year. He has asked you to prepare an announcement that can be sent to each member of the graduating class. He asks that you include a graphic of the school's mascot, an eagle. The reunion will be held at Fisher Country Club and will feature live entertainment by The Jazzicians, a local band. The reunion will be held on Saturday, October 27. The doors open at 6:00 p.m. with dinner at 7:00 p.m., followed by entertainment from 8:00 p.m. until 11:00 p.m. Cost is $50 per person. Guests will have the opportunity to reminisce about old times, catch up on current projects, and share future plans. More information can be obtained by calling Sue Nordic at 555-9808. Use the concepts and techniques presented in this project to create the announcement. Ask your instructor if you should bullet the list of paragraphs of the body copy.

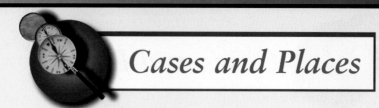

Cases and Places

4 ▶▶ Your parents own a campground called Quiet Oaks. With the new season just around the corner, they have asked you to prepare an announcement for their campground. Located at the intersection of I-293 and SR-35 in southern Louisiana, Quiet Oaks is a secluded campground situated in wooded, rolling hills. It has 75 paved pull-through sites and 46 gravel sites. All have city water and electric hook-ups. Facilities include restrooms, showers, dump, security, laundry, public telephone, and a data port. Recreation includes lake fishing, swimming pool, playground, horseshoes, and a game room. The campground is open from April 1 through October 31. Rates begin at $15 per night. Call 555-9393 for more information. Use the concepts and techniques presented in this project to create the announcement. Be sure to include an appropriate graphic from the Clip Gallery. Ask your instructor if you should bullet the list of paragraphs of the body copy.

5 ▶▶ You have a part-time job as the assistant to the Marketing Director at a new office supply store called Office World. The Director has asked you to prepare an announcement for the store's grand opening. Office World stocks thousands of office products including supplies, furniture, electronics, and computer software. Office World's low price guarantee states it will refund double a customer's money if the customer finds a comparable product for a lower price within ten days of purchase. Customers can purchase at the store, via fax or telephone, or on the Web at www.officeworld.com. Fax number is 555-2982 and telephone number is 555-2983. For purchases over $45.00, delivery is free. For a catalog, customers or potential customers can call 555-2900. Use the concepts and techniques presented in this project to create the announcement. Be sure to include an appropriate graphic from the Clip Gallery. Ask your instructor if you should bullet the list of paragraphs of the body copy.

6 ▶▶▶ Schools, churches, libraries, grocery stores, and other public places have bulletin boards for announcements and other postings. Often, these bulletin boards have so many announcements that some go unnoticed. At one of the above-mentioned organizations, find a posted announcement that you think might be overlooked. Copy the text from the announcement. Using this text, together with the techniques presented in this project, create an announcement that would be more likely to catch a reader's eye. Format the announcement effectively and include a bulleted list and suitable graphic from the Clip Gallery.

7 ▶▶▶ Advertisements are a company's way of announcing products or services to the public. You can find advertisements in printed media such as newspapers and magazines. Many companies also advertise on the World Wide Web. Find a printed advertisement or one on the Web that you feel lacks luster. Copy the text from the announcement. Using this text, together with the techniques presented in this project, create an announcement that would be more likely to catch a reader's eye. Format the announcement effectively and include a bulleted list and suitable graphic from the Clip Gallery.

Excel 2000

Microsoft Excel 2000

PROJECT

1

Creating a Worksheet and Embedded Chart

O B J E C T I V E S

You will have mastered the material in this project when you can:

- Start Excel
- Describe the Excel worksheet
- Reset menus and toolbars
- Select a cell or range of cells
- Enter text and numbers
- Use the AutoSum button to sum a range of cells
- Copy a cell to a range of cells using the fill handle
- Change the size of the font in a cell
- Bold cell entries
- Apply the AutoFormat command to format a range
- Center cell contents across a series of columns
- Use the Name box to select a cell
- Create a Column chart using the Chart Wizard
- Save a workbook
- Print a worksheet
- Quit Excel
- Open a workbook
- Use the AutoCalculate area to determine totals
- Correct errors on a worksheet
- Use the Office Assistant and other online Help tools to answer your questions

Get Smart

Smart Cards Open Convenience Doors

What can pay for your laundry, open your dorm door, feed the parking meter, and withdraw money from an automatic teller machine? Need a hint? It is smart, but it never went to college. It is a smart card, and it is coming soon to your wallet.

This ingenious card resembles a credit card in size, but instead of a magnetic strip on the back, it has a microprocessor chip inside. This chip gives the card its brains, while it gives its owner convenience and security.

University of Michigan and University of Illinois students are familiar with the card, as are students at 25 other schools across the United States and Canada. They use it for everything from calling Mom back home to checking out library books to debiting their checking accounts.

The nonprofit Smart Card Forum (www.smartcardforum.org) has helped bring this technology to education. The 200 members of this organization represent a cross-section of technology experts and smart card users who are working to increase multiple-application smart cards in the government, private, and education sectors.

Some visionaries predict 3.75 billion smart cards will be issued by 2005, with owners using them to make 25 billion transactions yearly. The cost to manufacture one card ranges from 80 cents to 15 dollars depending on the application and complexity.

Two types of smart cards are available. One is a memory card. The memory card contains a stored value that the owner can spend on transactions such as paying bus fare or making a call from a public telephone. When the value is depleted, the card is useless.

The second is an intelligent card. The intelligent card contains a central processing unit that can store data and make decisions. Owners begin with a set monetary value, such as $100, and then they can make a purchase that does not exceed this figure. If the amount is insufficient, they can add money to the balance. These functions are similar to the activities you will perform using Microsoft Excel in this project for the Fun-N-Sun Sojourn company, where you will enter numbers in predefined storage areas, or cells, and then calculate a sum.

The smart card originated in 1974 when Roland Moreno, a reporter and self-taught inventor, secured a chip on an epoxy card. His vision was for merchants to accept electronic payments by inserting three cards in his Take the Money and Run (TMR) machine. One card identified the merchant, the second contained the customer's electronic money, and the third had a list of deadbeat accounts that could not be used to make a transaction. Pictures and descriptions of Moreno's invention and other smart card developments are found in the Smart Card Museum (www.cardshow.com/museum).

Today, chips for the cards are manufactured by such industry leaders as Motorola, Gemplus, and Schlumberger. These companies are working to meet the demand for the cards, which is increasing at a rate of 30 percent annually. With an ever-growing global marketplace, smart cards are a smart way of doing business.

Microsoft **Excel 2000**

Microsoft Excel 2000

Creating a Worksheet and Embedded Chart

P R O J E C T

1

CASE PERSPECTIVE

While on spring break in the Bahamas four years ago, Kylie Waiter and three of her friends came up with the idea of creating a worldwide travel agency that catered to young adults. After graduation, they invested $3,000 each and started their dream company, Fun-N-Sun Sojourn. Thanks to their market savvy and the popularity of personal computers and the World Wide Web, the company has become the premier provider of student vacations.

As sales continue to grow, the management at Fun-N-Sun Sojourn has realized they need a better tracking system for first quarter sales. As a result, they have asked you to prepare a first quarter sales worksheet that shows the sales for the first quarter.

In addition, Kylie has asked you to create a graphical representation of the first quarter sales because she has little tolerance for lists of numbers.

What Is Microsoft Excel 2000?

Microsoft Excel is a powerful spreadsheet program that allows you to organize data, complete calculations, make decisions, graph data, develop professional looking reports, publish organized data to the Web, and access real-time data from Web sites. The four major parts of Excel are:

- ▶ **Worksheets** Worksheets allow you to enter, calculate, manipulate, and analyze data such as numbers and text. The term worksheet means the same as spreadsheet.
- ▶ **Charts** Charts pictorially represent data. Excel can draw a variety of two-dimensional and three-dimensional charts.
- ▶ **Databases** Databases manage data. For example, once you enter data onto a worksheet, Excel can sort the data, search for specific data, and select data that meets a criteria.
- ▶ **Web Support** Web support allows Excel to save workbooks or parts of a workbook in HTML format so they can be viewed and manipulated using a browser. You also can access real-time data using Web queries.

Project One — Fun-N-Sun Sojourn First Quarter Sales

From your meeting with Fun-N-Sun Sojourn's management, you have determined the following needs, source of data, calculations, and chart requirements.

Need: An easy-to-read worksheet (Figure 1-1) that shows Fun-N-Sun Sojourn's first quarter sales for each key vacation package (Bahamas Repose, Daytona Delight, Key West Haven, and South Padre Del Sol) by sales channel (Mail, Campus, Telephone, and Web). The worksheet also should include total sales for each vacation package, each sales channel, and total company sales for the first quarter.

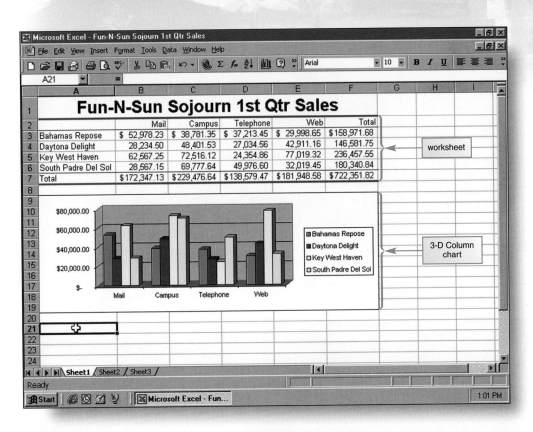

FIGURE 1-1

Source of Data: The data for the worksheet is available at the end of the first quarter from Eric Jacobs, chief financial officer (CFO) of Fun-N-Sun Sojourn.

Calculations: You have determined that the following calculations must be made for the worksheet: (a) total first quarter sales for each of the four vacation packages; (b) total first quarter sales for each of the four sales channels; and (c) total company first quarter sales.

Chart Requirements: Below the worksheet, construct a 3-D Column chart that compares the amount of sales to the four sales channels for each vacation package.

Starting Excel

To start Excel, Windows must be running. Perform the following steps to start Excel.

 To Start Excel

1 **Click the Start button on the taskbar and then point to New Office Document.**

The Start menu displays (Figure 1-2).

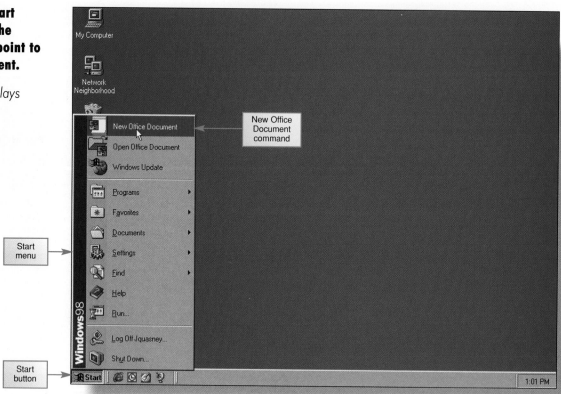

FIGURE 1-2

2 **Click New Office Document. If necessary, click the General tab, and then point to the Blank Workbook icon.**

The New Office Document dialog box displays (Figure 1-3).

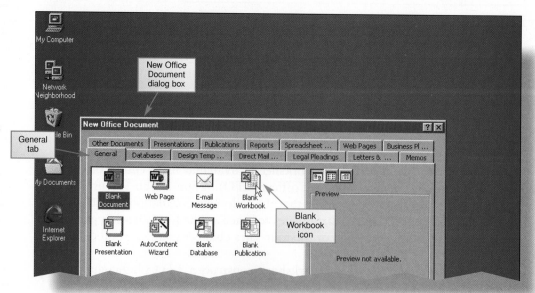

FIGURE 1-3

3 Double-click the Blank Workbook icon. If necessary, maximize the Excel window by double-clicking its title bar.

Excel displays an empty workbook titled Book1 (Figure 1-4).

FIGURE 1-4

4 If the Office Assistant displays (Figure 1-4), click Help on the menu bar and then click Hide the Office Assistant.

Excel hides the Office Assistant (Figure 1-5). The purpose of the Office Assistant will be discussed later in this project.

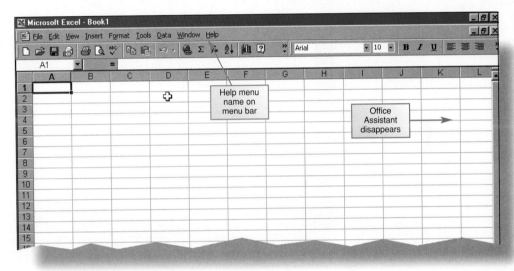

FIGURE 1-5

The Excel Worksheet

When Excel starts, it creates a new empty workbook, called Book1. The **workbook** (Figure 1-6 on the next page) is like a notebook. Inside the workbook are sheets, called **worksheets**. Each sheet name displays on a **sheet tab** at the bottom of the workbook. For example, Sheet1 is the name of the active worksheet displayed in the workbook called Book1. If you click the tab labeled Sheet2, Excel displays the Sheet2 worksheet. A new workbook opens with three worksheets. If necessary, you can add additional worksheets to a maximum of 255. This project uses only the Sheet1 worksheet. Later projects will use multiple worksheets in a workbook.

The Worksheet

The worksheet is organized into a rectangular grid containing columns (vertical) and rows (horizontal). A column letter above the grid, also called the **column heading**, identifies each **column**. A row number on the left side of the grid, also called the **row heading**, identifies each **row**. With the screen resolution set to 800 × 600, twelve columns (A through L) and twenty-five rows (1 through 25) of the worksheet display on the screen when the worksheet is maximized as shown in Figure 1-6 on the next page.

FIGURE 1-6

The intersection of each column and row is a cell. A **cell** is the basic unit of a worksheet into which you enter data. Each worksheet in a workbook has 256 columns and 65,536 rows for a total of 16,777,216 cells. The column headings begin with A and end with IV. The row headings begin with 1 and end with 65,536. Only a small fraction of the active worksheet displays on the screen at one time.

A cell is referred to by its unique address, or **cell reference**, which is the coordinates of the intersection of a column and a row. To identify a cell, specify the column letter first, followed by the row number. For example, cell reference C5 refers to the cell located at the intersection of column C and row 5 (Figure 1-6).

One cell on the worksheet, designated the **active cell**, is the one in which you can enter data. The active cell in Figure 1-6 is A1. Cell A1 is identified in three ways. First, a heavy border surrounds the cell; second, the **active cell reference** displays immediately above column A in the **Name box**; and third, the column heading A and row heading 1 light up so it is easy to see which cell is active (Figure 1-6).

The horizontal and vertical lines on the worksheet itself are called **gridlines**. Gridlines make it easier to see and identify each cell in the worksheet. If desired, you can turn the gridlines off so they do not display on the worksheet, but it is recommended that you leave them on.

The mouse pointer in Figure 1-6 has the shape of a block plus sign. The mouse pointer displays as a **block plus sign** whenever it is located in a cell on the worksheet. Another common shape of the mouse pointer is the block arrow. The mouse pointer turns into the **block arrow** whenever you move it outside the worksheet or when you drag cell contents between rows or columns. The other mouse pointer shapes are described when they display on the screen during this and subsequent projects.

Worksheet Window

You view the portion of the worksheet displayed on the screen through a **worksheet window** (Figure 1-6). Below and to the right of the worksheet window are **scroll bars**, **scroll arrows**, and **scroll boxes** that you can use to move the window around to view different parts of the active worksheet. To the right of the sheet tabs at the bottom of the screen is the **tab split box**. You can drag the tab split box (Figure 1-6) to increase or decrease the view of the sheet tabs. When you decrease the view of the sheet tabs, you increase the length of the horizontal scroll bar; and vice versa.

The menu bar, Standard toolbar, and Formatting toolbar display at the top of the screen just below the title bar (Figure 1-7a). The Standard toolbar and Formatting toolbar display on one row. Because both of these toolbars cannot fit entirely on a single row, a portion or all of the Standard toolbar displays on the left of the row and a portion or all of the Formatting toolbar displays on the right.

(a) Menu Bar and Toolbars

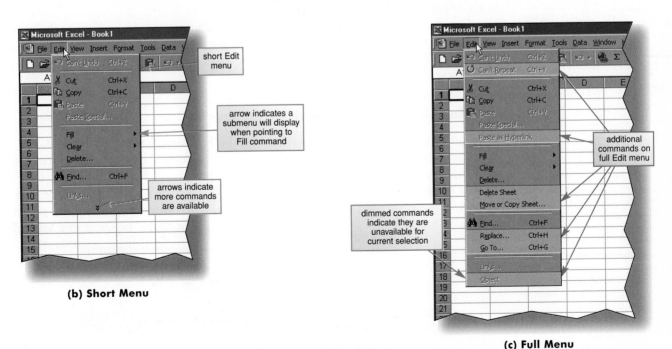

(b) Short Menu

(c) Full Menu

FIGURE 1-7

Menu Bar

The menu bar is a special toolbar that includes the Excel menu names (Figure 1-7a on the previous page). The menu bar that displays when you start Excel is the **Worksheet menu bar**. Each menu name represents a menu of commands that you can use to retrieve, store, print, and manipulate data on the worksheet. When you point to a menu name on the menu bar, the area of the menu bar containing the name changes to a button. To display a menu, such as the Edit menu, click the Edit menu name on the menu bar (Figures 1-7b and 1-7c on the previous page). If you point to a command with an arrow on the right, a submenu displays from which you can choose a command.

When you click a menu name on the menu bar, a **short menu** displays listing the most recently used commands (Figure 1-7b). If you wait a few seconds or click the arrows at the bottom of the short menu (Figure 1-7b), the full menu displays. The **full menu** lists all the commands associated with a menu (Figure 1-7c). You also can display a full menu immediately by double-clicking the menu name on the menu bar. In this book, when you display a menu, always display the full menu using one of the following techniques.

1. Click the menu name on the menu bar and then wait a few seconds.
2. Click the menu name and then click the arrows at the bottom of the short menu.
3. Click the menu name and then point to the arrows at the bottom of the short menu.
4. Double-click the menu name.

When a full menu displays, some of the commands are recessed into a shaded gray background and others are dimmed. A recessed command is called a **hidden command** because it does not display on the short menu. As you use Excel, it automatically personalizes the short menus for you based on how often you use commands. That is, as you use hidden commands, Excel unhides them and places them on the short menu. A **dimmed command** displays in a faint type, which indicates it is not available for the current selection.

The menu bar can change to include other menu names depending on the type of work you are doing in Excel. For example, if you are working with a chart sheet rather than a worksheet, the **Chart menu bar** displays with menu names that reflect charting commands.

Standard Toolbar and Formatting Toolbar

The Standard toolbar (Figure 1-8a) and the Formatting toolbar (Figure 1-8b) contain buttons and list boxes that allow you to perform frequent tasks more quickly than when using the menu bar. For example, to print a worksheet, you click the Print button on the Standard toolbar. Each button has a picture on the button face that helps you remember the button's function. Also, when you move the mouse pointer over a button or box, the name of the button or box displays below it in a **ScreenTip**.

FIGURE 1-8a Standard Toolbar

FIGURE 1-8b Formatting Toolbar

More About

Toolbars on Separate Rows

You can point to an empty location on the Formatting toolbar and drag it immediately below the Standard toolbar to display the toolbars on separate rows.

Figures 1-8a and 1-8b illustrate the Standard and Formatting toolbars and describe the functions of the buttons. Each of the buttons and list boxes will be explained in detail when they are used in the projects.

Both the Standard and Formatting toolbars are preset to display on the same row, immediately below the menu bar. To display the entire Standard toolbar, double-click the move handle on the left. Excel slides the Formatting toolbar to the right so the toolbars appear as shown in Figure 1-9a.

More About

Sizing Toolbar Buttons

If you have difficulty seeing the small buttons on the toolbars, you can increase their size by clicking View on the menu bar, pointing to Toolbars, clicking Customize on the Toolbars submenu, clicking the Options tab, clicking the Large icons check box, and clicking the Close button.

(a) Complete Standard Toolbar and Partial Formatting Toolbar

(b) Partial Standard Toolbar and Complete Formatting Toolbar

(c) More Buttons List

FIGURE 1-9

To display the entire Formatting toolbar, double-click the move handle on its left edge or drag the move handle to the left. When you display the complete Formatting toolbar, a portion of the Standard toolbar is hidden (Figure 1-9b on the previous page).

An alternative to sliding one toolbar over another is to use the **More Buttons button** on a toolbar to display the buttons that are hidden (Figure 1-9c on the previous page).

As with the menus, Excel will personalize the toolbars. That is, if you use a hidden button on a partially displayed toolbar, Excel will remove the button from the More Buttons list (Figure 1-9c) and promote it to the toolbar. For example, if you click the Bold button and then the Italic button on the Formatting toolbar in Figure 1-9c, Excel will promote these buttons to the Formatting toolbar and remove buttons from the Standard or Formatting toolbars to make room on the row.

Resetting Menus and Toolbars

Each project in this book begins with resetting the menus and toolbars to the settings as they were at the initial installation of the software. To reset your menus and toolbars so they display exactly as shown in this book, follow the steps outlined in Appendix C.

Formula Bar

Below the Standard and Formatting toolbars is the formula bar (Figure 1-10). As you type, the data displays in the **formula bar**. Excel also displays the active cell reference on the left side of the formula bar in the **Name box**.

Status Bar

Immediately above the Windows taskbar at the bottom of the screen is the status bar. The **status bar** displays a brief description of the command selected (highlighted) in a menu, the function of the button the mouse pointer is pointing to, or the current activity (mode) in progress (Figure 1-10). **Mode indicators**, such as Enter and Ready, display on the status bar and specify the current mode of Excel. When the mode is **Ready**, Excel is ready to accept the next command or data entry. When the mode indicator reads **Enter**, Excel is in the process of accepting data through the keyboard into the active cell.

In the middle of the status bar is the AutoCalculate area. The **AutoCalculate area** can be used in place of a calculator to view the sum, average, or other types of totals of a group of numbers on the worksheet. The AutoCalculate area is discussed in detail later in this project.

Keyboard indicators, such as NUM (Num Lock), CAPS (Caps Lock), and SCRL (Scroll) show which keys are engaged. Keyboard indicators display on the right side of the status bar within the small rectangular boxes (Figure 1-10).

More *About*

Resetting Toolbars

If your toolbars have a different set of buttons than shown in Figures 1-8a and 1-8b on the previous page, it is likely that a prior user added or deleted buttons. To reset the Standard or Formatting toolbars, click View on the menu bar, point to Toolbars, click Customize on the Toolbars submenu, click the Toolbars tab, click the name of the toolbar to reset, click the Reset button, and click the OK button. To remove promoted buttons, click the Options tab, click the Reset my usage data button, click the Yes button, and click the Close button.

FIGURE 1-10

Selecting a Cell

To enter data into a cell, you first must select it. The easiest way to **select a cell** (make it active) is to use the mouse to move the block plus sign to the cell and then click.

An alternative method is to use the **arrow keys** that are located just to the right of the typewriter keys on the keyboard. An arrow key selects the cell adjacent to the active cell in the direction of the arrow on the key.

You know a cell is selected (active) when a heavy border surrounds the cell (cell A1 in Figure 1-10) and the active cell reference displays in the Name box on the left side of the formula bar.

Entering Text

In Excel, any set of characters containing a letter, hyphen (as in a telephone number), or space is considered **text**. Text is used to place titles on the worksheet, such as worksheet titles, column titles, and row titles. In Project 1 (Figure 1-11 on the next page), the worksheet title, Fun-N-Sun Sojourn 1st Qtr Sales, identifies the worksheet. The column titles in row 2 (Mail, Campus, Telephone, Web, and Total) identify the data in each column. The row titles in column A (Bahamas Repose, Daytona Delight, Key West Haven, South Padre Del Sol, and Total) identify the data in each row.

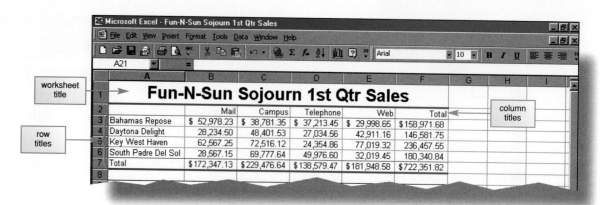

FIGURE 1-11

Entering the Worksheet Title

The following steps show how to enter the worksheet title in cell A1. Later in this project, the worksheet title will be formatted so it displays as shown in Figure 1-11.

 To Enter the Worksheet Title

1 Click cell A1.

Cell A1 becomes the active cell and a heavy border surrounds it (Figure 1-12).

FIGURE 1-12

2 Type Fun-N-Sun Sojourn 1st Qtr Sales **in cell A1.**

*The title displays in the formula bar and in cell A1. The text in cell A1 is followed by the insertion point (Figure 1-13). The **insertion point** is a blinking vertical line that indicates where the next character typed will display.*

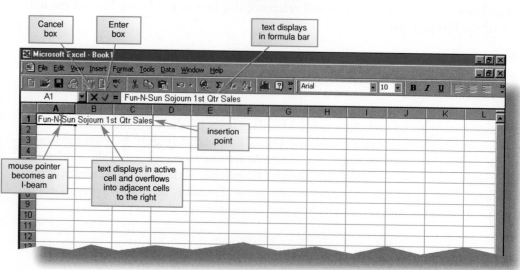

FIGURE 1-13

3 **Point to the Enter box (Figure 1-14).**

When you begin typing a cell entry, Excel displays two boxes in the formula bar: the Cancel box and the Enter box.

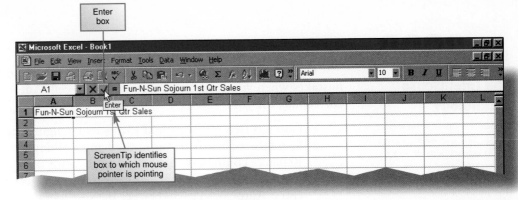

FIGURE 1-14

4 **Click the Enter box to complete the entry.**

Excel enters the worksheet title in cell A1 (Figure 1-15).

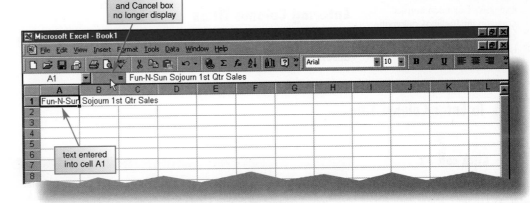

FIGURE 1-15

Other Ways

1. Click any cell other than active cell
2. Press ENTER
3. Press an arrow key
4. Press HOME, PAGE UP PAGE DOWN, or END

In Step 3, clicking the **Enter box** completes the entry. Clicking the **Cancel box** cancels the entry.

When you complete a text entry into a cell, a series of events occurs. First, Excel positions the text left-aligned in the cell. **Left-aligned** means the cell entry is positioned at the far left in the cell. Therefore, the F in the worksheet title, Fun-N-Sun Sojourn 1st Qtr Sales, begins in the leftmost position of cell A1.

Second, when the text is longer than the width of a column, Excel displays the overflow characters in adjacent cells to the right as long as these adjacent cells contain no data. In Figure 1-15, the width of cell A1 is approximately nine characters. The text consists of 31 characters. Therefore, Excel displays the overflow characters from cell A1 in cells B1, C1, and D1 because these cells are empty. If cell B1 contained data, only the first nine characters in cell A1 would display on the worksheet. Excel would hide the overflow characters, but they still would remain stored in cell A1 and display in the formula bar whenever cell A1 is the active cell.

Third, when you complete an entry by clicking the Enter box, the cell in which the text is entered remains the active cell.

Correcting a Mistake While Typing

If you type the wrong letter and notice the error before clicking the Enter box or pressing the **ENTER key**, use the **BACKSPACE key** to erase all the characters back to and including the one that is wrong. To cancel the entire entry before entering it into the cell, click the Cancel box in the formula bar or press the **ESC key**. If you see an error in a cell, select the cell and retype the entry. Later in this project, additional error-correction techniques are covered.

More About

Entering Data

Unless you are entering large amounts of data into a worksheet, you probably will want to set the ENTER key to complete an entry without changing the active cell location. If pressing the ENTER key changes the active cell location, you can change it by clicking Options on the Tools menu, clicking the Edit tab, removing the check mark from the Move Selection after Enter check box, and then clicking the OK button. If you want the ENTER key to change the active cell location, click the desired direction in the Move Selection after Enter list box and then click the OK button.

The IntelliSense Technology

Microsoft's IntelliSense technology is built into all the Office 2000 applications. It tries to understand what you are doing and helps you do it. The smart toolbars, adaptive menus, Office Assistant, and AutoCorrect are part of the IntelliSense technology. For example, Excel can correct common misspellings automatically. When you press the ENTER key, the corrected text is entered in the cell.

AutoCorrect

The **AutoCorrect feature** of Excel works behind the scenes, correcting common mistakes when you complete a text entry in a cell. AutoCorrect makes three types of corrections for you:

1. Corrects two initial capital letters by changing the second letter to lowercase.
2. Capitalizes the first letter in the names of days.
3. Replaces commonly misspelled words with their correct spelling. For example, it will change the misspelled word *recieve* to *receive* when you complete the entry. AutoCorrect will correct the spelling automatically of more than 400 commonly misspelled words.

Entering Column Titles

To enter the column titles, select the appropriate cell and then enter the text, as described in the following steps.

 To Enter Column Titles

① Click cell B2.

Cell B2 becomes the active cell. The active cell reference in the Name box changes from A1 to B2 (Figure 1-16).

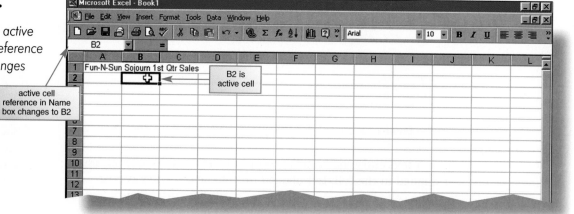

FIGURE 1-16

② Type Mail **in cell B2.**

Excel displays Mail in the formula bar and in cell B2 (Figure 1-17).

FIGURE 1-17

3 **Press the RIGHT ARROW key.**

Excel enters the column title, Mail, in cell B2 and makes cell C2 the active cell (Figure 1-18).

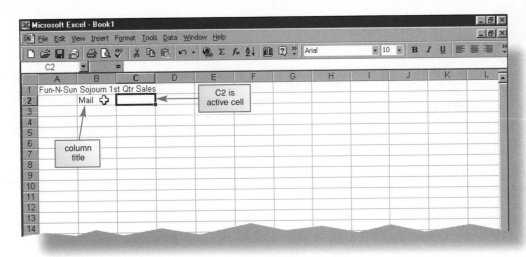

FIGURE 1-18

4 **Repeat Steps 2 and 3 for the remaining column titles in row 2. That is, enter Campus in cell C2, Telephone in cell D2, Web in cell E2, and Total in cell F2. Complete the last entry in cell F2 by pressing the ENTER key.**

The column titles display left-aligned as shown in Figure 1-19.

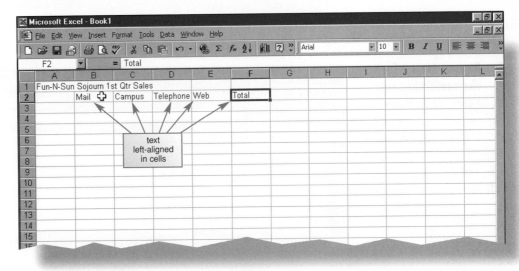

FIGURE 1-19

If the next entry is in an adjacent cell, use the arrow keys to complete the entry in a cell. When you press an arrow key to complete an entry, the adjacent cell in the direction of the arrow (up, down, left, or right) becomes the active cell. If the next entry is in a non-adjacent cell, click the next cell in which you plan to enter data, or click the Enter box, or press the ENTER key and then click the appropriate cell for the next entry.

Entering Row Titles

The next step in developing the worksheet in Project 1 is to enter the row titles in column A. This process is similar to entering the column titles and is described in the steps on the next page.

To Enter Row Titles

1 **Click cell A3. Type**
Bahamas
Repose **and then
press the DOWN
ARROW key.**

*Excel enters the row title
Bahamas Repose in cell A3
and cell A4 becomes the
active cell (Figure 1-20).*

FIGURE 1-20

2 **Repeat Step 1 for
the remaining row
titles in column A. Enter**
Daytona Delight **in cell
A4,** Key West Haven **in
cell A5,** South Padre Del
Sol **in cell A 6, and** Total
in cell A7.

*The row titles display as
shown in Figure 1-21.*

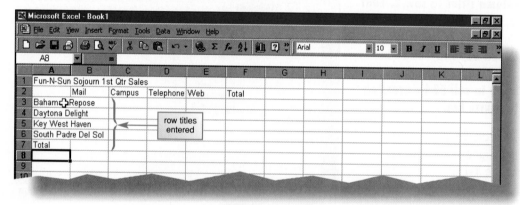

FIGURE 1-21

In Excel, text is left-aligned in a cell, unless you change it by realigning it. Excel treats any combination of numbers, spaces, and nonnumeric characters as text. For example, the following entries are text:

401AX21, 921-231, 619 321, 883XTY

Entering Data

When you type the first few letters of an entry in a cell, Excel can complete the entry for you, based on the entries already in that column. This is called the AutoComplete feature. If you want to pick an entry from a list of column entries, right-click a cell in the column and then click Pick from List on the shortcut menu.

Entering Numbers

In Excel, you can enter numbers into cells to represent amounts. **Numbers** can contain only the following characters:

0 1 2 3 4 5 6 7 8 9 + - ( ) , / . $ % E e

If a cell entry contains any other keyboard character (including spaces), Excel interprets the entry as text and treats it accordingly. The use of the special characters is explained when they are used in a project.

In Project 1, the Fun-N-Sun first quarter numbers are summarized in Table 1-1.

Table 1-1 Fun-N-Sun First Quarter Data				
	MAIL	CAMPUS	TELEPHONE	WEB
Bahamas Repose	52978.23	38781.35	37213.45	29998.65
Daytona Delight	28234.50	48401.53	27034.56	42911.16
Key West Haven	62567.25	72516.12	24354.86	77019.32
South Padre Del Sol	28567.15	69777.64	49976.60	32019.45

More About

Entering Numbers as Text

Some times, you will want Excel to treat numbers, such as ZIP codes, as text. To enter a number as text, start the entry with an apostrophe (').

These numbers, which represent first quarter sales for each of the sales channels and vacation packages, must be entered in rows 3, 4, 5, and 6. The following steps illustrate how to enter these values one row at a time.

 To Enter Numeric Data

1 **Click cell B3. Type** 52978.23 **and then press the RIGHT ARROW key.**

Excel enters the number 52978.23 in cell B3 and changes the active cell to cell C3 (Figure 1-22). The numbers are formatted with dollar signs and commas later in this project.

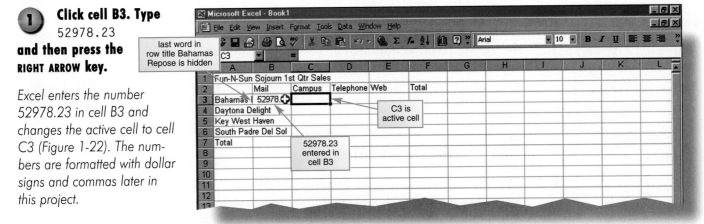

FIGURE 1-22

2 **Enter** 38781.35 **in cell C3,** 37213.45 **in cell D3, and** 29998.65 **in cell E3.**

Row 3 now contains the first quarter sales by sales channel for the vacation package Bahamas Repose (Figure 1-23). The numbers in row 3 are *right-aligned*, which means Excel displays the cell entry to the far right in the cell.

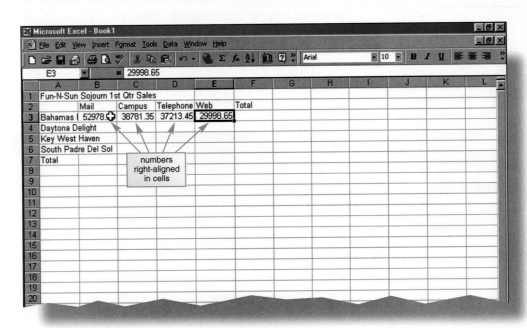

FIGURE 1-23

3 Click cell B4. Enter the remaining first quarter sales provided on the previous page in Table 1-1 by sales channel for each of the three remaining vacation packages in rows 4, 5, and 6.

The first quarter sales display as shown in Figure 1-24.

FIGURE 1-24

Number Limits

In Excel, a number can be between approximately -1 x 10^{308} and 1 x 10^{308}. That is, a negative 1 followed by 308 zeros or a positive 1 followed by 308 zeros. To enter a number such as 5,000,000,000,000, you can type 5,000,000,000,000 or you can type 5E12, which stands for 5 x 10^{12}.

As you can see in Figure 1-24, when you enter data into the cell in column B, the row titles in column A partially display. Later when the worksheet is formatted, the row titles will display in their entirety.

Steps 1 through 3 complete the numeric entries. You are not required to type dollar signs, commas, or trailing zeros. As you can see in Figure 1-24, if you typed the trailing zeros, as indicated in Table 1, they do not display. When you enter a number that has cents, however, you must add the decimal point and the numbers representing the cents when you enter the number. Later in this project, dollar signs, commas, and trailing zeros will be added to improve the appearance of the numbers.

Calculating a Sum

The next step in creating the first quarter sales worksheet is to determine the total first quarter sales by Mail in column B. To calculate this value in cell B7, Excel must add the numbers in cells B3, B4, B5, and B6. Excel's **SUM function** provides a convenient means to accomplish this task.

To use the SUM function, first you must identify the cell in which the sum will be stored after it is calculated. Then, you can use the **AutoSum button** on the Standard toolbar to enter the SUM function as shown in the following steps.

To Sum a Column of Numbers

1 Click cell B7 and then point to the AutoSum button on the Standard toolbar.

Cell B7 becomes the active cell (Figure 1-25).

FIGURE 1-25

2 **Click the AutoSum button.**

Excel responds by displaying = SUM(B3:B6) in the formula bar and in the active cell B7 (Figure 1-26). The B3:B6 within parentheses following the function name SUM is Excel's way of identifying the cells B3 through B6. Excel also surrounds the proposed cells to sum with a moving border, called a **marquee.**

FIGURE 1-26

3 **Click the AutoSum button a second time.**

Excel enters the sum of the first quarter sales in cell B7 (Figure 1-27). The SUM function assigned to cell B7 displays in the formula bar when cell B7 is the active cell.

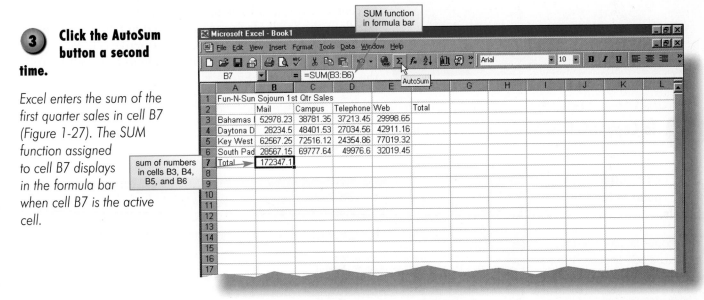

FIGURE 1-27

When you enter the SUM function using the AutoSum button, Excel automatically selects what it considers to be your choice of the group of cells to sum. The group of adjacent cells B3, B4, B5, and B6 is called a range. A **range** is a series of two or more adjacent cells in a column or row or a rectangular group of cells. Many Excel operations, such as summing numbers, take place on a range of cells.

When proposing the range to sum, Excel first looks for a range of cells with numbers above the active cell and then to the left. If Excel proposes the wrong range, you can drag through the correct range anytime prior to clicking the AutoSum button a second time. You also can enter the correct range by typing the beginning cell reference, a colon (:), and the ending cell reference.

Other Ways

1. Press ALT+EQUAL SIGN (=) twice
2. Click Edit Formula (=) box in formula bar, select SUM in Functions list, click OK button

Using the Fill Handle to Copy a Cell to Adjacent Cells

Excel also must calculate the totals for Campus in cell C7, Telephone in cell D7, and for Web in cell E7. Table 1-2 illustrates the similarities between the entry in cell B7 and the entries required for the totals in cells C7, D7, and E7.

To place the SUM functions in cells C7, D7, and E7, you can follow the same steps shown previously in Figures 1-25 through 1-27. A second, more efficient method is to copy the SUM function from cell B7 to the range C7:E7. The cell being copied is called the **copy area**. The range of cells receiving the copy is called the **paste area**.

Although the SUM function entries are similar in Table 1-2, they are not exact copies. The range in each SUM function entry to the right of cell B7 uses cell references that are one column to the right of the previous column. When you copy cell references, Excel automatically adjusts them for each new position, resulting in the SUM function entries illustrated in Table 1-2. Each adjusted cell reference is called a **relative reference**.

The easiest way to copy the SUM formula from cell B7 to cells C7, D7, and E7 is to use the fill handle. The **fill handle** is the small black square located in the lower-right corner of the heavy border around the active cell. Perform the following steps to use the fill handle to copy cell B7 to the adjacent cells C7:E7.

Table 1-2	SUM Function Entries in Row 7	
CELL	SUM FUNCTION ENTRIES	REMARK
B7	=SUM(B3:B6)	Sums cells B3, B4, B5, and B6
C7	=SUM(C3:C6)	Sums cells C3, C4, C5, and C6
D7	=SUM(D3:D6)	Sums cells D3, D4, D5, and D6
E7	=SUM(E3:E6)	Sums cells E3, E4, E5, and E6

 To Copy a Cell to Adjacent Cells in a Row

1 **With cell B7 active, point to the fill handle.**

The mouse pointer changes to a cross hair (Figure 1-28).

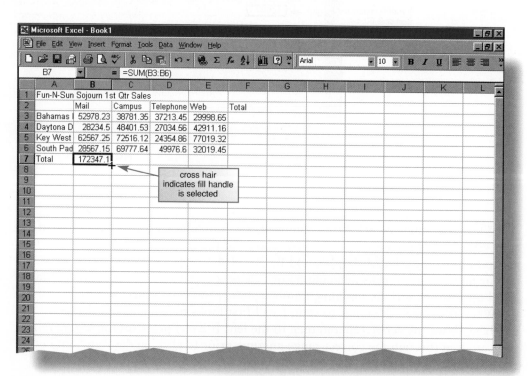

cross hair indicates fill handle is selected

FIGURE 1-28

2 **Drag the fill handle to select the paste area, range C7:E7.**

Excel displays a shaded border around the paste area, range C7:E7, and the copy area, cell B7 (Figure 1-29).

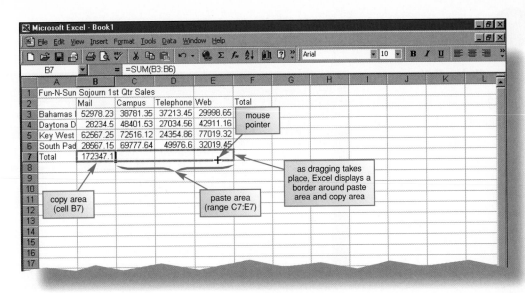

FIGURE 1-29

3 **Release the mouse button.**

Excel copies the SUM function in cell B7 to the range C7:E7 (Figure 1-30). In addition, Excel calculates the sums and enters the results in cells C7, D7, and E7.

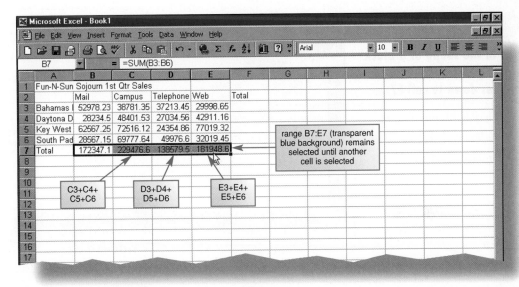

FIGURE 1-30

Once the copy is complete, Excel continues to display a heavy border and transparent (blue) background around cells B7:E7. The heavy border and transparent background indicate a selected range. Cell B7, the first cell in the range, does not display with the transparent background because it is the active cell. If you click any cell, Excel will remove the heavy border and transparent background. The heavy border and transparent (blue) background is called **see-through view**.

Determining Row Totals

The next step in building the worksheet is to determine totals for each vacation package and total first quarter sales for the company in column F. Use the SUM function in the same manner as you did when the sales by sales channel were totaled in row 7. In this example, however, all the rows will be totaled at the same time. The steps on the next page illustrate this process.

More *About*

Using the Mouse to Copy

Another way to copy a cell or range of cells is to select the copy area, point to the border of the copy area, and then, while holding down the CTRL key, drag the copy area to the paste area. If you drag without holding down the CTRL key, Excel moves the data, rather than copying it.

Steps **To Determine Multiple Totals at the Same Time**

1 **Click cell F3.**

Cell F3 becomes the active cell (Figure 1-31).

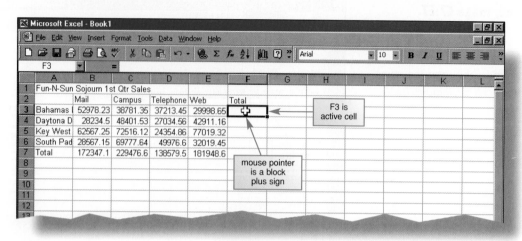

FIGURE 1-31

2 **With the mouse pointer in cell F3 and in the shape of a block plus sign, drag the mouse pointer down to cell F7.**

Excel highlights the range F3:F7 (Figure 1-32).

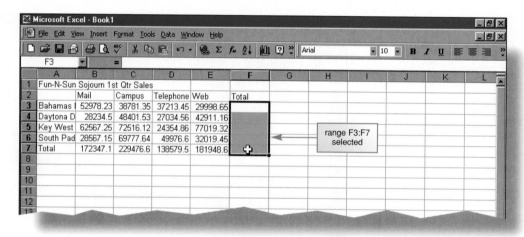

FIGURE 1-32

3 **Click the AutoSum button on the Standard toolbar.**

Excel assigns the appropriate SUM functions to cell F3, F4, F5, F6, and F7, and then calculates and displays the sums in the respective cells (Figure 1-33).

4 **Select cell A8 to deselect the range F3:F7.**

FIGURE 1-33

If each cell in the selected range is next to a row of numbers, Excel assigns the SUM function to each cell in the selected range when you click the AutoSum button. Thus, five SUM functions with different ranges were assigned to the selected range, one for each row. This same procedure could have been used earlier to sum the columns. That is, rather than selecting cell B7, clicking the AutoSum button twice, and then copying the SUM function to the range C7:E7, you could have selected the range B7:E7 and then clicked the AutoSum button once.

Formatting the Worksheet

The text, numeric entries, and functions for the worksheet now are complete. The next step is to format the worksheet. You **format** a worksheet to emphasize certain entries and make the worksheet easier to read and understand.

Figure 1-34a shows the worksheet before formatting. Figure 1-34b shows the worksheet after formatting. As you can see from the two figures, a worksheet that is formatted not only is easier to read, but also looks more professional.

More About

Summing Columns and Rows

A quick way to determine all of the totals in row 7 and column F shown in Figure 1-33 at once is to select the range (B3:F7) and then click the AutoSum button. The range B3:F7 includes the numbers to sum plus an additional row (row 7) and an additional column (column F), in which the totals will display.

(a) Before Formatting

(b) After Formatting

FIGURE 1-34

To change the unformatted worksheet in Figure 1-34a to the formatted worksheet in Figure 1-34b, the following tasks must be completed:

1. Bold the worksheet title in cell A1.
2. Enlarge the worksheet title in cell A1.
3. Format the body of the worksheet. The body of the worksheet, range A2:F7, includes the column titles, row titles, and numbers. Formatting the body of the worksheet results in numbers represented in a dollars-and-cents format, dollar signs in the first row of numbers and the total row, underlines that emphasize portions of the worksheet, and modified column widths.
4. Center the worksheet title in cell A1 across columns A through F.

The process required to format the worksheet is explained in the remainder of this section. Although the format procedures will be carried out in the order described above, you should be aware that you can make these format changes in any order.

More About

Changing Fonts

In general, use no more than two font types and font styles in a worksheet to maintain balance and simplicity.

Fonts, Font Size, and Font Style

Characters that display on the screen are a specific shape, size, and style. The **font type** defines the appearance and shape of the letters, numbers, and special characters. The **font size** specifies the size of the characters on the screen. Font size is gauged by a measurement system called points. A single **point** is about 1/72 of one inch in height. Thus, a character with a **point size** of 10 is about 10/72 of one inch in height.

Font style indicates how the characters are formatted. Common font styles include regular, bold, underlined, or italicized.

When Excel begins, the preset font type for the entire workbook is Arial with a size and style of 10-point regular. Excel allows you to change the font characteristics in a single cell, a range of cells, the entire worksheet, or the entire workbook.

Displaying the Formatting Toolbar in Its Entirety

Most of the formatting you will do in Excel can be accomplished using the buttons on the Formatting toolbar. Thus, before starting the formatting process display the Formatting toolbar in its entirety as shown in the following steps.

Steps | To Display the Formatting Toolbar in Its Entirety

1 **Double-click the move handle on the left side of the Formatting toolbar as shown earlier in Figure 1-33 on page E1.26.**

The entire Formatting toolbar displays and only a portion of the Standard toolbar displays (Figure 1-35).

FIGURE 1-35

Other Ways

1. Drag move handle to left
2. Click More Buttons button on Standard toolbar to display hidden buttons

Bolding a Cell

You **bold** an entry in a cell to emphasize it or make it stand out from the rest of the worksheet. Perform the following steps to bold the worksheet title in cell A1.

To Bold a Cell

1 **Click cell A1 and then point to the Bold button on the Formatting toolbar.**

The ScreenTip displays immediately below the Bold button to identify the function of the button (Figure 1-36).

FIGURE 1-36

2 **Click the Bold button.**

Excel applies a bold format to the worksheet title Fun-N-Sun Sojourn 1st Qtr Sales (Figure 1-37).

FIGURE 1-37

When the active cell is bold, the Bold button on the Formatting toolbar is recessed, or dimmed (Figure 1-37). Clicking the Bold button a second time removes the bold format.

Other Ways

1. Press CTRL+B
2. Right-click cell, click Format Cells on shortcut menu, click Font tab, click Bold, click OK button
3. On Format menu click Cells, click Font tab, click Bold, click OK button

Increasing the Font Size

Increasing the font size is the next step in formatting the worksheet title. You increase the font size of a cell so the entry stands out and is easier to read.

Steps **To Increase the Font Size of a Cell Entry**

1 **With cell A1 selected, click the Font Size box arrow on the Formatting toolbar and then point to 20 in the Font Size list (Figure 1-38).**

FIGURE 1-38

2 **Click 20.**

The font size of the characters in the worksheet title in cell A1 increase from 10 point to 20 point (Figure 1-39).

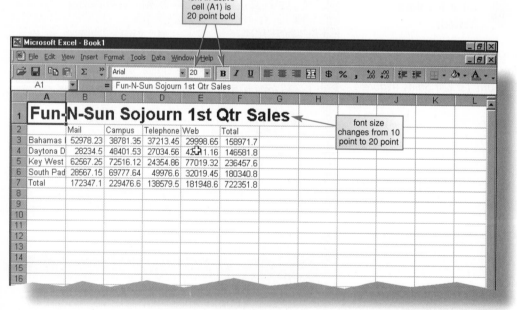

FIGURE 1-39

An alternative to clicking a font size in the Font Size list is to type the font size in the Font Size box and then press the ENTER key. With cell A1 selected (Figure 1-39), the Font Size box shows the new font size 20 and the recessed Bold button shows the active cell is bold.

According to the requirements, the worksheet title must be centered across columns A through F. Because the increased font size causes the worksheet title to exceed the length of the combined columns (Figure 1-39), the centering will be done after the body of the worksheet is formatted.

Using AutoFormat to Format the Body of a Worksheet

Excel has several customized format styles called **table formats** that allow you to format the body of the worksheet. Using table formats can give your worksheet a professional appearance. Follow these steps to format the range A2:F7 automatically using the **AutoFormat command** on the Format menu.

 Steps **To Use AutoFormat to Format the Body of a Worksheet**

1 Select cell A2, the upper-left corner cell of the rectangular range to format. Drag the mouse pointer to cell F7, the lower-right corner cell of the range to format.

Excel highlights the range to format with a heavy border and blue background (Figure 1-40).

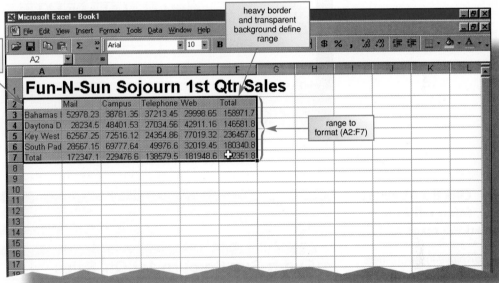

FIGURE 1-40

2 Click Format on the menu bar and then point to AutoFormat.

The Format menu displays (Figure 1-41).

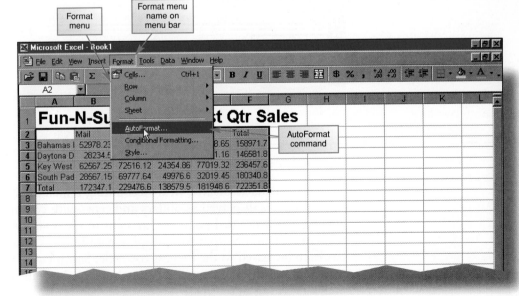

FIGURE 1-41

3 **Click AutoFormat. Click the Accounting 2 format (column 2, row 3) in the AutoFormat dialog box. Point to the OK button.**

The AutoFormat dialog box displays with a list of customized formats (Figure 1-42). Each format illustrates how the body of the worksheet will display if it is chosen.

FIGURE 1-42

4 **Click the OK button. Select cell A9 to deselect the range A2:F7.**

Excel displays the worksheet with the range A2:F7 using the customized format, Accounting 2 (Figure 1-43).

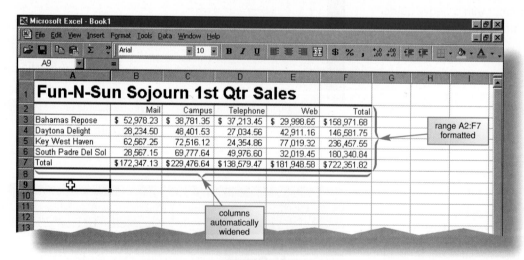

FIGURE 1-43

The formats associated with Accounting 2 include right-alignment of column titles, numbers displayed as dollars and cents with comma separators, numbers aligned on the decimal point, dollar signs in the first row of numbers and in the total row, and top and bottom rows display with borders. The width of column A also has been increased so the longest row title, South Padre Del Sol, just fits in the column. The widths of columns B through F have been increased so that the formatted numbers will fit in the cells.

The AutoFormat dialog box shown in Figure 1-42 includes 17 customized formats and five buttons. Use the scroll bar to view the 11 customized formats that do not display in the dialog box. Each one of these customized formats offers a different look. The one you choose depends on the worksheet you are creating.

The five buttons in the dialog box allow you to cancel, complete the entries, get Help, and adjust a customized format. The **Close button** terminates current activity without making changes. You also can use the **Cancel button**, immediately below the **OK button**, for this purpose. Use the **Question Mark button**, to obtain Help on any box or button located in the dialog box. The **Options button** allows you to select additional formats to assign as part of the selected customized format.

Centering the Worksheet Title Across Columns

With the column widths increased, the final step in formatting the worksheet title is to center it across columns A through F. Centering a worksheet title across the columns used in the body of the worksheet improves the worksheet's appearance.

 To Center a Cell's Contents Across Columns

1 **Click cell A1. Drag the block plus sign to the rightmost cell (F1) of the range to center (A1:F1). Point to the Merge and Center button on the Formatting toolbar.**

When you drag through the range A1:F1, Excel highlights the cells (Figure 1-44).

FIGURE 1-44

Click the Merge and Center button.

Excel merges the cells A1 through F1 to create a new cell A1 and centers the contents of cell A1 across columns A through F (Figure 1-45). After the merge, cells B1 through F1 no longer exist on the worksheet.

③ Click cell A9 to deselect cell A1.

A1 is active cell and heavy border indicates new dimensions of cell

contents of cell A1 centered across columns A through F

cells A1 through F1 are merged to create new cell A1

	Mail	Campus	Telephone	Web	Total
Fun-N-Sun Sojourn 1st Qtr Sales					
Bahamas Repose	$ 52,978.23	$ 38,781.35	$ 37,213.45	$ 29,998.65	$158,971.68
Daytona Delight	28,234.50	48,401.53	27,034.56	42,911.16	146,581.75
Key West Haven	62,567.25	72,516.12	24,354.86	77,019.32	236,457.55
South Padre Del Sol	28,567.15	69,777.64	49,976.60	32,019.45	180,340.84
Total	$172,347.13	$229,476.64	$138,579.47	$181,948.58	$722,351.82

FIGURE 1-45

More About

The Name Box

If you repeatedly select certain cells in a worksheet, consider naming the cells in the Name box. Select the cells one at a time and then type a name in the Name box for each, such as Company Total, for cell F7 shown in Figure 1-48. Then, when you want to select one of the named cells, click the Name box arrow and click the cell name in the Name box list.

Excel not only centers the worksheet title, but also merges cells A1 through F1 into one cell, cell A1. Thus, the heavy border that defines the active cell in Figure 1-45 covers what originally was cells A1 through F1. For the Merge and Center button to work properly, all the cells except the leftmost cell in the range of cells must be empty.

Most formats assigned to a cell will display on the Formatting toolbar when the cell is selected. For example, the font type and font size display in their appropriate boxes. Recessed buttons indicate an assigned format. To determine if less frequently used formats are assigned to a cell, point to the cell and right-click. Next, click Format Cells, and then click each of the tabs in the Format Cells dialog box.

The worksheet now is complete. The next step is to chart the first quarter sales for the four vacation packages by sales channel. To create the chart, you must select the cell in the upper-left corner of the range to chart (cell A2). Rather than clicking cell A2 to select it, the next section describes how to use the Name box to select the cell.

Using the Name Box to Select a Cell

The **Name box** is located on the left side of the formula bar. To select any cell, click the Name box and enter the cell reference of the cell you want to select. Perform the following steps to select cell A2.

Steps To Use the Name Box to Select a Cell

① **Click the Name box in the formula bar. Type** a2 **in the Name box.**

Even though cell A9 is the active cell, the Name box displays the typed cell reference a2 (Figure 1-46).

FIGURE 1-46

② **Press the ENTER key.**

Excel changes the active cell from cell A9 to cell A2 (Figure 1-47).

FIGURE 1-47

As you will see in later projects, besides using the Name box to select any cell in a worksheet, you also can use it to assign names to a cell or range of cells.

Excel supports several additional ways to select a cell, as summarized on the next page in Table 1-3.

Table 1-3   Selecting Cells in Excel

KEY, BOX, OR COMMAND	FUNCTION
ALT+PAGE DOWN	Selects the cell one window to the right and moves the window accordingly.
ALT+PAGE UP	Selects the cell one window to the left and moves the window accordingly.
ARROW	Selects the adjacent cell in the direction of the arrow on the key.
CTRL+ARROW	Selects the border cell of the worksheet in combination with the arrow keys and moves the window accordingly. For example, to select the rightmost cell in the row that contains the active cell, press CTRL+RIGHT arrow. You also can press the END key, release it, and then press the arrow key to accomplish the same task.
CTRL+HOME	Selects cell A1 or the cell one column and one row below and to the right of frozen titles and moves the the window accordingly.
Find command on Edit menu	Finds and selects a cell that contains specific contents that you enter in the Find dialog box. If necessary, Excel moves the window to display the cell. You can press SHIFT+F5 or CTRL+F to display the Find dialog box.
F5 or Go To command on Edit menu	Selects the cell that corresponds to the cell reference you enter in the Go To dialog box and moves the window accordingly. You can press CTRL+G to display the Find dialog box.
HOME	Selects the cell at the beginning of the row that contains the active cell and moves the window accordingly.
Name box	Selects the cell in the workbook that corresponds to the cell reference you enter in the Name box.
PAGE DOWN	Selects the cell down one window from the active cell and moves the window accordingly.
PAGE UP	Selects the cell up one window from the active cell and moves the window accordingly.

More About

Navigation

For more information on selecting cells that contain certain entries, such as constants or formulas, visit the Excel 2000 More About Web page (www.scsite.com/ex2000/more.htm) and click Using Go To Special.

Adding a 3-D Column Chart to the Worksheet

The 3-D Column chart (Figure 1-48) is called an **embedded chart** because it is drawn on the same worksheet as the data.

FIGURE 1-48

For the sales channel Mail, the light blue column represents the first quarter sales for the Bahamas Repose vacation package ($52,978.23); the purple column represents the first quarter sales for Daytona Delight ($28,234.50); the light yellow column represents the first quarter sales for Key West Haven ($62,567.25); and the turquoise column represents the first quarter sales for South Padre Del Sol ($28,567.15). For the sales channels Campus, Telephone, and Web, the columns follow the same color scheme to represent the comparable first quarter sales. The totals from the worksheet are not represented because the totals were not in the range specified for charting.

Excel derives the scale along the vertical axis (also called the **y-axis** or **value axis**) of the chart on the basis of the values in the worksheet. For example, no value in the range B3:E6 is less than zero or greater than $80,000.00. Excel also determines the $20,000.00 increments along the y-axis automatically. The format used by Excel for the numbers along the y-axis includes representing zero (0) with a dash (Figure 1-48).

With the range to chart selected, you click the **Chart Wizard button** on the Standard toolbar to initiate drawing the chart. The area on the worksheet where the chart displays is called the **chart location**. The chart location is the range A9:F20, immediately below the worksheet data.

Follow the steps below to draw a 3-D Column chart that compares the first quarter sales by vacation package for the four sales channels.

Steps To Add a 3-D Column Chart to the Worksheet

1 Double-click the move handle on the left side of the Standard toolbar to display the entire toolbar. With cell A2 selected, position the block plus sign within the cell's border and drag the mouse pointer to the lower-right corner cell (cell E6) of the range to chart (A2:E6). Point to the Chart Wizard button on the Standard toolbar.

Excel highlights the range to chart (Figure 1-49).

FIGURE 1-49

**Click the Chart
Wizard button.**

*The Chart Wizard – Step 1 of
4 – Chart Type dialog box
displays.*

**With Column
selected in the
Chart type list, click the
3-D Column chart sub-type
(column 1, row 2) in the
Chart sub-type area. Point
to the Finish button.**

*Column is highlighted in
the Chart type list and
Clustered column with a 3-D
visual effect is highlighted in
the Chart sub-type area
(Figure 1-50).*

FIGURE 1-50

**Click the Finish
button.**

*Excel draws the 3-D Column
chart (Figure 1-51). The chart
displays in the middle of the
window in a selection rectangle. The small sizing handles
at the corners and along the
sides of the selection
rectangle indicate the
chart is selected.*

FIGURE 1-51

5 Point to an open area in the lower-right section of the Chart Area so the ScreenTip, Chart Area, displays (Figure 1-51). The ScreenTip defines the area of the chart that the mouse pointer is pointing to. Drag the chart down and to the left to position the upper-left corner of the dotted line rectangle over the upper-left corner of cell A9 (Figure 1-52).

Excel displays a dotted line rectangle showing the new chart location. As you drag the selected chart, the mouse pointer changes to a cross hair with four arrowheads.

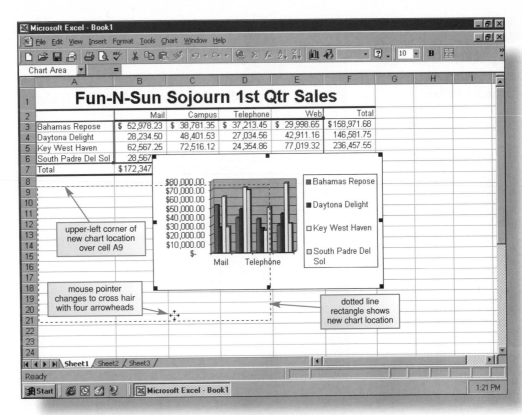

FIGURE 1-52

6 Release the mouse button. Point to the middle sizing handle on the right edge of the selection rectangle.

The chart displays in a new location (Figure 1-53). The mouse pointer changes to a horizontal line with two arrowheads when it points to a sizing handle.

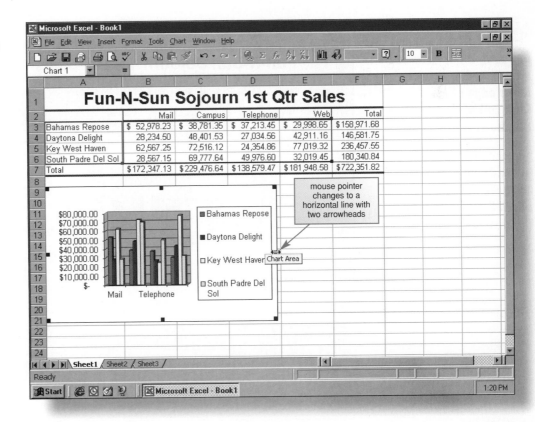

FIGURE 1-53

7 While holding down the ALT key, drag the sizing handle to the right edge of column F. Release the mouse button.

While you drag, the dotted line rectangle shows the new chart location (Figure 1-54). Holding down the ALT key while you drag a chart snaps (aligns) the new border to the worksheet gridlines.

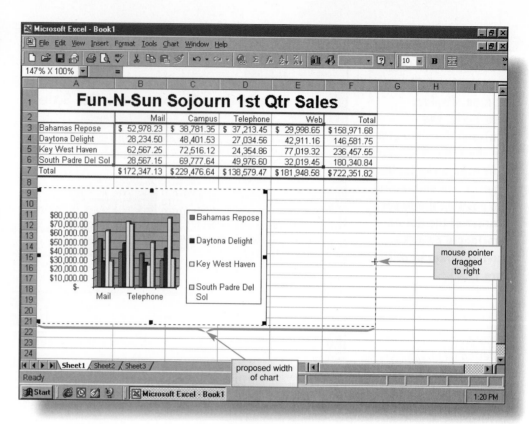

FIGURE 1-54

8 If necessary, hold down the ALT key and drag the lower-middle sizing handle up to the lower edge of row 19. Click cell A21 to deselect the chart.

The new chart location extends from the top of cell A9 to the bottom of cell F19 (Figure 1-55).

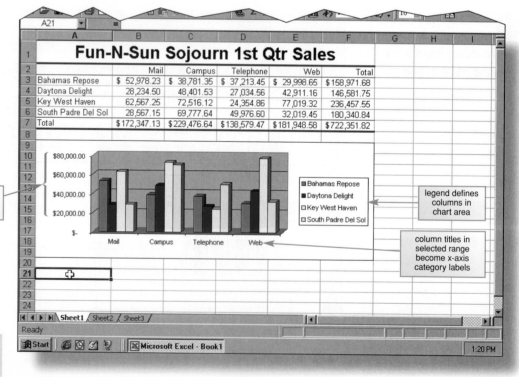

FIGURE 1-55

Other Ways

1. Select range, press F11
2. Select range, on Insert menu click Chart

The embedded 3-D Column chart in Figure 1-55 compares the first quarter sales for the four vacation packages within each sales channel. It also allows you to compare first quarter sales among the sales channels.

Excel automatically selects the entries in the topmost row of the range (row 2) as the titles for the horizontal axis (also called the **x-axis** or **category axis**) and draws a column for each of the 16 cells in the range containing numbers. The small box to the right of the column chart in Figure 1-55 contains the legend. The **legend** identifies each bar in the chart. Excel automatically selects the leftmost column of the range (column A) as titles within the legend. As indicated earlier, it also automatically scales the y-axis on the basis of the magnitude of the numbers in the chart range.

Excel offers 14 different chart types (Figure 1-50 on page E 1.38). The **default chart type** is the chart Excel draws if you click the Finish button in the first Chart Wizard dialog box. When you install Excel on a computer, the default chart type is the 2-D (two-dimensional) Column chart.

Saving a Workbook

While you are building a workbook, the computer stores it in memory. If the computer is turned off or if you lose electrical power, the workbook is lost. Hence, you must save on a floppy disk or hard disk any workbook that you will use later. A saved workbook is referred to as a **file** or **workbook**. The following steps illustrate how to save a workbook on a floppy disk in drive A using the Save button on the Standard toolbar.

More About

Changing the Chart Type

Excel has fourteen chart types from which to choose. You can change the embedded 3-D Column chart to another type by double-clicking the chart location. When a heavy gray border surrounds the chart location, right-click the chart and then click Chart Type on the shortcut menu. You also can use the shortcut menu to format the chart to make it look more professional. Subsequent projects will discuss changing charts, sizing charts, adding text to charts, and drawing a chart on a chart sheet.

Steps To Save a Workbook

1 With a floppy disk in drive A, click the Save button on the Standard toolbar.

The Save As dialog box displays (Figure 1-56). The preset Save in folder is My Documents, the preset file name is Book1, and the file type is Microsoft Excel Workbook. The buttons on the top and on the side are used to select folders and change the display of file names and other information.

FIGURE 1-56

2 **Type** Fun-N-Sun Sojourn 1st Qtr Sales **in the File name text box.**

The new file name replaces Book1 in the File name text box (Figure 1-57). A file name can be up to 255 characters and can include spaces.

FIGURE 1-57

3 **Click the Save in box arrow and then point to 3½ Floppy (A:).**

A list of available drives and folders displays (Figure 1-58).

FIGURE 1-58

4 Click 3½ Floppy (A:) and then point to the Save button in the Save As dialog box.

Drive A becomes the selected drive (Figure 1-59).

FIGURE 1-59

5 Click the Save button.

Excel saves the workbook on the floppy disk in drive A using the file name Fun-N-Sun Sojourn 1st Qtr Sales. Excel automatically appends the extension *.xls* to the file name you entered in Step 2, which stands for Excel workbook. Although the workbook is saved on a floppy disk, it also remains in memory and displays on the screen (Figure 1-60). Notice the file name in the title bar.

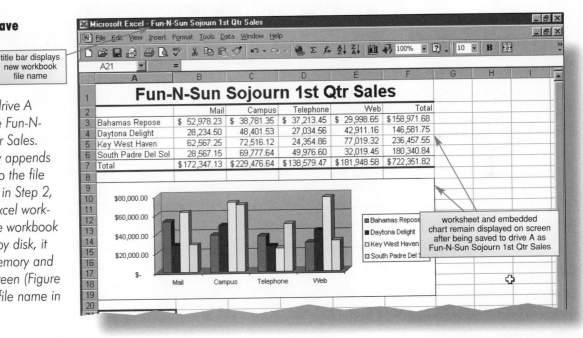

FIGURE 1-60

Other Ways

1. Press CTRL+S, type file name, select drive or folder, click OK button

2. Right-click workbook Control-menu icon on menu bar, click Save As on shortcut menu, type file name, select drive of folder, click OK button

3. On File menu click Save As, type file name, select drive of folder, click OK button

More About

Saving a Worksheet as a Web Page

Excel allows you to save a worksheet in HTML format so you can publish it to the World Wide Web. Click Save as Web Page on the File menu. You have the option to save the worksheet as a static Web page or as a dynamic Web page. A static Web page means you can view the worksheet on the World Wide Web, but you cannot change cell contents. A dynamic Web page means you can modify the worksheet using a browser.

More About

AutoSave

Are you worried about losing your work because your computer might crash? If so, you can use the AutoSave command on the Tools menu. The AutoSave command automatically saves your work every 10 minutes. If you prefer to change the time between saves, you can do so through the AutoSave dialog box that displays when you invoke the AutoSave command. AutoSave is an add-in program. If the AutoSave command does not display on your Tools menu, use the Add-Ins command on the Tools menu to add it.

While Excel is saving the workbook, it momentarily changes the word Ready on the status bar to Saving. It also displays a horizontal bar on the status bar indicating the amount of the workbook saved. After the save operation is complete, Excel changes the name of the workbook in the title bar from Book1 to Fun-N-Sun Sojourn 1st Qtr Sales (Figure 1-60 on the previous page).

When you click the **Tools button** in the Save As dialog box (Figure 1-59 on the previous page), a list box displays. The **General Options command** in the list allows you to save a backup copy of the workbook, create a password to limit access to the workbook, and carry out other functions that will be discussed later. Saving a **backup workbook** means that each time you save a workbook, Excel copies the current version of the workbook on disk to a file with the same name, but with the words, Backup of, appended to the front of the file name. In the case of a power failure or some other problem, use the backup version to restore your work.

You also can use the General Options command on the Tools list to assign a **password** to a workbook so others cannot open it. A password is case sensitive and can be up to 15 characters long. **Case sensitive** means Excel can differentiate between uppercase and lowercase letters. If you assign a password and forget the password, you cannot access the workbook.

The seven buttons at the top and to the right in the Save As dialog box (Figure 1-59) and their functions are summarized in Table 1-4.

Table 1-4	Save As Dialog Box Toolbar Buttons	
BUTTON	BUTTON NAME	FUNCTION
⇦	Default File Location	Displays contents of default file location
🔼	Up One Level	Displays contents of next level up folder
🔍	Search the Web	Starts browser and displays search engine
✕	Delete	Deletes selected file or folder
📁	Create New Folder	Creates new folder
▦▾	Views	Changes view of files and folders
Tools ▾	Tools	Lists commands to print or modify file names and folders

The five buttons on the left of the Save As dialog box in Figure 1-59 allow you to select frequently used folders. The **History button** displays a list of shortcuts (pointers) to the most recently used files in a folder titled Recent. You can not save workbooks to the Recent folder.

Printing the Worksheet

Once you have created the worksheet and saved it on a floppy disk or hard disk, you might want to print it. A printed version of the worksheet is called a **hard copy** or **printout**.

You might want a printout for several reasons. First, to present the worksheet and chart to someone who does not have access to a computer, it must be in printed form. A printout, for example, can be handed out in a management meeting about first quarter sales. In addition, worksheets and charts often are kept for reference by people other than those who prepare them. In many cases, worksheets and charts are printed and kept in binders for use by others. This section describes how to print a worksheet and an embedded chart.

Steps **To Print a Worksheet**

1 **Ready the printer according to the printer instructions. Point to the Print button on the Standard toolbar (Figure 1-61).**

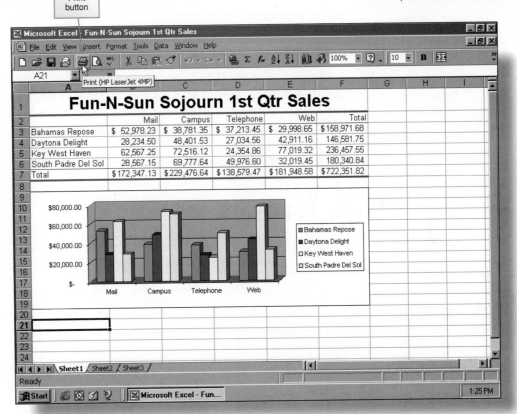

FIGURE 1-61

2 Click the Print button. When the printer stops printing the worksheet and the chart, retrieve the printout (Figure 1-62).

Excel displays the Printing dialog box that allows you to cancel the print job while the system is sending the worksheet and chart image to the printer.

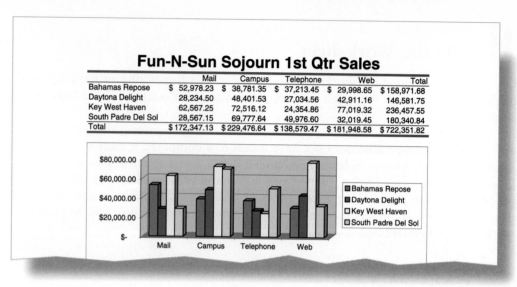

FIGURE 1-62

Other Ways

1. Press CTRL+P, click OK button
2. On File menu click Print, click OK button
3. Right-click workbook Control-menu icon on menu bar, click Print on shortcut menu, click OK button

Prior to clicking the Print button, you can select which columns and rows in the worksheet to print. The range of cells you choose to print is called the **print area**. If you do not select a print area, as was the case in the previous set of steps, Excel automatically selects a print area on the basis of used cells. As you will see in future projects, Excel has many different print options, such as allowing you to preview the printout on the screen to see if the printout is satisfactory prior to sending it to the printer. Several of these print options are discussed in Project 2.

Quitting Excel

After you build, save, and print the worksheet and chart, Project 1 is complete. To quit Excel, complete the following steps.

Steps **To Quit Excel**

1 Point to the Close button on the right side of the title bar (Figure 1-63).

FIGURE 1-63

2 **Click the Close button.**

If you made changes to the workbook, the Microsoft Excel dialog box displays the question, Do you want to save the changes you made to 'Fun-N-Sun Sojourn 1st Qtr Sales.xls'? (Figure 1-64). Clicking the Yes button saves the changes before quitting Excel. Clicking the No button quits Excel without saving the changes. Clicking the Cancel button stops the Exit command and returns to the worksheet.

3 **Click the No button.**

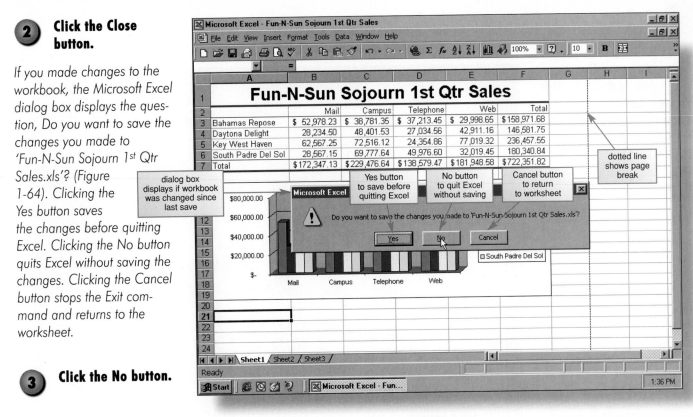

FIGURE 1-64

In Figure 1-63, you can see that two Close buttons and two Control-menu icons display. The Close button and Control-menu icon on the title bar close Excel. The Close button and Control-menu icon on the menu bar close the workbook.

Starting Excel and Opening a Workbook

Once you have created and saved a workbook, you often will have reason to retrieve it from a floppy disk. For example, you might want to review the calculations on the worksheet and enter additional or revised data on it. The steps on the next page assume Excel is not running.

Other Ways

1. Double-click Control-menu icon
2. Right-click Microsoft Excel button on taskbar, click Close on shortcut menu
3. On File menu click Exit

To Start Excel and Open a Workbook

① With your floppy disk in drive A, click the Start button on the taskbar and then point to Open Office Document (Figure 1-65).

FIGURE 1-65

② Click Open Office Document. If necessary, click the Look in box arrow and then click 3½ Floppy (A:).

The Open Office Document dialog box displays (Figure 1-66).

FIGURE 1-66

③ **Double-click the file name Fun-N-Sun Sojourn 1st Qtr Sales.**

Excel starts, opens the workbook Fun-N-Sun Sojourn 1st Qtr Sales.xls from drive A, and displays it on the screen (Figure 1-67). An alternative to double-clicking the file name is to click it and then click the Open button in the Open Office Document dialog box.

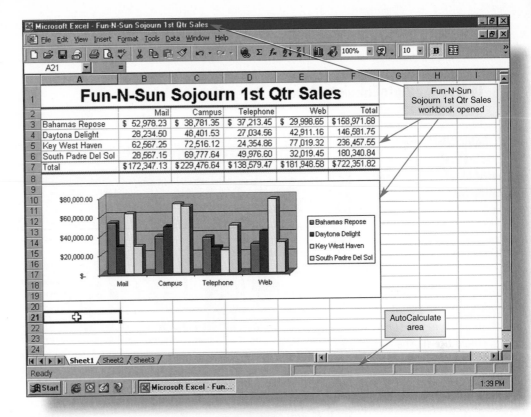

FIGURE 1-67

AutoCalculate

You easily can obtain a total, an average, or other information about the numbers in a range by using the **AutoCalculate area** on the status bar (bottom of Figure 1-67). All you need do is select the range of cells containing the numbers you want to check. Next, right-click the AutoCalculate area to display the shortcut menu (Figure 1-68 on the next page). The recessed check mark to the left of the active function (Sum) indicates that the sum of the selected range displays. The function commands on the AutoCalculate shortcut menu are described in Table 1-5.

Table 1-5	AutoCalculate Shortcut Menu Commands
COMMAND	FUNCTION
Average	Displays the average of the numbers in the selected range
Count	Displays the number of nonblank cells in the selected range
Count Nums	Displays the number of cells containing numbers in the selected range
Max	Displays the highest value in the selected range
Min	Displays the lowest value in the selected range
Sum	Displays the sum of the numbers in the selected range

The following steps show how to display the average first quarter sales by sales channel for the Bahamas Repose vacation package.

 To Use the AutoCalculate Area to Determine an Average

1 **Select the range B3:E3. Right-click the AutoCalculate area on the status bar.**

The sum of the numbers in the range B3:E3 displays ($158,971.68) as shown in Figure 1-68 because Sum is active in the AutoCalculate area (you may see a total other than the Sum in your AutoCalculate area). The shortcut menu listing the various types of functions displays over the AutoCalculate area.

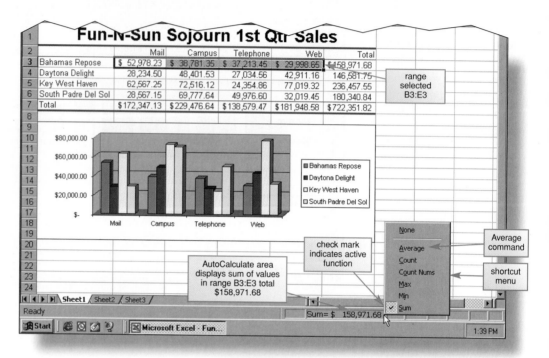

FIGURE 1-68

2 **Click Average on the shortcut menu.**

The average of the numbers in the range B3:E3 displays in the AutoCalculate area (Figure 1-69).

3 **Right-click the AutoCalculate area and then click Sum on the shortcut menu.**

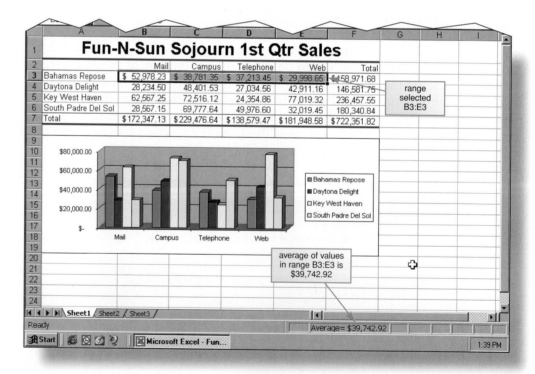

FIGURE 1-69

To change to any one of the other five functions for the range B3:E3, right-click the AutoCalculate area. Then click the desired function.

Correcting Errors

You can correct errors on a worksheet using one of several methods. The one you choose will depend on the extent of the error and whether you notice it while typing the data or after you have entered the incorrect data into the cell.

Correcting Errors While You Are Typing Data into a Cell

If you notice an error while you are typing data into a cell, press the BACKSPACE key to erase the portion in error and then type the correct characters. If the error is a major one, click the Cancel box in the formula bar or press the ESC key to erase the entire entry and then reenter the data from the beginning.

In-Cell Editing

If you find an error in the worksheet after entering the data, you can correct the error in one of two ways:

1. If the entry is short, select the cell, retype the entry correctly, and click the Enter box or press the ENTER key. The new entry will replace the old entry.
2. If the entry in the cell is long and the errors are minor, the **Edit mode** may be a better choice. Use the Edit mode as described below.
   a. Double-click the cell containing the error. Excel switches to Edit mode, the active cell contents display in the formula bar, and a flashing insertion point displays in the active cell (Figure 1-70). This editing procedure is called **in-cell editing** because you can edit the contents directly in the cell. The active cell contents also display in the formula bar.

FIGURE 1-70

b. Make your changes, as specified below.
   (1) To insert between two characters, place the insertion point between the two characters and begin typing. Excel inserts the new characters at the location of the insertion point.
   (2) To delete a character in the cell, move the insertion point to the left of the character you want to delete and then press the DELETE key, or place the insertion point to the right of the character you want to delete and then press the BACKSPACE key. You also can use the mouse to drag through the character or adjacent characters you want to delete and then press the DELETE key or click the **Cut button** on the Standard toolbar.

More About

Shortcut Menus

Shortcut menus display frequently used commands related to an object that the mouse pointer points to. To display a shortcut menu, right-click the object as shown in Step 1. In some cases, you also can display the shortcut menu by selecting the object, such as a cell or range of cells, and pressing SHIFT+F10. To hide a shortcut menu, click outside the shortcut menu or press the ESC key.

More About

Correcting Errors

Learning how to correct errors in a worksheet is critical to becoming proficient in Excel. Thus, carefully review this section on how to correct errors prior to entering data in a cell, how to perform in-cell editing, how to undo the last entry, and how to clear cells.

More About

In-Cell Editing

An alternative to double-clicking the cell to edit is to select the cell and then press F2.

More About

Editing the Contents of a Cell

Rather than using in-cell editing, you can select the cell and then click the formula bar to edit the contents.

(3) When you are finished editing an entry, click the Enter box or press the ENTER key.

When Excel enters the Edit mode, the keyboard usually is in Insert mode. In **Insert mode**, as you type a character, Excel inserts the character and moves all characters to the right of the typed character one position to the right. You can change to Overtype mode by pressing the INSERT key. In **Overtype mode**, Excel overtypes the character to the right of the insertion point. The INSERT key toggles the keyboard between Insert mode and Overtype mode.

While in Edit mode, you may have reason to move the insertion point to various points in the cell, select portions of the data in the cell, or switch from inserting characters to overtyping characters. Table 1-6 summarizes the most common tasks used during in-cell editing.

Table 1-6   Summary of In-Cell Editing Tasks

TASK	MOUSE	KEYBOARD
Move the insertion point to the beginning of data in a cell	Point to the left of the first character and click	Press HOME
Move the insertion point to the end of data in a cell	Point to the right of the last character and click	Press END
Move the insertion point anywhere in a cell	Point to the appropriate position and click the character	Press RIGHT ARROW or LEFT ARROW
Highlight one or more adjacent characters	Drag the mouse pointer through adjacent characters	Press SHIFT+RIGHT ARROW or SHIFT+LEFT ARROW
Select all data in a cell	Double-click the cell with the insertion point in the cell	
Delete selected characters	Click the Cut button on the Standard toolbar	Press DELETE
Toggle between Insert and Overtype modes		Press INSERT

Undoing the Last Entry

Excel provides the **Undo command** on the Edit menu and the **Undo button** on the Standard toolbar (Figure 1-71) that you can use to erase the most recent cell entry. Thus, if you enter incorrect data in a cell and notice it immediately, click the Undo command or Undo button and Excel changes the cell contents to what they were prior to entering the incorrect data.

FIGURE 1-71

If Excel cannot undo an action, then the Undo button is inoperative. Excel remembers the last 16 actions you have completed. Thus, you can undo up to 16 previous actions by clicking the Undo box arrow to display the Undo list and clicking the action to be undone (Figure 1-71). You also can click Undo on the Edit menu rather than using the Undo button.

Next to the Undo button on the Standard toolbar is the Redo button. The **Redo button** allows you to repeat previous actions. You also can click Redo on the Edit menu rather than using the Redo button.

Clearing a Cell or Range of Cells

If you enter data into the wrong cell or range of cells, you can erase, or clear, the data using one of several methods. **Never press the** SPACEBAR **to clear a cell.** Pressing the SPACEBAR enters a blank character. A blank character is text and is different from an empty cell, even though the cell may appear empty.

Excel provides four methods to clear the contents of a cell or a range of cells.

TO CLEAR CELL CONTENTS USING THE FILL HANDLE

1 Select the cell or range of cells and point to the fill handle so the mouse pointer changes to a cross hair.

2 Drag the fill handle back into the selected cell or range until a shadow covers the cell or cells you want to erase. Release the mouse button.

TO CLEAR CELL CONTENTS USING THE SHORTCUT MENU

1 Select the cell or range of cells to be cleared.

2 Right-click the selection.

3 Click Clear Contents on the shortcut menu.

TO CLEAR CELL CONTENTS USING THE DELETE KEY

1 Select the cell or range of cells to be cleared.

2 Press the DELETE key.

TO CLEAR CELL CONTENTS USING THE CLEAR COMMAND

1 Select the cell or range of cells to be cleared.

2 Click Edit on the menu bar and then click Clear.

3 Click All on the submenu.

You also can select a range of cells and click the Cut button on the Standard toolbar or click Cut on the Edit menu. Be aware, however, that the **Cut button** or **Cut command** not only deletes the contents from the range, but also copies the contents of the range to the Office Clipboard.

More About

Quick Reference

For a table that lists how to complete the tasks covered in this book using the mouse, menu, shortcut menu, and keyboard, visit the Shelly Cashman Series Office Web page (www.scsite.com/ off2000/qr.htm), and then click Microsoft Excel 2000.

Clearing the Entire Worksheet

Sometimes, everything goes wrong. If this happens, you may want to clear the worksheet entirely and start over. To clear the worksheet, follow these steps.

TO CLEAR THE ENTIRE WORKSHEET

1 Click the Select All button on the worksheet (Figure 1-71 on page E 1.52).

2 Press the DELETE key or on the Edit menu click Clear and then click All on the submenu.

The **Select All button** selects the entire worksheet. Instead of clicking the Select All button, you also can press CTRL+A. You also can clear an unsaved workbook by clicking the workbook's Close button or by clicking **Close** on the File menu. If you close the workbook, click the **New button** on the Standard toolbar or click **New** on the File menu to begin working on the next workbook.

TO DELETE AN EMBEDDED CHART

1 Click the chart to select it.

2 Press the DELETE key.

Excel Help System

At any time while you are using Excel, you can get answers to questions by using the **Excel Help system**. Used properly, this form of online assistance can increase your productivity and reduce your frustrations by minimizing the time you spend learning how to use Excel.

The following section shows how to get answers to your questions using the Office Assistant. For additional information on using the Excel Help system, see Appendix A and Table 1-7 on page E1.57.

More About

The Office Assistant

The Office Assistant unifies Excel Help, allows users to ask questions in their own words, and interactively provides tips and suggestions to let users discover the power of Excel 2000.

Using the Office Assistant

The **Office Assistant** answers your questions and suggests more efficient ways to complete a task. With the Office Assistant active, for example, you can type a question, word, or phrase in a text box and the Office Assistant provides immediate help on the subject. Also, as you create a worksheet, the Office Assistant accumulates tips that suggest more efficient ways to do the tasks you completed while building a worksheet, such as formatting, printing, and saving. This tip feature is part of the **IntelliSense™ technology** that is built into Excel, which understands what you are trying to do and suggests better ways to do it. When the light bulb displays above the Office Assistant, click it to see a tip.

The following steps show how to use the Office Assistant to obtain information on formatting a worksheet.

To Obtain Help Using the Office Assistant

1 If the Office Assistant is not on the screen, click Help on the menu bar and then click Show the Office Assistant. With the Office Assistant on the screen, click it. Type formatting in the What would you like to do? text box in the Office Assistant balloon. Point to the Search button (Figure 1-72).

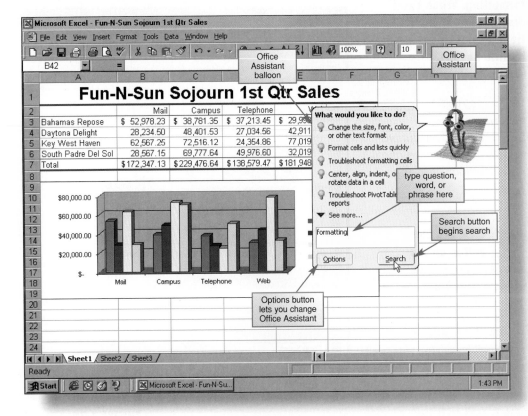

FIGURE 1-72

2 Click the Search button. Point to the topic About worksheet formatting in the Office Assistant balloon.

The Office Assistant displays a list of topics relating to the question, how do i format. The mouse pointer changes to a hand indicating it is pointing to a link (Figure 1-73).

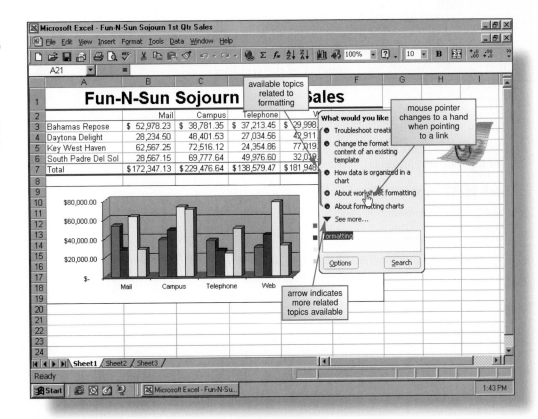

FIGURE 1-73

3 **Click About worksheet formatting. When Excel displays the Microsoft Excel Help window, double-click its title bar to maximize it.**

The Office Assistant displays a Microsoft Excel Help window that provides Help information about worksheet formatting (Figure 1-74).

4 **Click the Close button on the Microsoft Excel Help window title bar.**

The Microsoft Excel Help window closes and the worksheet is active.

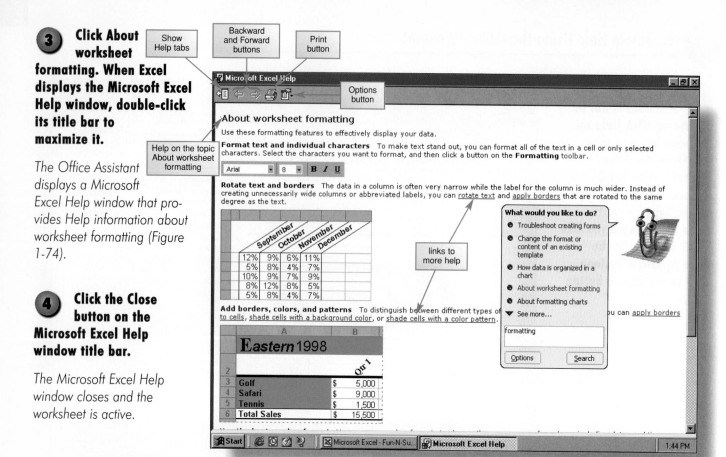

FIGURE 1-74

Use the buttons in the upper-left corner of the Microsoft Excel Help window (Figure 1-74) to navigate through the Help system, change the display, and print the contents of the window.

More About

Excel 2000 Tips

To receive a newsletter titled *ExcelTips* regularly via e-mail at no charge, visit the Excel 2000 More About Web page (www.scsite.com/ex2000/more.htm) and click ExcelTips.

Table 1-7 summarizes the nine categories of Help available to you. Because of the way the Excel Help system works, please review the right most column of Table 1-7 if you have difficulties activating the desired category of Help. For additional information on using the Excel Help system, see Appendix A.

Table 1-7 Excel Help System			
TYPE	DESCRIPTION	HOW TO ACTIVATE	TURNING THE OFFICE ASSISTANT ON AND OFF
Answer Wizard	Similar to the Office Assistant in that it answers questions that you type in your own words.	Click the Microsoft Excel Help button on the Standard toolbar. If necessary, maximize the Help window by double-clicking its title bar. Click the Answer Wizard tab.	If the Office Assistant displays, right-click it, click Options on the shortcut menu, click Use the Office Assistant to remove the check mark, click the OK button.
Contents sheet	Groups Help topics by general categories. Use when you know only the general category of the topic in question.	Click the Microsoft Excel Help button on the Standard toolbar. If necessary, maximize the Help window by double-clicking its title bar. Click the Contents tab.	If the Office Assistant displays, right-click it, click Options, click Use the Office Assistant to remove the check mark, click the OK button.
Detect and Repair	Automatically finds and fixes errors in the application.	Click Detect and Repair on the Help menu.	
Hardware and Software Information	Shows Product ID and allows access to system information and technical support information.	Click About Microsoft Excel on the Help menu and then click the appropriate button.	
Help for Lotus 1-2-3 Users	Used to assist Lotus 1-2-3 users who are learning Microsoft Excel.	Click Lotus 1-2-3 Help on the Help menu.	
Index sheet	Similar to an index in a book. Use when you know exactly what you want.	Click the Microsoft Excel Help button on the Standard toolbar. If necessary, maximize the Help window by double-clicking its title bar. Click the Index tab.	If the Office Assistant displays, right-click it, click Options, click Use the Office Assistant to remove the check mark, click the OK button.
Office Assistant	Answers questions that you type in your own words, offers tips, and provides Help for a variety of Excel features.	Click the Microsoft Excel Help button on the Standard toolbar or double-click the Office Assistant icon. Some dialog boxes also include the Microsoft Excel Help button.	If the Office Assistant does not display, click Show the Office Assistant on the Help menu.
Office on the Web	Used to access technical resources and download free product enhancements on the Web.	Click Office on the Web on the Help menu.	
Question Mark button and What's This? command	Used to identify unfamiliar items on the screen.	In a dialog box, click the Question Mark button and then click an item in the dialog box. Click What's This? on the Help menu, and then click an item on the screen.	

Quitting Excel

To quit Excel, complete the following steps.

TO QUIT EXCEL

1. Click the Close button on the right side of the title bar (see Figure 1-63 on page E 1.46).

2. If the Microsoft Excel dialog box displays, click the No button.

More About

Quitting Excel 2000

Do not forget to remove the floppy disk from drive A after quitting Excel, especially if you are working in a laboratory environment. Nothing can be more frustrating than leaving all of your hard work behind on a floppy disk for the next user.

C A S E   P E R S P E C T I V E   S U M M A R Y

The worksheet created in this project (Figure 1-1 on page E 1.7) allows the management of the Fun-N-Sun Sojourn company to examine the first quarter sales for the four key vacation packages. Furthermore, the 3-D Column chart should meet the needs of Kylie Waiter, who as you recall, has little tolerance for lists of numbers.

Project Summary

In creating the Fun-N-Sun Sojourn 1st Quarter Sales worksheet and chart in this project, you gained a broad knowledge about Excel. First, you were introduced to starting Excel. You learned about the Excel window and how to enter text and numbers to create a worksheet. You learned how to select a range and how to use the AutoSum button to sum numbers in a column or row. Using the fill handle, you learned how to copy a cell to adjacent cells.

Once the worksheet was built, you learned how to change the font size of the title, bold the title, and center the title across a range using buttons on the Formatting toolbar. Using the steps and techniques presented in the project, you formatted the body of the worksheet using the AutoFormat command, and you used the Chart Wizard to add a 3-D Column chart. After completing the worksheet, you saved the workbook on disk and printed the worksheet and chart. You learned how to edit data in cells. Finally, you learned how to use the Excel Help system to answer your questions.

What You Should Know

Having completed this project, you now should be able to perform the following tasks:

▶ Add a 3-D Column Chart to the Worksheet *(E 1.37)*
▶ Bold a Cell *(E 1.29)*
▶ Center a Cell's Contents Across Columns *(E 1.33)*
▶ Clear Cell Contents Using the Clear Command *(E 1.53)*
▶ Clear Cell Contents Using the DELETE Key *(E 1.53)*
▶ Clear Cell Contents Using the Fill Handle *(E 1.53)*
▶ Clear Cell Contents Using the Shortcut Menu *(E 1.53)*
▶ Clear the Entire Worksheet *(E 1.54)*

▶ Copy a Cell to Adjacent Cells in a Row *(E 1.24)*
▶ Delete an Embedded Chart *(E 1.54)*
▶ Determine Multiple Totals at the Same Time *(E 1.26)*
▶ Display the Formatting Toolbar in Its Entirety *(E 1.28)*
▶ Enter Column Titles *(E 1.18)*
▶ Enter Numeric Data *(E 1.21)*
▶ Enter Row Titles *(E 1.20)*
▶ Enter the Worksheet Title *(E 1.16)*
▶ Increase the Font Size of a Cell Entry *(E 1.30)*
▶ Obtain Help Using the Office Assistant *(E 1.55)*
▶ Print a Worksheet *(E 1.45)*
▶ Quit Excel *(E 1.46, E 1.57)*
▶ Save a Workbook *(E 1.41)*
▶ Start Excel *(E 1.8)*
▶ Start Excel and Open a Workbook *(E 1.48)*
▶ Sum a Column of Numbers *(E 1.22)*
▶ Use AutoFormat to Format the Body of a Worksheet *(E 1.31)*
▶ Use the AutoCalculate Area to Determine an Average *(E 1.50)*
▶ Use the Name Box to Select a Cell *(E 1.35)*

More *About*

Microsoft Certification

The Microsoft Office User Specialist (MOUS) Certification program provides an opportunity for you to obtain a valuable industry credential — proof that you have the Excel 2000 skills required by employers. For more information, see Appendix D or visit the Shelly Cashman Series MOUS Web page at www.scsite.com/off2000/cert.htm.

Apply Your Knowledge

Project Reinforcement at www.scsite.com/off2000/reinforce.htm

1 Changing Data in a Worksheet

Instructions: Start Excel. Open the workbook Trevor's Shady Tree Service from the Data Disk. See the inside back cover of this book for instructions for downloading the Data Disk or see your instructor for information on accessing the files required in this book.

Make the changes to the worksheet described in Table 1-8 so it appears as shown in Figure 1-75. As you edit the values in the cells containing numeric data, watch the values in the total income (row 6), the total expenses (row 11), and the profit (row 12). The numbers in these three rows are based on formulas. When you enter a new value, Excel automatically recalculates the formulas. After you have successfully made the changes listed in the table, the profits in cells C12 through F12 should equal $18,580.17, $45,452.34, $44,101.35, and $26,996.44, respectively.

Save the workbook. Use the file name, Eric's Arborescent Service. Print the revised worksheet and hand in the printout to your instructor.

FIGURE 1-75

| Microsoft Excel - Eric's Arborescent Service |

Eric's Arborescent Service

	A	B	C	D	E	F
2	INCOME:		Jan-Mar	Apr-June	July-Sept	Oct-Dec
3		Removal	$62,613.25	$95,324.56	$63,235.25	$95,324.56
4		Trimming	32,341.40	31,721.97	32,341.40	29,213.78
5		Treatment	26,945.30	32,090.21	42,982.90	14,213.75
6	TOTAL INCOME:		$121,899.95	$159,136.74	$138,559.55	$138,752.09
7	EXPENSES:					
8		Salaries	$54,430.00	$52,875.40	$48,430.00	$52,875.40
9		Rent	15,235.00	15,235.00	15,235.00	15,235.00
10		Cost of Goods	33,654.78	45,574.00	30,793.20	43,645.25
11	TOTAL EXPENSES:		$103,319.78	$113,684.40	$94,458.20	$111,755.65
12	PROFIT:		$18,580.17	$45,452.34	$44,101.35	$26,996.44

Table 1-8 New Worksheet Data

CELL	CHANGE CELL CONTENTS TO
A1	Eric's Arborescent Service
C3	62,613.25
D4	31,721.97
E5	42,982.90
F5	14,213.75
C8	54,430.00
E10	30,793.20
F10	43,645.25

In the Lab

1 Marvin's Music & Movie Mirage Sales Analysis Worksheet

Problem: The chief financial officer (CFO) of Marvin's Music & Movie Mirage needs a sales analysis worksheet similar to the one shown in Figure 1-76. Your task is to develop the worksheet. Table 1-9 provides the sales figures for the worksheet.

Instructions: Perform the following tasks.

1. Create the worksheet shown in Figure 1-76 using the title, sales amounts, and categories in Table 1-9.

2. Determine the totals for the types of products, sales channels, and company totals.

3. Format the worksheet title, Marvin's Music & Movie Mirage, in 18-point Arial, bold font, centered across columns A through F.

4. Format the range A2:F8 using the AutoFormat command on the Format menu as follows: (a) Select the range A2:F8 and then apply the table format Accounting 1; and (b) with the range A2:F8 still selected, apply the table format List 2. Excel 2000 appends the formats of List 2 to the formats of Accounting 1.

5. Select the range A2:E7 and then use the Chart Wizard button on the Standard toolbar to draw a Clustered column with a 3-D visual effect chart (column 1, row 2 in Chart sub-type list). Move the chart to the upper-left corner of cell A10 and then drag the lower-right corner of the chart location to cell F20.

6. Enter your name, course, laboratory assignment number, date, and instructor name in cells A24 through A28.

7. Save the workbook using the file name Marvin's Music & Movie Mirage.

8. Print the worksheet.

9. Make the following two corrections to the sales amounts: $35,987.99 for DVDs sold in a store and $36,498.33 for Videos sold over the telephone. After you enter the corrections, the company totals should equal $157,390.58 in cell C8 and $111,876.00 in cell D8.

10. Print the revised worksheet. Close the workbook without saving the changes.

FIGURE 1-76

Table 1-9 Marvin's Music & Movie Mirage Data

	MAIL ORDER	STORE	TELEPHONE	WEB
CDs	$23,789.34	$24,897.12	$34,612.89	$16,410.51
DVDs	35,912.54	23,908.23	9,219.42	29,900.32
Tapes	23,719.32	23,823.90	7,100.76	16,758.45
Videos	8,313.10	33,912.56	24,200.87	29,126.71
Other	25,310.55	38,769.01	24,444.60	22,318.75

In the Lab

2 Dollar Bill's Annual Software Sales Worksheet

Problem: As the assistant financial manager for Dollar Bill's Software, Inc., your supervisor has asked you to create a workbook to analyze the annual sales for the company by product group and store location. The software sales for the year are shown in Table 1-10.

Table 1-10 Dollar Bill's Data				
	SAN ANTONIO	**SAN FRANCISCO**	**CLEVELAND**	**CHARLOTTE**
Business	35,102.15	18,231.56	31,012.40	12,012.00
Database	42,970.50	57,210.00	29,089.12	29,765.23
Education	21,892.70	18,329.34	26,723.15	22,914.50
Graphics	9,312.45	12,923.21	9,012.56	8,910.32
Games	13,453.30	22,134.45	13,908.55	9,143.75

Instructions: Perform the following tasks.

1. Create the worksheet shown in Figure 1-77 using the sales amounts in Table 1-10.

2. Direct Excel to determine the totals for the four store locations, the product categories, and the company.

3. Format the worksheet title, Dollar Bill's Annual Software Sales, in 18-point Arial bold font, and centered across columns A through F.

4. Use the AutoFormat command on the Format menu to format the range A2:F8. Use the table format Accounting 2.

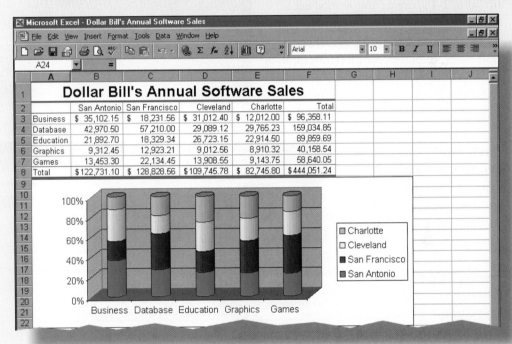

FIGURE 1-77

5. Use the ChartWizard button on the Standard toolbar to draw the 3-D Stacked Cylinder chart (column 3, row 1 in the Chart sub-type list), as shown in Figure 1-77. Chart the range A2:E7 and use the chart location A9:H22. Extend the chart location to the right, if necessary.

6. Enter your name in cell A25. Enter your course, computer laboratory assignment number, date, and instructor name in cells A26 through A29.

7. Save the workbook using the file name, Dollar Bill's Annual Software Sales. Print the worksheet.

8. Two corrections to the sales amounts were sent in from the accounting department. The correct sales amounts are $16,453.21 for Games in San Antonio and $42,781.50 for Database software in Charlotte. Enter the two corrections. After you enter the two corrections, the company total should equal $460,067.42 in cell F8. Print the revised worksheet.

9. Use the Undo button to change the worksheet back to the original numbers in Table 1-10.

10. Use the Redo button to change the worksheet back to the revised state.

11. Hand in all printouts to your instructor. Close the workbook without saving the changes.

In the Lab

3 Projected College Cash Flow Analysis

Problem: Attending college is an expensive proposition and your resources are limited. To plan for your four-year college career, you have decided to organize your anticipated expenses and resources in a worksheet. The data required to prepare your worksheet is shown in Table 1-11.

Part 1 Instructions: Using the numbers in Table 1-11, create the worksheet shown in Figure 1-78. Enter the worksheet title in cell A1 and the section titles, Expenses and Resources, in cells A2 and A10, respectively. Use the AutoSum button to calculate the totals in rows 9 and 16 and column F.

To format the worksheet, use the table format Accounting 1 for the range A3:F9 and again for the range A11:F16. Increase the font size of the worksheet title to 18 point and the section titles to 16 point. Bold the entire worksheet by first clicking the Select All button on the worksheet and then clicking the Bold button on the Formatting toolbar. Center the title across columns A through F. Enter your name in cell A19 and your course, laboratory assignment number, date, and instructor name in cells A20 through A23. Use Help to determine how to use the Font Color button on the Formatting toolbar to change the font color of the worksheet title and section titles as shown in Figure 1-78.

Save the workbook using the file name, College Expenses and Resources. Print the worksheet. Use the Office Assistant to learn how to print only a specific area of a worksheet and then print the selection A1:F9 of the worksheet.

Table 1-11	College Expenses and Resources			
EXPENSES	**FRESHMAN**	**SOPHOMORE**	**JUNIOR**	**SENIOR**
Room & Board	$3,290.00	$3,454.50	$3,627.23	$3,808.59
Tuition & Books	4,850.00	5,092.50	5,347.13	5,614.48
Clothes	490.00	514.50	540.23	567.24
Entertainment	635.00	666.75	700.09	735.09
Miscellaneous	325.00	341.25	358.31	376.23
RESOURCES	**FRESHMAN**	**SOPHOMORE**	**JUNIOR**	**SENIOR**
Savings	$1,600.00	$1,680.00	$1,764.00	$1,852.20
Parents	2,340.00	2,457.00	2,579.85	2,708.84
Job	1,450.00	1,522.50	1,598.64	1,678.56
Financial Aid	4,200.00	4,410.00	4,630.50	4,862.03

FIGURE 1-78

In the Lab

Increment all Junior-year expenses in column D by $500. Increment the financial aid for the Junior year by the amount required to cover the increase. The totals in cells F9 and F16 should equal $43,834.12. Print the worksheet. Close the workbook without saving changes. Hand in the three printouts to your instructor.

Part 2 Instructions: Open the workbook College Expenses and Resources created in Part 1. A close inspection of Table 1-11 shows a 5% increase each year over the previous year. Use the Office Assistant to determine how to enter the data for the last three years using a formula and the Copy command. For example, the formula to enter in cell C4 is =B4 * 1.5. Enter formulas to replace all the numbers in the range C4:E8 and C12:E15. If necessary, reformat the tables using Accounting 1 as you did in Part 1. The worksheet should appear as shown in Figure 1-78, except that some of the totals will be off by 0.01 due to round-off errors. Save the worksheet using the file name, College Expenses and Resources2. Print the worksheet. Press CTRL+` (left single quotation mark) to display the formulas. Print the formulas version. Hand in both printouts to your instructor.

Cases and Places

The difficulty of these case studies varies:
▶ are the least difficult; ▶▶ are more difficult; and ▶▶▶ are the most difficult.

1 ▶ You just started as a summer intern at the Blue Suede Music Company. Your manager, Elma Presley, has asked you to prepare a worksheet and chart to help her analyze the yearly guitar sales by region and by guitar type (Table 1-12). Use the concepts and techniques presented in this project to create the worksheet and chart.

Table 1-12	Blue Suede Music Company Data			
	NORTH	EAST	WEST	SOUTH
Classical	6734	7821	4123	7989
Steel String	5423	2134	6574	3401
Electric	3495	6291	7345	7098
Bass	5462	2923	8034	5135

2 ▶ The number of new cars and trucks has increased each year from 1996 through 2000, as indicated in Table 1-13. Create a worksheet and 3-D Column chart that illustrates these increases. Show model year and type car and truck totals. Use the concepts and techniques presented in this project to create the worksheet and chart.

Table 1-13	1996 - 2000 New Cars and Trucks Data			
YEAR	DOMESTIC CARS*	IMPORT CARS*	DOMESTIC TRUCKS*	IMPORT TRUCKS*
1996	7,323	2,231	6,125	225
1997	7,498	2,356	6,315	257
1998	7,615	2,489	6,727	313
1999	7,734	2,501	6,501	407
2000	7,944	2,578	6,623	661
* in thousands				

Cases and Places

3 ▸ You are a teaching assistant for the Computer Information Systems department. The department head has asked you to take her grade ledger (Table 1-14), which shows her grade distributions for all her spring classes, and separate them into categories based on the class and the grade. She wants a worksheet and 3-D Column chart to make it easier to view the grades as well as the totals at a glance. Use the concepts and techniques presented in this project to create the worksheet and chart.

Table 1-14	Semester Grade Summary			
GRADE	CIS 104	CIS 205	CIS 299	CIS 331
A	2	1	4	2
B	22	7	2	3
C	15	10	11	9
D	20	5	15	6
F	11	8	19	3

4 ▸ The CheeseHeads restaurant in Green Bay, Wisconsin is trying to decide whether it is feasible to open another restaurant in the neighboring community of Oshkosh, Wisconsin. The owner, G. B. Pack, has asked you to develop a worksheet totaling all the revenue received last year. The revenue by quarter is: Quarter 1, $94,342.98; Quarter 2, $81,500.65; Quarter 3, $158,220.09; and Quarter 4, $225,435.50. Create a 3-D Pie chart to illustrate revenue contribution by quarter. Use the AutoCalculate area to find the average annual revenue.

5 ▸▸ The Palace Theater is a small movie house that shows almost-current releases at weekday evening, weekend matinee, and weekend evening screenings. Three types of tickets are sold at each presentation: general admission, senior citizen, and children. The theater management has asked you to prepare a worksheet, based on the revenue from a typical week, that can be used in reevaluating its ticket structure. During an average week, weekday evening shows generate $7,540 from general admission ticket sales, $3,575 from senior citizen ticket sales, and $1,375 from children ticket sales. Weekend matinee shows make $5,500 from general admission ticket sales, $1,950 from senior citizen ticket sales, and $2,500 from children ticket sales. Weekend evening shows earn $8,540 from general admission ticket sales, $7,350 from senior citizen ticket sales, and $1,100 from children ticket sales. Use the concepts and techniques presented in this project to prepare a worksheet that includes total revenues for each type of ticket and for each presentation time, and a Bar chart illustrating ticket revenues.

6 ▸▸▸ Some academic disciplines appear to attract more students of one gender than the other. Visit the Registrar's office at your school and find out how many males and how many females have declared majors in five disciplines. Using this information, create a worksheet showing the number of male, female, and total number of majors in each discipline. Include totals for each numeric column. Include a Column chart to illustrate your data.

Access 2000

Microsoft **Access 2000**

Microsoft Access 2000

Creating a Database Using Design and Datasheet Views

OBJECTIVES

You will have mastered the material in this project when you can:

- Describe databases and database management systems
- Start Access
- Describe the features of the Access screen
- Create a database
- Create a table
- Define the fields in a table
- Open a table
- Add records to an empty table
- Close a table
- Close a database and quit Access
- Open a database
- Add records to a nonempty table
- Print the contents of a table
- Use a form to view data
- Create a custom report
- Use Microsoft Access Help
- Design a database to eliminate redundancy

A Match Made in Computer Heaven

Mentoring Unites Experts and Schools

E ducational issues dominate the airwaves and print media. From decorum in the classroom to equal access to the Internet, school-related topics are broadcast on the evening news and published in the morning newspapers. Then discussions take place around family dinner tables and at study sessions. Often these dialogues focus on improving the classroom experience by strengthening the relationship among educators, students, community members, and funding sources.

One effective way of enriching the learning process is to involve various groups in education. For example, college students are earning federal work-study funds by helping students in elementary grades learn to read and do math in the America Reads and the America Counts programs. More than 900 public schools have received grants in the 21st Century Community Learning Centers program to provide safe places for children to gather. Business leaders critique middle school students' writing samples as part of the National School Network Exchange, a grant-funded program that links more than 500 schools, companies, museums, and governmental agencies via the Internet.

In mythology, Mentor advised Odysseus, who lead the Greeks in the Trojan War. In today's world, mentors advise people needing direction and coaching. These partnerships are common in the computer field. For example, network experts collaborate with a culturally diverse school district to network classrooms throughout the region. Technology buffs develop a distance education program for students living in remote areas. Software experts install donated copies of Microsoft Office in computer labs and then train teachers.

Building these partnerships requires superb technological and organizational skills, strong marketing, and dedicated staff members. Various local, regional, and national organizations have the right mix of technology expertise and qualified personnel to meet these requirements. The nation's largest nonprofit computerization assistance center, CompuMentor, is one of these successful partnering organizations. CompuMentor has linked its staff with more than 6,000 schools and other nonprofit organizations since 1987.

The heart of its success is matching computer experts with the appropriate school or organization. Some mentors volunteer long term, while others agree to work intensively for a few days, particularly in telecommunications areas. Potential mentors complete an application at CompuMentor's Web site (www.compumentor.org) by entering specific information in boxes, called fields, pertaining to their knowledge of operating systems, networking, and hardware repair. They give additional information about their available working hours, training experience, and special skills in office and accounting applications, databases, and desktop publishing.

This information structures records in the CompuMentor database. The staff then can search these records to find a volunteer whose skills match the school's or organization's needs. Similarly, in Project 1, you will use the Access database management system to enter records in the Bavant Marine Services database so the marina staff can match service technicians with boat owners whose vessels need repairs.

Uniting schools with appropriate experts increases awareness of educational issues and ultimately improves the learning process. For more information on building mentoring relationships, visit the U.S. Department of Education Web site (www.ed.gov) or call 1-800-USA-LEARN.

Microsoft Access 2000

Creating a Database Using Design and Datasheet Views

C A S E   P E R S P E C T I V E

With the popularity of water sports increasing, the number of recreational boaters has risen dramatically! Boats come in all shapes and sizes and are often stored at a marina.

Larger, full-service marinas typically have a service department. The department performs the requested work, such as engine repair, and bills the owner's account. Smaller marinas usually cannot provide on-site service departments, but can offer the same convenience to boat owners by contracting with Bavant Marine Services. A boat owner requiring service notifies the marina, which then contacts Bavant. Bavant sends a technician to perform the required labor and bills the marina.

To ensure operations run smoothly, Bavant Marine Services needs to maintain data on its technicians and their assigned marinas. Bavant wants to organize the data in a database, managed by a database management system such as Access. In this way, Bavant can keep its data current and accurate while management can analyze the data for trends and produce a variety of useful reports. Your task is to help Bavant Marine Services in creating and using their database.

What Is Microsoft Access 2000?

Microsoft Access 2000 is a powerful database management system (DBMS) that functions in the Windows environment and allows you to create and process data in a database. Some of the key features are:

- **Data entry and update** Access provides easy mechanisms for adding data, changing data, and deleting data, including the ability to make mass changes in a single operation.
- **Queries** (questions) Using Access, it is easy to ask complex questions concerning the data in the database and receive instant answers.
- **Forms** In Access, you can produce attractive and useful forms for viewing and updating data.
- **Reports** Access contains a feature to allow you to easily create sophisticated reports for presenting your data.
- **Web Support** Access allows you to save objects (reports, tables) in HTML format so they can be viewed using a browser. You also can create data access pages to allow real-time access to data in the database via the Internet.

Project One — Bavant Marine Services Database

Creating, storing, sorting, and retrieving data are important tasks. In their personal lives, many people keep a variety of records such as names, addresses, and telephone numbers of friends and business associates, records of investments, records of expenses for tax purposes, and so on. These records must be arranged for quick access. Businesses also must be able to store and access information quickly and easily. Personnel and inventory records, payroll information, client records, order data, and accounts receivable information all are crucial and must be available readily.

The term **database** describes a collection of data organized in a manner that allows access, retrieval, and use of that data. A database management system, such as Access, allows you to use a computer to create a database; add, change, and delete data in the database; sort the data in the database; retrieve data in the database; and create forms and reports using the data in the database.

In Access, a database consists of a collection of tables. Figure 1-1 shows a sample database for Bavant Marine Services. It consists of two tables. The Marina table contains information about the marinas that Bavant Marine Services provides service for. Each marina is assigned to a specific technician. The Technician table contains information about the technicians to whom these marinas are assigned.

fields

marinas of technician Trista Anderson

Marina table

MARINA NUMBER	NAME	ADDRESS	CITY	STATE	ZIP CODE	WARRANTY	NON-WARRANTY	TECH NUMBER
AD57	Alan's Docks	314 Central	Burton	MI	49611	$1,248.00	$597.75	23
AN75	Afton's Marina	21 West 8th	Glenview	MI	48121	$1,906.50	$831.25	36
BL72	Brite's Landing	281 Robin	Burton	MI	49611	$217.00	$0.00	36
EL25	Elend Marina	462 River	Torino	MI	48268	$413.50	$678.75	49
FB96	Fenton's Boats	36 Bayview	Cavela	MI	47926	$923.20	$657.50	23
FM22	Fedder Marina	283 Waterfront	Burton	MI	49611	$432.00	$0.00	36
JB92	JT Boat Club	28 Causeway	Torino	MI	48268	$0.00	$0.00	36
NW72	Nelson's Wharf	27 Lake	Masondale	MI	49832	$608.50	$520.00	23
SM72	Solton's Marine	867 Bay Ridge	Glenview	MI	48121	$462.50	$295.00	49
TR72	The Reef	92 East Bay	Woodview	MI	47212	$219.00	$0.00	36

records

Technician table

TECH NUMBER	LAST NAME	FIRST NAME	ADDRESS	CITY	STATE	ZIP CODE	HOURLY RATE	YTD EARNINGS
23	Anderson	Trista	283 Belton	Port Anton	MI	47989	$24.00	$17,862.00
36	Nichols	Ashton	978 Richmond	Hewitt	MI	47618	$21.00	$19,560.00
49	Gomez	Teresa	2855 Parry	Ashley	MI	47711	$22.00	$21,211.50

technician Trista Anderson

FIGURE 1-1

More *About*

Databases in Access 2000

In some DBMS's, every table, query, form, or report is stored in a separate file. This is not the case in Access 2000, in which a database is stored in a single file on disk. The file contains all the tables, queries, forms, reports, and programs that you create for this database.

The rows in the tables are called **records**. A record contains information about a given person, product, or event. A row in the Marina table, for example, contains information about a specific marina.

The columns in the tables are called fields. A **field** contains a specific piece of information within a record. In the Marina table, for example, the fourth field, City, contains the city where the marina is located.

The first field in the Marina table is the Marina Number. This is a code assigned by Bavant Marine Services to each marina. Like many organizations, Bavant Marine Services calls it a *number* although it actually contains letters. The marina numbers have a special format. They consist of two uppercase letters followed by a two-digit number.

These numbers are unique; that is, no two marinas will be assigned the same number. Such a field can be used as a **unique identifier**. This simply means that a given marina number will appear only in a single record in the table. Only one record exists, for example, in which the marina number is BL72. A unique identifier also is called a **primary key**. Thus, the Marina Number field is the primary key for the Marina table.

The next eight fields in the Marina table are Name, Address, City, State, Zip Code, Warranty, Non-warranty, and Tech Number. The Warranty field contains the amount billed to the Marina that should be covered by the boat owner's warranty. The Non-warranty field contains the amount that is not covered by warranty.

For example, marina AD57 is Alan's Docks. It is located at 314 Central in Burton, Michigan. The zip code is 49611. The marina has been billed $1,248.00 that should be covered by warranty and $597.75 that will not be covered by warranty.

Each marina is assigned to a single technician. The last field in the Marina table, Tech Number, gives the number of the marina's technician.

The first field in the Technician table, Tech Number, is the number assigned by Bavant Marine Services to the technician. These numbers are unique, so Tech Number is the primary key of the Technician table.

The other fields in the Technician table are Last Name, First Name, Address, City, State, Zip Code, Hourly Rate, and YTD Earnings. The Hourly Rate field gives the technician's hourly billing rate, and the YTD Earnings field contains the total amount that has been paid to the technician for services so far this year.

For example, Technician 23 is Trista Anderson. She lives at 283 Belton in Port Anton, Michigan. Her zip code is 47989. Her hourly billing rate is $24.00 and her YTD earnings are $17,862.00.

The tech number displays in both the Marina table and the Technician table. It is used to relate marinas and technicians. For example, in the Marina table, you see that the tech number for marina AD57 is 23. To find the name of this technician, look for the row in the Technician table that contains 23 in the Tech Number field. Once you have found it, you know the marina is assigned to Trista Anderson. To find all the marinas assigned to Trista Anderson, on the other hand, look through the Marina table for all the marinas that contain 23 in the Tech Number field. Her marinas are AD57 (Alan's Docks), FB96 (Fenton's Boats), and NW72 (Nelson's Wharf).

Together with the management of Bavant Marine Services, you have determined the data that must be maintained in the database is that shown in Figure 1-1 on page A 1.7. You first must create the database and the tables it contains. In the process, you must define the fields included in the two tables, as well as the type of data each field will contain. You then must add the appropriate records to the tables. You also must print the contents of the tables. Finally, you must create a report with the Marina Number, Name, Warranty, and Non-warranty fields for each marina served by Bavant Marine Services. Other reports and requirements for the database at Bavant Marine Services will be addressed with the Bavant Marine Services management in the future.

Starting Access and Creating a New Database

In Access, all the tables, reports, forms, and queries that you create are stored in a single file called a database. Thus before creating any of these objects, you must first start Access and create the database that will hold them. To start Access, first make sure that Windows is running. Once you have done so, perform the following steps to start Access, create a new database, and save the database on a floppy disk.

More About

Creating a Database

Access 2000 includes a Database Wizard that can guide you by suggesting some commonly used databases. If you already know the tables and fields you need, however, you simply create the database yourself. For more information, visit the Access 2000 More About Web page (www.scsite.com/ac2000/more.htm) and then click Database Wizard.

 To Start Access

1 **Place a formatted floppy disk in drive A, click the Start button, and then point to New Office Document on the Start menu.**

The Start menu displays (Figure 1-2).

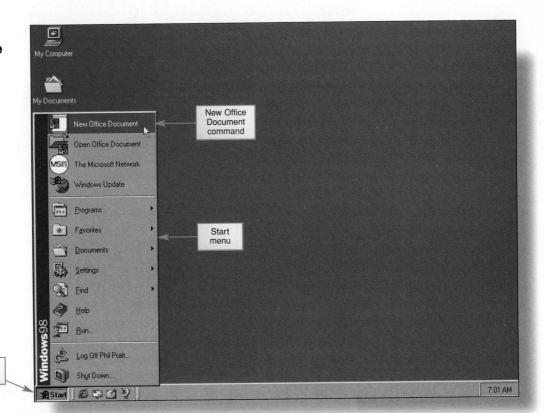

FIGURE 1-2

2 Click New Office Document. If the General tab is not selected, that is, if it does not display in front of the other tabs, click the General tab. Click the Blank Database icon and then point to the OK button.

The New Office Document dialog box displays (Figure 1-3). The Blank Database icon is selected.

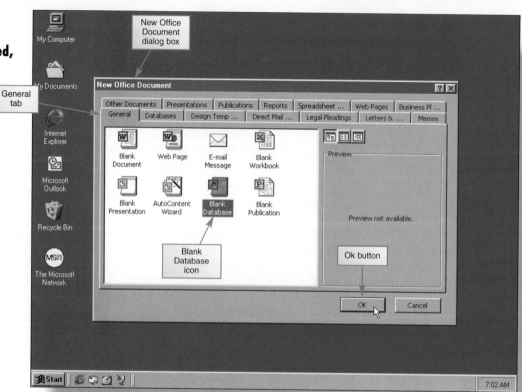

FIGURE 1-3

3 Click the OK button and then point to the Save in box arrow.

The File New Database dialog box displays (Figure 1-4).

FIGURE 1-4

4 **Click the Save in box arrow and then point to 3½ Floppy (A:).**

The Save in list displays (Figure 1-5).

FIGURE 1-5

5 **Click 3½ Floppy (A:). Click the File name text box. Repeatedly press the BACKSPACE key to delete db1 (your number may be different) and then type** Bavant Marine Services **as the file name. Point to the Create button.**

The file name is changed to Bavant Marine Services (Figure 1-6).

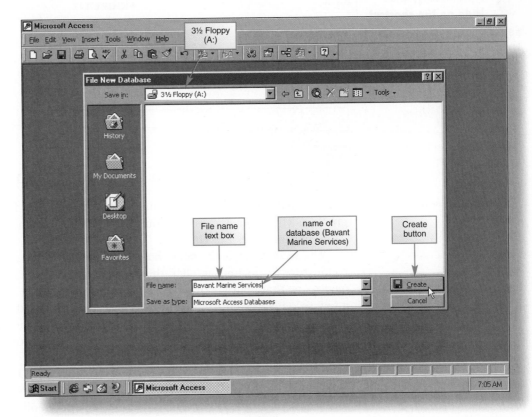

FIGURE 1-6

6 **Click the Create button to create the database. If the Office Assistant displays, right-click the Office Assistant and then point to Hide on the shortcut menu.**

*The Bavant Marine Services database is created. The Bavant Marine Services : Database window displays on the desktop (Figure 1-7). The **Office Assistant,** a tool you can use to obtain help while working with Microsoft Access may display. (You will see how to use the Office Assistant later in this project.)*

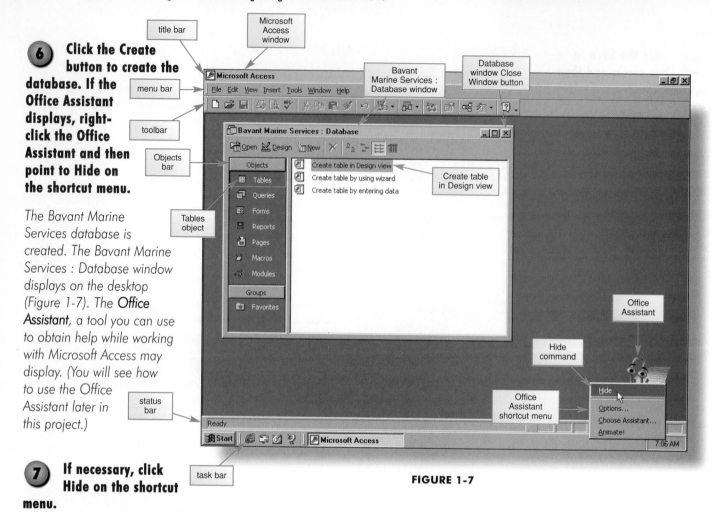

FIGURE 1-7

7 **If necessary, click Hide on the shortcut menu.**

The Office Assistant no longer displays.

Other Ways

1. Right-click Start button, click Open, double-click New Office Document
2. On Start menu click Programs, click Microsoft Access

More About 2000

Toolbars

Normally, the correct Access 2000 toolbar automatically will display. If it does not, click View on the menu bar, and then click Toolbars. Click the toolbar for the activity in which you are engaged. See Appendix C for additional details.

The Access Desktop and the Database Window

The first bar on the desktop (Figure 1-7) is the **title bar.** It displays the title of the product, Microsoft Access. The button on the right is the **Close button.** Clicking the Close button closes the window.

The second bar is the **menu bar.** It contains a list of menu names. To open a menu from the menu bar, click the menu name. Initially a personalized version of the menu, one that consists of commands you have selected most recently, displays. After a few seconds, the entire menu displays. If the command you wish to select is on the personalized menu, you can select it immediately. If not, wait a few seconds to view the entire menu. (The menus shown throughout this book are the full menus, the ones that display after a few seconds.)

The third bar is the **Database window toolbar.** The Database window toolbar contains buttons that allow you to perform certain tasks more quickly than using the menu bar. Each button contains a picture, or **icon,** depicting its function. The specific buttons on the Database window toolbar will vary, depending on the task on which you are working.

The **taskbar** at the bottom of the screen displays the Start button, any active windows, and the current time.

Immediately above the Windows taskbar is the **status bar** (Figure 1-7). It contains special information that is appropriate for the task on which you are working. Currently, it contains the word, Ready, which means Access is ready to accept commands.

The **Database window**, referred to in Figure 1-7 as the Bavant Marine Services : Database window, is a special window that allows you to access easily and rapidly a variety of objects such as tables, queries, forms, and reports. To do so, you will use the various components of the window.

Creating a Table

An Access database consists of a collection of tables. Once you have created the database, you must create each of the tables within it. In this project, for example, you must create both the Marina and Technician tables shown in Figure 1-1 on page A 1.7.

To create a table, you describe the **structure** of the table to Access by describing the fields within the table. For each field, you indicate the following:

1. **Field name** — Each field in the table must have a unique name. In the Marina table (Figure 1-8), for example, the field names are Marina Number, Name, Address, City, State, Zip Code, Warranty, Non-warranty, and Tech Number.

> **More About**
>
> **Creating a Table**
>
> Access 2000 includes **Table Wizards** that guide you by suggesting some commonly used tables and fields. If you already know the fields you need, however, it usually is easier to simply create the table yourself. For more information, visit the Access 2000 More About Web page (www.scsite.com/ac2000/ more.htm) and then click Table Wizards.

Structure of Marina table

FIELD NAME	DATA TYPE	FIELD SIZE	PRIMARY KEY?	DESCRIPTION
Marina Number	Text	4	Yes	Marina Number (Primary Key)
Name	Text	20		Marina Name
Address	Text	15		Street Address
City	Text	15		City
State	Text	2		State (Two-Character Abbreviation)
Zip Code	Text	5		Zip Code (Five-Character Version)
Warranty	Currency			Current Warranty Amount
Non-warranty	Currency			Current Non-warranty Amount
Tech Number	Text	2		Number of Marina's Technician

Data for Marina table

MARINA NUMBER	NAME	ADDRESS	CITY	STATE	ZIP CODE	WARRANTY	NON-WARRANTY	TECH NUMBER
AD57	Alan's Docks	314 Central	Burton	MI	49611	$1,248.00	$597.75	23
AN75	Afton's Marina	21 West 8th	Glenview	MI	48121	$1,906.50	$831.25	36
BL72	Brite's Landing	281 Robin	Burton	MI	49611	$217.00	$0.00	36
EL25	Elend Marina	462 River	Torino	MI	48268	$413.50	$678.75	49
FB96	Fenton's Boats	36 Bayview	Cavela	MI	47926	$923.20	$657.50	23
FM22	Fedder Marina	283 Waterfront	Burton	MI	49611	$432.00	$0.00	36
JB92	JT Boat Club	28 Causeway	Torino	MI	48268	$0.00	$0.00	36
NW72	Nelson's Wharf	27 Lake	Masondale	MI	49832	$608.50	$520.00	23
SM72	Solton's Marine	867 Bay Ridge	Glenview	MI	48121	$462.50	$295.00	49
TR72	The Reef	92 East Bay	Woodview	MI	47212	$219.00	$0.00	36

FIGURE 1-8

Data Types (General)

Different database management systems have different available data types. Even data types that are essentially the same can have different names. The Access 2000 Text data type, for example, is referred to as Character in some systems and Alpha in others.

Data Types (Access 2000)

Access 2000 offers a wide variety of data types, some of which have special options associated with them. For more information on data types, visit the Access 2000 More About Web page (www.scsite.com/ac2000/more.htm) and then click Data Types.

2. **Data type** — Data type indicates to Access the type of data the field will contain. Some fields can contain letters of the alphabet and numbers. Others contain only numbers. Others, such as Warranty and Non-warranty, can contain numbers and dollar signs.
3. **Description** — Access allows you to enter a detailed description of the field.

You also can assign field widths to text fields (fields whose data type is Text). This indicates the maximum number of characters that can be stored in the field. If you do not assign a width to such a field, Access assumes the width is 50.

You also must indicate which field or fields make up the **primary key**; that is, the unique identifier, for the table. In the sample database, the Marina Number field is the primary key of the Marina table and the Tech Number field is the primary key of the Technician table.

The rules for field names are:

1. Names can be up to 64 characters in length.
2. Names can contain letters, digits, and spaces, as well as most of the punctuation symbols.
3. Names cannot contain periods, exclamation points (!), or square brackets ([ ]).
4. The same name cannot be used for two different fields in the same table.

Each field has a **data type**. This indicates the type of data that can be stored in the field. The data types you will use in this project are:

1. **Text** — The field can contain any characters.
2. **Number** — The field can contain only numbers. The numbers either can be positive or negative. Fields are assigned this type so they can be used in arithmetic operations. Fields that contain numbers but will not be used for arithmetic operations usually are assigned a data type of Text. The Tech Number field, for example, is a text field because the tech numbers will not be involved in any arithmetic.
3. **Currency** — The field can contain only dollar amounts. The values will be displayed with dollar signs, commas, decimal points, and with two digits following the decimal point. Like numeric fields, you can use currency fields in arithmetic operations. Access assigns a size to currency fields automatically.

The field names, data types, field widths, primary key information, and descriptions for the Marina table are shown in Figure 1-8. With this information, you are ready to begin creating the table. To create the table, use the following steps.

Steps To Create a Table

 1 **Right-click Create table in Design view and then point to Open on the shortcut menu.**

The shortcut menu for creating a table in Design view displays (Figure 1-9).

FIGURE 1-9

2 Click Open.

The Table1 : Table window displays (Figure 1-10).

3 Click the Maximize button for the Table1 : Table window.

A maximized Table1 : Table window displays.

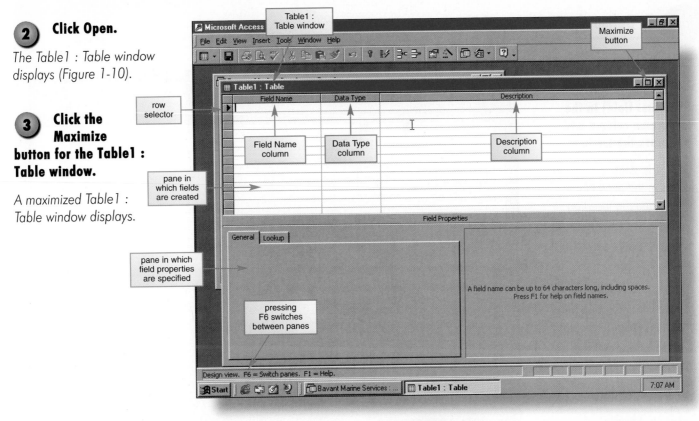

FIGURE 1-10

Defining the Fields

The next step in creating the table is to define the fields by specifying the required details in the Table window. Make entries in the Field Name, Data Type, and Description columns. Enter additional information in the Field Properties box in the lower portion of the Table window. Press the F6 key to move from the upper **pane** (portion of the screen), the one where you define the fields, to the lower pane, the one where you define field properties. Enter the appropriate field size and then press the F6 key to return to the upper pane. As you define the fields, the row selector (Figure 1-10) indicates the field you currently are describing. The **row selector** is a small box or bar that, when clicked, selects the entire row. It is positioned on the first field, indicating Access is ready for you to enter the name of the first field in the Field Name column.

Perform the steps on the next page to define the fields in the table.

Other Ways

1. Click New Object: AutoForm button arrow on Database window toolbar, click Table
2. On Insert menu click Table
3. Double-click Create table in Design view
4. Press ALT+N

More About

Primary Keys

In some cases, the primary key consists of a combination of fields rather than a single field. For more information on determining primary keys in such situations, visit the Access 2000 More About Web page (www.scsite.com/ac2000/more.htm) and then click Primary Key.

To Define the Fields in a Table

1 **Type** Marina Number **(the name of the first field) in the Field Name column and then press the TAB key.**

The words, Marina Number, display in the Field Name column and the insertion point advances to the Data Type column, indicating you can enter the data type (Figure 1-11). The word, Text, one of the possible data types, currently displays. The arrow in the Data Type column indicates a list of data types is available by clicking the arrow.

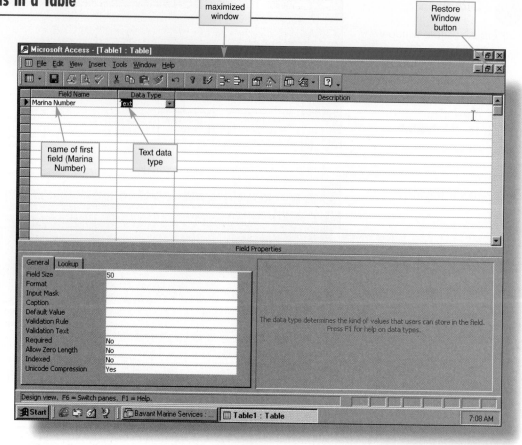

FIGURE 1-11

2 **Because Text is the correct data type, press the TAB key to move the insertion point to the Description column, type** Marina Number (Primary Key) **as the description and then point to the Primary Key button on the Database window toolbar.**

A ScreenTip, which is a description of the button, displays partially obscuring the description of the first field (Figure 1-12).

FIGURE 1-12

3 Click the Primary Key button to make Marina Number the primary key and then press the F6 key to move the insertion point to the Field Size text box.

The Marina Number field is the primary key as indicated by the key symbol that displays in the row selector (Figure 1-13). The current entry in the Field Size text box (50) is selected.

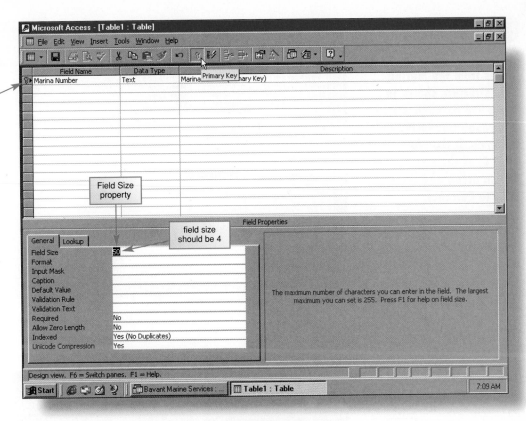

FIGURE 1-13

4 Type 4 as the size of the Marina Number field. Press the F6 key to return to the Description column for the Marina Number field and then press the TAB key to move to the Field Name column in the second row.

The row selector moves to the second row just below the field name Marina Number (Figure 1-14).

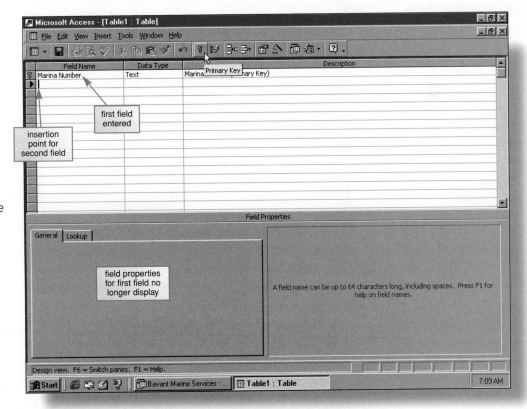

FIGURE 1-14

5 Use the techniques illustrated in Steps 1 through 4 to make the entries from the Marina table structure shown in Figure 1-8 on page A 1.13 up through and including the name of the Warranty field. Click the Data Type column arrow and then point to Currency.

The additional fields are entered (Figure 1-15). A list of available data types displays in the Data Type column for the Warranty field.

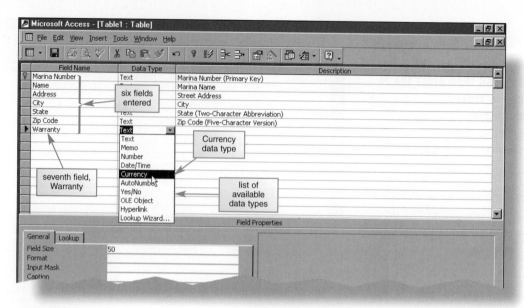

FIGURE 1-15

6 Click Currency and then press the TAB key. Make the remaining entries from the Marina table structure shown in Figure 1-8.

The fields are all entered (Figure 1-16).

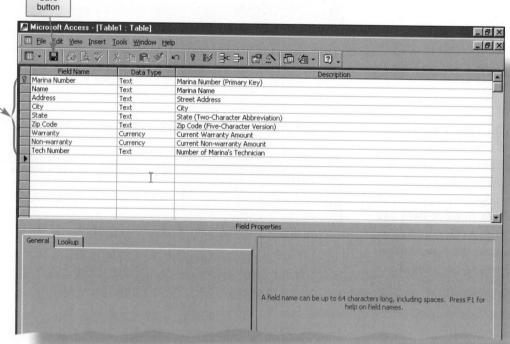

FIGURE 1-16

Correcting Errors in the Structure

When creating a table, check the entries carefully to ensure they are correct. If you make a mistake and discover it before you press the TAB key, you can correct the error by repeatedly pressing the BACKSPACE key until the incorrect characters are removed. Then, type the correct characters. If you do not discover a mistake until later, you can click the entry, type the correct value, and then press the ENTER key.

If you accidentally add an extra field to the structure, select the field by clicking the row selector (the leftmost column on the row that contains the field to be deleted). Once you have selected the field, press the DELETE key. This will remove the field from the structure.

If you forget a field, select the field that will follow the field you wish to add by clicking the row selector, and then press the INSERT key. The remaining fields move down one row, making room for the missing field. Make the entries for the new field in the usual manner.

If you made the wrong field a primary key field, click the correct primary key entry for the field and then click the Primary Key button on the Database window toolbar.

As an alternative to these steps, you may want to start over. To do so, click the Close button for the Table1 : Table window and then click No. The original desktop displays and you can repeat the process you used earlier.

More About

Correcting Errors

Even after you have entered data, it still is possible to correct errors in the structure. Access 2000 will make all the necessary adjustments to the structure of the table as well as to the data within it. (It is simplest to make the correction, however, before any data is entered.)

Saving a Table

The Marina table structure now is complete. The final step is to save the table within the database. At this time, you should give the table a name.

Table names are from one to 64 characters in length and can contain letters, numbers, and spaces. The two table names in this project are Marina and Technician.

To save the table, complete the following steps.

Steps To Save a Table

1 **Click the Save button on the Database window toolbar (see Figure 1-16 on page A 1.18). Type** Marina **as the name of the table in the Table Name text box and then point to the OK button.**

The Save As dialog box displays (Figure 1-17). The name of the table displays in the Table Name text box.

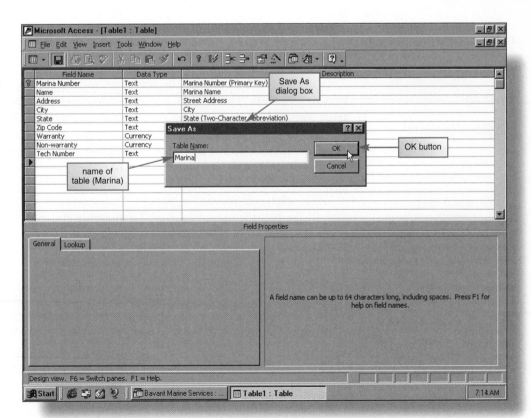

FIGURE 1-17

2 **Click the OK button and then point to the Close Window button for the Marina : Table window.**

The table is saved on the floppy disk in drive A. The name of the table is now Marina as indicated on the title bar (Figure 1-18).

3 **Click the Close Window button for the Marina : Table window. (Be sure not to click the Close button on the Microsoft Access title bar, because this would close Microsoft Access.)**

The Marina : Table window no longer displays.

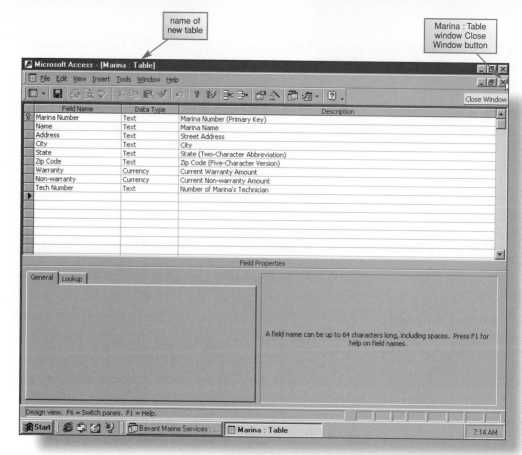

name of new table

Marina : Table window Close Window button

FIGURE 1-18

More *About*

Adding Records

As soon as you have entered or modified a record and moved to another record, the original record is saved. This is different from other tools. The rows entered in a spreadsheet, for example, are not saved until the entire spreadsheet is saved.

Adding Records to a Table

Creating a table by building the structure and saving the table is the first step in a two-step process. The second step is to add records to the table. To add records to a table, the table must be open. To open a table, right-click the table in the Database window and then click Open on the shortcut menu. The table displays in Datasheet view. In **Datasheet view**, the table is represented as a collection of rows and columns called a **datasheet**. It looks very much like the tables shown in Figure 1-1 on page A 1.7.

You often add records in phases. You may, for example, not have enough time to add all the records in one session. To illustrate this process, this project begins by adding the first two records in the Marina table (Figure 1-19). The remaining records are added later.

Marina table (first 2 records)

MARINA NUMBER	NAME	ADDRESS	CITY	STATE	ZIP CODE	WARRANTY	NON-WARRANTY	TECH NUMBER
AD57	Alan's Docks	314 Central	Burton	MI	49611	$1,248.00	$597.75	23
AN75	Afton's Marina	21 West 8th	Glenview	MI	48121	$1,906.50	$831.25	36

FIGURE 1-19

To open the Marina table and then add records, use the following steps.

Steps To Add Records to a Table

1 **Right-click Marina in the Bavant Marine Services : Database window and then point to Open on the shortcut menu.**

The shortcut menu for the Marina table displays (Figure 1-20). The Bavant Marine Services : Database window is maximized because the previous window, the Marina : Table window, was maximized. (If you wanted to restore the Database window to its original size, you would click the Restore Window button.)

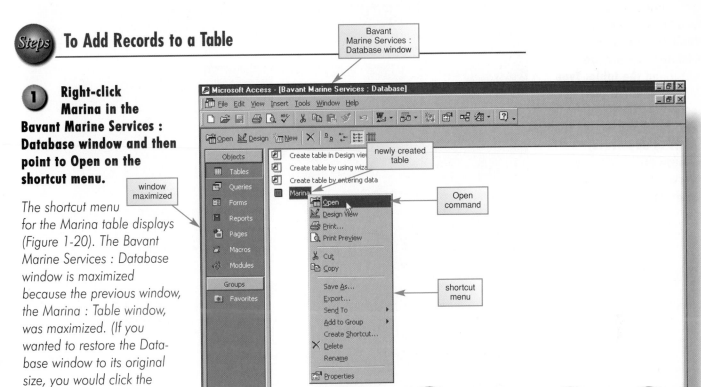

FIGURE 1-20

2 **Click Open on the shortcut menu.**

The Marina : Table window displays (Figure 1-21). The window contains the Datasheet view for the Marina table. The **record selector** is positioned on the first record. The record selector is the small box or bar to the left of the record. The status bar at the bottom of the window also indicates that the record selector is positioned on record 1.

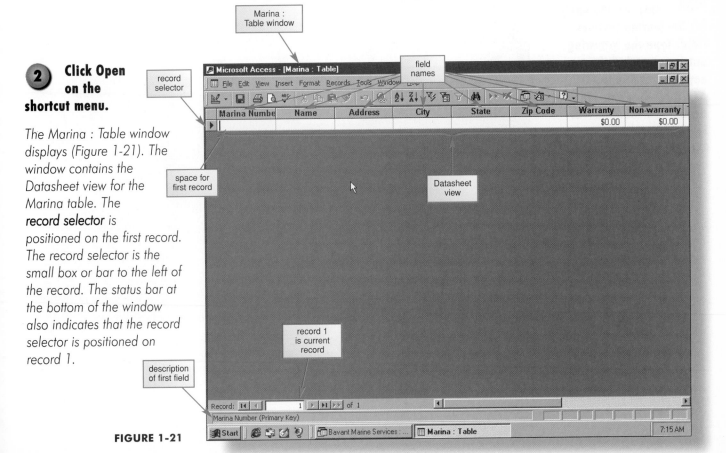

FIGURE 1-21

3 If your window is not already maximized, click the Maximize button to maximize the window containing the table. Type AD57 as the first marina number, as shown in Figure 1-19. Be sure you type the letters in uppercase, because that is the way they are to be entered in the database.

The marina number is entered, but the insertion point is still in the Marina Number field (Figure 1-22).

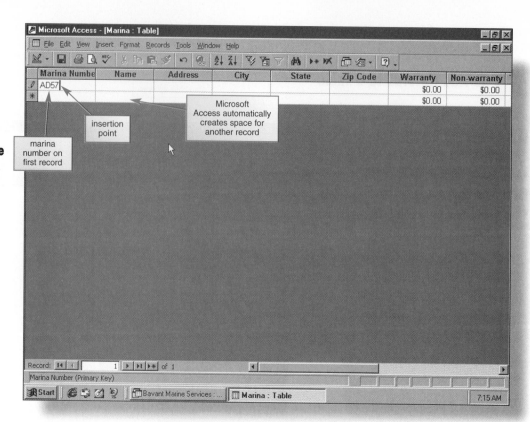

FIGURE 1-22

4 Press the TAB key to complete the entry for the Marina Number field. Type the following entries, pressing the TAB key after each one: Alan's Docks as the name, 314 Central as the address, Burton as the city, MI as the state, and 49611 as the zip code.

The Name, Address, City, State, and Zip Code fields are entered (Figure 1-23).

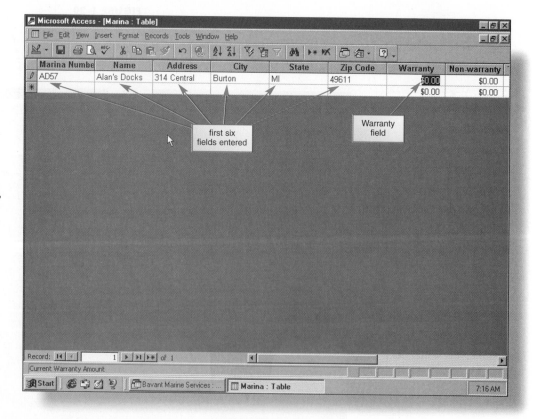

FIGURE 1-23

5 Type 1248 as the warranty amount and then press the TAB key. (You do not need to type dollar signs or commas. In addition, because the digits to the right of the decimal point were both zeros, you did not need to type the decimal point.) Type 597.75 as the non-warranty amount and then press the TAB key. Type 23 as the tech number to complete the record.

The fields have shifted to the left (Figure 1-24). The Warranty and Non-warranty values display with dollar signs and decimal points. The insertion point is positioned in the Tech Number field.

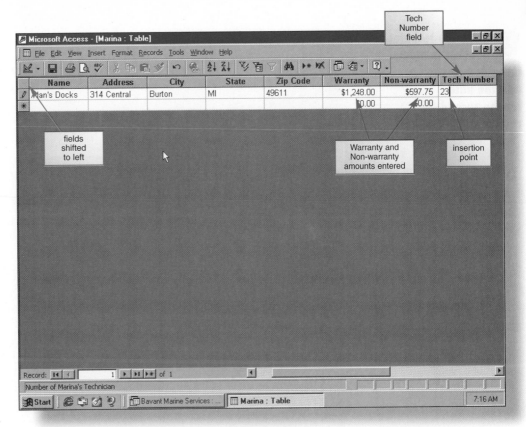

FIGURE 1-24

6 Press the TAB key.

The fields shift back to the right, the record is saved, and the insertion point moves to the marina number on the second row (Figure 1-25).

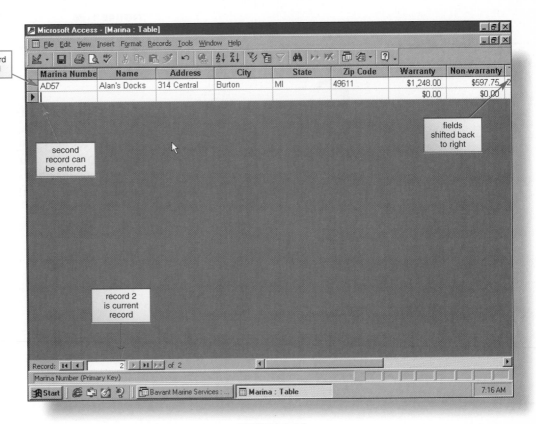

FIGURE 1-25

7 Use the techniques shown in Steps 3 through 6 to add the data for the second record in Figure 1-19.

The second record is added and the insertion point moves to the marina number on the third row (Figure 1-26).

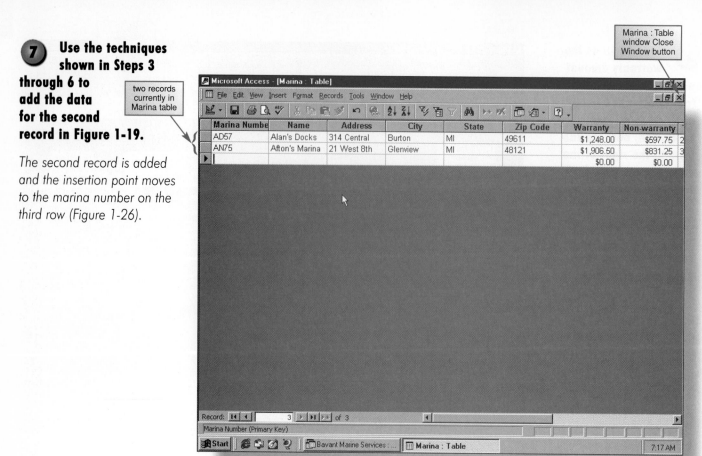

FIGURE 1-26

Closing a Table and a Database and Quitting Access

It is a good idea to close a table as soon as you have finished working with it. It keeps the screen from getting cluttered and prevents you from making accidental changes to the data in the table. If you no longer will work with the database, you should close the database as well. With the creation of the Marina table complete, you can quit Access at this point.

Perform the following steps to close the table and the database and then quit Access.

To Close a Table and Database and Quit Access

1 **Click the Close Window button for the Marina : Table window (see Figure 1-26 on page A 1.24).**

The datasheet for the Marina table no longer displays (Figure 1-27).

2 **Click the Close button for the Bavant Marine Services : Database window (see Figure 1-27).**

The Bavant Marine Services : Database window no longer displays.

3 **Click the Close button for the Microsoft Access window.**

The Microsoft Access window no longer displays.

FIGURE 1-27

Opening a Database

To work with any of the tables, reports, or forms in a database, the database must be open. To open a database from the Windows desktop, click Open Office Document on the Start menu by performing the following steps. (The Other Ways box indicates ways to open a database from within Access.)

To Open a Database

1 **Click the Start button and then point to Open Office Document (Figure 1-28).**

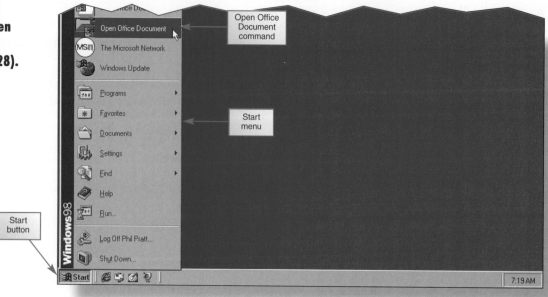

FIGURE 1-28

2 **Click Open Office Document. If necessary, click the Look in box arrow and then click 3½ Floppy (A:) in the Look in box. If it is not already selected, click the Bavant Marine Services database name. Point to the Open button.**

The Open Office Document dialog box displays (Figure 1-29). The 3½ Floppy (A:) folder displays in the Look in box and the files on the floppy disk in drive A display. Your list may be different.

3 **Click the Open button.**

The database opens and the Bavant Marine Services : Database window displays.

FIGURE 1-29

Other Ways

1. Click Open button on Database window toolbar
2. On File menu click Open
3. Press CTRL+O

Adding Additional Records

You can add records to a table that already contains data using a process almost identical to that used to add records to an empty table. The only difference is that you place the insertion point after the last data record before you enter the additional data. To do so, use the **Navigation buttons** found near the lower-left corner of the screen. The purpose of each of the Navigation buttons is described in Table 1-1.

Table 1-1	Navigation Buttons in Datasheet View
BUTTON	*PURPOSE*
First Record	Moves to the first record in the table
Previous Record	Moves to the previous record
Next Record	Moves to the next record
Last Record	Moves to the last record in the table
New Record	Moves to the end of the table to a position for entering a new record

Complete the following steps to add the remaining records (Figure 1-30) to the Marina table.

Marina table (last 8 records)								
MARINA NUMBER	*NAME*	*ADDRESS*	*CITY*	*STATE*	*ZIP CODE*	*WARRANTY*	*NON-WARRANTY*	*TECH NUMBER*
BL72	Brite's Landing	281 Robin	Burton	MI	49611	$217.00	$0.00	36
EL25	Elend Marina	462 River	Torino	MI	48268	$413.50	$678.75	49
FB96	Fenton's Boats	36 Bayview	Cavela	MI	47926	$923.20	$657.50	23
FM22	Fedder Marina	283 Waterfront	Burton	MI	49611	$432.00	$0.00	36
JB92	JT Boat Club	28 Causeway	Torino	MI	48268	$0.00	$0.00	36
NW72	Nelson's Wharf	27 Lake	Masondale	MI	49832	$608.50	$520.00	23
SM72	Solton's Marine	867 Bay Ridge	Glenview	MI	48121	$462.50	$295.00	49
TR72	The Reef	92 East Bay	Woodview	MI	47212	$219.00	$0.00	36

FIGURE 1-30

Steps | **To Add Additional Records to a Table**

1 **Right-click Marina in the Bavant Marine Services : Database window and then click Open on the shortcut menu.**

2 **When the Marina table displays, maximize the window by clicking the Maximize button. Point to the New Record button.**

The datasheet displays (Figure 1-31).

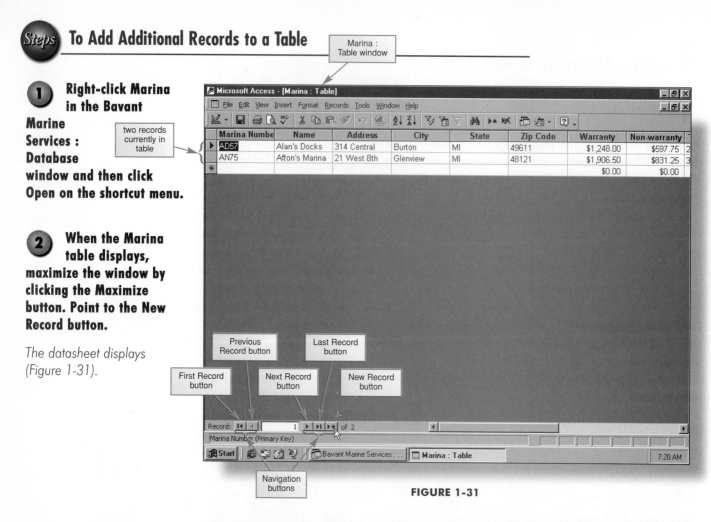

FIGURE 1-31

3 **Click the New Record button.**

Access places the insertion point in position to enter a new record (Figure 1-32).

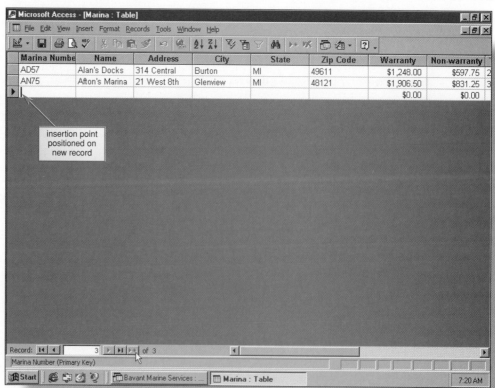

FIGURE 1-32

4 Add the remaining records from Figure 1-30 on page A 1.27 using the same techniques you used to add the first two records. Point to the Close Window button.

The additional records are added (Figure 1-33).

5 Click the Close Window button.

The window containing the table closes.

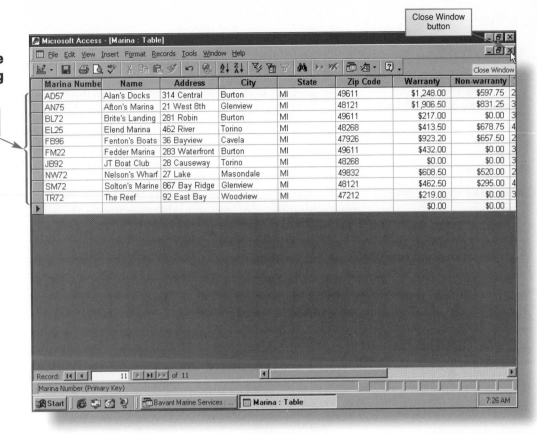

FIGURE 1-33

Correcting Errors in the Data

Check your entries carefully to ensure they are correct. If you make a mistake and discover it before you press the TAB key, correct it by pressing the BACKSPACE key until the incorrect characters are removed and then typing the correct characters.

If you discover an incorrect entry later, correct the error by clicking the incorrect entry and then making the appropriate correction. If the record you must correct is not on the screen, use the Navigation buttons (Next Record, Previous Record, and so on) to move to it. If the field you want to correct is not visible on the screen, use the horizontal scroll bar along the bottom of the screen to shift all the fields until the one you want displays. Then make the correction.

If you add an extra record accidentally, select the record by clicking the record selector that immediately precedes the record. Then, press the DELETE key. This will remove the record from the table. If you forget a record, add it using the same procedure as for all the other records. Access will place it in the correct location in the table automatically.

If you cannot determine how to correct the data, you are, in effect, stuck on the record. Access neither allows you to move to any other record until you have made the correction, nor allows you to close the table. If you encounter this situation, simply press the ESC key. Pressing the ESC key will remove from the screen the record you are trying to add. You then can move to any other record, close the table, or take any other action you desire.

Other Ways

1. Click New Record button on Database window toolbar
2. On Insert menu click New Record

Printing the Contents of a Table

You can change the paper size, paper source, or the printer that will be used to print the report. To change any of these, select the Page sheet in the Page Setup dialog box.

Previewing and Printing the Contents of a Table

When working with a database, you often will need to print a copy of the table contents. Figure 1-34 shows a printed copy of the contents of the Marina table. (Yours may look slightly different, depending on your printer.) Because the Marina table is wider substantially than the screen, it also will be wider than the normal printed page in portrait orientation. **Portrait orientation** means the printout is across the width of the page. **Landscape orientation** means the printout is across the length of the page. Thus, to print the wide database table, use landscape orientation. If you are printing the contents of a table that fits on the screen, you will not need landscape orientation. A convenient way to change to landscape orientation is to **preview** what the printed copy will look like by using Print Preview. This allows you to determine whether landscape orientation is necessary and, if it is, to change easily the orientation to landscape. In addition, you also can use Print Preview to determine whether any adjustments are necessary to the page margins.

Marina   9/7/2001

Marina Number	Name	Address	City	State	Zip Code	Warranty	Non-warranty	Tech Number
AD57	Alan's Docks	314 Central	Burton	MI	49611	$1,248.00	$597.75	23
AN75	Afton's Marina	21 West 8th	Glenview	MI	48121	$1,906.50	$831.25	36
BL72	Brite's Landing	281 Robin	Burton	MI	49611	$217.00	$0.00	36
EL25	Elend Marina	462 River	Torino	MI	48268	$413.50	$678.75	49
FB96	Fenton's Boats	36 Bayview	Cavela	MI	47926	$923.20	$657.50	23
FM22	Fedder Marina	283 Waterfront	Burton	MI	49611	$432.00	$0.00	36
JB92	JT Boat Club	28 Causeway	Torino	MI	48268	$0.00	$0.00	36
NW72	Nelson's Wharf	27 Lake	Masondale	MI	49832	$608.50	$520.00	23
SM72	Solton's Marina	867 Bay Ridge	Glenview	MI	48121	$462.50	$295.00	49
TR72	The Reef	92 East Bay	Woodview	MI	47212	$219.00	$0.00	36

Page 1

FIGURE 1-34

Perform the following steps to use Print Preview to preview and then print the Marina table.

 To Preview and Print the Contents of a Table

1 **Right-click Marina and then point to Print Preview on the shortcut menu.**

The shortcut menu for the Marina table displays (Figure 1-35).

FIGURE 1-35

2 **Click Print Preview on the shortcut menu. Point anywhere in the upper-right portion of the report.**

The preview of the report displays (Figure 1-36).

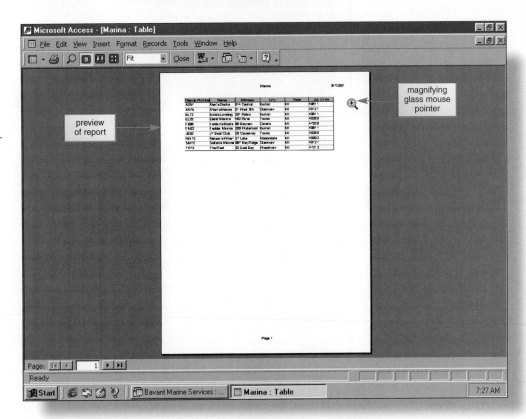

FIGURE 1-36

3 **Click the magnifying glass mouse pointer in the approximate position shown in Figure 1-36.**

The portion surrounding the mouse pointer is magnified (Figure 1-37). The last field that displays is the Zip Code field. The Warranty, Nonwarranty, and Tech Number fields do not display. To display the additional fields, you will need to switch to landscape orientation.

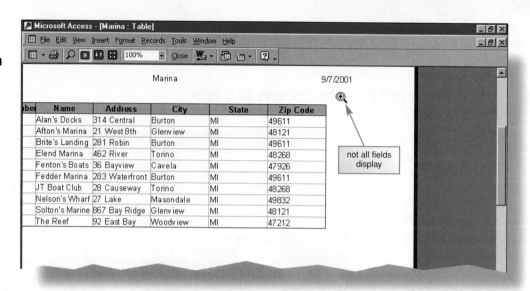

FIGURE 1-37

4 **Click File on the menu bar and then point to Page Setup. (Remember that you might have to wait a few seconds for the entire menu to display.)**

The File menu displays (Figure 1-38).

FIGURE 1-38

5 **Click Page Setup and then point to the Page tab.**

The Page Setup dialog box displays (Figure 1-39).

FIGURE 1-39

Step 6

Click the Page tab and then point to the Landscape option button.

The Page sheet displays (Figure 1-40). The Portrait option button currently is selected. (*Option button* refers to the round button that indicates choices in a dialog box. When the corresponding option is selected, the button contains within it a solid circle. Clicking an option button selects it, and deselects all others.)

FIGURE 1-40

Step 7

Click Landscape and then click the OK button. Click the mouse pointer anywhere within the report to view the entire report.

The orientation is changed to landscape as shown by the report that displays on the screen (Figure 1-41). The characters in the report are so small that it is difficult to determine whether all fields currently display. To zoom in on a portion of the report, click the desired portion of the report.

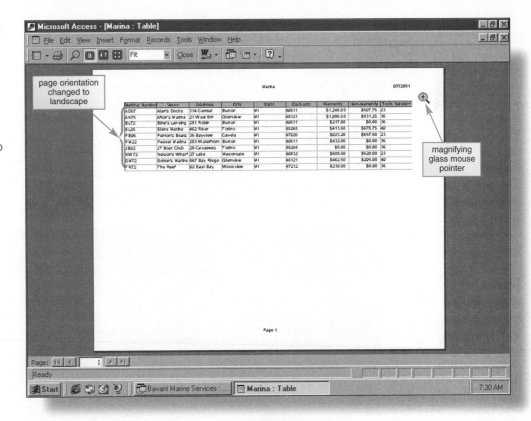

FIGURE 1-41

8 **Click the magnifying glass mouse pointer in the approximate position shown in Figure 1-41.**

The portion surrounding the mouse pointer is magnified (Figure 1-42). The last field that displays is the Tech Number field, so all fields currently display. If they did not, you could decrease the left and right margins; that is, the amount of space left by Access on the left and right edges of the report.

9 **Click the Print button to print the report. Click the Close button when the report has been printed to close the Print Preview window.**

The Print Preview window no longer displays.

FIGURE 1-42

Creating Additional Tables

A database typically consists of more than one table. The sample database contains two, the Marina table and the Technician table. You need to repeat the process of creating a table and adding records for each table in the database. In the sample database, you need to create and add records to the Technician table. The structure and data for the table are given in Figure 1-43. The steps to create the table follow.

Structure of Technician table				
FIELD NAME	DATA TYPE	FIELD SIZE	PRIMARY KEY?	DESCRIPTION
Tech Number	Text	2	Yes	Technician Number (Primary Key)
Last Name	Text	10		Last Name of Technician
First Name	Text	8		First Name of Technician
Address	Text	15		Street Address
City	Text	15		City
State	Text	2		State (Two-Character Abbreviation)
Zip Code	Text	5		Zip Code (Five-Character Version)
Hourly Rate	Currency			Hourly Rate of Technician
YTD Earnings	Currency			YTD Earnings of Technician

FIGURE 1-43

Data for Technician table

TECH NUMBER	LAST NAME	FIRST NAME	ADDRESS	CITY	STATE	ZIP CODE	HOURLY RATE	YTD EARNINGS
23	Anderson	Trista	283 Belton	Port Anton	MI	47989	$24.00	$17,862.00
36	Nichols	Ashton	978 Richmond	Hewitt	MI	47618	$21.00	$19,560.00
49	Gomez	Teresa	2855 Parry	Ashley	MI	47711	$22.00	$21,211.50

FIGURE 1-43 (continued)

Steps To Create an Additional Table

1 **Make sure the Bavant Marine Services database is open. Right-click Create table in Design view and then click Open on the shortcut menu. Enter the data for the fields for the Technician table from Figure 1-43. Be sure to click the Primary Key button when you enter the Tech Number field. Point to the Save button on the Database window toolbar after you have entered all the fields.**

The entries display (Figure 1-44).

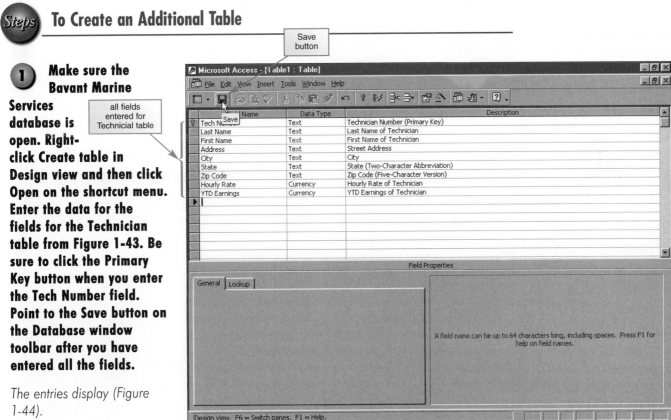

FIGURE 1-44

2 **Click the Save button, type Technician as the name of the table, and then click the OK button. Click the Close Window button.**

The table is saved in the Bavant Marine Services database. The Technician : Table window no longer displays.

Adding Records to the Additional Table

Now that you have created the Technician table, use the steps on the next page to add records to it.

To Add Records to an Additional Table

1 **Right-click Technician and point to Open on the shortcut menu.**

The shortcut menu for the Technician table displays (Figure 1-45).

FIGURE 1-45

2 **Click Open on the shortcut menu and then enter the Technician data from Figure 1-43 on page A 1.34 into the Technician table.**

The datasheet displays with three records entered (Figure 1-46).

3 **Click the Close Window button for the Technician : Table window.**

Access closes the table and removes the datasheet from the screen.

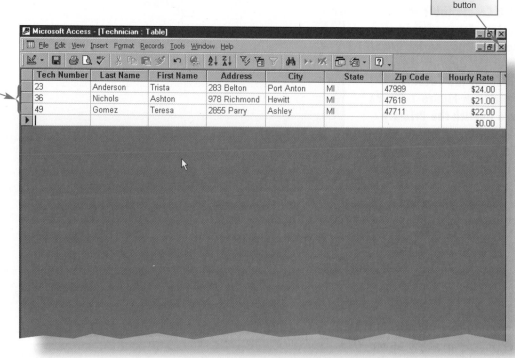

FIGURE 1-46

Using a Form to View Data

In creating tables, you have used Datasheet view; that is, the data on the screen displayed as a table. You also can use **Form view**, in which you see a single record at a time.

The advantage with Datasheet view is you can see multiple records at once. It has the disadvantage that, unless you have few fields in the table, you cannot see all the fields at the same time. With Form view, you see only a single record, but you can see all the fields in the record. The view you choose is a matter of personal preference.

Creating a Form

To use Form view, you first must create a form. The simplest way to create a form is to use the New Object: AutoForm button on the Database window toolbar. To do so, first select the table for which the form is to be created in the Database window and then click the New Object: AutoForm button. A list of available objects displays. Click AutoForm in the list to select it.

Perform the following steps using the New Object: AutoForm button to create a form for the Marina table.

More About

Forms

Attractive and functional forms can improve greatly the data entry process. Forms are not restricted to data from a single table, but can incorporate data from multiple tables as well as special types of data like pictures and sounds. A good DBMS like Access 2000 furnishes an easy way to create sophisticated forms.

Steps **To Use the New Object: AutoForm Button to Create a Form**

1 Make sure the Bavant Marine Services database is open, the Database window displays, and the Marina table is selected. Point to the New Object: AutoForm button arrow on the Database window toolbar (Figure 1-47).

FIGURE 1-47

2 Click the New Object: AutoForm button arrow and then point to AutoForm.

A list of objects that can be created displays (Figure 1-48).

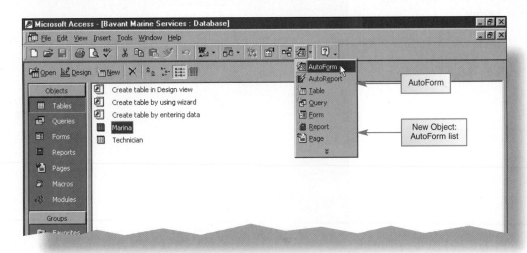

FIGURE 1-48

3 **Click AutoForm in the New Object: AutoForm list.**

The form displays (Figure 1-49). An additional toolbar, the Formatting toolbar, also displays. (When you close the form, this toolbar no longer displays.)

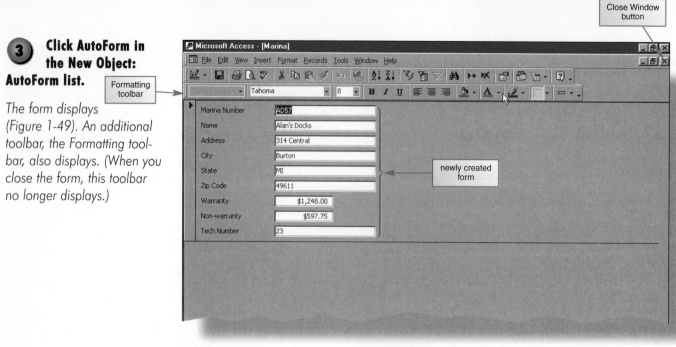

FIGURE 1-49

Closing and Saving the Form

Closing a form is similar to closing a table. The only difference is that you will be asked if you want to save the form unless you previously have saved it. Perform the following steps to close the form and save it as Marina.

 To Close and Save a Form

1 **Click the Close Window button for the Marina window (see Figure 1-49). Point to the Yes button.**

The Microsoft Access dialog box displays (Figure 1-50).

FIGURE 1-50

Click the Yes button and then point to the OK button.

The Save As dialog box displays (Figure 1-51). The name of the table (Marina) becomes the name of the form automatically. This name can be replaced with any name.

 Click the OK button in the Save As dialog box.

The form is saved as part of the database and is removed from the screen. The Bavant Marine Services : Database window again displays.

FIGURE 1-51

Other Ways

1. On File menu click Close

Opening the Saved Form

Once you have saved a form, you can use it at any time in the future by opening it. Opening a form is similar to opening a table; that is, make sure the form to be opened is selected, right-click, and then click Open on the shortcut menu. Before opening the form, however, the Forms object, rather than the Tables object, must be selected.

Perform the following steps to open the Marina form.

Steps To Open a Form

 With the Bavant Marine Services database open and the Database window on the screen, point to Forms on the Objects bar (Figure 1-52).

FIGURE 1-52

2 **Click Forms, right-click Marina, and then point to Open on the shortcut menu.**

The Forms object is selected and the list of available forms displays (Figure 1-53). Currently, the Marina form is the only form. The shortcut menu for the Marina form displays.

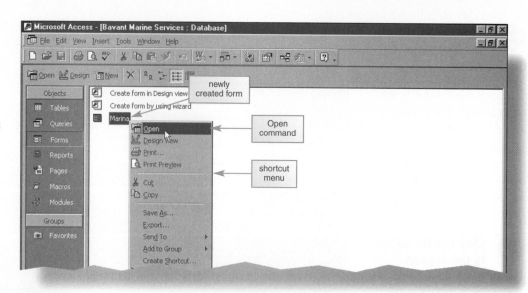

FIGURE 1-53

3 **Click Open on the shortcut menu.**

The Marina form displays (Figure 1-54).

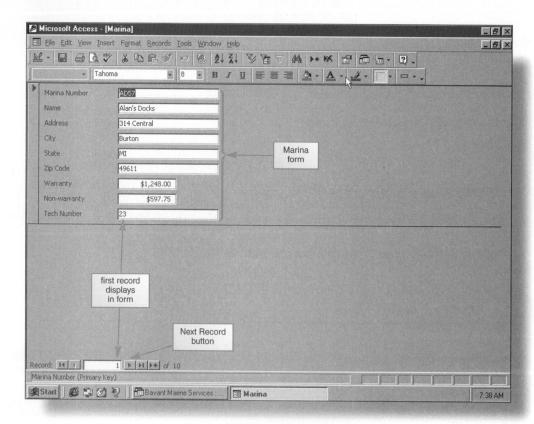

FIGURE 1-54

Other Ways

1. Click Forms object, double-click desired form
2. Click desired form, click Open button
3. Click desired from, press ALT+O

Using the Form

You can use the form just as you used Datasheet view. You use the Navigation buttons to move between records. You can add new records or change existing ones. To delete the record displayed on the screen, after selecting the record by clicking its record selector, press the DELETE key. Thus, you can perform database operations using either Form view or Datasheet view.

Because you can see only one record at a time in Form view, to see a different record, such as the fifth record, use the Navigation buttons to move to it. To move from record to record in Form view, perform the following step.

Steps To Use a Form

1 **Click the Next Record button four times.**

The fifth record displays on the form (Figure 1-55).

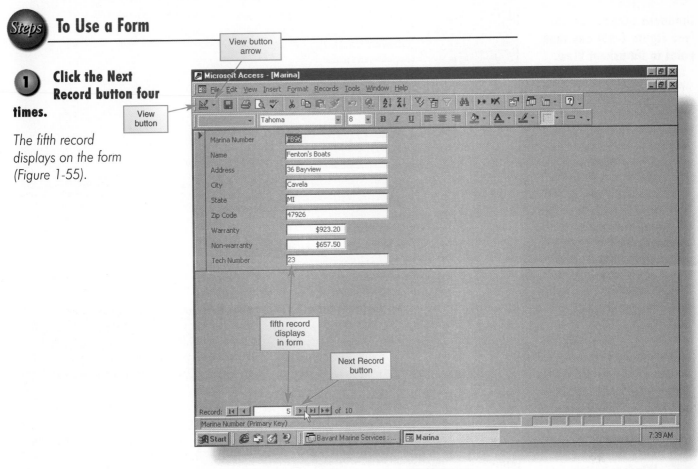

FIGURE 1-55

Switching Between Form View and Datasheet View

In some cases, once you have seen a record in Form view, you will want to move to Datasheet view to again see a collection of records. To do so, click the View button arrow on the Database window toolbar and then click Datasheet View in the list that displays.

Perform the steps on the next page to switch from Form view to Datasheet view.

Steps To Switch from Form View to Datasheet View

 Click the View button arrow on the Database window toolbar (see Figure 1-55) and then point to Datasheet View.

The list of available views displays (Figure 1-56).

FIGURE 1-56

 Click Datasheet View.

The table displays in Datasheet view (Figure 1-57). The record selector is positioned on the fifth record.

3 Click the Close Window button.

The Marina window closes and the datasheet no longer displays.

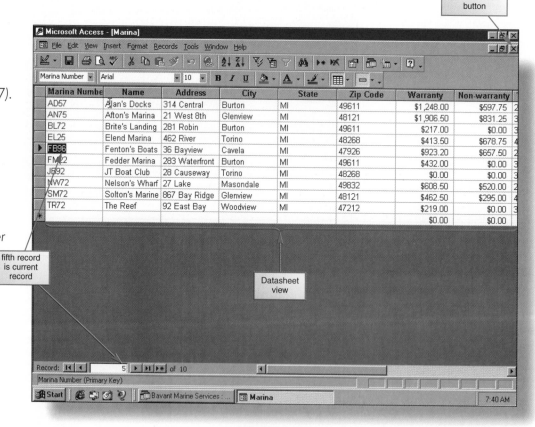

FIGURE 1-57

Other Ways

1. On View menu click Datasheet View

Creating a Report

Earlier in this project, you printed a table using the Print button. The report you produced was shown in Figure 1-34 on page A 1.30. While this type of report presented the data in an organized manner, it was not very flexible. It included all the fields, but in precisely the same order in which they occurred in the table. A way to change the title was not presented; it remained Marina.

In this section, you will create the report shown in Figure 1-58. This report features significant differences from the one in Figure 1-34 on page A 1.30. The portion at the top of the report in Figure 1-58, called a **page header**, contains a custom title. The contents of this page header display at the top of each page. The **detail lines**, which are the lines that are printed for each record, contain only those fields you specify and in the order you specify.

Perform the following steps to create the report in Figure 1-58.

More *About*

Reports

Custom reports represent one of the more important ways of presenting the data in a database. Reports can incorporate data from multiple tables and can be formatted in a wide variety of ways. The ability to create sophisticated custom reports is one of the major benefits of a DBMS like Access 2000.

Billing Summary Report

Marina Number	Name	Warranty	Non-warranty
AD57	Alan's Docks	$1,248.00	$597.75
AN75	Afton's Marina	$1,906.50	$831.25
BL72	Brite's Landing	$217.00	$0.00
EL25	Elend Marina	$413.50	$678.75
FB96	Fenton's Boats	$923.20	$657.50
FM22	Fedder Marina	$432.00	$0.00
JB92	JT Boat Club	$0.00	$0.00
NW72	Nelson's Wharf	$608.50	$520.00
SM72	Solton's Marina	$462.50	$295.00
TR72	The Reef	$219.00	$0.00

FIGURE 1-58

Steps **To Create a Report**

① **Click Tables on the Objects bar. Make sure the Marina table is selected. Click the New Object: AutoForm button arrow on the Database window toolbar.**

The list of available objects displays (Figure 1-59).

FIGURE 1-59

2 **Click Report and then point to Report Wizard.**

The New Report dialog box displays (Figure 1-60).

FIGURE 1-60

3 **Click Report Wizard and then click the OK button. Point to the Add Field button.**

The Report Wizard dialog box displays (Figure 1-61).

FIGURE 1-61

1. On Insert menu click Report
2. On Objects bar click Reports, click New

Selecting the Fields for the Report

To select a field for the report; that is, to indicate the field is to be included in the report, click the field in the Available Fields list. Next, click the Add Field button. This will move the field from the Available Fields box to the Selected Fields box, thus including the field in the report. If you wanted to select all fields, a shortcut is available simply by clicking the Add All Fields button.

To select the Marina Number, Name, Warranty, and Non-warranty fields for the report, perform the following steps.

Steps To Select the Fields for a Report

1 **Click the Add Field button to add the Marina Number field. Add the Name field by clicking it and then clicking the Add Field button. Add the Warranty and Non-warranty fields just as you added the Marina Number and Name fields.**

The fields for the report display in the Selected Fields box (Figure 1-62).

FIGURE 1-62

2 **Click the Next button.**

The Report Wizard dialog box displays (Figure 1-63).

FIGURE 1-63

Other Ways

1. Double-click field

Completing the Report

Several additional steps are involved in completing the report. With the exception of changing the title, the Access selections are acceptable, so you simply will click the Next button.

Perform the following steps to complete the report.

 To Complete a Report

1 **Because you will not specify any grouping, click the Next button in the Report Wizard dialog box (see Figure 1-63). Click the Next button a second time because you will not need to make changes on the screen that follows.**

The Report Wizard dialog box displays (Figure 1-64). In this dialog box, you can change the layout or orientation of the report.

FIGURE 1-64

2 **Make sure that Tabular is selected as the layout and Portrait is selected as the orientation and then click the Next button.**

The Report Wizard dialog box displays (Figure 1-65). In this dialog box, you can select a style for the report.

FIGURE 1-65

3 Be sure that the Corporate style is selected and then click the Next button.

The Report Wizard dialog box displays (Figure 1-66). In this dialog box, you can specify a title for the report.

FIGURE 1-66

4 Type Billing Summary Report as the new title and then click the Finish button.

A preview of the report displays (Figure 1-67). Yours may look slightly different, depending on your printer.

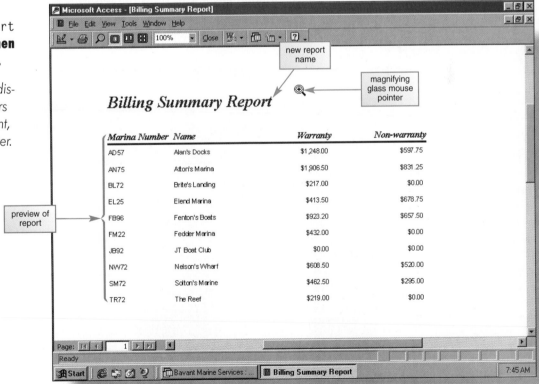

FIGURE 1-67

5 Click anywhere within the report to see the entire report.

The entire report displays (Figure 1-68).

6 Click the Close Window button in the Billing Summary Report window.

The report no longer displays. It has been saved automatically using the name Billing Summary Report.

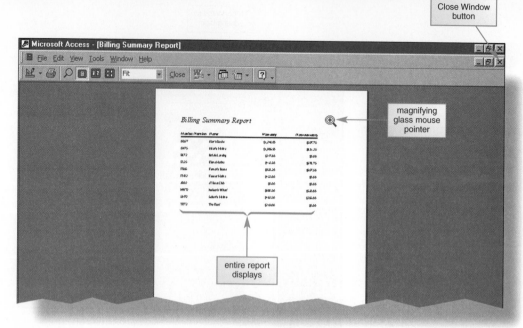

FIGURE 1-68

Printing the Report

To print a report from the Database window, first right-click the report. Then click Print on the shortcut menu to print the report or click Print Preview on the shortcut menu to see a preview of the report on the screen.

Perform the following steps to print the report.

Steps **To Print a Report**

1 If necessary, click Reports on the Objects bar in the Database window, right-click Billing Summary Report, and then point to Print on the shortcut menu.

The shortcut menu for the Billing Summary Report displays (Figure 1-69).

2 Click Print on the shortcut menu.

The report prints. It should look similar to the one shown in Figure 1-58 on page A 1.43.

FIGURE 1-69

Closing the Database

Once you have finished working with a database, you should close it. The following step closes the database by closing its Database window.

TO CLOSE A DATABASE

 Click the Close Window button for the Bavant Marine Services : Database window.

Access Help System

At any time while you are using Access, you can get answers to questions by using the **Access Help system**. Used properly, this form of online assistance can increase your productivity and reduce your frustrations by minimizing the time you spend learning how to use Access. Table 1-2 on page A 1.51, summarizes the eight categories of help available to you. Because of the way the Access Help system works, please review the rightmost column of Table 1-2 if you have difficulties activating the desired category of help.

The following section shows how to get answers to your questions using the Office Assistant. For additional information on using the Access Help system, see Appendix A.

Using the Office Assistant

The **Office Assistant** answers your questions and suggests more efficient ways to complete a task. With the Office Assistant active, for example, you can type a question, word, or phrase in a text box and the Office Assistant provides immediate help on the subject. Also, as you create a database, the Office Assistant accumulates tips that suggest more efficient ways to do the tasks you completed while creating a database, such as printing and saving. This tip feature is part of the **IntelliSense™ technology** built into Access, which understands what you are trying to do and suggests better ways to do it. When the light bulb displays above the Office Assistant, click it to see a tip.

The steps on the next page show how to use the Office Assistant to obtain information on setting and changing the primary key.

More About

Quick Reference

For a table that lists how to complete the tasks covered in this book using the mouse, menu, shortcut menu, and keyboard, visit the Shelly Cashman Series Office Web page (www.scsite.com/off2000/qr.htm), and then click Microsoft Access 2000.

Steps **To Obtain Help Using the Office Assistant**

1 **If the Office Assistant does not display, click Show the Office Assistant on the Help menu. With the Office Assistant on the screen, click it. Type** how do i set the primary key **in the What would you like to do? text box in the Office Assistant balloon. Point to the Search button (Figure 1-70).**

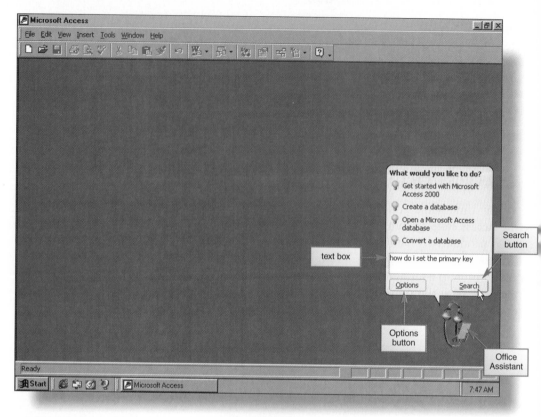

FIGURE 1-70

2 **Click the Search button. Point to the topic Set or change the primary key.**

The Office Assistant displays a list of topics relating to the question, "how do i set the primary key." (Your list may be different.) The mouse pointer changes to a hand (Figure 1-71).

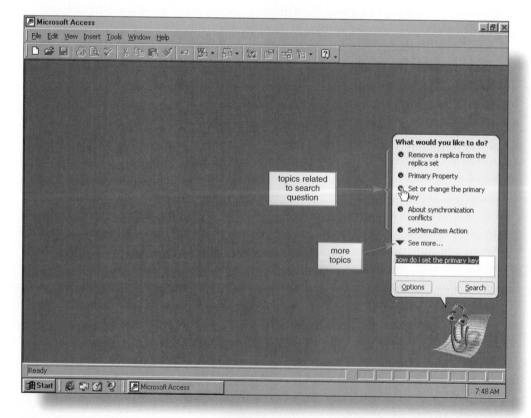

FIGURE 1-71

3 **Click Set or change the primary key.**

The Office Assistant displays a Microsoft Access Help window that provides Help information on setting or changing the primary key (Figure 1-72).

4 **Click the Close Window button on the Microsoft Access Help window title bar.**

The Microsoft Access Help window closes.

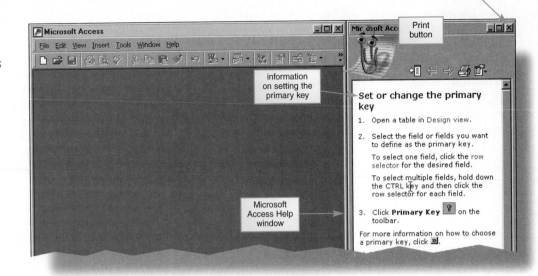

FIGURE 1-72

Table 1-2 summarizes the eight categories of Help available in Access 2000.

Table 1-2	Access Help System		
TYPE	**DESCRIPTION**	**HOW TO ACTIVATE**	**TURNING THE OFFICE ASSISTANT ON AND OFF**
Answer Wizard	Similar to the Office Assistant in that it answers questions that you type in your own words.	Click the Microsoft Access Help button on the Database window toolbar. If necessary, maximize the Help window by double-clicking its title bar. Click the Answer Wizard tab.	If the Office Assistant displays, right-click it, click Options, click the Use the Office Assistant check box, and click the OK button.
Contents sheet	Groups Help topics by general categories. Use when you know only the general category of the topic in question.	Click the Microsoft Access Help button on the Database window toolbar. If necessary, maximize the Help window by double-clicking its title bar. Click the Contents tab.	If the Office Assistant displays, right-click it, click Options, click the Use the Office Assistant check box, and then click the OK button.
Detect and Repair	Automatically finds and fixes errors in the application.	Click Detect and Repair on the Help menu.	
Hardware and Software Information	Shows Product ID and allows access to system information and technical support information.	Click About Microsoft Access on the Help menu and then click the appropriate button.	
Index sheet	Similar to an index in a book; use when you know exactly what you want.	Click the Microsoft Access Help button on the Database window toolbar. If necessary, maximize the window by double-clicking its title bar. Click the Index tab.	If the Office Assistant displays, right-click it, click Options, click the Use the Office Assistant check box, and then click the OK button.
Office Assistant	Answers questions that you type in your own words, offers tips, and provides Help for a variety of Access features.	Click the Microsoft Access Help button on the Database window toolbar.	If the Office Assistant does not display, close the Microsoft Access Help window and then click Show the Office Assistant on the Help menu.
Office on the Web	Used to access technical resources and download free product enhancements on the Web.	Click Office on the Web on the Help menu.	
Question Mark button and What's This? command	Used to identify unfamiliar items on the screen.	Click the Question Mark button and click an item in the dialog box. Click What's This? on the Help menu, and then click an item on the screen.	

More About

Database Design (Normalization)

There is a special technique for identifying and eliminating redundancy, called **normalization**. For more information on normalization, visit the Access 2000 More About Web page (www.scsite.com/ac2000/more.htm) and then click Normalization.

Designing a Database

Database design refers to the arrangement of data into tables and fields. In the example in this project, the design is specified, but in many cases, you will have to determine the design based on what you want the system to accomplish.

With large, complex databases, the database design process can be extensive. Major sections of advanced database textbooks are devoted to this topic. Often, however, you should be able to design a database effectively by keeping one simple principle in mind: Design to remove redundancy. **Redundancy** means storing the same fact in more than one place.

To illustrate, you need to maintain the following information shown in Figure 1-73 on the next page. In the figure, all the data is contained in a single table. Notice that the data for a given technician (number, name, and so on) occurs on more than one record.

Marina table

MARINA NUMBER	NAME	ADDRESS	CITY	STATE	ZIP CODE	WARRANTY	NON WARRANTY	TECH NUMBER	LAST NAME	FIRST NAME
AD57	Alan's Docks	314 Central	Burton	MI	49611	$1,248.00	$597.75	23	Anderson	Trista
AN75	Afton's Marina	21 West 8th	Glenview	MI	48121	$1,906.50	$831.25	36	Nichols	Ashton
BL72	Brite's Landing	281 Robin	Burton	MI	49611	$217.00	$0.00	36	Nichols	Ashton
EL25	Elend Marina	462 River	Torino	MI	48268	$413.50	$678.75	49	Gomez	Teresa
FB96	Fenton's Boats	36 Bayview	Cavela	MI	47926	$923.20	$657.50	23	Anderson	Trista
FM22	Fedder Marina	283 Waterfront	Burton	MI	49611	$432.00	$0.00	36	Nichols	Ashton
JB92	JT Boat Club	28 Causeway	Torino	MI	48268	$0.00	$0.00	36	Nichols	Ashton
NW72	Nelson's Wharf	27 Lake	Masondale	MI	49832	$608.50	$520.00	23	Anderson	Trista
SM72	Solton's Marine	867 Bay Ridge	Glenview	MI	48121	$462.50	$295.00	49	Gomez	Teresa
TR72	The Reef	92 East Bay	Woodview	MI	47212	$219.00	$0.00	36	Nichols	Ashton

FIGURE 1-73

duplicate technician names

More About

Database Design (Design Method)

There are a variety of methods that have been developed for designing complex databases given a set of input and output requirements. For more information on database design methods, visit the Access 2000 More About Web page (www.scsite.com/ac2000/more.htm) and then click Database Design.

Storing this data on multiple records is an example of redundancy, which causes several problems, including:

1. Redundancy wastes space on the disk. The address of technician 23 (Trista Anderson), for example, should be stored only once. Storing this fact several times is wasteful.
2. Redundancy makes updating the database more difficult. If, for example, Trista Anderson moves, her address would need to be changed in several different places.
3. A possibility of inconsistent data exists. Suppose, for example, that you change the address of Trista Anderson on marina FB96's record to 146 Valley, but do not change it on marina AD57's record. In both cases, the tech number is 23, but the addresses are different. In other words, the data is inconsistent.

The solution to the problem is to place the redundant data in a separate table, one in which the data will no longer be redundant. If, for example, you place the data for technicians in a separate table (Figure 1-74), the data for each technician will appear only once.

technician data is in separate table →

Technician table

TECH NUMBER	LAST NAME	FIRST NAME	ADDRESS	CITY	STATE	ZIP CODE	HOURLY RATE	YTD EARNINGS
23	Anderson	Trista	283 Belton	Port Anton	MI	47989	$24.00	$17,862.00
36	Nichols	Ashton	978 Richmond	Hewitt	MI	47618	$21.00	$19,560.00
49	Gomez	Teresa	2855 Parry	Ashley	MI	47711	$22.00	$21,211.50

Marina table

MARINA NUMBER	NAME	ADDRESS	CITY	STATE	ZIP CODE	WARRANTY	NON-WARRANTY	TECH NUMBER
AD57	Alan's Docks	314 Central	Burton	MI	49611	$1,248.00	$597.75	23
AN75	Afton's Marina	21 West 8th	Glenview	MI	48121	$1,906.50	$831.25	36
BL72	Brite's Landing	281 Robin	Burton	MI	49611	$217.00	$0.00	36
EL25	Elend Marina	462 River	Torino	MI	48268	$413.50	$678.75	49
FB96	Fenton's Boats	36 Bayview	Cavela	MI	47926	$923.20	$657.50	23
FM22	Fedder Marina	283 Waterfront	Burton	MI	49611	$432.00	$0.00	36
JB92	JT Boat Club	28 Causeway	Torino	MI	48268	$0.00	$0.00	36
NW72	Nelson's Wharf	27 Lake	Masondale	MI	49832	$608.50	$520.00	23
SM72	Solton's Marine	867 Bay Ridge	Glenview	MI	48121	$462.50	$295.00	49
TR72	The Reef	92 East Bay	Woodview	MI	47212	$219.00	$0.00	36

FIGURE 1-74

Notice that you need to have the tech number in both tables. Without it, no way exists to tell which technician is associated with which marina. All the other technician data, however, was removed from the Marina table and placed in the Technician table. This new arrangement corrects the problems of redundancy in the following ways:

1. Because the data for each technician is stored only once, space is not wasted.
2. Changing the address of a technician is easy. You have only to change one row in the Technician table.
3. Because the data for a technician is stored only once, inconsistent data cannot occur.

Designing to omit redundancy will help you to produce good and valid database designs.

CASE PERSPECTIVE SUMMARY

In Project 1, you assisted Bavant Marine Service in their efforts to place their data in a database. You created the database that Bavant will use. Within this database, you created the Marina and Technician tables by defining the fields within them. You then added records to these tables. Once you created the tables, you printed the contents of the tables. You also used a form to view the data in the table. Finally, you used the Report Wizard to create a report containing the Marina Number, Name, Warranty, and Non-warranty fields for each marina served by Bavant Marine Services.

Project Summary

In Project 1, you learned about databases and database management systems. You learned how to create a database and how to create the tables within a database. You saw how to define the fields in a table by specifying the characteristics of the fields. You learned how to open a table, how to add records to it, and how to close it. You also printed the contents of a table. You created a form to view data on the screen and also created a custom report. You learned how to use Microsoft Access Help. Finally, you learned how to design a database to eliminate redundancy.

What You Should Know

Having completed this project, you now should be able to perform the following tasks:

▶ Add Additional Records to a Table *(A 1.27)*
▶ Add Records to a Table *(A 1.20)*
▶ Add Records to an Additional Table *(A 1.35)*
▶ Close a Database *(A 1.49)*
▶ Close a Table and Database and Quit Access *(A 1.24)*
▶ Close and Save a Form *(A 1.38)*
▶ Complete a Report *(A 1.46)*
▶ Create a Report *(A 1.43)*

▶ Create a Table *(A 1.13)*
▶ Create an Additional Table *(A 1.34)*
▶ Define the Fields in a Table *(A 1.15)*
▶ Obtain Help Using the Office Assistant *(A 1.50)*
▶ Open a Database *(A 1.25)*
▶ Open a Form *(A 1.39)*
▶ Preview and Print the Contents of a Table *(A 1.30)*
▶ Print a Report *(A 1.48)*
▶ Save a Table *(A 1.19)*
▶ Select the Fields for a Report *(A 1.45)*
▶ Start Access *(A 1.9)*
▶ Switch from Form View to Datasheet View *(A 1.41)*
▶ Use a Form *(A 1.36)*
▶ Use the New Object: AutoForm Button to Create a Form *(A 1.37)*

More About

Microsoft Certification

The Microsoft Office User Specialist (MOUS) Certification program provides an opportunity for you to obtain a valuable industry credential — proof that you have the Access 2000 skills required by employers. For more information, see Appendix D or visit the Shelly Cashman Series MOUS Web page at www.scsite.com/off2000/cert.htm.

Apply Your Knowledge

Project Reinforcement at www.scsite.com/off2000/reinforce.htm

1 Changing Data and Creating Reports

Instructions: Start Access. Open the Sidewalk Scrapers database from the Access Data Disk. See the inside back cover for instructions for downloading the Access Data Disk or see your instructor for information on accessing the files required for this book. Sidewalk Scrapers is a snow removal service that was started by two high school juniors looking for ways to earn money for college. Sidewalk Scrapers provides snow removal to residences and businesses in a city that receives lots of snow during the winter months. The business has expanded rapidly and now employs high school and college students to shovel sidewalks, steps, and driveways. Sidewalk Scrapers has a database that keeps track of its workers and customers. The database has two tables. The Customer table contains data on the customers who use the services of Sidewalk Scrapers. The Worker table contains data on the students employed by Sidewalk Scrapers. The structure and data are shown for the Customer table in Figure 1-75 and for the Worker table in Figure 1-76.

Structure of Customer table

FIELD NAME	DATA TYPE	FIELD SIZE	PRIMARY KEY?	DESCRIPTION
Customer Number	Text	4	Yes	Customer Number (Primary Key)
Name	Text	20		Customer Name
Address	Text	15		Street Address
Telephone	Text	8		Telephone Number (999-9999 Version)
Balance	Currency			Amount Owed by Customer
Worker Id	Text	2		Id of Customer's Worker

Data for Customer table

CUSTOMER NUMBER	NAME	ADDRESS	TELEPHONE	BALANCE	WORKER ID
AL25	Arders, Lars	205 Norton	555-2050	$45.00	03
AT43	Atari Cleaners	147 Main	555-7410	$80.00	10
BH81	Bond, Laura	407 Scott	555-0704	$0.00	10
CH65	Chan's Bootery	154 Main	555-0504	$70.00	14
CI05	Cinco Gallery	304 Secord	555-1304	$29.00	03
JB51	Jordach, Ben	203 Norton	555-0213	$60.00	10
LK44	Lee, Kim	605 Thurston	555-5061	$0.00	10
MD60	Martinez, Dan	410 Orange	555-4110	$95.00	03
ME02	Meat Shoppe	75 Edgewater	555-7557	$0.00	14
ST21	Styling Salon	406 Secord	555-6454	$40.00	10

FIGURE 1-75

(continued)

Apply Your Knowledge

➕ Project Reinforcement at www.scsite.com/off2000/reinforce.htm

Changing Data and Creating Reports (continued)

Structure of Worker table

FIELD NAME	DATA TYPE	FIELD SIZE	PRIMARY KEY?	DESCRIPTION
Worker Id	Text	2	Yes	Worker Identification Number (Primary Key)
Last Name	Text	15		Last Name of Worker
First Name	Text	10		First Name of Worker
Address	Text	20		Street Address
Telephone	Text	8		Telephone Number (999-9999 Version)
Pay Rate	Currency			Hourly Pay Rate

Data for Worker table

WORKER ID	LAST NAME	FIRST NAME	ADDRESS	TELEPHONE NUMBER	PAY RATE
03	Carter	Chris	467 Norton	555-7641	$4.50
10	Lau	John	56 Parker	555-5656	$4.25
14	Sanchez	Elena	211 Thurston	555-1122	$4.75

FIGURE 1-76

Perform the following tasks.

1. Open the Worker table in Datasheet view and add the following record to the table:

07	Ferrens	Louis	24 Scott	555-2442	4.25

Close the Worker table.

2. Open the Worker table again. Notice that the record you just added has been moved. It is no longer at the end of the table. The records are in order by the primary key, Worker Id.

3. Print the Worker table.

4. Open the Customer table.

5. Change the Worker Id for customer LK44 to 07.

6. Print the Customer table.

7. Create the report shown in Figure 1-77 for the Customer table.

8. Print the report.

Balance Due Report

Customer Number	Name	Balance
AL25	Arders, Lars	$45.00
AT43	Atari Cleaners	$80.00
BH81	Bond, Laura	$0.00
CH65	Chan's Bootery	$70.00
CI05	Cinco Gallery	$29.00
JB51	Jordach, Ben	$60.00
LK44	Lee, Kim	$0.00
MD60	Martinez, Dan	$95.00
ME02	Meat Shoppe	$0.00
ST21	Styling Salon	$40.00

FIGURE 1-77

In the Lab

1 Creating the School Connection Database

Problem: The Booster's Club at the local high school raises money by selling merchandise imprinted with the school logo to alumni. The Booster's Club purchases products from vendors that deal in school specialty items. The database consists of two tables. The Item table contains information on items available for sale. The Vendor table contains information on the vendors.

Instructions: Perform the following tasks.

1. Create a new database in which to store all the objects related to the merchandise data. Call the database School Connection.
2. Create the Item table using the structure shown in Figure 1-78. Use the name Item for the table.
3. Add the data shown in Figure 1-78 to the Item table.
4. Print the Item table.
5. Create the Vendor table using the structure shown in Figure 1-79. Use the name Vendor for the table.
6. Add the data shown in Figure 1-79 on the next page to the Vendor table.
7. Print the Vendor table.
8. Create a form for the Item table. Use the name Item for the form.

Structure of Item table

FIELD NAME	DATA TYPE	FIELD SIZE	PRIMARY KEY?	DESCRIPTION
Item Id	Text	4	Yes	Item Id Number (Primary Key)
Description	Text	25		Description of Item
On Hand	Number	Long Integer		Number of Units On Hand
Cost	Currency			Cost of Item
Selling Price	Currency			Selling Price of Item
Vendor Code	Text	2		Code of Item Vendor

Data for Item table

ITEM ID	DESCRIPTION	ON HAND	COST	SELLING PRICE	VENDOR CODE
BA02	Baseball Cap	15	$12.50	$15.00	AL
CM12	Coffee Mug	20	$3.75	$5.00	GG
DM05	Doormat	5	$14.25	$17.00	TM
OR01	Ornament	25	$2.75	$4.00	GG
PL05	Pillow	8	$13.50	$15.00	TM
PN21	Pennant	22	$5.65	$7.00	TM
PP20	Pen and Pencil Set	12	$16.00	$20.00	GG
SC11	Scarf	17	$8.40	$12.00	AL
TT12	Tie	10	$8.90	$12.00	AL
WA34	Wastebasket	3	$14.00	$15.00	GG

FIGURE 1-78

(continued)

In the Lab

Creating the School Connection Database *(continued)*

Structure of Vendor table

FIELD NAME	DATA TYPE	FIELD SIZE	PRIMARY KEY?	DESCRIPTION
Vendor Code	Text	2	Yes	Vendor Code (Primary Key)
Name	Text	30		Name of Vendor
Address	Text	20		Street Address
City	Text	20		City
State	Text	2		State (Two-Character Abbreviation)
Zip Code	Text	5		Zip Code (Five-Character Version)
Telephone Number	Text	12		Telephone Number (999-999-9999 Version)

Data for Vendor table

VENDOR CODE	NAME	ADDRESS	CITY	STATE	CODE	TELEPHONE NUMBER
AL	Alum Logo Inc.	1669 Queen	Aurora	WI	53595	608-555-9753
GG	GG Gifts	5261 Stream	Brisbane	NM	88061	505-555-8765
TM	Trinkets 'n More	541 Maple	Kentwood	VA	20147	804-555-1234

FIGURE 1-79

9. Create and print the report shown in Figure 1-80 for the Item table.

Inventory Report

Item Id	Description	On Hand	Cost
BA02	Baseball Cap	15	$12.50
CM12	Coffee Mug	20	$3.75
DM05	Doormat	5	$14.25
OR01	Ornament	25	$2.75
PP20	Pen and Pencil Set	12	$16.00
PN21	Pennant	22	$5.65
PL05	Pillow	8	$13.50
SC11	Scarf	17	$8.40
TT12	Tie	10	$8.90
WA34	Wastebasket	3	$14.00

FIGURE 1-80

In the Lab

2 Creating the City Area Bus Company Database

Problem: Like many urban transportation companies, the City Area Bus Company sells advertising. Local firms buy advertising from ad sales representatives who work for the bus company. Ad sales representatives receive a commission based on the advertising revenues they generate. The database consists of two tables. The Advertiser table contains information on the organizations that advertise on the buses. The Sales Rep table contains information on the representative assigned to the advertising account.

Instructions: Perform the following tasks.

1. Create a new database in which to store all the objects related to the advertising data. Call the database City Area Bus Company.
2. Create the Advertiser table using the structure shown in Figure 1-81. Use the name Advertiser for the table.
3. Add the data shown in Figure 1-81 to the Advertiser table.

Structure of Advertiser table

FIELD NAME	DATA TYPE	FIELD SIZE	PRIMARY KEY?	DESCRIPTION
Advertiser Id	Text	4	Yes	Advertiser Id (Primary Key)
Name	Text	20		Name of Advertiser
Address	Text	15		Street Address
City	Text	15		City
State	Text	2		State (Two-Character Abbreviation)
Zip Code	Text	5		Zip Code (Five-Character Version)
Balance	Currency			Amount Currently Owed
Amount Paid	Currency			Amount Paid Year-to-Date
Sales Rep Number	Text	2		Number of Advertising Sales Representative

Data for Advertiser table

ADVERTISER ID	NAME	ADDRESS	CITY	STATE	ZIP CODE	BALANCE	AMOUNT PAID	SALES REP NUMBER
AC25	Alia Cleaners	223 Michigan	Crescentville	MA	05431	$85.00	$585.00	24
BB99	Bob's Bakery	1939 Jackson	Richmond	MA	05433	$435.00	$1,150.00	29
CS46	Cara's Salon	787 Ottawa	Cheltenham	CT	06470	$35.00	$660.00	29
FS78	Franz and Sons	3294 Campeau	Richmond	MA	05434	$185.00	$975.00	31
GR75	G's Restaurant	1632 Shue	Manyunk	CT	06471	$0.00	$1,500.00	24
HC11	Hilde's Cards	3140 Main	Crescentville	MA	05431	$250.00	$500.00	29
MC34	Mom's Cookies	1805 Broadway	Crescentville	MA	05431	$95.00	$1,050.00	29
NO10	New Orient	2200 Lawrence	Manyunk	CT	06471	$150.00	$350.00	24
PJ24	Pajama Store	13 Monroe	Cheltenham	CT	06470	$0.00	$775.00	31
TM89	Tom's Market	39 Albert	Richmond	MA	05433	$50.00	$500.00	24

FIGURE 1-81

(continued)

In the Lab

Creating the City Area Bus Company Database (continued)

4. Print the Advertiser table.

5. Create the Sales Rep table using the structure shown in Figure 1-82. Use the name Sales Rep for the table. Be sure that the field size for the Comm Rate field is Double.

6. Add the data shown in Figure 1-82 to the Sales Rep table.

7. Print the Sales Rep table.

8. Create a form for the Advertiser table. Use the name Advertiser for the form.

Structure of Sales Rep table

FIELD NAME	DATA TYPE	FIELD SIZE	PRIMARY KEY?	DESCRIPTION
Sales Rep Number	Text	2	Yes	Advertising Sales Rep Number (Primary Key)
Last Name	Text	15		Last Name of Advertising Sales Rep
First Name	Text	10		First Name of Advertising Sales Rep
Address	Text	15		Street Address
City	Text	15		City
State	Text	2		State (Two-Character Abbreviation)
Zip Code	Text	5		Zip Code (Five-Character Version)
Comm Rate	Number	Double		Commission Rate
Commission	Currency			Year-to-Date Total Commissions

Data for Sales Rep table

SALES REP NUMBER	LAST NAME	FIRST NAME	ADDRESS	CITY	STATE	ZIP CODE	COMM RATE	COMMISSION
24	Chou	Peter	34 Second	Crescentville	MA	05431	0.09	$7,500.00
29	Ortiz	Elvia	45 Belmont	Cheltenham	CT	06470	0.09	$8,450.00
31	Reed	Pat	78 Farmwood	Richmond	MA	05433	0.08	$7,225.00

FIGURE 1-82

9. Open the form you created and change the address for Advertiser Number HC11 to 340 Mainline.

10. Change to Datasheet view and delete the record for Advertiser Number GR75.

11. Print the Advertiser table.

12. Create and print the report shown in Figure 1-83 for the Advertiser table.

Advertiser Status Report

Advertiser Id	Name	Balance	Amount Paid
AC25	Alia Cleaners	$85.00	$585.00
BB99	Bob's Bakery	$435.00	$1,150.00
CS46	Cara's Salon	$35.00	$660.00
FS78	Franz and Sons	$185.00	$975.00
HC11	Hilde's Cards	$250.00	$500.00
MC34	Mom's Cookies	$95.00	$1,050.00
NO10	New Orient	$150.00	$350.00
PJ24	Pajama Store	$0.00	$775.00
TM89	Tom's Market	$50.00	$500.00

FIGURE 1-83

In the Lab

3 Creating the Resort Rental Database

Problem: A real estate company located in an ocean resort community provides a rental service for apartment/ condo owners. The company rents units by the week to interested tourists and "snowbirds" (people who spend their winters in warmer climates). The database consists of two tables. The Rental Unit table contains information on the units available for rent. The Owner table contains information on the owners of the rental units.

Instructions: Perform the following tasks.

1. Create a new database in which to store all the objects related to the rental data. Call the database Resort Rentals.
2. Create the Rental Unit table using the structure shown in Figure 1-84. Use the name Rental Unit for the table. Note that the table uses a new data type, Yes/No for the Pool and Ocean View fields.
3. Add the data shown in Figure 1-84 to the Rental Unit table.

Structure of Rental Unit table

FIELD NAME	DATA TYPE	FIELD SIZE	PRIMARY KEY?	DESCRIPTION
Rental Id	Text	3	Yes	Rental Id (Primary Key)
Address	Text	20		Street Address of Rental Unit
City	Text	20		City
Bedrooms	Number			Number of Bedrooms
Bathrooms	Number			Number of Bathrooms
Sleeps	Number			Maximum Number that can sleep in rental unit
Pool	Yes/No			Does the rental unit have a pool?
Ocean View	Yes/No			Does the rental unit have an ocean view?
Weekly Rate	Currency			Weekly Rental Rate
Owner Id	Text	4		Id of Rental Unit's Owner

Data for Rental Unit table

RENTAL ID	ADDRESS	CITY	BED-ROOMS	BATH-ROOMS	SLEEPS	POOL	OCEAN VIEW	WEEKLY RATE	OWNER ID
101	521 Ocean	Hutchins	2	1	4	Y	Y	$750.00	ML10
103	783 First	Gulf Breeze	3	3	8	Y		$1,000.00	FH15
105	684 Beach	San Toma	1	1	3		Y	$700.00	PR23
108	96 Breeze	Gulf Breeze	1	1	2		Y	$650.00	PR23
110	523 Ocean	Hutchins	2	2	6	Y		$900.00	LD45
112	345 Coastal	Shady Beach	2	2	5		Y	$900.00	LD45
116	956 First	Gulf Breeze	2	2	6	Y	Y	$1,100.00	ML10
121	123 Gulf	San Toma	3	2	8	Y	Y	$1,300.00	FH15
134	278 Second	Shady Beach	2	1	4		Y	$1,000.00	FH15
144	24 Plantation	Hutchins	1	1	2	Y		$650.00	PR23

FIGURE 1-84

(continued)

In the Lab

Creating the Resort Rental Database *(continued)*

4. Use Microsoft Access Help to learn how to resize column widths in Datasheet view and then reduce the size of the Rental Id, Bedrooms, Bathrooms, Sleeps, Pool, Ocean View, Weekly Rate, and Owner Id columns.

5. Print the Rental Unit table.

6. Create the Owner table using the structure shown in Figure 1-85. Use the name Owner for the table.

7. Add the data shown in Figure 1-85 to the Owner table.

8. Print the Owner table.

Structure of Owner table

FIELD NAME	DATA TYPE	FIELD SIZE	PRIMARY KEY?	DESCRIPTION
Owner Id	Text	4	Yes	Owner Id (Primary Key)
Last Name	Text	15		Last Name of Owner
First Name	Text	10		First Name of Owner
Address	Text	15		Street Address
City	Text	15		City
State	Text	2		State (Two-Character Abbreviation)
Zip Code	Text	5		Zip Code (Five-Character Version)
Telephone	Text	12		Telephone Number (999-999-9999 Version)

Data for Owner table

OWNER ID	LAST NAME	FIRST NAME	ADDRESS	CITY	STATE	ZIP CODE	TELEPHONE NO
FH15	Franco	Hilda	1234 Oakley	Middleville	PA	19063	610-555-7658
LD45	Lakos	Daniel	45 Fanshawe	Grenard	MI	49441	616-555-9080
ML10	Manuel	Larry	78 Unruh	Dalute	CA	95518	916-555-8787
PR23	Peoples	Rita	5489 South	Johnson	LA	58345	504-555-9845

FIGURE 1-85

9. Create a form for the Rental Unit table. Use the name Rental Unit for the form.

10. Open the form you created and change the weekly rate for Rental Id 144 to $675.00.

11. Print the Rental Unit table.

12. Create and print the report shown in Figure 1-86 for the Rental Unit table.

Available Rental Units Report

Rental Id	Address	City	Weekly Rate
101	521 Ocean	Hutchins	$750.00
103	783 First	Gulf Breeze	$1,000.00
105	684 Beach	San Toma	$700.00
108	96 Breeze	Gulf Breeze	$650.00
110	523 Ocean	Hutchins	$900.00
112	345 Coastal	Shady Beach	$900.00
116	956 First	Gulf Breeze	$1,100.00
121	123 Gulf	San Toma	$1,300.00
134	278 Second	Shady Beach	$1,000.00
144	24 Plantation	Hutchins	$675.00

FIGURE 1-86

Cases and Places

The difficulty of these case studies varies:
▌ are the least difficult; ▌▌ are more difficult; and ▌▌▌ are the most difficult.

1 ▌ As a fund-raising project, the local college's Computer Science Club sells small computer accessories to students. Disks, disk cases, and mouse pads are some of the items that the club sells from a small kiosk in the student computer lab. The club has asked you to create a database that keeps track of their inventory and suppliers. The current inventory is shown in Figure 1-87.

Design and create a database to store the club's inventory. Then create the necessary tables, enter the data from Figure 1-87, and print the tables.

ITEM ID	DESCRIPTION	UNITS ON HAND	COST	SELLING PRICE	SUPPLIER CODE	SUPPLIER NAME	SUPPLIER TELEPHONE
1663	Antistatic Wipes	30	$0.15	$0.25	ER	Ergonomics Ltd.	517-555-3853
1683	CD Wallet	12	$3.45	$4.00	HI	Human Interface	317-555-4747
2563	Desktop Holder	4	$3.85	$4.75	ER	Ergonomics Ltd.	517-555-3853
2593	Disks	175	$0.20	$.75	HI	Human Interface	317-555-4747
3923	Disk Cases	12	$2.20	$2.75	HI	Human Interface	317-555-4747
3953	Mouse Holder	10	$0.80	$1.00	MT	Mouse Tracks	616-555-9228
4343	Mouse Pad	25	$2.25	$3.00	MT	Mouse Tracks	616-555-9228
5810	PC Tool Kit	9	$7.80	$9.00	ER	Ergonomics Ltd.	517-555-3853
5930	Wrist Rest	3	$2.90	$3.25	ER	Ergonomics Ltd.	517-555-3853

FIGURE 1-87

2 ▌ Sci-Fi Scene is a local bookstore that specializes in Science Fiction. The owner has asked you to create and update a database that she can use to keep track of the books she has in stock. You gather the information shown in Figure 1-88.

Design and create a database to store the book data. Then create the necessary tables, enter the data from Figure 1-88, and print the tables.

Cases and Places

BOOK CODE	TITLE	AUTHOR	UNITS ON HAND	PRICE	YEAR PUBLISHED	PUBLISHER CODE	PUBLISHER NAME
0488	Robot Wars	H Brawley	1	$5.95	1997	SI	Simpson-Ivan
0533	Albert's Way	H Brawley	2	$4.75	1999	SI	Simpson-Ivan
1019	Stargaze	G Chou	3	$5.50	1996	BB	Bertrand Books
128X	Comet Dust	R Eaton	2	$5.95	2000	PB	Peabody Books
1668	Android	E Dearling	3	$6.95	1999	VN	VanNester
3495	Dark Wind	G Chou	4	$4.95	1998	BB	Bertrand Books
3859	Infinity	R Torres	1	$4.75	1997	VN	VanNester
4889	The Galaxy	E Dearling	2	$6.75	2000	VN	VanNester
6517	Strange Alien	R Eaton	2	$9.95	1998	PB	Peabody Books
7104	Secret City	R Torres	1	$5.75	1997	VN	VanNester

FIGURE 1-88

3 ▶▶ The marching band director of your school has asked you to create a database of band members. He wants to keep track of the following data on each band member: name, address, telephone number, age, sex, emergency contact name, emergency telephone number, type of band instrument, band instrument number, whether the student owns or leases the instrument, and number of years in the band.

Design and create a database to meet the band director's needs. Create the necessary tables, enter some sample data, and print the tables to show the director.

4 ▶▶ You have been hired as an intern by the local humane society. The humane society would like you to computerize their adoption files. Currently, they keep all the information about animals that are placed for adoption on index cards. The cards include information on the family, for example, name, address, telephone number, number of children, any previous animal adoptions, and other family pets. Information on the animal also is kept, for example, type of animal, sex, age, name, and any medical problems.

Design and create a database to meet the humane society's needs. Create the necessary tables, enter some sample data, and print the tables to show the director of the humane society.

5 ▶▶▶ The Intramural Sports Club has decided that a good way to make money and help students would be to set up a used sports equipment co-operative similar to the secondhand sporting goods stores. As a member of the club, you are asked to create a database that can store data related to the sports equipment and the students who wish to sell their items.

Determine the type of data you will need, then design and create a database to meet the club's needs. Create the necessary tables, enter some sample data, and print the tables.

PowerPoint 2000

1
2
3
4
5
6

Microsoft **PowerPoint 2000**

Microsoft PowerPoint 2000

P R O J E C T

1

Using a Design Template and AutoLayouts to Create a Presentation

O B J E C T I V E S

You will have mastered the material in this project when you can:

- Start a presentation as a New Office document
- Describe the PowerPoint window
- Select a design template
- Create a title slide
- Describe and use text attributes such as font size and font style
- Save a presentation
- Add a new slide
- Create a multi-level bulleted list slide
- Move to another slide in normal view
- End a slide show with a black slide
- View a presentation in slide show view
- Quit PowerPoint
- Open a presentation
- Check the spelling and consistency of a presentation
- Edit a presentation
- Change line spacing on the slide master
- Display a presentation in black and white
- Print a presentation in black and white
- Use the PowerPoint Help system

Puttin' on the Glitz

Presentations Help COMDEX Shine

Microsoft's Bill Gates will be there. So will thousands of the world's computer industry executives. And they will be joined by hundreds of thousands of curious technology affectionados seeking the latest trends in hardware, software, and the Internet.

They will be attending COMDEX, North America's largest trade show. COMDEX/Fall is held in Las Vegas each November, and COMDEX/Spring is held in Chicago in April. Both shows feature speeches by industry leaders, tutorials on the latest technologies, and thousands of square feet of exhibits showcasing the latest in computer technology.

Information technology (IT) experts headline COMDEX as the premier IT event in the world. Indeed, more than 10,000 new products are unveiled at the Fall show. Since COMDEX's inception in 1979, some of the more notable product launches have been the IBM PC in 1981, COMPAQ's suitcase-sized portable computer, Microsoft's first version of Windows, Apple's original Macintosh computer, and CD-ROM drives.

Attendance and industry representation have grown steadily. The first show featured 150 exhibitions seen by 4,000 curious visitors. Six years later, more than 1,000 companies displayed their wares for more than 100,000 techies. Recent shows have produced as many as 2,400 booths visited by 250,000-plus attendees.

Computer companies realize their sales forces need to capture their audiences' attention, so they add sensory cues to their exhibits. They treat the trade show visitors to a multimedia blitz of sound, visuals, and action with the help of presentation software such as Microsoft PowerPoint 2000. This program enhances the presenters' speeches by highlighting keywords in the presentation, displaying graphs, pictures, and diagrams, and playing sound and video clips.

In this project, you will learn to use PowerPoint 2000 to create a presentation, which also is called a slide show, concerning effective study skills. You then will run the slide show and print handouts for the audience. In later projects you will add animation, pictures, and sound.

PowerPoint's roots stem from the innovative work performed by a small company called Forethought, Inc. Programmers at this pioneering business coined the phrase, desktop presentation graphics, for formal slide shows and created a complete software package that automated creating slides containing text, charts, and graphics. Microsoft liked the visual appeal of the software and acquired Forethought in 1987. Company executives decided to market the software to Apple Macintosh users because Mac computers were considered clearly superior to IBM-based personal computers for graphics applications.

Microsoft PowerPoint became a favorite among Mac users. Meanwhile, Lotus Freelance Graphics and Software Publishing Harvard Graphics were popular within the PC community. This division ceased, however, when Microsoft released Windows 3.0 in 1990 and subsequently developed a Windows version of PowerPoint to run on PCs.

Since that time, Macintosh and PC users alike have utilized the presentation power of PowerPoint. The package has grown to include animation, audio and video clips, and Internet integration. Certainly the technology gurus at COMDEX have realized PowerPoint's dazzling visual appeal. So will you as you complete the exercises in this textbook.

Microsoft PowerPoint 2000

Using a Design Template and AutoLayouts to Create a Presentation

Microsoft PowerPoint 2000

C A S E   P E R S P E C T I V E

Excellent study habits are the keys to college success. What matters is not how long people study — it is how well they use their time. Students who study well can maximize their hours, have time for other activities, make the highest grades, and have a better chance to get accepted to their desired school. Ultimately, they generally earn higher incomes because their good study habits carry over to the working environment.

Advisers in Seaview College's Counseling Department spend many hours each semester helping students organize their study times, maximize their classroom experiences, and read their textbooks for ultimate comprehension. Dr. Ramon Martinez, the dean of counseling, has asked you to develop a short presentation to run at next semester's Freshmen Orientation sessions. You agree to create the presentation using a computer and PowerPoint software with the theme of effective study habits. In addition, you will print handouts of the presentation for the incoming students and also print a copy of the presentation on transparency film to enable the advisers to project the slides using an overhead projector.

What Is Microsoft PowerPoint 2000?

Microsoft PowerPoint 2000 is a complete presentation graphics program that allows you to produce professional-looking presentations. A PowerPoint **presentation** also is called a **slide show**. PowerPoint gives you the flexibility to make presentations using a projection device attached to a personal computer (Figure 1-1a) and using overhead transparencies (Figure 1-1b). In addition, you can take advantage of the World Wide Web and run virtual presentations on the Internet (Figure 1-1c). PowerPoint also can create paper printouts of the individual slides, outlines, and speaker notes.

PowerPoint contains several features to simplify creating a slide show. For example, you can instruct PowerPoint to create a predesigned presentation, and then you can modify the presentation to fulfill your requirements. You quickly can format a slide show using one of the professionally designed presentation design templates. To make your presentation more impressive, you can add tables, charts, pictures, video, sound, and, animation effects. You also can check the spelling of your slide show as you type or after you have completed designing the presentation. For example, you can instruct PowerPoint to restrict the number of bulleted items on a slide or limit the number of words in each paragraph. Additional PowerPoint features include the following:

▶ **Word processing** — create bulleted lists, combine words and images, find and replace text, and use multiple fonts and type sizes.
▶ **Outlining** — develop your presentation using an outline format. You also can import outlines from Microsoft Word or other word processing programs.
▶ **Charting** — create and insert charts into your presentations. The two chart types are: standard, which includes bar, line, pie, and xy (scatter) charts; and custom, which displays floating bars, colored lines, and three-dimensional cones.

(a) Projection Device Connected to a Personal Computer

(b) Overhead Transparencies

FIGURE 1-1

(c) PowerPoint Presentation Over the World Wide Web

More About

Projection Devices

Multimedia projectors have become the standard for today's presenters. The newest devices are about the size of a deli sandwich, weigh just five pounds, and fill the room with brilliant, clear images. For more information, visit the PowerPoint 2000 More About Web page (www.scsite.com/ pp2000/more.htm) and click Projection.

▶ **Drawing** —form and modify diagrams using shapes such as arcs, arrows, cubes, rectangles, stars, and triangles.

▶ **Inserting multimedia** — insert artwork and multimedia effects into your slide show. Clip Gallery 5.0 contains hundreds of clip art images, pictures, photos, sounds, and video clips. You can search for clips by entering words or phrases that describe the subject you want, by looking for clips with similar artistic styles, colors, or shapes, or by connecting to a special Web site reserved for Clip Gallery users. You also can import art from other applications.

▶ **Web support** — save presentations or parts of a presentation in HTML format so they can be viewed and manipulated using a browser. You can publish your slide show to the Internet or to an intranet. You also can insert action buttons and hyperlinks to create a self-running or interactive Web presentation.

▶ **E-mailing** — send an individual slide as an e-mail message or your entire slide show as an attachment to an e-mail message.

▶ **Using Wizards** — quickly and efficiently create a presentation by answering prompts for specific content criteria. For example, the **AutoContent Wizard** gives prompts for the type of slide show you are planning, such as communicating bad news or motivating a team, and the type of output, such as an on-screen presentation or black and white overheads. If you are planning to run your presentation on another computer, the **Pack and Go Wizard** helps you bundle everything you need, including any objects associated with that presentation. If you cannot confirm that this other computer has PowerPoint installed, you also can include the **PowerPoint Viewer**, a program that allows you to run, but not edit, a PowerPoint slide show.

Project One — Effective Study Skills

This book presents a series of projects using PowerPoint to produce slides similar to those you would develop in an academic or business environment. Project 1 uses PowerPoint to create the presentation shown in Figures 1-2a through 1-2d. The objective is to produce a presentation, called Effective Study Skills, to be displayed using an overhead projector. As an introduction to PowerPoint, this project steps you through the most common type of presentation, which is a bulleted list. A **bulleted list** is a list of paragraphs, each preceded by a bullet. A **bullet** is a symbol such as a heavy dot (•) or other character that precedes text when the text warrants special emphasis.

Effective Study Skills

Strategies for College Success
Presented by
Seaview College

(a) Slide 1

Managing Your Time

◆ Make a weekly schedule
  ■ List specific study times for all subjects
  ■ Plan time for recreation and sleep
  ■ Spread study times throughout the week
◆ Stick to your schedule
◆ Revise your schedule when necessary

(b) Slide 2

Attending Class

◆ Sit in the front of the room
◆ Ask questions at appropriate times
◆ Take notes
  ■ Rephrase ideas in your own words
  ■ Review immediately after class

(c) Slide 3

Reading Your Textbooks

◆ Survey the assignment
  ■ Read the summary and chapter questions
◆ Read the chapter carefully
◆ Recite the material in your own words
◆ Write brief notes in the margins
◆ Review the entire assignment

(d) Slide 4

FIGURE 1-2

Starting a Presentation as a New Office Document

The quickest way to begin a new presentation is to use the **Start button** on the **taskbar** at the bottom of your screen. When you click the Start button, the **Start menu** displays several commands for simplifying tasks in Windows. When Microsoft Office 2000 is installed, the Start menu displays the New Office Document and Open Office Document commands. You use the **New Office Document command** to designate the type of Office document you are creating. The Open Office Document command is discussed later in this project. Perform these steps to start a new presentation, or ask your instructor how to start PowerPoint on your system.

 To Start a New Presentation

1 **Click the Start button on the taskbar and then point to New Office Document.**

The programs on the Start menu display above the Start button (Figure 1-3). The New Office Document command is highlighted on the Start menu. Your computer system displays the time on the clock in the tray status area on the taskbar.

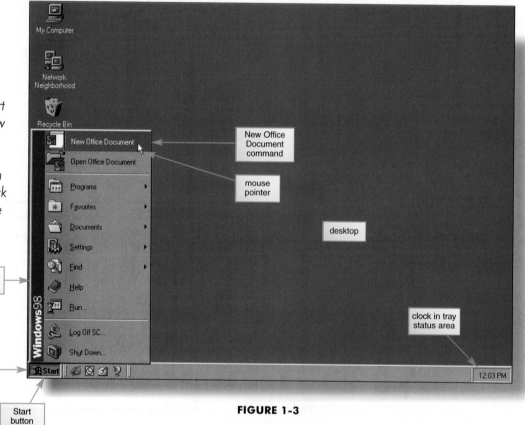

FIGURE 1-3

2 **Click New Office Document. If necessary, click the General tab in the New Office Document dialog box, and then click the Blank Presentation icon.**

Office displays several icons on the General sheet in the New Office Document dialog box (Figure 1-4). Each icon represents a different type of document you can create in Microsoft Office. In this project, you will create a new presentation using Microsoft PowerPoint, starting with a blank presentation.

FIGURE 1-4

3 **Click the OK button. If necessary, enlarge the PowerPoint window by double-clicking its title bar. If the Office Assistant displays, right-click the Office Assistant and then click Hide on the shortcut menu. Point to the OK button in the New Slide dialog box.**

The New Slide dialog box displays (Figure 1-5). The Title Slide AutoLayout is selected, and its name displays in the lower-right corner of the New Slide dialog box. The Office Assistant will be discussed later in this project.

FIGURE 1-5

4 **Click the OK button.**

PowerPoint displays the Title Slide AutoLayout and the Default Design template on Slide 1 (Figure 1-6). The title bar identifies this window as a Microsoft PowerPoint presentation currently titled [Presentation1]. The status bar displays information about the current slide: the slide number and the name of the current design template.

FIGURE 1-6

When an application is open, its name displays on a button in the **taskbar button area**. The **active application** is the one displaying on the foreground of the desktop. That application's corresponding button in the taskbar button area displays recessed.

The basic unit of a PowerPoint presentation is a **slide**. A slide contains one or many **objects**, such as a title, text, graphics, tables, charts, and drawings. An object is the building block for a PowerPoint slide. PowerPoint assumes the first slide in a new presentation is the **title slide**. The title slide's purpose is to introduce the presentation to the audience.

The PowerPoint Window

In PowerPoint, you have the option of using the PowerPoint default settings or establishing your own. A **default setting** is a particular value for a variable that PowerPoint assigns initially. It controls the placement of objects, the color scheme, the transition between slides, and other slide attributes, and it remains in effect unless you cancel or override it. **Attributes** are the properties or characteristics of an object. For example, if you underline the title of a slide, the title is the object, and the underline is the attribute. When you start PowerPoint, the default **slide layout** is **landscape orientation**, where the slide width is greater than its height. In landscape orientation, the slide size is preset to 10 inches wide and 7.5 inches high. The slide layout can be changed to **portrait orientation**, so that the slide height is greater than its width, by clicking Page Setup on the File menu. In portrait orientation, the slide width is 7.5 inches, and the height is 10 inches.

PowerPoint Views

PowerPoint has five views: normal view, outline view, slide view, slide sorter view, and slide show. A **view** is the mode in which the presentation displays on the screen. You may use any or all views when creating your presentation, but you can use only one at a time. Change views by clicking one of the view buttons found in the lower-left of the PowerPoint window above the status bar (Figure 1-6). The PowerPoint window display is dependent on the view. Some views are graphical while others are textual.

You generally will use normal view and slide sorter view when you are creating your presentation. Normal view is composed of three panes, which are the **outline pane**, **slide pane**, and **notes pane**. You can drag the pane borders to adjust the size of the panes. They allow you to work on various aspects of your presentation simultaneously (Figure 1-6). You can type the text of your presentation in the outline pane and easily rearrange bulleted lists, paragraphs, and individual slides. As you type in the outline pane, you can view this text in the slide pane. You also can enter text, graphics, animations, and hyperlinks directly in the slide pane. You can type notes and additional information in the notes pane. This text can consist of notes to yourself or remarks to share with your audience. After you have created at least two slides, **scroll bars**, **scroll arrows**, and **scroll boxes** will display below and to the right of the windows, and you can use them to view different parts of the panes.

Slide sorter view is helpful when you want to see all the slides in your presentation simultaneously. A miniature version of each slide displays, and you can rearrange their order, add transitions and timings to switch from one side to the next in your presentation, add and delete slides, and preview animations.

Table 1-1 identifies the view buttons and provides an explanation of each view.

More About

PowerPoint Views

The three panes in normal, outline, and slide views allow you to work on all aspects of your presentation simultaneously. You can drag the pane borders to make each area larger or smaller.

Table 1-1	View Buttons and Functions	
BUTTON	*NAME*	*FUNCTION*
	Normal View	Displays three panes: the outline pane, the slide pane, and the notes pane.
	Outline View	Displays a presentation in an outline format showing slide titles and text. It is best used for organizing and developing the content of your presentation. You can rearrange paragraphs and bullet points in this view.
	Slide View	Displays a single slide as it appears in your presentation. Slide view is used to incorporate text, graphics, video, audio, hyperlinks, and animation and also to create line-by-line progressive disclosure, called build effects. Use slide view to create or edit a presentation.
	Slide Sorter View	Displays miniature versions of all slides in your presentation. You then can copy, cut, paste, or otherwise change slide position to modify your presentation. Slide sorter view also is used to add timings, to select animated transitions, and to preview animations.
	Slide Show View	Displays your slides as an electronic presentation on the full screen of your computer's monitor. Looking much like a slide projector display, you can see the effect of transitions, build effects, slide timings, and animations.

Placeholders, Title Area, Object Area, Mouse Pointer, and Scroll Bars

The PowerPoint window contains elements similar to the document windows in other Microsoft Office 2000 applications. Other features are unique to PowerPoint. The main elements are the Title Area and Object Area placeholders, the mouse pointer, and scroll bars.

PLACEHOLDERS **Placeholders** are boxes that display when you create a new slide. All AutoLayouts except the Blank AutoLayout contain placeholders. Depending on the particular slide layout selected, placeholders display for the slide title, text, charts, tables, organization charts, media clips, and clip art. You type titles, body text, and bulleted lists in **text placeholders**; you place graphic elements in chart placeholders, table placeholders, organizational chart placeholders, and clip art placeholders. A placeholder is considered an **object**, which is a single element of your slide. An empty placeholder is called an **unfilled object**; a placeholder containing text or graphics is called a **filled object**. When a filled object contains text, it is called a **text object**.

TITLE AREA Surrounded by a dotted outline, the **Title Area** is the location of the text placeholder where you will type the main heading of a new slide (Figure 1-6 on page PP 1.12).

OBJECT AREA Surrounded by a dotted outline, the **Object Area** is the empty area that displays below the Title Area on a slide. It can contain various placeholders for displaying subtitle or supporting information such as clip art and charts (Figure 1-6).

MOUSE POINTER The **mouse pointer** can have a different shape depending on the task you are performing in PowerPoint and the pointer's location on the screen. The different shapes are discussed when they display in subsequent projects.

SCROLL BARS When you add a second slide to your presentation, **vertical scroll bars** display on the right side of the outline and slide panes. PowerPoint allows you to use the scroll bars to move forward or backward through your presentation.

The **horizontal scroll bar** also displays when you add a second slide to your presentation. It is located on the bottom of the slide pane and allows you to display a portion of the slide when the entire slide does not fit on the screen.

More About

The Mouse Pointer

The Microsoft IntelliMouse® pointing device can help you build presentations efficiently. For example, you can roll the wheel forward or backward instead of clicking a scroll bar. You also can have your document scroll automatically. For more information, visit the PowerPoint 2000 More About Web page (www.scsite.com/pp2000/more.htm) and click IntelliMouse.

Menu Bar, Standard Toolbar, Formatting Toolbar, Drawing Toolbar, and Status Bar

The menu bar, Standard toolbar, and Formatting toolbar display at the top of the screen just below the title bar (Figure 1-6). The Standard and Formatting toolbars are by default on one row. The Drawing toolbar and status bar display at the bottom of the screen above the Windows taskbar.

MENU BAR The menu bar displays the PowerPoint menu names (Figure 1-7a). Each menu name represents a menu of commands that you can use to retrieve, store, print, and manipulate objects in your presentation. When you point to a menu name on the menu bar, the area of the menu bar containing the name changes to a button. To display a menu, such as the Insert menu, click the Insert menu name on the menu bar (Figures 1-7b and 1-7c). If you point to a command with an arrow on the right, a submenu displays from which you can choose a command.

When you click a menu name on the menu bar, a **short menu** displays listing the most recently used commands (Figure 1-7b). If you wait a few seconds or click the arrows at the bottom of the short menu (Figure 1-7b), the full menu displays. The **full menu** shows all the commands associated with a menu (Figure 1-7c). As you use PowerPoint, it automatically personalizes the menus for you based on how often you use commands. In this book, when you display a menu, wait a few seconds or click the arrows at the bottom of the menu so the long menu displays. The **hidden commands** that display on the full menu are recessed. **Dimmed commands** (gray background) indicate they are not available for the current selection.

The menu bar can change to include other menu names depending on the type of work you are doing. For example, if you are adding a chart to a slide, Data and Chart menu names are added to the menu bar with commands that reflect charting options.

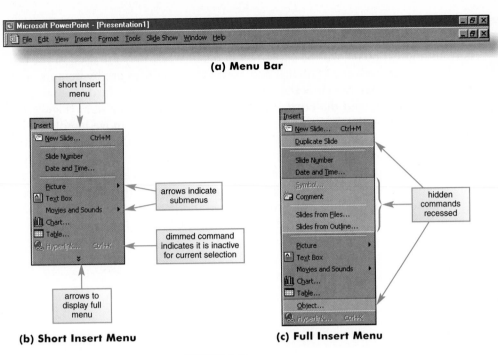

(a) Menu Bar

short Insert menu

arrows indicate submenus

dimmed command indicates it is inactive for current selection

arrows to display full menu

(b) Short Insert Menu

hidden commands recessed

(c) Full Insert Menu

FIGURE 1-7

STANDARD, FORMATTING, AND DRAWING TOOLBARS The Standard toolbar (Figure 1-8a), Formatting toolbar (Figure 1-8b), and Drawing toolbar (Figure 1-8c) contain buttons and list boxes that allow you to perform frequent tasks more quickly than when using the menu bar. For example, to print a slide show, you click the Print button on the Standard toolbar. Each button has an image on the button that helps you remember the button's function. When you move the mouse pointer over a button or box, the name of the button or box also displays below it. This name is called a **ScreenTip**.

(a) Standard Toolbar

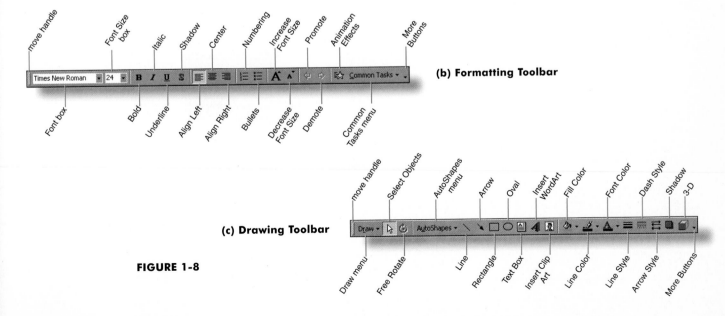

(b) Formatting Toolbar

(c) Drawing Toolbar

FIGURE 1-8

Toolbars

To display more of the PowerPoint window, you can hide a toolbar you no longer need. To hide a toolbar, right-click any toolbar and then click the check mark next to the toolbar you want to hide.

Figures 1-8a, 1-8b, and 1-8c on the previous page illustrate the Standard, Formatting, and Drawing toolbars and describe the functions of the buttons. Each of the buttons and list boxes will be explained in detail when they are used in the projects.

Remember, both the Standard and Formatting toolbars are by default on the same row immediately below the menu bar. Usually, the Standard toolbar displays on the left of the row and the Formatting toolbar displays on the right (Figure 1-9a).

To view the entire Formatting toolbar, double-click the move handle on its left edge or drag the move handle to the left. When you show the complete Formatting toolbar, a portion of the Standard toolbar is hidden (Figure 1-9b). To display the entire Standard toolbar, double-click its move handle. PowerPoint slides the Formatting toolbar to the right so the toolbars return to the way they look in Figure 1-9a.

An alternative to sliding one toolbar over another is to use the More Buttons button on a toolbar to display the buttons that are hidden (Figure 1-9c).

FIGURE 1-9

As with the menus, PowerPoint will personalize the toolbars. That is, if you use a hidden button on a partially displayed toolbar, PowerPoint will remove the button from the More Buttons list (Figure 1-9c) and place it on the toolbar. For example, if you click the Spelling button and then the Grayscale Preview button on the Standard toolbar (Figure 1-9c), PowerPoint will display these buttons on the Standard toolbar and remove buttons from the Standard or Formatting toolbars to make room on the row.

STATUS BAR Immediately above the Windows taskbar at the bottom of the screen is the status bar. The **status bar** consists of a message area and a presentation design template identifier (Figure 1-11 on page PP 1.18). Generally the message area displays the current slide number and the total number of slides in the slide show. For example, in Figure 1-11 the message area displays Slide 1 of 1. Slide 1 is the current slide, and of 1 indicates the slide show contains only 1 slide. The template identifier displays Default Design, which is the template PowerPoint uses initially.

PowerPoint has several additional toolbars you can display by pointing to Toolbars on the View menu and then clicking the respective name on the Toolbars submenu. You also can display a toolbar by pointing to a toolbar and right-clicking to display a shortcut menu, which lists the available toolbars. A **shortcut menu** contains a list of commands or items that relate to the item to which you are pointing when you right-click.

Resetting Menus and Toolbars

Each project in this book begins with the menu bars and toolbars appearing as they did at initial installation of the software. To reset your toolbars and menus so they appear exactly as shown in this book, follow the steps outlined in Appendix C.

Displaying the Formatting Toolbar in Its Entirety

Perform the following steps to display the entire Formatting toolbar.

 To Display the Formatting Toolbar in Its Entirety

1 Point to the move handle on the Formatting toolbar (Figure 1-10).

FIGURE 1-10

Double-click the move handle on the Formatting toolbar.

The entire Formatting toolbar displays (Figure 1-11).

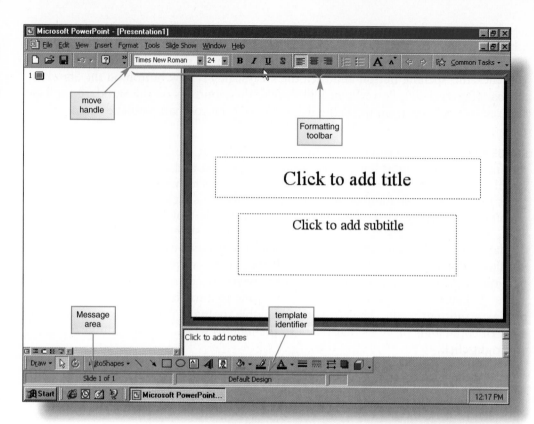

FIGURE 1-11

Choosing a Design Template

A **design template** provides consistency in design and color throughout the entire presentation. It determines the color scheme, font and font size, and layout of your presentation. Perform the following steps to choose a design template.

Steps To Choose a Design Template

① Click the Common Tasks menu button on the Formatting toolbar and then point to Apply Design Template (Figure 1-12).

FIGURE 1-12

Click Apply Design Template.

The Apply Design Template dialog box displays (Figure 1-13). Numerous design template names display in the list box. Artsy is highlighted in the list, and a thumbnail view of the Artsy design template displays in the preview area. If the preview area does not display, click the Views button arrow and then click Preview. The Cancel button or the Close button can be used to close the Apply Design Template dialog box if you do not want to apply a new template.

FIGURE 1-13

 Click the down scroll arrow to scroll down the list of design templates until Straight Edge appears. Click Straight Edge. Point to the Apply button.

A preview of the Straight Edge design template displays in the preview area (Figure 1-14).

FIGURE 1-14

Click the Apply button.

Slide 1 displays with the Straight Edge design template (Figure 1-15).

FIGURE 1-15

1. Double-click Straight Edge in list
2. On Format menu click Apply Design Template, scroll down to select Straight Edge, click Apply
3. Double-click Default Design on status bar, scroll down to select Straight Edge, click Apply

Creating a Title Slide

With the exception of a blank slide, PowerPoint also assumes every new slide has a title. To make creating your presentation easier, any text you type after a new slide displays becomes the title object. The AutoLayout for the title slide has a Title Area placeholder near the middle of the window and an Object Area placeholder directly below the Title Area placeholder (Figure 1-15).

Entering the Presentation Title

The presentation title for Project 1 is Effective Study Skills. As you begin typing in the Title Area placeholder, the title text displays immediately after the Slide 1 icon in the outline pane. Perform the following steps to create the title slide for this project.

Steps **To Enter the Presentation Title**

1 **Click the label, Click to add title, located inside the Title Area placeholder.**

*The insertion point is in the Title Area placeholder (Figure 1-16). The **insertion point** is a blinking vertical line (|), which indicates where the next character will display. The mouse pointer changes to an I-beam. A **selection rectangle** displays around the Title Area placeholder. The placeholder is selected as indicated by the border and sizing handles displaying on the edges.*

FIGURE 1-16

2 **Type** Effective Study Skills **in the Title Area placeholder. Do not press the ENTER key.**

The title text, Effective Study Skills, displays in the Title Area placeholder and in the outline pane (Figure 1-17). The current title text displays with the default font (Times New Roman) and default font size (40).

FIGURE 1-17

Enhancements

Microsoft touts the AutoFit text feature as an important PowerPoint 2000 upgrade. Other ease-of-use enhancements are the tri-pane view, the ability to create tables easily, and the self-paced introduction, which gives a useful overview of PowerPoint's key features. For more information, visit the PowerPoint 2000 More About Web page (www.scsite.com/pp2000/more.htm) and click Enhancements.

Notice that you do not press the ENTER key after the word Skills. If you press the ENTER key after typing the title, PowerPoint creates a new line, which would be a new second paragraph in the Title Area. You want only one paragraph in this text placeholder. A **paragraph** is a segment of text with the same format that begins when you press the ENTER key and ends when you press the ENTER key again. Therefore, do not press the ENTER key unless you want to create a two-paragraph title. Additionally, PowerPoint **line wraps** text that exceeds the width of the placeholder. For example, if the slide title was Effective College Study Skills, it would exceed the width of the Title Area placeholder and display on two lines.

One of PowerPoint's new features is **AutoFit text**. If you are creating your slide and need to squeeze an extra line in the text placeholder, PowerPoint will resize the existing text in the placeholder so that this extra line will fit on the screen.

Correcting a Mistake When Typing

If you type the wrong letter and notice the error before pressing the ENTER key, press the BACKSPACE key to erase all the characters back to and including the one that is incorrect. If you mistakenly press the ENTER key after entering the title and the insertion point is on the new line, simply press the BACKSPACE key to return the insertion point to the right of the letter s in the word Skills.

When you install PowerPoint, the default setting allows you to reverse up to the last 20 changes by clicking the **Undo button** on the Standard toolbar. The ScreenTip that displays when you point to the Undo button changes to indicate the type of change just made. For example, if you type text in the Title Area placeholder and then point to the Undo button, the ScreenTip that displays is Undo Typing. For clarity, when referencing the Undo button in this project, the name displaying in the ScreenTip is referenced. Another way to reverse changes is to click the Undo command on the Edit menu. Like the Undo button, the Undo command reflects the last type of change made to the presentation.

You can reapply a change that you reversed with the Undo button by clicking the Redo button on the Standard toolbar. Clicking the **Redo button** reverses the last undo action. The ScreenTip name reflects the type of reversal last performed.

Entering the Presentation Subtitle

The next step in creating the title slide is to enter the subtitle text into the Object Area placeholder. Perform the following steps to enter the presentation subtitle.

Steps **To Enter the Presentation Subtitle**

1 **Click the label, Click to add subtitle, located inside the Object Area placeholder.**

The insertion point is in the Object Area placeholder (Figure 1-18). The mouse pointer changes to an I-beam indicating the mouse is in a text placeholder. The selection rectangle indicates the placeholder is selected. The default Object Area text font size is 32.

FIGURE 1-18

2 **Type** Strategies for College Success **and then press the ENTER key. Type** Presented by **and then press the ENTER key. Type** Seaview College **but do not press the ENTER key.**

The text displays in the Object Area placeholder and the outline pane (Figure 1-19). The insertion point displays after the letter e in College. A red wavy line displays under the word, Seaview, to indicate a possible spelling error. A light bulb may display in the top-left corner of the text placeholder, depending on your computer's settings. The Office Assistant generates this light bulb to give you design tips.

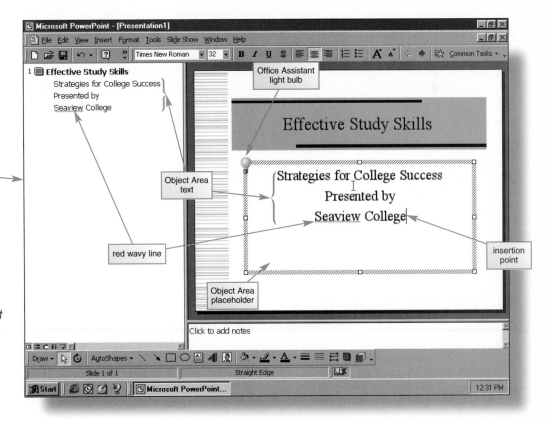

FIGURE 1-19

The previous section created a title slide using an AutoLayout for the title slide. PowerPoint displayed the title slide layout because you created a new presentation. You clicked the Title Area placeholder to select it and then typed your title. In general, to type text in any text placeholder, click the text placeholder and begin typing. You could, however, enter text in the Title Area placeholder without selecting this placeholder because PowerPoint assumes every slide has a title. You also added subtitle text in the Object Area placeholder. While this information identifying the presenter is not required, it often is useful for the audience.

Text Attributes

More About

Text Attributes

An extensive glossary of typography terms is available at the Microsoft Web site. The information includes a diagram illustrating the text attributes. For more information, visit the PowerPoint 2000 More About Web page (www.scsite.com/pp2000/more.htm) and click Attributes.

This presentation is using the Straight Edge design template. Each design template has its own text attributes. A **text attribute** is a characteristic of the text, such as font, font size, font style, or text color. You can adjust text attributes any time before, during, or after you type the text. Recall that a design template determines the color scheme, font and font size, and layout of your presentation. Most of the time, you use the design template's text attributes and color scheme. Occasionally you may want to change the way your presentation looks, however, and still keep a particular design template. PowerPoint gives you that flexibility. You can use the design template and change the text's color, font size, font, and font style. Table 1-2 explains the different text attributes available in PowerPoint.

Table 1-2	Design Template Text Attributes
ATTRIBUTE	**DESCRIPTION**
Color	Defines the color of text. Displaying text in color requires a color monitor. Printing text in color requires a color printer or plotter.
Font	Defines the appearance and shape of letters, numbers, and special characters.
Font size	Specifies the size of characters on the screen. Character size is gauged by a measurement system called points. A single point is about 1/72 of an inch in height. Thus, a character with a point size of eighteen is about 18/72 (or 1/4) of an inch in height.
Font style	Defines text characteristics. Font styles include plain, italic, bold, shadowed, and underlined. Text may have one or more font styles at a time.
Subscript	Defines the placement of a character in relationship to another. A subscript character displays or prints slightly below and immediately to one side of another character.
Superscript	Defines the placement of a character in relationship to another. A superscript character displays or prints above and immediately to one side of another character.

The next two sections explain how to change the font size and font style attributes.

Changing the Font Size

The Straight Edge design template default font size is 40 points for title text and 32 points for body text. A point is 1/72 of an inch in height. Thus, a character with a point size of 40 is about 40/72 (or 5/9) of an inch in height. Slide 1 requires you to increase the font size for the paragraph, Effective Study Skills. Perform the following steps to increase the font size.

To Increase Font Size

① **Position the mouse pointer in the Title Area placeholder and then triple-click.**

PowerPoint selects the entire line (Figure 1-20). You select an entire line quickly by triple-clicking any area within the Title Area placeholder.

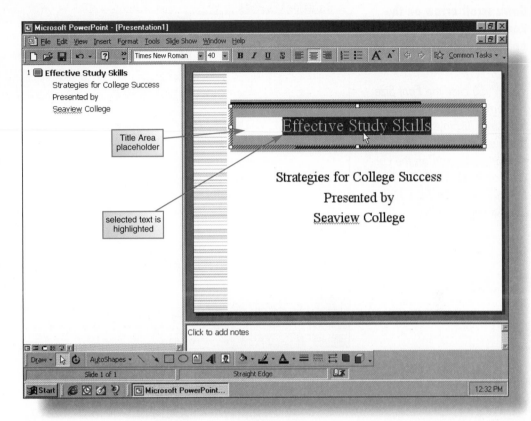

FIGURE 1-20

③ **With Effective Study Skills highlighted, point to the Font Size box arrow in the Font Size box on the Formatting toolbar.**

*When you point to a button or other areas on a toolbar, PowerPoint displays a Screen-Tip. A **ScreenTip** contains the name of the tool to which you are pointing. When pointing to the Font Size box or the Font Size box arrow, the ScreenTip displays the words, Font Size (Figure 1-21). The **Font Size box** indicates that the title text is 40 points.*

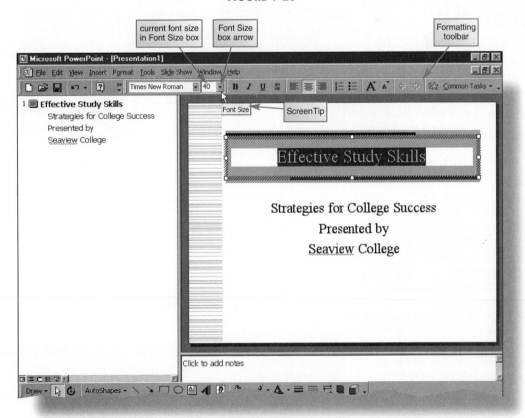

FIGURE 1-21

4 **Click the Font Size box arrow, click the down scroll arrow on the Font Size scroll bar until 54 appears, and then point to 54.**

When you click the Font Size box arrow, a list of available font sizes displays in the Font Size list box. The font sizes displayed depend on the current font, which is Times New Roman. Font size 54 is highlighted (Figure 1-22).

FIGURE 1-22

5 **Click 54.**

The title text, Effective Study Skills, increases in font size to 54 points (Figure 1-23). The Font Size box on the Formatting toolbar displays 54, indicating the selected text has a font size of 54.

Other Ways

1. Right-click selected text, click Font on shortcut menu, type new font size in Size box
2. Click Increase Font Size button on Formatting toolbar
3. Click Font Size box on Formatting toolbar, type font size between 1 and 4000
4. On Format menu click Font, click new font size in Size box, or type font size between 1 and 4000

FIGURE 1-23

You also can use the **Increase Font Size button** on the Formatting toolbar to increase the font size. Each time you click the button, the font size becomes larger in preset increments. If you need to decrease the font size, click the Font Size box arrow and select a size smaller than 40. Another method is to click the **Decrease Font Size button** on the Formatting toolbar. The font size will become smaller in preset increments each time you click the button.

Changing the Style of Text to Italic

Text font styles include plain, italic, bold, shadowed, and underlined. PowerPoint allows you to use one or more text font styles in your presentation. Perform the following steps to add emphasis to the title slide by changing plain text to italic text.

Steps To Change the Text Font Style to Italic

1 **Triple-click the paragraph, Presented by, in the Object Area text placeholder, and then point to the Italic button on the Formatting toolbar.**

The paragraph, Presented by, is highlighted (Figure 1-24). The Italic button is three-dimensional.

FIGURE 1-24

2 Click the Italic button.

The text is italicized in both the slide and outline panes, and the Italic button is recessed on the Formatting toolbar (Figure 1-25).

Italic button recessed

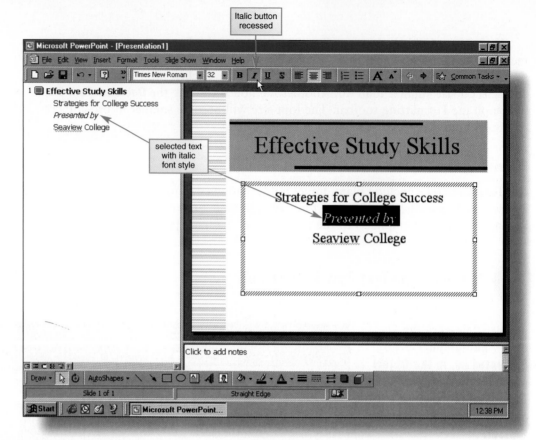

FIGURE 1-25

Other Ways

1. Right-click selected text, click Font on shortcut menu, click Italic in Font style list
2. On Format menu click Font, click Italic in Font style list
3. Press CTRL+I

To remove italics from text, select the italicized text and then click the Italic button. As a result, the Italic button is not recessed, and the text does not have the italic font style.

Saving the Presentation on a Floppy Disk

While you are building your presentation, the computer stores it in main memory. It is important to save your presentation frequently because the presentation will be lost if the computer is turned off or you lose electrical power. Another reason to save your work is that if you run out of lab time before completing your project, you may finish the project later without starting over. You must, therefore, save any presentation you will use later. Before you continue with Project 1, save the work completed thus far. Perform the following steps to save a presentation on a floppy disk using the Save button on the Standard toolbar.

To Save a Presentation on a Floppy Disk

1 **Insert a formatted floppy disk in drive A and then click the Save button on the Standard toolbar.**

The Save As dialog box displays (Figure 1-26). The default folder, My Documents, displays in the Save in box. Effective Study Skills displays highlighted in the File name box because PowerPoint uses the words in the Title Area placeholder as the default file name. Presentation displays in the Save as type box. Clicking the Cancel button closes the Save As dialog box.

FIGURE 1-26

2 **Type** Studying **in the File name box. Do not press the ENTER key after typing the file name.**

The name, Studying, displays in the File name box (Figure 1-27).

FIGURE 1-27

3 Click the Save in box arrow. Point to 3½ Floppy (A:) in the Save in list.

The Save in list displays a list of locations to which you can save your presentation (Figure 1-28). Your list may look different depending on the configuration of your system. 3½ Floppy (A:) is highlighted.

FIGURE 1-28

4 Click 3½ Floppy (A:) and then point to the Save button.

Drive A becomes the destination location for the presentation (Figure 1-29).

FIGURE 1-29

Click the Save button.

PowerPoint saves the presentation to your floppy disk in drive A. The title bar displays the file name, Studying, used to save the presentation (Figure 1-30).

file name displays on title bar

FIGURE 1-30

PowerPoint automatically appends the extension .ppt to the file name, Studying. The **.ppt** extension stands for **P**ower**P**oint. Although the slide show, Studying, is saved on a floppy disk, it also remains in main memory and displays on the screen.

It is a good practice to save periodically while you are working on a project. By doing so, you protect yourself from losing all the work you have done since the last time you saved.

Adding a New Slide to a Presentation

The title slide for your presentation is created. The next step is to add the first bulleted list slide immediately after the current slide in Project 1. Usually when you create your presentation, you add slides with text, graphics, or charts. When you add a new slide, PowerPoint displays a dialog box for you to choose one of the 24 different AutoLayouts. These AutoLayouts have placeholders for various objects. Some placeholders allow you to double-click the placeholder and then access other PowerPoint objects. More information about using AutoLayout placeholders to add graphics follows in subsequent projects. Perform the steps on the next page to add a new slide using the Bulleted List AutoLayout.

Other Ways

1. On File menu click Save As
2. Press CTRL+S or press SHIFT+F12

Steps **To Add a New Slide Using the Bulleted List AutoLayout**

1 Double-click the move handle on the Standard toolbar and then point to the New Slide button (Figure 1-31).

FIGURE 1-31

2 Click the New Slide button. When the New Slide dialog box displays, point to the OK button.

The New Slide dialog box displays (Figure 1-32). The Bulleted List AutoLayout is selected, and the AutoLayout title, Bulleted List, displays at the bottom-right corner of the New Slide dialog box.

FIGURE 1-32

3 **Click the OK button.**

Slide 2 displays keeping the attributes of the Straight Edge design template using the Bulleted List AutoLayout (Figure 1-33). Slide 2 of 2 displays on the status bar. The vertical scroll bar displays in the slide pane. The bullet appears as a diamond.

FIGURE 1-33

Because the Bulleted List AutoLayout was selected, PowerPoint displays Slide 2 with a Title Area placeholder and an Object Area placeholder with a bullet. You can change the layout for a slide at any time during the creation of your presentation by clicking the Common Tasks menu button on the Formatting toolbar and then clicking the Slide Layout button. You then can double-click the AutoLayout of your choice.

Other Ways

1. Click Common Tasks menu button on Formatting toolbar, click New Slide
2. On Insert menu click New Slide
3. Press CTRL+M

Creating a Bulleted List Slide

The bulleted list slides in Figure 1-2 on page PP 1.9 contain more than one level of bulleted text. A slide with more than one level of bulleted text is called a **multi-level bulleted list slide**. A **level** is a position within a structure, such as an outline, that indicates a magnitude of importance. PowerPoint allows for five paragraph levels. Each paragraph level has an associated bullet. The bullet font is dependent on the design template. Figure 1-34 on the next page identifies the five paragraph levels and the bullet fonts for the Straight Edge design template. Beginning with the Second level, each paragraph indents to the right of the preceding level.

FIGURE 1-34

An indented paragraph is **demoted**, or pushed down to a lower level. For example, if you demote a First level paragraph, it becomes a Second level paragraph. This lower-level paragraph is a subset of the higher-level paragraph. It usually contains information that supports the topic in the paragraph immediately above it. You demote a paragraph by clicking the **Demote button** on the Formatting toolbar.

When you want to raise a paragraph from a lower level to a higher level, you **promote** the paragraph by clicking the **Promote button** on the Formatting toolbar.

Creating a multi-level bulleted list slide requires several steps. Initially, you enter a slide title in the Title Area placeholder. Next, you select the Object Area text placeholder. Then you type the text for the multi-level bulleted list, demoting and promoting paragraphs as needed. The next several sections explain how to add a multi-level bulleted list slide.

Entering a Slide Title

PowerPoint assumes every new slide has a title. The title for Slide 2 is Managing Your Time. Perform the following step to enter this title.

Slide Masters

Each design template has a corresponding slide master designed by Microsoft graphic artists. The text attributes and color schemes are developed to coordinate with each other and to evoke audience reactions, such as excitement or relaxation.

Steps To Enter a Slide Title

1 **If necessary, click the Title Area placeholder and then type** Managing your Time **as the title. Do not press the ENTER key.**

The title, Managing Your Time, displays in the Title Area placeholder and in the outline pane (Figure 1-35). The insertion point displays after the e in Time.

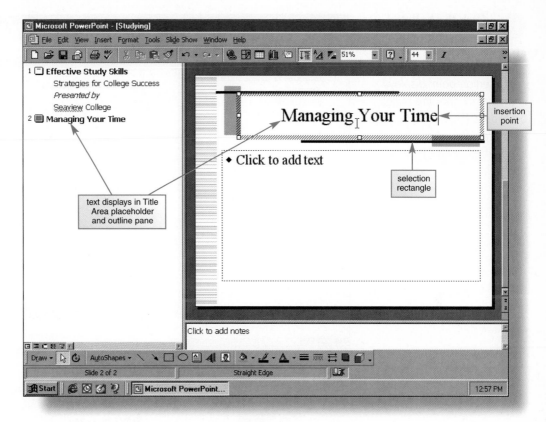

FIGURE 1-35

Selecting an Object Area Placeholder

Before you can type text in the Object Area placeholder, you first must select it. Perform the step on the next page to select the Object Area placeholder on Slide 2.

To Select an Object Area Placeholder

1 **Click the bulleted paragraph labeled, Click to add text.**

The insertion point displays immediately after the bullet on Slide 2 (Figure 1-36). The mouse pointer may change shape if you move it away from the bullet.

FIGURE 1-36

1. Press CTRL+ENTER

Typing a Multi-level Bulleted List

Recall that a bulleted list is a list of paragraphs, each of which is preceded by a bullet. Also recall that a paragraph is a segment of text ended by pressing the ENTER key. The next step is to type the multi-level bulleted list, which consists of the six entries (Figure 1-2 on page PP 1.9). Perform the following steps to type a multi-level bulleted list.

To Type a Multi-level Bulleted List

1 **Double-click the move handle on the Formatting toolbar. Type** Make a weekly schedule **and then press the ENTER key.**

The paragraph, Make a weekly schedule, displays (Figure 1-37). The font size is 32. The insertion point displays after the second bullet. When you press the ENTER key, PowerPoint ends one paragraph and begins a new paragraph. Because you are using the Bulleted List Auto-Layout, PowerPoint places a diamond bullet in front of the new paragraph.

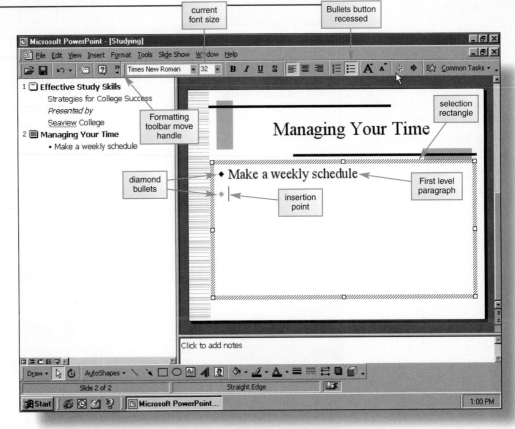

FIGURE 1-37

2 **Point to the Demote button (Figure 1-38).**

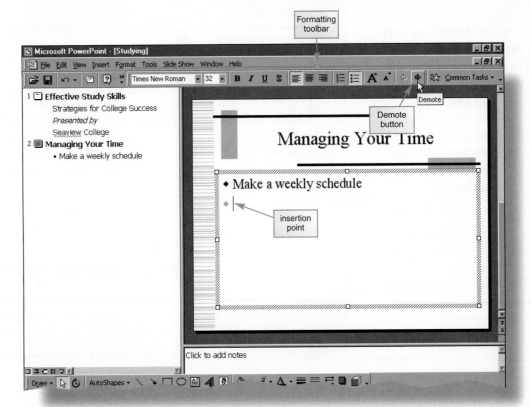

FIGURE 1-38

3 **Click the Demote button.**

The second paragraph indents under the first and becomes a Second level paragraph (Figure 1-39). Notice the bullet in front of the second paragraph changes from a diamond to a box, and the font size for the demoted paragraph now is 28. The insertion point displays after the box.

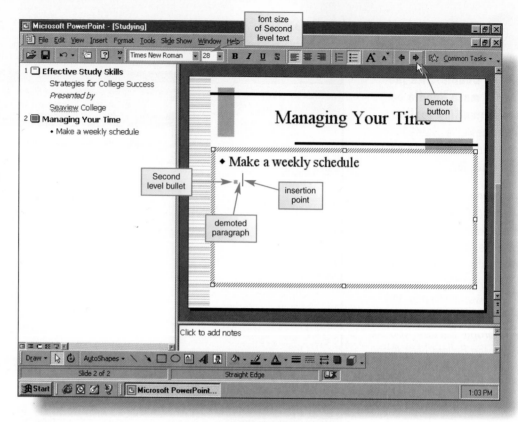

FIGURE 1-39

4 **Type** List specific study times for all subjects **and then press the ENTER key. Type** Plan time for recreation and sleep **and then press the ENTER key. Type** Spread study times throughout the week **and then press the ENTER key. Point to the Promote button.**

Three new Second level paragraphs display with boxes in both the slide and outline panes (Figure 1-40). When you press the ENTER key, PowerPoint adds a new paragraph at the same level as the previous paragraph.

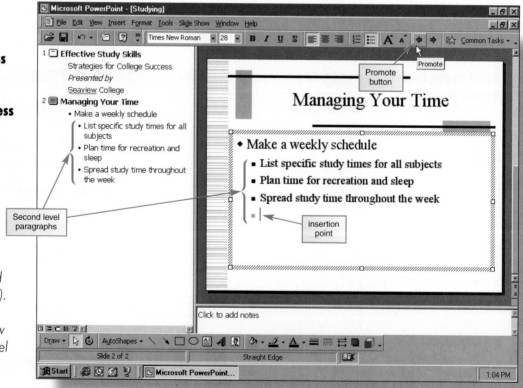

FIGURE 1-40

⑤ Click the Promote button.

The Second level paragraph becomes a First level paragraph (Figure 1-41). The bullet in front of the new paragraph changes from a box to a diamond, and the font size for the promoted paragraph is 32. The insertion point displays after the diamond bullet.

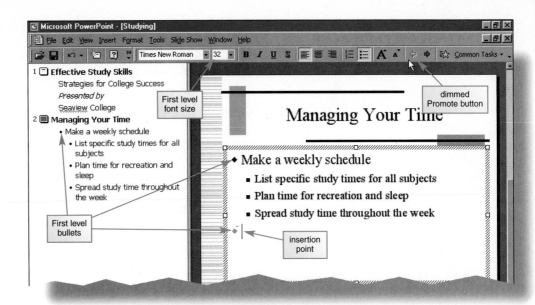

FIGURE 1-41

Perform the following steps to complete the text for Slide 2.

TO TYPE THE REMAINING TEXT FOR SLIDE 2

① Type Stick to your schedule and then press the ENTER key.

② Type Revise your schedule when necessary but do not press the ENTER key.

The insertion point displays after the y in necessary (Figure 1-42).

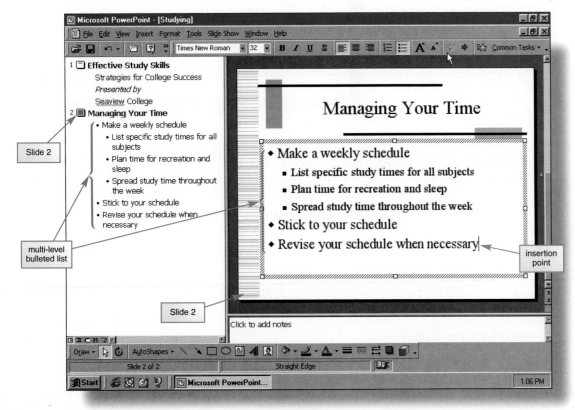

FIGURE 1-42

Notice that you did not press the ENTER key after typing the last bullet line in Step 2. If you press the ENTER key, a new bullet displays after the last entry on this slide. To remove an extra bullet, press the BACKSPACE key.

Adding New Slides with the Same AutoLayout

When you add a new slide to a presentation and want to keep the same AutoLayout used on the previous slide, PowerPoint gives you a shortcut. Instead of clicking the New Slide button and clicking an AutoLayout in the New Slide dialog box, you can press and hold down the SHIFT key and then click the New Slide button. Perform the following step to add a new slide (Slide 3) and keep the Bulleted List AutoLayout used on the previous slide.

 To Add a New Slide with the Same AutoLayout

1 **Press and hold down the SHIFT key, click the New Slide button on the Standard toolbar, and then release the SHIFT key.**

Slide 3 displays the Bulleted List AutoLayout (Figure 1-43). Slide 3 of 3 displays on the status bar.

FIGURE 1-43

1. Press SHIFT+CTRL+M

Slide 3 is added to the presentation. Perform the following steps to add text to Slide 3 and to create a multi-level bulleted list.

TO COMPLETE SLIDE 3

1 Type Attending Class in the Title Area placeholder.

2 Press CTRL+ENTER to move the insertion point to the Object Area placeholder.

(3) Type Sit in the front of the room and then press the ENTER key.

(4) Type Ask questions at appropriate times and then press the ENTER key.

(5) Type Take notes and then press the ENTER key.

(6) Click the Demote button.

(7) Type Rephrase ideas in your own words and then press the ENTER key.

(8) Type Review immediately after class but do not press the ENTER key.

Slide 3 displays as shown in Figure 1-44. The Office Assistant light bulb may display to offer design help. If so, you may click the light bulb next to the Office Assistant to see a tip. For additional help on using the Office Assistant, refer to Appendix A.

FIGURE 1-44

Slide 4, also a multi-level bulleted list, is the last slide in this presentation. Perform the following steps to create Slide 4.

TO CREATE SLIDE 4

(1) Press and hold down the SHIFT key, click the New Slide button on the Standard toolbar, and then release the SHIFT key.

(2) Type Reading Your Textbooks in the Title Area placeholder.

(3) Press CTRL+ENTER to move the insertion point to the Object Area placeholder.

(4) Type Survey the assignment and then press the ENTER key.

(5) Click the Demote button. Type Read the summary and chapter questions and then press the ENTER key.

6 Click the Promote button. Type Read the chapter carefully and then press the ENTER key.

7 Type Recite the material in your own words and then press the ENTER key.

8 Type Write brief notes in the margins and then press the ENTER key.

9 Type Review the entire assignment but do not press the ENTER key.

The Title Area and Object Area text objects display in the slide and outline panes (Figure 1-45). The Office Assistant light bulb may display to offer design help.

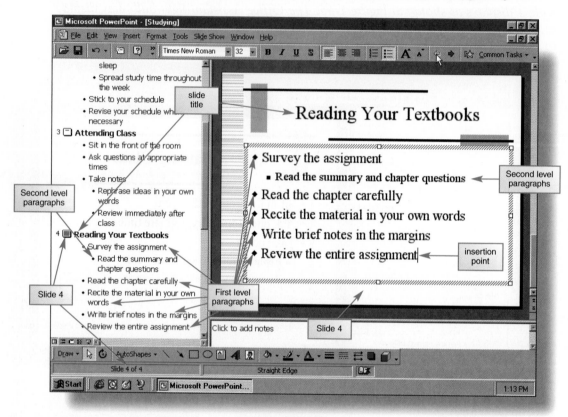

FIGURE 1-45

All slides for the Studying presentation are created. This presentation consists of a title slide and three multi-level bulleted list slides.

More *About* 2000

Black Slides

Insert a blank, black slide between sections of a large presentation or when you want to pause for discussion. The black slide focuses the audience's attention on you, the speaker, and away from the screen display.

Ending a Slide Show with a Black Slide

After the last slide in the slide show displays, the default PowerPoint setting is to end your presentation with a black slide. This black slide displays only when the slide show is running and concludes your slide show gracefully so your audience never sees the PowerPoint window. A black slide ends all slide shows until the option setting is deactivated. Perform the following steps to verify the End with black slide option is activated.

Steps **To End a Slide Show with a Black Slide**

① **Click Tools on the menu bar and then point to Options (Figure 1-46).**

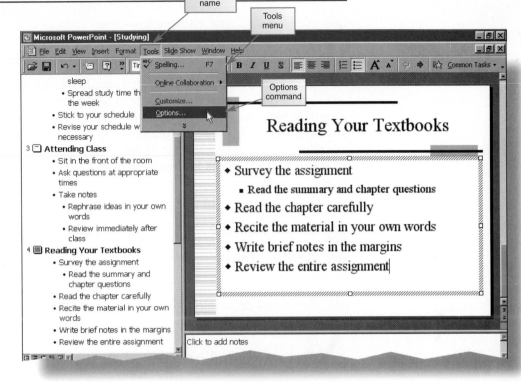

FIGURE 1-46

② **Click Options. If necessary, click the View tab when the Options dialog box opens. Verify a check mark displays in the End with black slide check box. If a check mark does not display, click the End with black slide check box.**

The Options dialog box displays (Figure 1-47). The View sheet contains settings for the overall PowerPoint display and for a particular slide show.

③ **Click the OK button.**

The End with black slide option is activated.

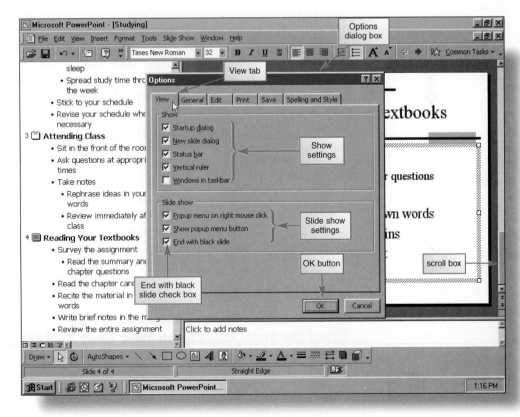

FIGURE 1-47

Now that all aspects of the presentation are complete, you need to save the additions and changes you have made to your Studying presentation.

Saving a Presentation with the Same File Name

Saving frequently cannot be overemphasized. When you first saved the presentation, you clicked the Save button on the Standard toolbar and the Save dialog box displayed. When you want to save the changes made to the presentation after your last save, you again click the Save button. This time, however, the Save dialog box does not display because PowerPoint updates the document called Studying.ppt on your floppy disk. Perform the following steps to save the presentation again.

TO SAVE A PRESENTATION WITH THE SAME FILE NAME

 Be sure your floppy disk is in drive A.

 Click the Save button on the Standard toolbar.

PowerPoint overwrites the old Studying.ppt document on the floppy disk in drive A with the revised presentation document. Slide 4 displays in the PowerPoint window.

Moving to Another Slide in Normal View

When creating or editing a presentation in normal view, you often want to display a slide other than the current one. You can move to another slide using several methods. In the outline pane, you can point to any of the text in a particular slide to display that slide in the slide pane, or you can drag the scroll box on the vertical scroll bar up or down to move through the text in your presentation. In the slide pane, you can click the **Previous Slide** or **Next Slide** buttons on the vertical scroll bar. Clicking the Next Slide button advances to the next slide in the presentation. Clicking the Previous Slide button backs up to the slide preceding the current slide. You also can drag the scroll box on the vertical scroll bar. When you drag the scroll box, the **slide indicator** displays the number and the title of the slide you are about to display. Releasing the mouse button displays the slide.

A slide's **Zoom setting** affects the portion of the slide displaying in the slide pane. PowerPoint defaults to a setting of approximately 50% so the entire slide displays. This percentage depends on the size and type of your monitor. If you want to display a small portion of the current slide, you would zoom in by clicking the Zoom box arrow and then clicking the desired magnification. You can display the entire slide in the slide pane by clicking Fit in the Zoom list. The Zoom setting affects the action of the vertical and horizontal scroll bars. If Zoom is set so that the entire slide is not visible in the slide pane, clicking the up scroll arrow on the vertical scroll bar displays the next portion of your slide, not the previous slide.

Using the Scroll Box on the Slide Pane to Move to Another Slide

Before continuing with Project 1, you want to display the title slide. Perform the following steps to move from Slide 4 to the Slide 1 using the scroll box on the slide pane vertical scroll bar.

More About

Zoom

You can increase your Zoom setting to as large as 400% when you want to see details on small objects. Likewise, you can decrease your Zoom setting to as small as 10%.

Steps | **To Use the Scroll Box on the Slide Pane to Move to Another Slide**

1 **Position the mouse pointer on the scroll box. Press and hold down the left mouse button.**

Slide: 4 of 4 Reading Your Textbooks displays in the slide indicator (Figure 1-48). The Slide 4 icon is shaded in the outline pane.

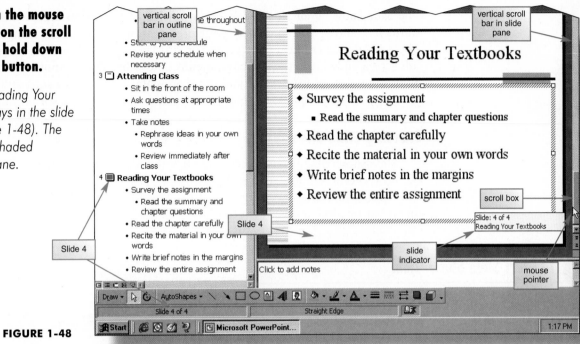

FIGURE 1-48

2 **Drag the scroll box up the vertical scroll bar until Slide: 1 of 4 Effective Study Skills displays in the slide indicator.**

Slide: 1 of 4 Effective Study Skills displays in the slide indicator (Figure 1-49). Slide 4 still displays in the PowerPoint window, and the Slide 4 icon is shaded in the outline pane.

3 **Release the left mouse button.**

Slide 1, titled Effective Study Skills, displays in the PowerPoint window. The Slide 1 icon is shaded in the outline pane.

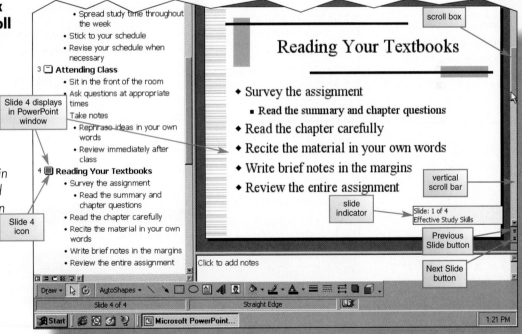

FIGURE 1-49

Other Ways

1. Click Next Slide button or Previous Slide button to move forward or back one slide

2. Press PAGE DOWN or PAGE UP to move forward or back one slide

Viewing the Presentation Using Slide Show

The **Slide Show button**, located at the lower-left of the PowerPoint window above the status bar, allows you to display your presentation electronically using a computer. The computer acts like a slide projector, displaying each slide on a full screen. The full screen slide hides the toolbars, menus, and other PowerPoint window elements. Slide show view is used when making a presentation. You can start slide show view from any view: normal view, outline view, slide view, or slide sorter view.

Starting Slide Show View

Slide show view begins when you click the Slide Show button in the lower-left of the PowerPoint window above the status bar. PowerPoint then displays the current slide on the full screen without any of the PowerPoint window objects, such as the menu bar or toolbars. Perform the following steps to start slide show view.

 To Start Slide Show View

1 **Point to the Slide Show button in the lower-left of the PowerPoint window above the status bar.**

The Normal View button is recessed because you still are in normal view (Figure 1-50).

FIGURE 1-50

Click the Slide Show button.

The title slide fills the screen (Figure 1-51). The PowerPoint window is hidden.

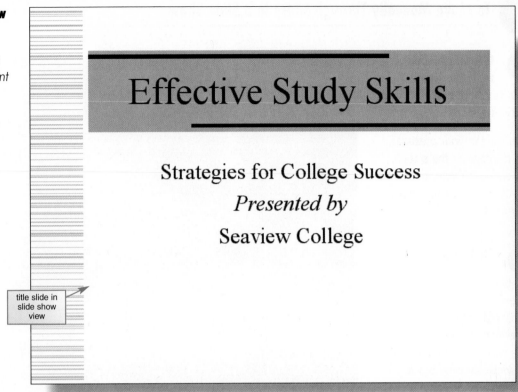

title slide in slide show view

Effective Study Skills

Strategies for College Success
Presented by
Seaview College

FIGURE 1-51

Other Ways

1. On View menu click Slide Show
2. Press F5

Advancing Through a Slide Show Manually

After you begin slide show view, you can move forward or backward through your slides. PowerPoint allows you to advance through your slides manually or automatically. Automatic advancing is discussed in a later project. Perform the steps on the next page to move manually through your slides.

Steps **To Move Manually Through Slides in a Slide Show**

 1 **Click each slide until the Reading Your Textbooks slide (Slide 4) displays.**

Each slide in your presentation displays on the screen, one slide at a time. Each time you click the mouse button, the next slide displays.

2 **Click Slide 4.**

The black slide displays (Figure 1-52). The message at the top of the slide announces the end of the slide show. To return to normal view, click the black slide.

FIGURE 1-52

Other **Ways**

1. Press PAGE DOWN to advance one slide at a time, or press PAGE UP to go backward one slide at a time
2. Press RIGHT ARROW key to advance one slide at a time, or press LEFT ARROW key to go backward one slide at a time

Using the Popup Menu to Go to a Specific Slide

Slide show view has a shortcut menu, called **Popup menu**, that displays when you right-click a slide in slide show view. This menu contains commands to assist you during a slide show. For example, clicking the **Next command** moves you to the next slide. Clicking the **Previous command** moves you to the previous slide. You can go to any slide in your presentation by pointing to the **Go command** and then clicking Slide Navigator. The **Slide Navigator dialog box** contains a list of the slides in your presentation. Go to the requested slide by double-clicking the name of that slide.

Perform the following steps to go to the title slide (Slide 1) in your presentation.

To Display the Popup Menu and Go to a Specific Slide

1 **With the black slide displaying in slide show view, right-click the slide. Point to Go on the Popup menu, and then point to Slide Navigator on the Go submenu.**

The Popup menu displays on the black slide, and the Go submenu displays (Figure 1-53). Your screen may look different because the Popup menu displays near the location of the mouse pointer at the time you right-click.

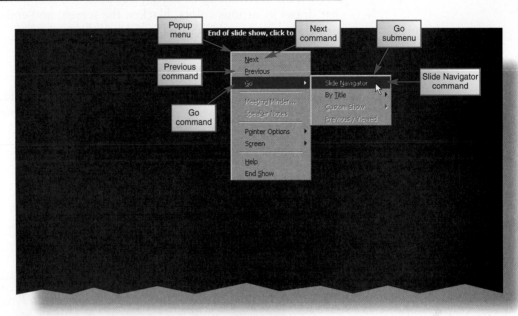

FIGURE 1-53

2 **Click Slide Navigator. When the Slide Navigator dialog box displays, point to 1. Effective Study Skills in the Slide titles list.**

The Slide titles list contains the title text of the slides in your presentation (Figure 1-54). You want to go to Slide 1 in your presentation. Slide 4 is the last slide viewed during your slide show.

3 **Double-click 1. Effective Study Skills.**

The title slide, Effective Study Skills, displays.

FIGURE 1-54

Other Ways

1. Right-click, point to Go, click Slide Navigator, type slide number, press ENTER

Additional Popup menu commands allow you to write meeting minutes or to create a list of action items during a slide show, change the mouse pointer to a pen that draws in various colors, blacken the screen, and end the slide show. Popup menu commands are discussed in subsequent projects.

Using the Popup Menu to End a Slide Show

The **End Show command** on the Popup menu exits slide show view and returns to the view you were in when you clicked the Slide Show button. Perform the following steps to end slide show view and return to normal view.

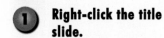 **To Use the Popup Menu to End a Slide Show**

1 **Right-click the title slide.**

The Popup menu displays on Slide 1.

2 **Point to End Show on the Popup menu.**

Your Popup menu may display in a different location (Figure 1-55).

3 **Click End Show.**

PowerPoint exits slide show view and returns to normal view. Slide 1 displays because it is the last slide displayed in slide show view.

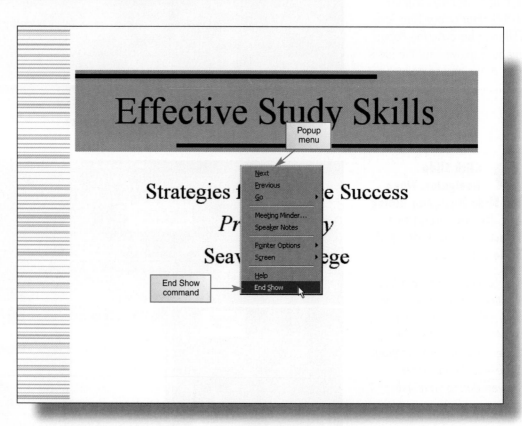

FIGURE 1-55

Other Ways

1. Click last slide in presentation to return to slide at which you began slide show view
2. Press ESC to display slide last viewed in slide show view

Quitting PowerPoint

The Studying presentation now is complete. When you quit PowerPoint, PowerPoint prompts you to save any changes made to the presentation since the last save, closes all PowerPoint windows, and then quits PowerPoint. Closing PowerPoint returns control to the desktop. Perform the following steps to quit PowerPoint.

Steps To Quit PowerPoint

1 **Point to the Close button on the title bar (Figure 1-56).**

2 **Click the Close button.**

PowerPoint closes and the Windows desktop displays. If you made changes to the presentation since your last save, a Microsoft PowerPoint dialog box displays the question, Do you wish to save the changes you made to Studying?. Click the Yes button to save the changes to the presentation before closing PowerPoint. Click the No button to quit PowerPoint without saving the changes. Click the Cancel button to return to the presentation.

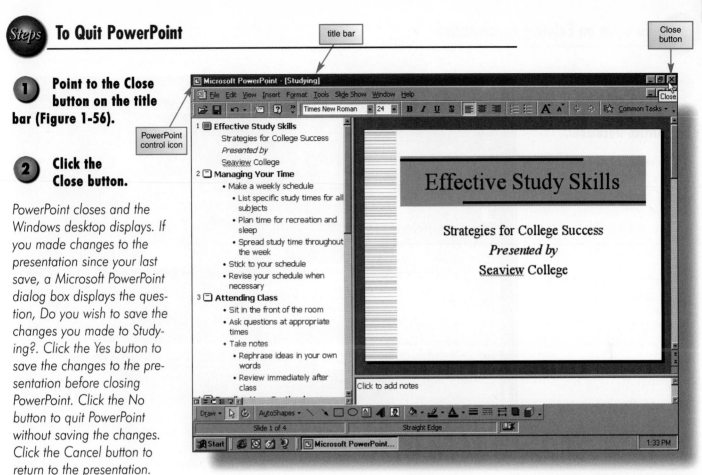

FIGURE 1-56

Opening a Presentation

Earlier, you saved the presentation on a floppy disk using the file name, Studying.ppt. Once you create and save a presentation, you may need to retrieve it from the floppy disk to make changes. For example, you may want to replace the design template or modify some text. Recall that a presentation is a PowerPoint document. Use the **Open Office Document command** to open an existing presentation.

Opening an Existing Presentation

Ensure that the floppy disk used to save Studying.ppt is in drive A. Then perform the steps on the next page to open the Studying presentation using the Open Office Document command on the Start menu.

Steps To Open an Existing Presentation

1 **Click the Start button on the taskbar and then point to Open Office Document.**

The Windows Start menu displays (Figure 1-57). Open Office Document is highlighted.

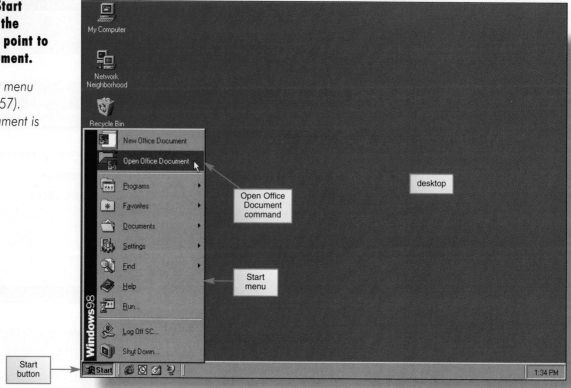

FIGURE 1-57

2 **Click Open Office Document. When the Open Office Document dialog box displays, if necessary, click the Look in box arrow and then click 3½ Floppy (A:) (see Figures 1-28 and 1-29 on page 1.30 to review this process).**

The Open Office Document dialog box displays (Figure 1-58). A list of existing files on drive A displays because your floppy disk is in drive A. Notice that Office Files displays in the Files of type box. The file, Studying, is highlighted. Your list of existing files may be different depending on the files saved on your floppy disk.

FIGURE 1-58

3 **Double-click Studying.**

PowerPoint starts, opens Studying.ppt from drive A into main memory, and displays the first slide on the screen. The presentation displays in normal view because PowerPoint opens a presentation in the same view in which it was saved.

Other Ways

1. Click Open Office Document button on Microsoft Office Shortcut Bar, click folder or drive name in Look in list, double-click document name
2. On Start menu click Documents, click document name

When you start PowerPoint and open Studying.ppt, this application and the file name display on a recessed button in the taskbar button area. When more than one application is open, you can switch between applications by clicking the button labeled with the name of the application to which you want to switch.

Checking a Presentation for Spelling and Consistency

After you create a presentation, you should check it visually for spelling errors and style consistency. In addition, you can use PowerPoint's Spelling and Style tools to identify possible misspellings and inconsistencies.

Checking a Presentation for Spelling Errors

PowerPoint checks your entire presentation for spelling mistakes using a standard dictionary contained in the Microsoft Office group. This dictionary is shared with the other Microsoft Office applications such as Word and Excel. A **custom dictionary** is available if you want to add special words such as proper names, cities, and acronyms. When checking a presentation for spelling errors, PowerPoint opens the standard dictionary and the custom dictionary file, if one exists. When a word displays in the Spelling dialog box, you perform one of the actions listed in Table 1-3.

More About

Dictionaries

Microsoft has partnered with publishing companies to produce the world's first global dictionary. More than 250 people worked to compile the three million English words contained in this work. The terms are used worldwide, for more than 80 percent of the world's computer-based communication uses the English language.

Table 1-3 Summary of Spelling Checker Actions	
FEATURE	*DESCRIPTION*
Ignore the word	Click Ignore when the word is spelled correctly but not found in the dictionaries. PowerPoint continues checking the rest of the presentation.
Ignore all occurrences of the word	Click Ignore All when the word is spelled correctly but not found in the dictionaries. PowerPoint ignores all occurrences of the word and continues checking the rest of the presentation.
Select a different spelling	Click the proper spelling of the word from the list in the Suggestions box. Click Change. PowerPoint corrects the word and continues checking the rest of the presentation.
Change all occurrences of the misspelling to a different spelling	Click the proper spelling of the word from the list in the Suggestions box. Click Change All. PowerPoint changes all occurrences of the misspelled word and continues checking the rest of the presentation.
Add a word to the custom dictionary	Click Add. PowerPoint opens the custom dictionary, adds the word, and continues checking the rest of the presentation.
View alternative spellings	Click Suggest. PowerPoint lists suggested spellings. Click the correct word from the Suggestions box or type the proper spelling. Then click Change. PowerPoint continues checking the rest of the presentation.
Add spelling error to AutoCorrect list	Click AutoCorrect. PowerPoint adds the spelling error and its correction to the AutoCorrect list. Any future misspelling of the word is corrected automatically as you type.
Close	Click Close to exit from the spelling checker and to return to the PowerPoint window.

The standard dictionary contains commonly used English words. It does not, however, contain proper names, abbreviations, technical terms, poetic contractions, or antiquated terms. PowerPoint treats words not found in the dictionaries as misspellings.

Starting the Spelling Checker

Start the Spelling checker by clicking the Spelling command on the Tools menu. Perform the following steps to start the Spelling checker and check your entire presentation.

Steps To Start the Spelling Checker

1 Double-click the move handle on the Standard toolbar. Point to the Spelling button on the Standard toolbar (Figure 1-59).

FIGURE 1-59

2 Click the Spelling button. When the Spelling dialog box displays, point to the Ignore button.

PowerPoint launches the Spelling checker and displays the Spelling dialog box (Figure 1-60). The word, Seaview, displays in the Not in Dictionary box. Depending on your custom dictionary, Seaview may not be recognized as a misspelled word.

FIGURE 1-60

Click the Ignore button.

PowerPoint ignores the word, Seaview, and continues searching for additional misspelled words. PowerPoint may stop on additional words depending on your typing accuracy. When PowerPoint has checked all slides for misspellings, it displays the Microsoft PowerPoint dialog box informing you that the spelling check is complete (Figure 1-61).

Click the OK button.

PowerPoint closes the Spelling checker and returns to the current slide, Slide 1, or to the slide where a possible misspelled word appeared.

FIGURE 1-61

1. Press ALT+T, press S; when finished, press ENTER

The red wavy line under the word, Seaview, is gone because you instructed PowerPoint to ignore that word, which does not appear in the standard dictionary. You also could have added that word to the dictionary so it would not be flagged as a possible misspelled word in subsequent presentations you create using that word.

Checking a Presentation for Style Consistency

Recall that the Office Assistant may have generated a light bulb in the text placeholder when you were typing your title slide (see Figure 1-19 on page PP 1.23). The Office Assistant recognized you were starting to prepare a slide show and offered design tips. These tips can range from suggesting clip art to ensuring your presentation meets predefined criteria for style consistency. For example, in this Studying presentation the first word in each line of text begins with a capital letter, and each line does not end with a period. The Office Assistant automatically checks for case and end punctuation consistency and for visual clarity. It identifies problems on a screen by displaying a light bulb. You then can choose to correct or to ignore the elements PowerPoint flags. You can change the options to suit your design specifications. Table 1-4 identifies each option available in the Style checker and each default setting.

Table 1-4 Style Checker Options and Default Settings	
OPTION	**SETTING**
CASE	
Slide title style	Title Case
Body text style	Sentence case
END PUNCTUATION	
Slide title punctuation	Paragraphs have punctuation
Body punctuation	Paragraphs have consistent punctuation
VISUAL CLARITY	
Number of fonts should not exceed	3
Title text size should be at least	36
Body text size should be at least	20
Number of bullets should not exceed	6
Number of lines per title should not exceed	2
Number of lines per bullet should not exceed	2

Correcting Errors

After creating a presentation and running the Spelling checker, you may find that you must make changes. Changes may be required because a slide contains an error, the scope of the presentation shifts, or the style is inconsistent. This section explains the types of errors that commonly occur when creating a presentation.

Types of Corrections Made to Presentations

You generally make three types of corrections to text in a presentation: additions, deletions, and replacements.

- **Additions** — are necessary when you omit text from a slide and need to add it later. You may need to insert text in the form of a sentence, word, or single character. For example, you may want to add the rest of the presenter's first name on your title slide.
- **Deletions** — are required when text on a slide is incorrect or is no longer relevant to the presentation. For example, one of your slides may look cluttered. Therefore, you may want to remove one of the bulleted paragraphs to add more space.
- **Replacements** — are needed when you want to revise the text in your presentation. For example, you may want to substitute the word, their, for the word, there.

Editing text in PowerPoint is basically the same as editing text in a word process ing package. The following sections illustrate the most common changes made to text in a presentation.

Deleting Text

You can delete text using one of three methods. One is to use the BACKSPACE key to remove text just typed. The second is to position the insertion point to the left of the text you wish to delete and then press the DELETE key. The third method is to drag through the text you wish to delete and then press the DELETE key. (Use the third method when deleting large sections of text.)

Replacing Text in an Existing Slide

When you need to correct a word or phrase, you can replace the text by selecting the text to be replaced and then typing the new text. As soon as you press any key on the keyboard, the highlighted text is deleted and the new text displays.

PowerPoint inserts text to the left of the insertion point. The text to the right of the insertion point moves to the right (and shifts downward if necessary) to accommodate the added text.

Changing Line Spacing

The bulleted lists on Slides 2, 3, and 4 look crowded; yet, there is ample blank space that could be used to separate the paragraphs. You can adjust the spacing on each slide, but when several slides need to be changed, you should change the slide master. Each PowerPoint component (slides, title slides, audience handouts, and speaker's notes) has a **master**, which controls its appearance. Slides have two masters, title master and slide master. The **title master** controls the appearance of the title slide. The **slide master** controls the appearance of the other slides in your presentation.

Table 1-5   Summary of Slide Master Components

ELEMENT	DESCRIPTION
Background items	Any object other than the title object or text object. Typical items include borders and graphics such as a company logo, page number, date, and time.
Color scheme	A coordinated set of eight colors designed to complement each other. Color schemes consist of background color, line and text color, shadow color, title text color, object fill color, and three different accent colors.
Date	Inserts the special symbol used to print the date the presentation was printed.
Font	Defines the appearance and shape of letters, numbers, and special characters.
Font size	Specifies the size of the characters on the screen. Character size is gauged by a measurement system called points. A single point is about 1/72 of an inch in height. Thus, a character with a point size of eighteen is about 18/72 of an inch in height.
Font style	Font styles include plain, italic, bold, shadowed, and underlined. Text may have more than one font style at a time.
Slide number	Inserts the special symbol used to print the slide number.
Text alignment	Position of text in a paragraph is left-aligned, right-aligned, centered, or justified. Justified text is proportionally spaced across the object.
Time	Inserts the special symbol used to print the time the presentation was printed.

Each design template has a specially designed slide master. If you select a design template but want to change one of its components, you can override that component by changing the slide master. Any change to the slide master results in changing every slide in the presentation, except the title slide. For example, if you change the line spacing to .5 inches before each paragraph on the slide master, each slide (except the title slide) changes line spacing after each paragraph to .5 inches. The slide master components more frequently changed are listed in Table 1-5.

Additionally, each view has its own master. You can access the master by holding down the SHIFT key while clicking the appropriate view button. For example, holding down the SHIFT key and clicking the Slide View button displays the slide master. To exit a master, click the view button to which you wish to return. To return to slide view, for example, click the Slide View button.

Displaying the Slide Master

Before you can change line spacing on the slide master, you first must display it. Perform the following steps to display the slide master.

Steps **To Display the Slide Master**

1 **Click the Next Slide button on the slide pane to display Slide 2. Press and hold down the SHIFT key and then point to the Slide View button.**

When you hold down the SHIFT key, the ScreenTip displays Slide Master View (Figure 1-62).

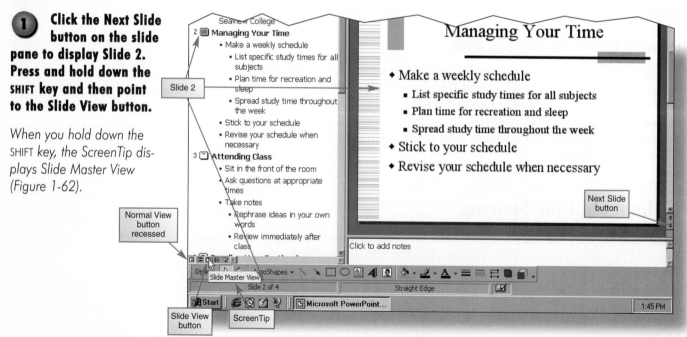

FIGURE 1-62

② **While holding down the SHIFT key, click the Slide Master View button. Then release the SHIFT key.**

The slide master and Master toolbar display (Figure 1-63).

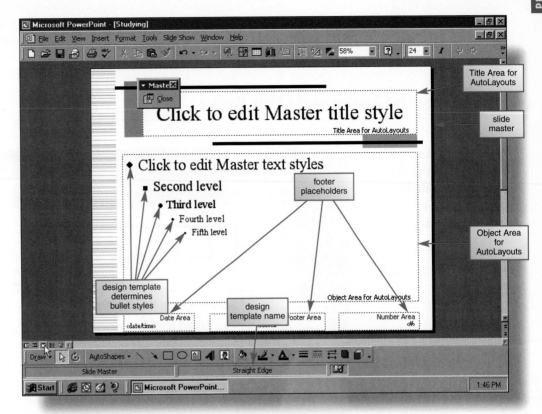

FIGURE 1-63

Changing Line Spacing on the Slide Master

Change line spacing by clicking the Line Spacing command on the Format menu. When you click the **Line Spacing command**, the Line Spacing dialog box displays. The Line Spacing dialog box contains three boxes, Line spacing, Before paragraph, and After paragraph, which allow you to adjust line spacing within a paragraph, before a paragraph, and after a paragraph, respectively.

Before paragraph line spacing is controlled by establishing the number of units before a paragraph. Units are either lines or points; lines are the default unit. Points may be selected by clicking the down arrow next to the Before paragraph box (see Figure 1-66 on page PP 1.61). Recall from page PP 1.24 that a single point is about 1/72 of an inch in height.

The Line spacing, Before paragraph, and After paragraph boxes each contain an amount of space box and a unit of measure box. To change the amount of space displaying between paragraphs, click the amount of space box up arrow or down arrow in the Line spacing box. To change the amount of space displaying before a paragraph, as you did in this project, click the amount of space box up arrow or down arrow in the Before paragraph box. To change the amount of space displaying after a paragraph, click the amount of space box up arrow or down arrow in the After paragraph box. To change the unit of measure from Lines to Points in the Line Spacing dialog box, click the arrow next to the appropriate unit of measure box and then click Points in the list.

In this project, you change the number in the amount of space box to increase the amount of space that displays before every paragraph, except the first paragraph, on every slide. For example, increasing the amount of space box to 0.5 lines increases the amount of space that displays before each paragraph.

Other **Ways**

1. On View menu point to Master, click Slide Master

More **About** 2000

Line Spacing

Blank space on a slide can be advantageous. The absence of text, called white space, helps the viewer focus attention on the presenter. Do not be afraid to increase line spacing to give your text some breathing room.

The first paragraph on every slide, however, does not change because of its position in the Object Area placeholder. Perform the following steps to change the line spacing.

Steps To Change Line Spacing on the Slide Master

1 **Click the bulleted paragraph in the Object Area placeholder labeled, Click to edit Master text styles.**

The insertion point displays at the point you clicked (Figure 1-64). The Object Area placeholder is selected.

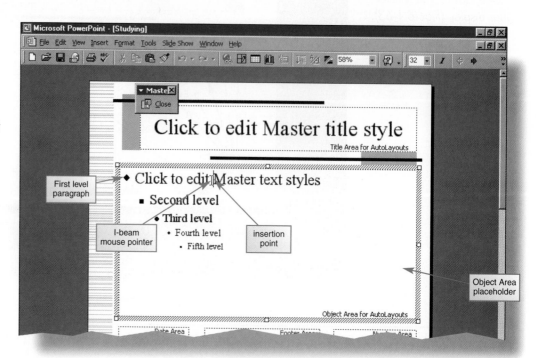

FIGURE 1-64

2 **Click Format on the menu bar and then point to Line Spacing. (Remember that you might have to wait a few seconds for the entire menu to display.)**

The Format menu displays (Figure 1-65).

FIGURE 1-65

3 **Click Line Spacing. Point to the Before Paragraph amount of space box up arrow.**

PowerPoint displays the Line Spacing dialog box (Figure 1-66). The default Before paragraph line spacing is set at 0.2 Lines.

FIGURE 1-66

4 **Click the Before paragraph amount of space box up arrow six times.**

The Before paragraph amount of space box displays 0.5 (Figure 1-67). The Preview button is available after this change is made in the Line Spacing dialog box. If you click the Preview button, PowerPoint temporarily updates your presentation with the new amount of space setting. This new setting is not actually applied until you click the OK button.

FIGURE 1-67

5 **Click the OK button.**

The slide master Object Area placeholder displays the new line spacing (Figure 1-68). Depending on the video drivers installed, the spacing on your screen may appear slightly different than this figure.

FIGURE 1-68

 6 **Click the Close button on the Master toolbar to return to normal view.**

Slide 2 displays with the Before paragraph line spacing set to 0.5 Lines (Figure 1-69).

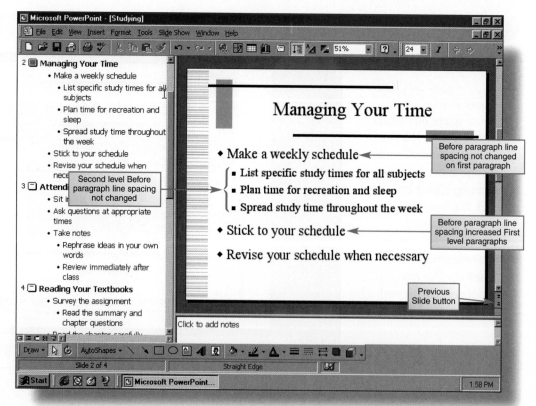

FIGURE 1-69

To display line spacing changes without making them permanent, click the Preview button in the Line Spacing dialog box. If you want to close the Line Spacing dialog box without applying the changes, click the Cancel button.

The placeholder at the top of the slide master (Figure 1-68) is used to edit the Master title style. The Object Area placeholder under the Master Title Area placeholder is used to edit the Master text styles. Here you make changes to the various bullet levels. Changes can be made to line spacing, bullet font, text and line color, alignment, and text shadow.

Displaying a Presentation in Black and White

You want to print handouts of your presentation and create overhead transparencies. The **Grayscale Preview button** allows you to display the presentation in black and white before you print. Table 1-6 identifies how PowerPoint objects display in black and white.

Perform the following steps to display the presentation in black and white.

Table 1-6 Appearance in Black and White View	
OBJECT	DISPLAY
Text	Black
Text shadows	Hidden
Embossing	Hidden
Fills	Grayscale
Frame	Black
Pattern fills	Grayscale
Lines	Black
Object shadows	Grayscale
Bitmaps	Grayscale
Slide backgrounds	White

Steps To Display a Presentation in Black and White

1 **Click the Previous Slide button to display Slide 1. Point to the Grayscale Preview button on the Standard toolbar.**

Slide 1 displays. The Grayscale Preview ScreenTip displays (Figure 1-70).

FIGURE 1-70

2 **Click the Grayscale Preview button.**

Slide 1 displays in black and white (Figure 1-71). The Grayscale Preview button is recessed on the Standard toolbar.

3 **Click the Next Slide button three times to view all slides in the presentation in black and white.**

4 **Click the Grayscale Preview button.**

Slide 4 displays with the default Straight Edge color scheme.

FIGURE 1-71

Other Ways

1. On View menu click Black and White

After you view the text objects in your presentation in black and white, you can make any changes that will enhance printouts produced from a black and white printer or photocopier.

Printing a Presentation

After you create a presentation, you often want to print it. A printed version of the presentation is called a **hard copy**, or **printout**. The first printing of the presentation is called a **rough draft**. The rough draft allows you to proofread the presentation to check for errors and readability. After correcting errors, you print the final copy of your presentation.

Saving a Presentation Before Printing

Prior to printing your presentation, you should save your work in the event you experience difficulties with the printer. You occasionally may encounter system problems that can be resolved only by restarting the computer. In such an instance, you will need to reopen your presentation. As a precaution, always save your presentation before you print. Perform the following steps to save the presentation before printing.

TO SAVE A PRESENTATION BEFORE PRINTING

 Verify that your floppy disk is in drive A.

② Click the Save button on the Standard toolbar.

All changes made after your last save now are saved on a floppy disk.

Printing the Presentation

After saving the presentation, you are ready to print. Clicking the **Print button** on the Standard toolbar causes PowerPoint to print all slides in the presentation. Perform the following steps to print the presentation slides.

Steps) To Print a Presentation

1 **Ready the printer according to the printer instructions. Then click the Print button on the Standard toolbar.**

The printer icon in the tray status area on the taskbar indicates a print job is processing (Figure 1-72). After several moments, the slide show begins printing on the printer. When the presentation is finished printing, the printer icon in the tray status area on the taskbar no longer displays.

FIGURE 1-72

When the printer stops, retrieve the printouts of the slides.

The presentation, Studying, prints on four pages (Figures 1-73a through 1-73d).

Effective Study Skills

Strategies for College Success

Presented by

Seaview College

(a) Slide 1

Managing Your Time

- ◆ Make a weekly schedule
  - ▪ List specific study times for all subjects
  - ▪ Plan time for recreation and sleep
  - ▪ Spread study times throughout the week
- ◆ Stick to your schedule
- ◆ Revise your schedule when necessary

(b) Slide 2

Attending Class

- ◆ Sit in the front of the room
- ◆ Ask questions at appropriate times
- ◆ Take notes
  - ▪ Rephrase ideas in your own words
  - ▪ Review immediately after class

(c) Slide 3

Reading Your Textbooks

- ◆ Survey the assignment
  - ▪ Read the summary and chapter questions
- ◆ Read the chapter carefully
- ◆ Recite the material in your own words
- ◆ Write brief notes in the margins
- ◆ Review the entire assignment

(d) Slide 4

FIGURE 1-73

Other Ways

1. On File menu click Print
2. Press CTRL+P or press CTRL+SHIFT+F12

You can click the printer icon next to the clock in the tray status area on the taskbar to obtain information about the presentations printing on your printer and to delete files in the print queue that are waiting to be printed.

Making a Transparency

Now that you have printed handouts, you want to make overhead transparencies. You can make transparencies using one of several devices. One device is a printer attached to your computer, such as an ink-jet printer or a laser printer. Transparencies produced on a printer may be in black and white or color, depending on the printer. Another device is a photocopier. Because each of these devices requires a special transparency film, check the user's manual for the film requirement of your specific device, or ask your instructor.

PowerPoint Help System

You can get answers to PowerPoint questions at any time by using the **PowerPoint Help system**. Used properly, this form of online assistance can increase your productivity and reduce your frustrations by minimizing the time you spend learning how to use PowerPoint. The following section shows how to get answers to your questions using the Office Assistant.

Using the Office Assistant

The **Office Assistant** answers your questions and suggests more efficient ways to complete a task. With the Office Assistant active, for example, you can type a question, word, or phrase in a text box and the Office Assistant provides immediate help on the subject. Also, as you create a worksheet, the Office Assistant accumulates tips that suggest more efficient ways to do the tasks you completed while building a presentation, such as formatting, printing, and saving. This tip feature is part of the **IntelliSense™ technology** that is built into PowerPoint, which understands what you are trying to do and suggests better ways to do it. When the light bulb displays above the Office Assistant, click it to see a tip.

The following steps show how to use the Office Assistant to obtain information on formatting a presentation.

Steps To Obtain Help Using the Office Assistant

1 If the Office Assistant is not on the screen, click Show the Office Assistant on the Help menu. With the Office Assistant on the screen, click it. Type how do i take meeting minutes in the What would you like to do? text box in the Office Assistant balloon. Point to the Search button (Figure 1-74).

FIGURE 1-74

2 **Click the Search button. Point to the topic Take notes or meeting minutes during a slide show in the Office Assistant balloon.**

The Office Assistant displays a list of topics relating to the question how do i take meeting minutes (Figure 1-75). The mouse pointer changes to a hand.

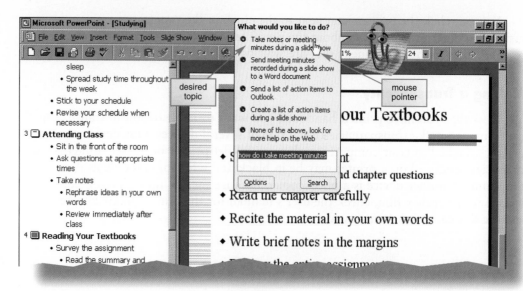

FIGURE 1-75

3 **Click Take notes or meeting minutes during a slide show.**

The Office Assistant displays a Microsoft PowerPoint Help window that provides Help information on taking notes or meeting minutes during a slide show (Figure 1-76).

4 **Click the Close button on the Microsoft PowerPoint Help window title bar.**

The Microsoft PowerPoint Help window closes, and the worksheet again is active.

FIGURE 1-76

Table 1-7 summarizes the eight categories of help available to you. Because of the way the PowerPoint Help system works, please review the right-most column of Table 1-7 if you have difficulties activating the desired category of help.

Table 1-7 PowerPoint Help System

TYPE	DESCRIPTION	HOW TO ACTIVATE	TURNING THE OFFICE ASSISTANT ON AND OFF
Answer Wizard	Similar to the Office Assistant in that it answers questions that you type in your own words.	Click the Microsoft PowerPoint Help button on the Standard toolbar. If necessary, maximize the Help window by double-clicking its title bar. Click the Answer Wizard tab.	If the Office Assistant displays, right-click it, click Options, click the Use the Office Assistant check box, and then click the OK button.
Contents sheet	Groups Help topics by general categories. Use when you know only the general category of the topic in question.	Click the Office Assistant button on the Standard toolbar. If necessary, maximize the Help window by double-clicking its title bar. Click the Contents tab.	If the Office Assistant displays, right-click it, click Options, click the Use the Office Assistant check box, and then click the OK button.
Detect and Repair	Automatically finds and fixes errors in the application.	Click Detect and Repair on the Help menu.	
Hardware and Software Information	Shows Product ID and allows access to system information and technical support information.	Click About Microsoft PowerPoint on the Help menu and then click the System Information or Technical Information button.	
Index sheet	Similar to an index in a book; use when you know exactly what you want.	Click the Microsoft PowerPoint Help button on the Standard toolbar. If necessary, maximize the Help window by double-clicking its title bar. Click the Index tab.	If the Office Assistant displays, right-click it, click Options, click Use the Office Assistant check box, and then click the OK button.
Office Assistant	Answers questions that you type in your own words, offers tips, and provides Help for a variety of PowerPoint features.	Click the Microsoft PowerPoint Help button on the Standard toolbar.	If the Office Assistant does not display, close the Microsoft PowerPoint Help window and then click Show the Office Assistant on the Help menu.
Office on the Web	Accesses technical resources and download free product enhancements on the Web.	Click Office on the Web on the Help menu.	
Question Mark button and What's This? command	Identifies unfamiliar items on the screen.	Click the Question Mark button and then click an item in the dialog box. Click What's This? on the Help menu, and then click an item on the screen.	

You can use the Office Assistant to search for Help on any topic concerning PowerPoint. For additional information on using the PowerPoint Help system, see Appendix A.

Quitting PowerPoint

Project 1 is complete. The final task is to close the presentation and quit PowerPoint. Perform the following steps to quit PowerPoint.

TO QUIT POWERPOINT

 Click the Close button on the title bar.

 If prompted to save the presentation before quitting PowerPoint, click the Yes button in the Microsoft PowerPoint dialog box.

More About

Quick Reference

For a table that lists how to complete the tasks covered in this book using the mouse, menu, shortcut menu, and keyboard, visit the Shelly Cashman Series Office Web page (www.scsite.com/off2000/qr.htm) and then click Microsoft PowerPoint 2000.

CASE PERSPECTIVE SUMMARY

Your Effective Study Skills PowerPoint slide show should help Dr. Martinez and the counseling staff present essential college survival skills to incoming freshmen attending orientation sessions at your school. The four slides display the key study habits all students need to succeed throughout college. The title slide identifies the topic of the presentation, and the next three slides give key pointers regarding time management, class attendance, and textbook usage. The counselors will use your overhead transparencies to organize their speeches, and the students will keep handouts of your slides for future reference.

Project Summary

Project 1 introduced you to starting PowerPoint and creating a multi-level bulleted list presentation. You learned about PowerPoint design templates, objects, and attributes. This project illustrated how to create an interesting introduction to a presentation by changing the text font style to italic and increasing font size on the title slide. Completing these tasks, you saved your presentation. Then, you created three multi-level bulleted list slides to explain how to study effectively in college. Next, you learned how to view the presentation in slide show view. Then you learned how to quit PowerPoint and how to open an existing presentation. You used the Spelling checker to search for spelling errors and learned how the Office Assistant Style checker identifies inconsistencies in design specifications. Using the slide master, you quickly adjusted the Before paragraph line spacing on every slide to make better use of white space. You learned how to display the presentation in black and white. Then, you learned how to print hard copies of your slides in order to make overhead transparencies. Finally, you learned how to use the PowerPoint Help system.

What You Should Know

Having completed this project, you now should be able to perform the following tasks:

▶ Add a New Slide Using the Bulleted List AutoLayout *(PP 1.32)*
▶ Add a New Slide with the Same AutoLayout *(PP 1.40)*
▶ Change Line Spacing on the Slide Master *(PP 1.60)*
▶ Change the Text Font Style to Italic *(PP 1.27)*

More About

Microsoft Certification

You can prove to your employer that you have essential PowerPoint 2000 skills. The Microsoft Office User Specialist (MOUS) Certification program allows you to obtain this valuable credential known throughout the computer industry. For more information, see Appendix D or visit the Shelly Cashman Series MOUS Web page at www.scsite.com/off2000/cert.htm.

▶ Choose a Design Template *(PP 1.18)*
▶ Complete Slide 3 *(PP 1.40)*
▶ Create Slide 4 *(PP 1.41)*
▶ Display a Presentation in Black and White *(PP 1.63)*
▶ Display the Formatting Toolbar in its Entirety *(PP 1.17)*
▶ Display the Popup Menu and Go to a Specific Slide *(PP 1.49)*
▶ Display the Slide Master *(PP 1.58)*
▶ End a Slide Show with a Black Slide *(PP 1.43)*
▶ Enter a Slide Title *(PP 1.35)*
▶ Enter the Presentation Subtitle *(PP 1.23)*
▶ Enter the Presentation Title *(PP 1.21)*
▶ Increase Font Size *(PP 1.25)*
▶ Move Manually Through Slides in a Slide Show *(PP 1.48)*
▶ Obtain Help Using the Office Assistant *(PP 1.67)*
▶ Open an Existing Presentation *(PP 1.52)*

▶ Print a Presentation *(PP 1.65)*
▶ Quit PowerPoint *(PP 1.51, 1.69)*
▶ Save a Presentation Before Printing *(PP 1.65)*
▶ Save a Presentation on a Floppy Disk *(PP 1.29)*
▶ Save a Presentation with the Same File Name *(PP 1.44)*
▶ Select an Object Area Placeholder *(PP 1.36)*
▶ Start a New Presentation *(PP 1.10)*
▶ Start Slide Show View *(PP 1.46)*
▶ Start the Spelling Checker *(PP 1.55)*
▶ Type a Multi-level Bulleted List *(PP 1.37)*
▶ Type the Remaining Text for Slide 2 *(PP 1.39)*
▶ Use the Popup Menu to End a Slide Show *(PP 1.50)*
▶ Use the Scroll Box on the Slide Pane to Move to Another Slide *(PP 1.45)*

Apply Your Knowledge

Project Reinforcement at www.scsite.com/off2000/reinforce.htm

1 Computer Buying Basics

Instructions: Start PowerPoint. Open the presentation Apply-1 from the PowerPoint Data Disk. See the inside back cover for instructions for downloading the PowerPoint Data Disk or see your instructor for information on accessing the files required for this book. This slide lists questions to consider when buying a computer. Perform the following tasks to change the slide so it looks like the one in Figure 1-77.

Buying a Computer?

- Ask these questions:
  - Hardware
    - How fast is the microprocessor?
    - How large is the hard drive?
    - How much RAM is included?
  - Software
    - Will I be using graphics?
    - Will I be computing my finances and taxes?

FIGURE 1-77

1. Click the Common Tasks menu button on the Formatting toolbar, and then click the Apply Design Template command. Choose the Blends design template.
2. Press and hold down the SHIFT key, and then click the Slide Master View button to display the slide master. Click the paragraph, Click to edit Master text styles. Click Format on the menu bar and then click Line Spacing. Increase the Before paragraph line spacing to 1 Lines. Click the OK button. Then click the Close button on the Master toolbar to return to normal view.
3. Select the text in the Title Area placeholder. Click the Bold button on the Formatting toolbar.
4. If necessary, select the text in the Title Area placeholder. Click the Font Size box arrow on the Font Size button on the Formatting toolbar. Click the down scroll arrow and then scroll down and click font size 48.
5. Click the paragraph in the Object Area placeholder, How fast is the microprocessor?. Click the Demote button on the Formatting toolbar.
6. Demote the four other paragraphs that end with a question mark.
7. Click File on the menu bar and then click Save As. Type Buying a Computer in the File name box. If drive A is not already displaying in the Save in box, click the Save in box arrow, and then click 3½ Floppy (A:). Click the Save button.
8. Click the Grayscale Preview button on the Standard toolbar to display the presentation in black and white.
9. Click the Print button on the Standard toolbar.
10. Click the Close button on the menu bar to quit PowerPoint.
11. Write your name on the printout, and hand it in to your instructor.

In the Lab

NOTE: These labs require you to create presentations based on notes. When you design these slide shows, use the 7 x 7 rule, which states that each line should have a maximum of seven words, and each slide should have a maximum of seven lines.

1 Financial Freedom at Community Savings & Loan

Problem: You work at the Community Savings & Loan. The institution's vice president wants you to help her prepare a presentation for an upcoming seminar for the community regarding achieving financial freedom. She hands you the notes in Figure 1-78, and you create the presentation shown in Figures 1-79a through 1-79d.

I) Money Sense –
Gaining Financial Freedom
  A) Presented by:
  B) Rich Jackson
  C) Community Savings & Loan
II) Start Saving Now
  A) Use the benefits of compounding interest
    1) Search for investments with high returns
    2) Consider stocks and stock mutual funds
  B) Have an emergency money fund
    1) Try to save six months' living expenses
    2) Put in easily liquidated accounts
III) Spend Within Your Means
  A) Make a budget and stick to it
  B) Watch for bargains
    1) Shop at pre-season and post-season sales
  C) Buy classic clothes and furnishings
    1) They will not seem dated years later
IV) Pay Yourself First
  A) You are your primary financial obligation
    1) Be completely committed to saving regularly
  B) Save 10 percent of your gross income
    1) As your salary grows, increase this amount
  C) Use direct deposit to ensure a transaction

FIGURE 1-78

In the Lab

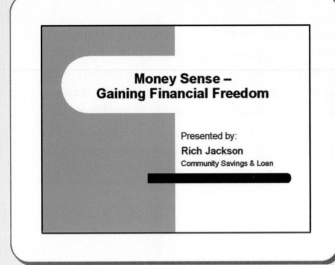

**Money Sense –
Gaining Financial Freedom**

Presented by:
Rich Jackson
Community Savings & Loan

(a) Slide 1

Start Saving Now

- Use the benefits of compounding interest
  - Search for investments with high returns
  - Consider stocks and stock mutual funds

- Have an emergency money fund
  - Try to save six months' living expenses
  - Put in easily liquidated accounts

(b) Slide 2

Spend Within Your Means

- Make a budget and stick to it

- Watch for bargains
  - Shop at pre-season and post-season sales

- Buy classic clothes and furnishings
  - They will not seem dated years later

(c) Slide 3

Pay Yourself First

- You are your primary financial obligation
  - Be completely committed to saving regularly

- Save 10 percent of your gross income
  - As your salary grows, increase this amount

- Use direct deposit to ensure a transaction

(d) Slide 4

FIGURE 1-79

Instructions: Perform the following tasks.

1. Create a new presentation using the Capsules design template.
2. Using the typed notes illustrated in Figure 1-78, create the title slide shown in Figure 1-79a using your name in place of Rich Jackson. Decrease the font size of the paragraph, Presented by:, to 24. Decrease the font size of the paragraph, Community Savings & Loan, to 20.
3. Using the typed notes in Figure 1-78, create the three bulleted list slides shown in Figures 1-79b through 1-79d. Increase the Before paragraph spacing to .8 Lines.
4. Click the Spelling button on the Standard toolbar. Correct any errors.
5. Save the presentation on a floppy disk using the file name, Money Freedom.
6. Display the presentation in black and white.
7. Print the black and white presentation. Quit PowerPoint.

In the Lab

2 Lake Shore Mall Fashion Show

Problem: You work in a clothing store at Lake Shore Mall, and your manager has asked you to participate in the annual fashion show. You decide to get involved with the segment promoting clothing to wear on job interviews. You determine that a PowerPoint presentation would help the commentator present key points as the models display accompanying clothing. You interview fashion coordinators at various stores in the mall and organize the list in Figure 1-80. Then you select a PowerPoint design template and decide to modify it. *Hint*: Use the PowerPoint Help system to solve this problem.

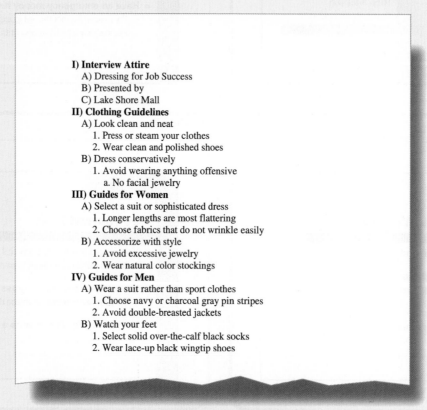

I) Interview Attire
   A) Dressing for Job Success
   B) Presented by
   C) Lake Shore Mall
II) Clothing Guidelines
   A) Look clean and neat
      1. Press or steam your clothes
      2. Wear clean and polished shoes
   B) Dress conservatively
      1. Avoid wearing anything offensive
         a. No facial jewelry
III) Guides for Women
   A) Select a suit or sophisticated dress
      1. Longer lengths are most flattering
      2. Choose fabrics that do not wrinkle easily
   B) Accessorize with style
      1. Avoid excessive jewelry
      2. Wear natural color stockings
IV) Guides for Men
   A) Wear a suit rather than sport clothes
      1. Choose navy or charcoal gray pin stripes
      2. Avoid double-breasted jackets
   B) Watch your feet
      1. Select solid over-the-calf black socks
      2. Wear lace-up black wingtip shoes

FIGURE 1-80

Instructions: Perform the following tasks.

1. Create a new presentation using the Post Modern design template.
2. Using the notes in Figure 1-80, create the title slide shown in Figure 1-81a. Increase the font size of the paragraph, Dressing for Job Success, to 36. Decrease the font size of the paragraph, Presented by, to 28.
3. Using the notes in Figure 1-80, create the three multi-level bulleted list slides shown in Figures 1-81b through 1-81d.
4. Display the slide master. Click the paragraph, Click to edit Master title style. Click the Bold button on the Formatting toolbar.
5. Click the paragraph, Click to edit Master text styles. On the Format menu, click Line Spacing, and then increase the Before paragraph line spacing to 0.75 Lines. Click the paragraph, Second level. On the Format menu, click Line Spacing, and then increase the After paragraph spacing to 0.25 Lines.

In the Lab

Interview Attire

Dressing for Job Success

Presented by

Lake Shore Mall

9/12/01   Student Name   1

(a) Slide 1

Clothing Guidelines

- Look clean and neat
  - Press or steam your clothes
  - Wear clean and polished shoes
- Dress conservatively
  - Avoid wearing anything offensive
    - No facial jewelry

9/12/01   Student Name   2

(b) Slide 2

Guides for Women

- Select a suit or sophisticated dress
  - Longer lengths are most flattering
  - Choose fabrics that do not wrinkle easily
- Accessorize with style
  - Avoid excessive jewelry
  - Wear natural color stockings

9/12/01   Student Name   3

(c) Slide 3

Guides for Men

- Wear a suit rather than sport clothes
  - Choose navy or charcoal gray pin stripes
  - Avoid double-breasted jackets
- Watch your feet
  - Select solid over-the-calf black socks
  - Wear lace-up black wingtip shoes

9/12/01   Student Name   4

(d) Slide 4

FIGURE 1-81

6. Drag the scroll box in the slide pane down to display the title master. Click the paragraph, Click to edit Master title style. Click the Bold button on the Formatting toolbar.

7. Return to normal view. On the View menu, click Header and Footer. If necessary, click the Slide tab. Add the date (so it updates automatically), a slide number, and your name to the footer. Display the footer on all slides.

8. Drag the scroll box to display Slide 1. Click the Slide Show button to start slide show view. Then click to display each slide.

9. Save the presentation on a floppy disk using the file name, Interview Attire. Display and print the presentation in black and white. Quit PowerPoint.

In the Lab

3 Cholesterol Basics at the Community Wellness Center

Problem: At your visit to the South Suburban Community Wellness Center last week, staff nurse Debbie Ortiz explained the fundamentals of cholesterol to you and several other patients. You decide she can use a presentation and handouts to better educate clinic visitors. *Hint*: Use the PowerPoint Help system to solve this problem.

Instructions: Using the list in Figure 1-82, design and create a presentation. The presentation must include a title slide and three bulleted list slides. Perform the following tasks.

1. Create a new presentation using the Dad's Tie design template.

2. Create a title slide titled, Cholesterol Highs and Lows. Include a subtitle, using your name in place of Debbie Ortiz. Decrease the font size for paragraphs Presented by: and South Suburban Wellness Center to 32. Italicize your name.

3. Using Figure 1-82, create three multi-level bulleted list slides. On Slide 2, use check marks instead of square bullets for the three main Cholesterol Basics paragraphs.

4. Adjust Before paragraph and After paragraph line spacing to utilize the available white space.

5. Insert a footer on every slide except the title slide that includes the current date, your name, and the slide number.

> **I) Cholesterol Highs and Lows**
>   A) Presented by:
>   B) Debbie Ortiz
>   C) South Suburban Wellness Center
> **II) Cholesterol Basics**
>   A) Needed by:
>   1) Every cell in your body
>   B) Builds:
>   1) Brain and nerve tissues; bile
>   C) Manufactured by:
>   1) Liver and small intestine
> **III) HDL (high density lipids)**
>   A) H stands for "Healthy"
>   B) Good for your heart
>   1) Delivers cholesterol deposits in body to liver
>   a) Liver disposes or recycles these deposits
> **IV) LDL (low density lipoproteins)**
>   A) L stands for "Lethal"
>   B) Enemy of the heart
>   1) Transports needed cholesterol to cells
>   2) Dumps excess on arterial walls and tissues

FIGURE 1-82

6. View the presentation in slide show view to look for errors. Correct any errors.

7. Check the presentation for spelling errors.

8. Save the presentation to a floppy disk with the file name, Cholesterol Basics. Print the presentation slides in black and white. Quit PowerPoint.

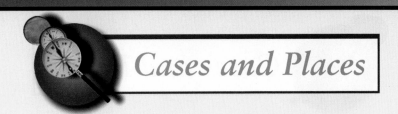

Cases and Places

The difficulty of these case studies varies:
▶ are the least difficult; ▶▶ are more difficult; and ▶▶▶ are the most difficult.

1 ▶ Dr. Doug Gordon, chief ophthalmologist at the North Shore Eye Clinic, knows that many people take their eyesight for granted. They visit an eye doctor only when they are having difficulties, such as eye pain or extreme redness. He urges everyone, from newborns to senior citizens, to preserve their eyesight by scheduling regular eye exams. The times for these checkups varies by age. Dr. Gordon has contacted you to help him prepare a presentation that will be delivered at community fairs and at the local shopping mall. He has prepared the notes in Figure 1-83 and has asked you to use them to develop a title slide and additional slides that can be used on an overhead projector. Use the concepts and techniques introduced in this project to create the presentation.

The Eyes Have It
When Is Checkup Time?
Dr. Doug Gordon
North Shore Eye Clinic

Children
Newborns
  When: In nursery
  Potential problems: infections, abnormalities
Infants (to 6 months)
  When: once
  Potential problems: eye misalignment
Youngsters (ages 1 to 6)
  When: every 1 to 3 years
  Potential problems: nearsightedness, farsightedness, astigmatism, lazy eye
School-age children (ages 7 to 17)
  When: every 1 to 2 years
  Potential problems: nearsightedness, farsightedness, astigmatism
Adults
Ages 18 to 40
  When: every 1 to 2 years
  Potential problems: needing reading glasses, early stages of glaucoma
Ages 41 – 64
  When: every 1 to 2 years
  Potential problems: glaucoma, cataracts, macular degeneration
Seniors (ages 65+)
  When: annually
  Potential problems: glaucoma, cataracts, macular degeneration

FIGURE 1-83

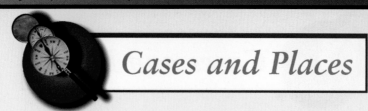
Cases and Places

2 ▶▶ This past holiday season, the Highland Shores police and fire departments experienced an unusually high number of calls for assistance. Many of these problems were the result of mishaps that easily could have been prevented. Police Chief Victor Halen and Fire Chief Norton Smits want to inform community residents at local block parties next summer about how they can follow a few safety precautions to reduce their chances of injuries. The chiefs want you to help them prepare a slide show and handouts for the community. They have typed safety tips for you (Figure 1-84), and they have asked you to prepare five slides that can be used on an overhead projector and as handouts. They want the title slide to introduce them and their topic. Use the concepts and techniques introduced in this project to create the presentation.

Seasonal Safety

Using Candles
Never burn unattended or in drafts
Burn on a heat-resistant surface
Trim wick to ¼ inch before lighting
    Do not drop wick trimming into candle
Burn for 2 – 3 hours at a time
    Allow to cool before relighting

Decorating
Be mindful of children
    Hang ornaments, tinsel on high branches
    Keep dangerous plants out of reach
        Mistletoe, poinsettia, and holly contain toxic substances

Lighting
Use the right lights
    Choose lights with the UL label
    Check for defects
        Cracked sockets, frayed wires, loose connections
    Turn off lights before leaving house

Cooking
Reduce the risk of bacterial growth
    Keep food on table two hours maximum
        Egg dishes should be refrigerated hourly
        Rotate foods occasionally
Do not leave food unattended on stovetops

FIGURE 1-84

Cases and Places

3 ▶▶ CPU-4-U is a computer repair store near campus that specializes in repairing computer systems and building custom computers. The co-owners, Warren Shilling and Mary Burg, want to attract new customers, and they have asked you to help them design a PowerPoint advertising campaign. Having graduated from your college, they are familiar with the hardware and software students need for their classes. Computer users can make appointments to bring their computers to the shop or to arrange for on-site service 24 hours a day. CPU-4-U also carries a complete line of supplies, including toner cartridges, paper, and labels. Many students consult with the technicians to plan for future computer purchases and to arrange financing for their new systems. The store is located in Tinley Mall, 6302 South State Street, Ypsilanti, Michigan. For more information call 555-2297. Using the techniques presented in this project, prepare a title slide and three bulleted list slides to be used for their presentation and for handouts.

4 ▶▶ The Poochy Humane Society in your town wants to increase community awareness of its services and facilities. The society's director, Jennifer Durkin, has decided that one way she can promote the shelter is by informing community residents on how they should react when a loose dog approaches them. She decides to address residents who regularly participate in activities at the local park district and who are walking, jogging, and biking in the community park. She wants to inform them that they can react in one of three ways when a stray dog approaches. They can be friendly by talking softly and by extending one of their hands palm down. Another behavior is to assert dominance. Using this approach, they should look at the dog sternly and yell, "Go away!" A third reaction is to act submissively by relaxing their muscles and glancing to the side. This technique is especially useful for an encounter with a big dog that thinks it is in control. The Poochy Humane Society is located at 10836 Windy Terrace; the telephone number is 555-DOGS. Using the concepts and techniques presented in this project, prepare a title slide and three bulleted list slides to be used on an overhead projector and as handouts for community residents.

5 ▶▶ Fat is one of the three essential components your body needs. The other two are protein and carbohydrates. Unfortunately, many people throughout the world consume too much fat in their diets. Although fat intake needs vary based on age and weight, following a low-fat diet can reduce the risk of heart disease. Some fats are healthy and actually help give energy, prevent blood clotting, and reduce cholesterol and triglyceride levels. These fats, commonly called essential fatty acids (EFAs) or Vitamin F, are found in cold-water fish and cold-temperature plant oils, such as flax seed and black currant. Monounsaturated fats also are healthy for the body. They are found in olive, almond, and canola oils, they all are liquid at room temperature, and they generally come from plant seeds. Although polyunsaturated fats can decrease cholesterol levels, they also can decrease the percentage of healthy HDL cholesterol (see In the Lab Project 3). Like monounsaturated fats, they come from plant seeds and are liquid at room temperature. They are found in safflower oil and corn oil. Saturated fats and hydrogenated fats are unhealthy because they can clog arteries and elevate cholesterol levels. They are found in animal foods, such as butter, margarine, and meat. Using the concepts and techniques presented in this project, prepare a presentation describing the various type of fats in our foods and their benefits or dangers to our health. Create a title slide and at least three additional slides that can be used with an overhead projector and as handouts.

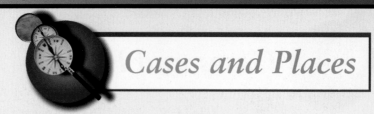

Cases and Places

6 ▶▶ Every day, two Americans are killed in collisions between trains and cars or between trains and pedestrians. Many more people suffer serious injuries from these accidents. Lighting is not a significant factor, for more than 50 percent of these accidents occur at crossings marked with gates and flashing lights, and more than 70 percent occur during the day. People involved in train accidents have one or more of these three personality traits: impatient, and not wanting to wait for a train; inattentive, and daydreaming or listening to loud music; or ignorant, and not aware of the impending danger. Drivers and pedestrians can reduce the risk of train accidents by looking both ways before crossing the tracks, never walking down a track, and assuming that a train can come at any time in either direction on any track. If your car stalls on a railroad track when a train is approaching, get out immediately and run away from the track in the same direction from which the train is coming. (If you run in the same direction the train is traveling, the train will hit your car, which can potentially hit you.) Using the concepts and techniques presented in this project, prepare a presentation to warn drivers and pedestrians of the dangers involved in crossing railroad tracks. Create a title slide and at least three additional slides that can be used with an overhead projector and as handouts.

7 ▶▶▶ In the Lab Project 1 discusses the need for developing techniques to achieve financial freedom. One of the suggestions is to invest in stocks or in stock mutual funds. These mutual funds pool shareholders' money and invest in a diversified portfolio of funds. Interview a financial planner or research the Internet for information on the various types of mutual funds and how they are managed. Determine the fees and expenses involved in this type of investment. Then, using the concepts and techniques presented in this project, prepare a presentation to report your findings. Create a title slide and at least three additional slides that can be used with an overhead projector and as handouts.

APPENDIX A
Microsoft Office 2000 Help System

Using the Microsoft Office Help System

This appendix demonstrates how you can use the Microsoft Office 2000 Help system to answer your questions. At any time while you are using one of the Microsoft Office 2000 applications, you can interact with the Help system to display information on any topic associated with the application. To illustrate the use of the Microsoft Office 2000 Help system, the Microsoft Word 2000 application will be used in this appendix. The Help systems in other Microsoft Office applications respond in a similar fashion.

The two primary forms of Help available in each Microsoft Office application are the Office Assistant and the Microsoft Help window. The one you use will depend on your preference. As shown in Figure A-1, you access either form of Help in Microsoft Word by pressing the F1 key, clicking Microsoft Word Help on the Help menu, or clicking the Microsoft Word Help button on the Standard toolbar. Word responds in one of two ways:

1. If the Office Assistant is turned on, then the Office Assistant displays with a balloon (lower-right side of Figure A-1).
2. If the Office Assistant is turned off, then the Microsoft Word Help window displays (lower-left side of Figure A-1)

Table A-1 on the next page summarizes the nine categories of Help available to you. Because of the way the Word Help system works, please review the rightmost column of Table A-1 if you have difficulties activating the desired category of Help.

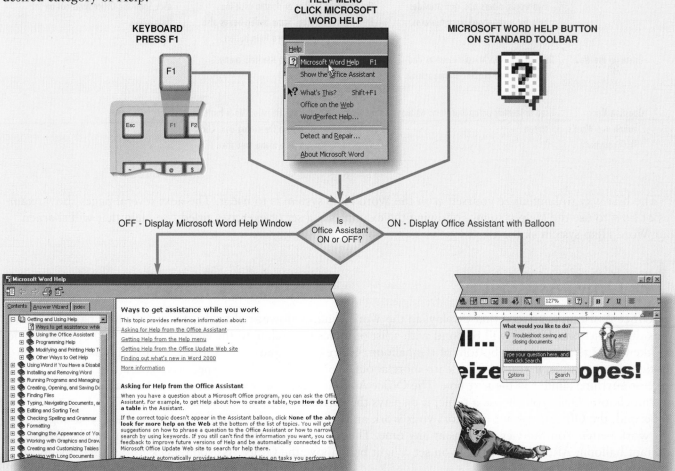

FIGURE A-1

Table A-1   Word Help System

TYPE	DESCRIPTION	HOW TO ACTIVATE	TURNING THE OFFICE ASSISTANT ON AND OFF
Answer Wizard	Similar to the Office Assistant in that it answers questions that you type in your own words.	Click the Microsoft Word Help button on the Standard toolbar. If necessary, maximize the Help window by double-clicking its title bar. Click the Answer Wizard tab.	If the Office Assistant displays, right-click it, click Options on the shortcut menu, click Use the Office Assistant to remove the check mark, click the OK button.
Contents sheet	Groups Help topics by general categories. Use when you know only the general category of the topic in question.	Click the Microsoft Word Help button on the Standard toolbar. If necessary, maximize the Help window by double-clicking its title bar. Click the Contents tab.	If the Office Assistant displays, right-click it, click Options, click Use the Office Assistant to remove the check mark, click the OK button.
Detect and Repair	Automatically finds and fixes errors in the application.	Click Detect and Repair on the Help menu.	
Hardware and Software Information	Shows Product ID and allows access to system information and technical support information.	Click About Microsoft Word on the Help menu and then click the appropriate button.	
Help for WordPerfect Users	Used to assist WordPerfect users who are learning Microsoft Word.	Click WordPerfect Help on the Help menu.	
Index sheet	Similar to an index in a book; use when you know exactly what you want.	Click the Microsoft Word Help button on the Standard toolbar. If necessary, maximize the Help window by double-clicking its title bar. Click the Index tab.	If the Office Assistant displays, right-click it, click Options, click Use the Office Assistant to remove the check mark, click the OK button.
Office Assistant	Answers questions that you type in your own words, offers tips, and provides Help for a variety of Word features.	Click the Microsoft Word Help button on the Standard toolbar or double-click the Office Assistant icon. Some dialog boxes also include the Microsoft Word Help button.	If the Office Assistant does not display, click Show the Office Assistant on the Help menu.
Office on the Web	Used to access technical resources and download free product enhancements on the Web.	Click Office on the Web on the Help menu.	
Question Mark button and What's This? command	Used to identify unfamiliar items on the screen.	In a dialog box, click the Question Mark button and then click an item in the dialog box. Click What's This? on the Help menu, and then click an item on the screen.	

The best way to familiarize yourself with the Word Help system is to use it. The next several pages show examples of how to use the Help system. Following the examples is a set of exercises titled Use Help that will sharpen your Word Help system skills.

The Office Assistant

The **Office Assistant** is an icon that displays in the Word window (lower-right side of Figure A-1 on page MO A.1). It has dual functions. First, it will respond with a list of topics that relate to the entry you make in the What would you like to do? text box at the bottom of the balloon. This entry can be in the form of a word, phrase, or written question. For example, if you want to learn more about saving a file, you can type, save, save a file, how do I save a file, or anything similar in the text box. The Office Assistant responds by displaying a list of topics from which you can choose. Once you choose a topic, it displays the corresponding information.

Second, the Office Assistant monitors your work and accumulates tips during a session on how you might do your work better. You can view the tips at any time. The accumulated tips display when you activate the Office Assistant balloon. Also, if at any time you see a light bulb above the Office Assistant, click it to display the most recent tip.

You may or may not want the Office Assistant to display on the screen at all times. You can hide it, and then show it at a later time. You may prefer not to use the Office Assistant at all. In this case, you use the Microsoft Word Help window (lower-left side of Figure A-1 on page MO A.1). Thus, not only do you need to know how to show and hide the Office Assistant, but you also need to know how to turn the Office Assistant on and off.

Showing and Hiding the Office Assistant

When Word is first installed, the Office Assistant displays in the Word window. You can move it to any location on the screen. You can click it to display the Office Assistant balloon, which allows you to request Help. If the Office Assistant is on the screen and you want to hide it, you click the **Hide the Office Assistant command** on the Help menu. You also can right-click the Office Assistant to display its shortcut menu and then click the **Hide command** to hide it. When the Office Assistant is hidden, then the **Show the Office Assistant command** replaces the Hide the Office Assistant command on the Help menu. Thus, you can show or hide the Office Assistant at any time.

Turning the Office Assistant On and Off

The fact that the Office Assistant is hidden, does not mean it is turned off. To turn the Office Assistant off, it must be displayed in the Word window. You right-click it to display its shortcut menu (right side of Figure A-2). Next, click Options on the shortcut menu. Invoking the **Options command** causes the Office Assistant dialog box to display (left side of Figure A-2).

FIGURE A-2

The top check box in the Options sheet determines whether the Office Assistant is on or off. To turn the Office Assistant off, remove the check mark from the **Use the Office Assistant check box** and then click the OK button. As shown in Figure A-1 on page MO A.1, if the Office Assistant is off when you invoke Help, then the Microsoft Word Help window displays instead of the Office Assistant. To turn the Office Assistant on at a later time, click the Show the Office Assistant command on the Help menu.

Through the Options command on the Office Assistant shortcut menu, you can change the look and feel of the Office Assistant. For example, you can hide the Office Assistant, turn the Office Assistant off, change the way it works, choose a different Office Assistant icon, or view an animation of the current one. These options also are available by clicking the Options button that displays in the Office Assistant balloon (Figure A-3 on the next page).

The **Gallery sheet** (Figure A-2) in the Office Assistant dialog box allows you to change the appearance of the Office Assistant. The default is the paper clip (Clippit). You can change it to a bouncing red happy face (The Dot), a robot (F1), a professor (The Genius), the Microsoft Office logo (Office Logo), the earth (Mother Nature), a cat (Links), or a dog (Rocky).

Using the Office Assistant

As indicated earlier, the Office Assistant allows you to enter a word, phrase, or question and then responds by displaying a list of topics from which you can choose to display Help. The following steps show how to use the Office Assistant to obtain Help about online meetings.

Steps **To Use the Office Assistant**

1 If the Office Assistant is not turned on, click Help on the menu bar and then click Show the Office Assistant. Click the Office Assistant. When the Office Assistant balloon displays, **type** what are online meetings **in the text box. Point to the Search button.**

The Office Assistant balloon displays as shown in Figure A-3.

FIGURE A-3

2 Click the Search button. When the Office Assistant balloon redisplays, point to the topic, About online meetings (Figure A-4).

FIGURE A-4

③ **Click the topic, About online meetings. Double-click the Microsoft Word Help window title bar to maximize it. If necessary, move or hide the Office Assistant so you can view all of the text in the Microsoft Word Help window.**

The Microsoft Word Help window displays the information about online meetings (Figure A-5).

FIGURE A-5

When the Microsoft Word Help window displays, you can choose to read it or print it. To print the information, click the Print button on the Microsoft Word Help toolbar. Table A-2 lists the function of each button on the toolbar in the Microsoft Word Help window. To close the Microsoft Word Help window shown in Figure A-5, click the Close button on the title bar.

Table A-2	Microsoft Word Help Toolbar Buttons	
BUTTON	**NAME**	**FUNCTION**
or	Show or Hide	Displays or hides the Contents, Answer Wizard, Index tabs
	Back	Displays the previous Help topic
	Forward	Displays the next Help topic
	Print	Prints the current Help topic
	Options	Displays a list of commands

Other Ways

1. If Office Assistant is turned on, on Help menu click Microsoft Word Help, or click Microsoft Word Help button on Standard toolbar to display Office Assistant balloon

The Microsoft Word Help Window

If the Office Assistant is turned off and you click the Microsoft Word Help button on the Standard toolbar, the **Microsoft Word Help window** displays (Figure A-6 on the next page). This window contains three tabs on the left side: Contents, Answer Wizard, and Index. Each tab displays a sheet with powerful look-up capabilities. Use the Contents sheet as you would a table of contents at the front of a book to look up Help. The Answer Wizard sheet answers your queries in the same manner as the Office Assistant. You use the Index sheet in the same manner as an index in a book.

Click the tabs to move from sheet to sheet. The five buttons on the toolbar, Show or Hide, Back, Forward, Print, and Options also are described in Table A-2.

Besides clicking the Microsoft Word Help button on the Standard toolbar, you also can click the Microsoft Word Help command on the Help menu or press the F1 key to display the Microsoft Word Help window to gain access to the three sheets. To close the Microsoft Word Help window, click the Close button in the upper-right corner on the title bar.

Using the Contents Sheet

The **Contents sheet** is useful for displaying Help when you know the general category of the topic in question, but not the specifics. The following steps show how to use the Contents sheet to obtain information about Web folders.

TO OBTAIN HELP USING THE CONTENTS SHEET

1 With the Office Assistant turned off, click the Microsoft Word Help button on the Standard toolbar (Figure A-3 on page MO A.4).

2 When the Microsoft Word Help window displays, double-click the title bar to maximize the window. If necessary, click the Show button to display the tabs.

3 Click the Contents tab.

4 Double-click the Working with Online and Internet Documents book on the left side of the window.

5 Double-click the Creating Web Pages book below the Working with Online and Internet Documents book.

6 Click the About Web Folders subtopic below the Creating Web Pages book.

Word displays Help on the subtopic, About Web Folders (Figure A-6).

FIGURE A-6

Once the information on the subtopic displays, you can scroll through the window and read it or you can click the Print button to obtain a hard copy. If you decide to click another subtopic on the left or a link on the right, you can get back to the Help page shown in Figure A-6 by clicking the Back button as many times as necessary.

Each topic in the Contents list is preceded by a book icon or question mark icon. A **book icon** indicates subtopics are available. A **question mark icon** means information on the topic will display if you double-click the title. The book icon opens when you double-click the book (or its title) or click the plus sign (+) to the left of the book icon.

Using the Answer Wizard Sheet

The **Answer Wizard sheet** works like the Office Assistant in that you enter a word, phrase, or question and it responds with topics from which you can choose to display Help. The following steps show how to use the Answer Wizard sheet to obtain Help about discussions in a Word document.

TO OBTAIN HELP USING THE ANSWER WIZARD SHEET

1 With the Office Assistant turned off, click the Microsoft Word Help button on the Standard toolbar (Figure A-3 on page MO A.4).

2 When the Microsoft Word Help window displays, double-click the title bar to maximize the window. If necessary, click the Show button to display the tabs.

3 Click the Answer Wizard tab. Type what are discussions in the What would you like to do? text box on the left side of the window. Click the Search button.

4 When a list of topics displays in the Select topic to display list box, click About discussions in Word.

Word displays Help about discussions (Figure A-7).

FIGURE A-7

If the topic, About discussions in Word, does not include the information you are searching for, click another topic in the list. Continue to click topics until you find the desired information.

Using the Index Sheet

The third sheet in the Microsoft Word Help window is the Index sheet. Use the **Index sheet** to display Help when you know the keyword or the first few letters of the keyword you want to look up. The following steps show how to use the Index sheet to obtain Help on understanding the readability statistics available to evaluate the reading level of a document.

TO OBTAIN HELP USING THE INDEX SHEET

1 With the Office Assistant turned off, click the Microsoft Word Help button on the Standard toolbar (Figure A-3 on page MO A.4).

2 When the Microsoft Word Help window displays, double-click the title bar to maximize the window. If necessary, click the Show button to display the tabs.

3 Click the Index tab. Type readability in the Type keywords text box on the left side of the window. Click the Search button.

Word highlights the first topic (Readability scores) on the left side of the window and displays information about two readability tests on the right side of the window (Figure A-8).

FIGURE A-8

In the Choose a topic list box on the left side of the window, you can click another topic to display additional Help.

An alternative to typing a keyword in the Type keywords text box is to scroll through the Or choose keywords list box (the middle list box on the left side of the window). When you locate the keyword you are searching for, double-click it to display Help on the topic. Also in the Or choose keywords list box, the Word Help system displays other topics that relate to the new keyword. As you begin typing a new keyword in the Type keywords text box, Word jumps to that point in the middle list box. To begin a new search, click the Clear button.

What's This? Command and Question Mark Button • MO A.9

APPENDIX A

What's This? Command and Question Mark Button

Use the What's This command on the Help menu or the Question Mark button in a dialog box when you are not sure what an object on the screen is or what it does.

What's This? Command

You use the **What's This? command** on the Help menu to display a detailed ScreenTip. When you invoke this command, the mouse pointer changes to an arrow with a question mark. You then click any object on the screen, such as a button, to display the ScreenTip. For example, after you click the What's This? command on the Help menu and then click the Zoom box on the Standard toolbar, a description of the Zoom box displays (Figure A-9). You can print the ScreenTip by right-clicking it and clicking Print Topic on the shortcut menu.

FIGURE A-9

Question Mark Button

In a response similar to the What's This? command, the **Question Mark button** displays a ScreenTip. You use the Question Mark button with dialog boxes. It is located in the upper-right corner on the title bar of dialog boxes, next to the Close button. For example, in Figure A-10, the Print dialog box displays on the screen. If you click the Question Mark button, and then click the Print to file check box, an explanation of the Print to file check box displays in a ScreenTip. You can print the ScreenTip by right-clicking it and clicking Print Topic on the shortcut menu.

If a dialog box does not include a Question Mark button, press the SHIFT+F1 keys. This combination of keys will change the mouse pointer to an arrow with a question mark. You then can click any object in the dialog box to display the ScreenTip.

FIGURE A-10

Office on the Web Command

The **Office on the Web command** on the Help menu displays a Microsoft Web page containing up-to-date information on a variety of Office-related topics. To use this command, you must be connected to the Internet. Once the page displays, you can click the Word link on the left side of the window and then click the Assistance link (Figure A-11). The Word Assistance Web page contains several links such as Knowledge Base Articles about Word and Frequently Asked Questions about Word.

FIGURE A-11

Other Help Commands

Three additional commands available on the Help menu are WordPerfect Help, Detect and Repair, and About Microsoft Word. The WordPerfect Help command is available only if it was included as part of a Custom install of Word 2000. The Help menu of the other Office applications have similar commands that are useful when using each Office application.

WordPerfect Help Command

The **WordPerfect Help command** on the Help menu offers assistance to WordPerfect users switching to Word. When you choose this command, Word displays the Help for WordPerfect Users dialog box. The instructions in the dialog box step the user through the appropriate selections. A similar command is available in each of the other Office applications.

Detect and Repair Command

Use the **Detect and Repair command** on the Help menu if Word is not running properly or if it is generating errors. When you invoke this command, the Detect and Repair dialog box displays. Click the Start button in the dialog box to initiate the detect and repair process.

About Microsoft Word Command

The **About Microsoft Word command** on the Help menu displays the About Microsoft Word dialog box. The dialog box lists the owner of the software and the product identification. You need to know the product identification if you call Microsoft for assistance. The two buttons below the OK button are the System Info button and the Tech Support button. The **System Info button** displays system information, including hardware resources, components, software environment, and applications. The **Tech Support button** displays technical assistance information.

Use Help

1 Using the Office Assistant

Instructions: Perform the following tasks using the Word Help system.

1. If the Office Assistant is turned on, click it to display the Office Assistant balloon. If the Office Assistant is not turned on, click Help on the menu bar, and click Show the Office Assistant.
2. Right-click the Office Assistant and then click Options on the shortcut menu. Click the Gallery tab in the Office Assistant dialog box and then click the Next button to view all the Office Assistants. Click the Options tab in the Office Assistant dialog box and review the different options for the Office Assistant. Click the Question Mark button and then display ScreenTips for the first two check boxes (Use the Office Assistant and Respond to F1 key). Right-click the ScreenTips to print them. Hand them in to your instructor. Close the Office Assistant dialog box.
3. Click the Office Assistant and then type show me the keyboard shortcuts in the What would you like to do? text box at the bottom of the balloon. Click the Search button.
4. Click Keyboard shortcuts in the Office Assistant balloon. If necessary, double-click the title bar to maximize the Microsoft Word Help window. Click the Function keys link and then click the SHIFT+Function key link to view the set of shortcut keys using the SHIFT key and function keys. Click the Print button on the Microsoft Word Help toolbar to print the list of shortcut keys. Hand in the printouts to your instructor.
5. Close all open Help windows.
6. Click the Office Assistant. If it is not turned on, click Show the Office Assistant on the Help menu. Search for the topic, what is a netmeeting. Click the Use NetMeeting for an online meeting link. When the Microsoft Word Help window displays, maximize the window and then click the the Start an impromptu online meeting with Microsoft Word link. Read and print the information. Close the Microsoft Word Help window.

2 Expanding on the Word Help System Basics

Instructions: Use the Word Help system to understand the topics better and answer the questions listed below. Answer the questions on your own paper, or hand in the printed Help information to your instructor.

1. Right-click the Office Assistant. If it is not turned on, click Show the Office Assistant on the Help menu. When the shortcut menu displays, click Options. Click Use the Office Assistant to remove the check mark, and then click the OK button.
2. Click the Microsoft Word Help button on the Standard toolbar. Maximize the Microsoft Word Help window. If the tabs are hidden on the left side, click the Show button. Click the Index tab. Type undo in the Type keywords text box. Click the Search button. Click Reset built-in menus and toolbars. Print the information. Click the Hide button and then the Show button. Click the four links below What do you want to do? Read and print the information for each link. Close the Microsoft Word Help window. Hand in the printouts to your instructor.
3. Press the F1 key. Maximize the Microsoft Word Help window. Click the Answer Wizard tab. Type help in the What would you like to do? text box, and then click the Search button. Click Ways to get assistance while you work. Read through the information that displays. Print the information. Click the first two links. Read and print the information for both.
4. Click the Contents tab. Click the plus sign (+) to the left of the Typing, Navigating Documents, and Selecting Text book. Click the plus sign (+) to the left of the Selecting Text book. One at a time, click the three topics below the Selecting Text book. Read and print each one. Close the Microsoft Word Help window. Hand in the printouts to your instructor.
5. Click Help on the menu bar and then click What's This? Click the E-mail button on the Standard toolbar. Right-click the ScreenTip to print the ScreenTip. Click Format on the menu bar and then click Paragraph. When the Paragraph dialog box displays, click the Question Mark button on the title bar. Click the Special box. Right-click the ScreenTip to print the ScreenTip. Hand in the printouts to your instructor. Close the Paragraph dialog box and the Microsoft Word window.

APPENDIX B
Publishing Office Web Pages to a Web Server

With a Microsoft Office 2000 program, such as Word, Excel, Access, or PowerPoint, you use the **Save as Web Page command** on the File menu to save the Web page to a Web server using one of two techniques: Web folders or File Transfer Protocol. A **Web folder** is an Office 2000 shortcut to a Web server. **File Transfer Protocol (FTP)** is an Internet standard that allows computers to exchange files with other computers on the Internet.

You should contact your network system administrator or technical support staff at your ISP to determine if their Web server supports Web folders, FTP, or both, and to obtain necessary permissions to access the Web server. If you decide to publish Web pages using a Web folder, you must have the Office Server Extensions (OSE) installed on your computer. OSE comes with the Standard, Professional, and Premium editions of Office 2000.

Using Web Folders to Publish Office Web Pages

If you are granted permission to create a Web folder (shortcut) on your computer, you must obtain the URL of the Web server, and a user name and possibly a password that allows you to access the Web server. You also must decide on a name for the Web folder. Table B-1 explains how to create a Web folder.

Office adds the name of the Web folder to the list of current Web folders. You can save to this folder, open files in the folder, rename the folder, or perform any operations you would to a folder on your hard disk. You can use your Office program or Windows Explorer to access this folder. Table B-2 explains how to save to a Web folder.

Using FTP to Publish Office Web Pages

When publishing a Web page using FTP, you first add the FTP location to your computer and then you can save to it. An **FTP location**, also called an **FTP site**, is a collection of files that resides on an FTP server. In this case, the FTP server is the Web server.

To add an FTP location, you must obtain the name of the FTP site, which usually is the address (URL) of the FTP server, and a user name and a password that allows you to access the FTP server. You save and open the Web pages on the Web server using the name of the FTP site. Table B-3 explains how to add an FTP site.

Office adds the name of the FTP site to the FTP locations in the Save As and Open dialog boxes. You can open and save files on this FTP location. Table B-4 explains how to save using an FTP location.

Table B-1   Creating a Web Folder

1. Click File on the menu bar and then click Save As; or click File on the menu bar and then click Open.
2. When the Save As dialog box or the Open dialog box displays, click the Web Folders shortcut on the Places Bar along the left side of the dialog box.
3. Click the Create New Folder button.
4. When the first dialog box of the Add Web Folder wizard displays, type the URL of the Web server and then click the Next button.
5. When the Enter Network Password dialog box displays, type the user name and, if necessary, the password in the respective text boxes and then click the OK button.
6. When the last dialog box of the Add Web Folder wizard displays, type the name you would like to use for the Web folder. Click the Finish button.
7. Close the Save As or the Open dialog box.

Table B-2   Saving to a Web Folder

1. Click File on the menu bar and then click Save As.
2. When the Save As dialog box displays, type the Web page file name in the File name text box. Do not press the ENTER key.
3. Click Web Folders shortcut on the Places Bar along the left side of the dialog box.
4. Double-click the Web folder name in the Save in list.
5. When the Enter Network Password dialog box displays, type the user name and password in the respective text boxes and then click the OK button.
6. Click the Save button in the Save As dialog box.

Table B-3   Adding an FTP Location

1. Click File on the menu bar and then click Save As; or click File on the menu bar and then click Open.
2. In the Save As dialog box, click the Save in box arrow and then click Add/Modify FTP Locations in the Save in list; or in the Open dialog box, click the Look in box arrow and then click Add/Modify FTP Locations in the Look in list.
3. When the Add/Modify FTP Locations dialog box displays, type the name of the FTP site in the Name of FTP site text box. If the site allows anonymous logon, click Anonymous in the Log on as area; if you have a user name for the site, click User in the Log on as area and then type the user name. Type the password in the Password text box. Click the OK button.
4. Close the Save As or the Open dialog box.

Table B-4   Saving to an FTP Location

1. Click File on the menu bar and then click Save As.
2. When the Save As dialog box displays, type the Web page file name in the File name text box. Do not press the ENTER key.
3. Click the Save in box arrow and then click FTP Locations.
4. Double-click the name of the FTP site you want to save to.
5. When the FTP Log On dialog box displays, type your user name and password and then click the OK button.
6. Click the Save button in the Save As dialog box.

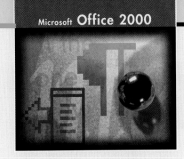

APPENDIX C
Resetting the Menus and Toolbars

When you first install Microsoft Office 2000, the Standard and Formatting toolbars display on one row in some of the applications. As you use the buttons on the toolbars and commands on the menus, Office personalizes the toolbars and the menus based on their usage. Each time you start an application, the toolbars and menus display in the same settings as the last time you used the application. The following steps show how to reset the Word menus and toolbars to their installation settings.

 To Reset My Usage Data and Toolbar Buttons

1 **Click View on the menu bar and then point to Toolbars. Point to Customize on the Toolbars submenu.**

The View menu and Toolbars submenu display (Figure C-1).

FIGURE C-1

2 **Click Customize. When the Customize dialog box displays, click the Options tab. Make sure the three check boxes in the Personalized Menus and Toolbars area have check marks and then point to the Reset my usage data button.**

The Customize dialog box displays as shown in Figure C-2.

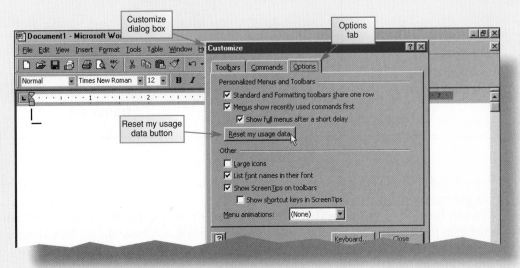

FIGURE C-2

3 Click the Reset my usage data button. When the Microsoft Word dialog box displays explaining the function of the Reset my usage data button, click the Yes button. In the Customize dialog box, click the Toolbars tab.

The Toolbars sheet displays (Figure C-3).

4 Click Standard in the Toolbars list and then click the Reset button. When the Reset Toolbar dialog box displays, click the OK button. Click Formatting in the Toolbars list and then click the Reset button. When the Reset Toolbar dialog box displays, click the OK button.

5 Click the Close button in the Customize dialog box.

The toolbars display as shown in Figure C-4.

FIGURE C-3

FIGURE C-4

Steps 3 and 4 display or remove any buttons that were added or deleted through the use of the Add or Remove Buttons button on the More Buttons menu.

You can turn off both the toolbars sharing a single row and the short menus by removing the check marks from the two top check boxes in the Options sheet in the Customize dialog box (Figure C-2 on the previous page). If you remove these check marks, Word will display the toolbars on two separate rows below the menu bar and will show only full menus.

Microsoft Office 2000

APPENDIX D

Microsoft Office User Specialist Certification Program

The Microsoft Office User Specialist (MOUS) Certification Program provides a framework for measuring your proficiency with the Microsoft Office 2000 applications, such as Word 2000, Excel 2000, Access 2000, and PowerPoint 2000. Three levels of certification are available — Master, Expert, and Core. The three levels of certification are described in Table D-1.

Table D-1	Three Levels of MOUS Certification		
LEVEL	DESCRIPTION	REQUIREMENTS	CREDENTIAL AWARDED
Master	Indicates that you have a comprehensive understanding of Microsoft Office 2000	Pass all FIVE of the required exams: Microsoft Word 2000 Expert Microsoft Excel 2000 Expert Microsoft PowerPoint 2000 Core Microsoft Access 2000 Core Microsoft Outlook 2000 Core	Candidates will be awarded one certificate for passing all five of the required Microsoft Office 2000 exams: Microsoft Office User Specialist: Microsoft Office 2000 Master
Expert	Indicates that you have a comprehensive understanding of the advanced features in a specific Microsoft Office 2000 application	Pass any ONE of the Expert exams: Microsoft Word 2000 Expert Microsoft Excel 2000 Expert	Candidates will be awarded one certificate for each of the Expert exams they have passed: Microsoft Office User Specialist: Microsoft Word 2000 Expert Microsoft Office User Specialist: Microsoft Excel 2000 Expert
Core	Indicates that you have a comprehensive understanding of the core features in a specific Microsoft Office 2000 application	Pass any ONE of the Core exams: Microsoft Word 2000 Core Microsoft Excel 2000 Core Microsoft PowerPoint 2000 Core Microsoft Access 2000 Core Microsoft Outlook 2000 Core	Candidates will be awarded one certificate for each of the Core exams they have passed: Microsoft Office User Specialist: Microsoft Word 2000 Microsoft Office User Specialist: Microsoft Excel 2000 Microsoft Office User Specialist: Microsoft PowerPoint 2000 Microsoft Office User Specialist: Microsoft Access 2000 Microsoft Office User Specialist: Microsoft Outlook 2000

Why Should You Get Certified?

Being a Microsoft Office User Specialist provides a valuable industry credential — proof that you have the Office 2000 applications skills required by employers. By passing one or more MOUS certification exams, you demonstrate your proficiency in a given Office application to employers. With nearly 80 million copies of Office in use around the world, Microsoft is targeting Office certification to a wide variety of companies. These companies include temporary employment agencies that want to prove the expertise of their workers, large corporations looking for a way to measure the skill set of employees, and training companies and educational institutions seeking Microsoft Office teachers with appropriate credentials.

The MOUS Exams

You pay $50 to $100 each time you take an exam, whether you pass or fail. The fee varies among testing centers. The Expert exams, which you can take up to 60 minutes to complete, consist of between 40 and 60 tasks that you perform online. The tasks require you to use the application just as you would in doing your job. The Core exams contain fewer tasks, and you will have slightly less time to complete them. The tasks you will perform differ on the two types of exams.

How Can You Prepare for the MOUS Exams?

The Shelly Cashman Series® offers several Microsoft-approved textbooks that cover the required objectives on the MOUS exams. For a listing of the textbooks, visit the Shelly Cashman Series MOUS Web page at www.scsite.com/off2000/cert.htm and click the Shelly Cashman Office Series 2000 Microsoft-Approved MOUS Textbooks link (Figure D-1). After using any of the books listed in an instructor-led course, you will be prepared to take the MOUS exam indicated.

How to Find an Authorized Testing Center

You can locate a testing center by calling 1-800-933-4493 in North America or visiting the Shelly Cashman Series MOUS Web page at www.scsite.com/off2000/cert.htm and then clicking the Locate an Authorized Testing Center Near You link (Figure D-1). At this Web page, you can look for testing centers around the world.

Shelly Cashman Series MOUS Web Page

The Shelly Cashman Series MOUS Web page (Figure D-1) has more than fifteen Web pages you can visit to obtain additional information on the MOUS Certification Program. The Web page (www.scsite.com/off2000/cert.htm) includes links to general information on certification, choosing an application for certification, preparing for the certification exam, and taking and passing the certification exam.

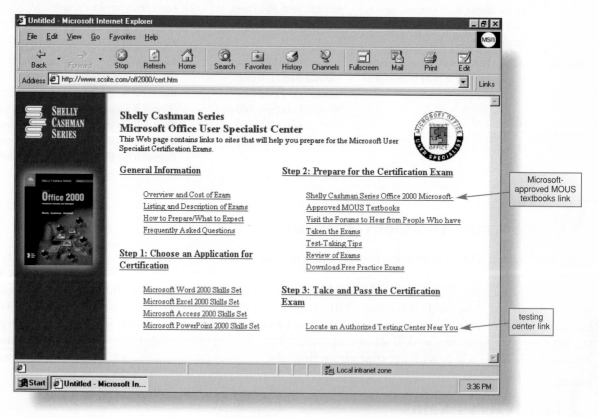

FIGURE D-1

Index